Introduction to Statistics

HARPERCOLLINS COLLEGE OUTLINE

Introduction to Statistics

Susan F. Wagner, Ph.D.
Northern Virginia Community College

HarperPerennial
A Division of HarperCollinsPublishers

An American BookWorks Corporation Production
Project Manager: Mary Mooney
Editor: Robert A. Weinstein

Library of Congress Catalog Card Number: 91-58278
ISBN: 0-06-467134-8

92 93 94 95 96 ABW/RRD 10 9 8 7 6 5 4 3 2 1

Contents

Preface

This statistics book is intended as a supplement to your textbook in a one or two semester statistics course. The course this book complements does not require calculus and is generally offered for social science, business, accounting, biology, education, and other students who need to know how to use different statistical methods. The derivations of these methods are outlined, but the emphasis here is on use, not mathematical rigor.

The book is organized into fourteen chapters; the entire fourteen would comprise a full two semester college statistics course. Chapter 1 is a review of the mathematics (arithmetic, algebra, and some notation) which will be needed for statistics.

The rest of this book is organized in much the same way as a similar college course is. Chapters 2, 3, and 4 discuss descriptive statistics: describing data sets as to their shape, central measure, and variability. Chapters 5 and 6 concern probability and probability distributions. Chapter 7 lays the foundation for inferential statistics by discussing sampling theory and the Central Limit Theorem.

Inferential statistics, making reasonable quantitative hypotheses about real world data, is the theme of the last half of the book. Chapters 8 through 14 discuss hypothesis testing using large samples (chapter 8), proportions (9), small samples (10), more than two samples (11), and count data samples (12). Chapter 13 deals with the strength of a linear relationship between two variables, linear regression analysis. Chapter 14 discusses how to test hypotheses concerning populations whose characteristics are not known using nonparametric (non-measure based) statistics.

There is an introduction for each of these chapters. New material is developed through concrete examples, step by step. Theory is introduced where needed, to help explain difficult concepts. Exercises are presented and model solutions given after each new concept is thoroughly explained and illustrated. Each chapter ends with a summary and a summary exercise, which in most cases combines several of the concepts discussed in that chapter.

It is hoped that this book will help college students to better understand and apply the material in their statistics course(s) and to get a clearer idea of the scope and uses of statistics in today's world.

Introduction to Statistics

1

Review of Mathematics for Statistics

*This book will introduce you to the branch of mathematics called "statistics."
In order to make sure you are familiar with arithmetic and algebra and with
the notation and terminology needed to understand statistics, this chapter will
highlight some of the important mathematical ideas you must know before
beginning your study. Most of these ideas, perhaps all of them, should be a
review for you.*

ARITHMETIC CONCEPTS

Although most people are familiar with arithmetic, we will review a few
topics that will be used frequently in statistics. The first of these is order of
operations.

**Order of
Operations**

We all know how to add, subtract, multiply, and divide. If we don't always
get it right, our calculators can help us. But the calculators can only do what we
want them to do if we tell them correctly. And what happens if a problem
consists of several of the above operations (+, −, ×, ÷), along with some
parentheses and exponents thrown in for good measure?

Suppose we want to evaluate (find the value of) the following expression:

$$4 + 3 (5 - 6/2) - 2^3$$

Which part of the problem is done first? Do we add the 4 and 3? And what is that 3 floating over the 2? How about the "/"? What operation does it represent? This is an *order of operations* problem.

Although some Eastern countries and most computers do arithmetic operations in a different order, the order of operations used for evaluating arithmetic expressions in the Western world is the following:

P   (work in parentheses)

E   (exponentiation)

MD   (multiplication and/or division: left to right)

AS   (addition and/or subtraction: left to right)

A useful mnemonic (memory device) to remember this order is "Please Excuse My Dear Aunt Sally": PEMDAS.

To show how this rule operates, each arithmetic step will be shown in order on the left with the operation discussed on the right:

$4 + 3 (5 - 6/2) - 2^3 =$
$4 + 3 (5 - 3) - 2^3 =$

Work inside parentheses first. In the parentheses, the order of operations prevails. Since there are no exponents inside the parentheses, the division indicated by 6/2 is completed. (Note: division can be indicated in 3 different ways:

$6/2, 6 \div 2, \text{or } \dfrac{6}{2}$).

$4 + 3 (2) - 2^3 =$

Work in parentheses is completed by subtracting 3 from 5.

$4 + 3 (2) - 8 =$

With no more parentheses, go to the next level, which is evaluating expressions with exponents: $2^3 = 2 \cdot 2 \cdot 2 = 8$ since 2^3 means multiplying the base 2 by itself three times.

$4 + 6 - 8 =$

Multiply $3(2) = 6$. Multiplication also can be indicated in three different ways: $3(2)$, 3×2, or $3 \cdot 2$.

$10 - 8 = 2$

Add and/or subtract from left to right.

Thus, $4 + 3 (5 - 6/2) - 2^3 = 2$. No other answer is correct.

Exercise 1.1:   Evaluate the following expressions, using order of operations.
a. $32 + 60 \div 4 + 2 - 2 \cdot 3^2$
b. $32 + 60 \div (4 + 2) - (2 \cdot 3)^2$
c. $(32 + 60) \div 4 + (2 - 2) \cdot 3^2$

Answers: Notice that the numbers and operations are the same for all three parts of the problem; only the parentheses are different. However, since the rules for order of operations state that work in parentheses is always done first, the answers are different.

a. $32 + 60 \div 4 + 2 - 2 \cdot 3^2 =$

     $32 + 60 \div 4 + 2 - 2 \cdot 9 =$ Exponentiation.

     $32 + 15 + 2 - 18 =$ Multiply and divide, left to right.

     $49 - 18 = 31$ Add and subtract, left to right.

b. $32 + 60 \div (4 + 2) - (2 \cdot 3)^2 =$

     $32 + 60 \div 6 - 6^2 =$ Parentheses work.

     $32 + 60 \div 6 - 36 =$ Exponentiation.

     $32 + 10 - 36 =$ Multiply and divide.

     $42 - 36 = 6$ Add and subtract.

c. $(32 + 60) \div 4 + (2 - 2) \cdot 3^2 =$

     $92 \div 4 + 0 \cdot 3^2 =$ Parentheses work.

     $92 \div 4 + 0 \cdot 9 =$ Exponentiation.

     $23 + 0 =$ Multiply and divide.

     23 Add and subtract.

Operations with Fractions

Recall that fractions are pairs of numbers, a numerator (top) and a denominator (bottom), which are expressed like a division problem. One half, or one over two, is expressed as 1/2 or $\frac{1}{2}$. Fractions are also called *rational numbers*. They can be added, subtracted, multiplied, divided, and raised to powers.

Unlike a whole number, however, a fraction can have several names. For example,

$\frac{1}{2} = \frac{3}{6} = \frac{4}{8} = \frac{10}{20}$. This is because all these fractions are equivalent. The equivalency can be shown by factoring and equating to 1 the fractions with the same numerator and denominator:

$\frac{10}{20} = \frac{10 \cdot 1}{10 \cdot 2} = \frac{10}{10} \cdot \frac{1}{2} = \frac{1}{2}$ since any number (10) divided by itself (10) is 1.

ADDING AND SUBTRACTING FRACTIONS

Fractions whose denominators are identical can be added. For example, $\frac{5}{8} + \frac{1}{8} + \frac{3}{8} = \frac{5 + 1 + 3}{8} = \frac{9}{8} = 1\frac{1}{8}$ (a mixed number). If the denominators of fractions are not identical, the fractions cannot be added until their denominators are made identical. This is done by changing each fraction to an equivalent fraction with the same (common) denominator as the others. For example, to add $\frac{3}{4} + \frac{1}{8}$, change $\frac{3}{4}$ to the equivalent fraction $\frac{6}{8}$ by multiplying the numerator and denominator by 2. Since $\frac{2}{2} = 1$, the value of the fraction remains the same. Then add $\frac{6}{8} + \frac{1}{8} = \frac{7}{8}$.

Similarly, to subtract fractions, the denominators must be the same. Then the numerators can be subtracted. For example, $\frac{3}{4} - \frac{1}{8} = \frac{6}{8} - \frac{1}{8} = \frac{5}{8}$.

MULTIPLYING AND DIVIDING FRACTIONS

When multiplying fractions, multiply the numerators together and the denominators together. The result is a fraction whose numerator is the product of all the numerators and whose denominator is the product of all the denominators. However, if the fractions have a common factor, both in the numerator and in the denominator of any of the fractions to be multiplied, this factor can be cancelled to avoid having to reduce to lowest terms at the end of the problem.

For example, to multiply $\frac{4}{15} \cdot \frac{9}{14}$, we could multiply the numerators together $(4 \cdot 9 = 36)$ and the denominators together $(14 \cdot 15 = 210)$. Then, to reduce the answer to lowest terms: $\frac{36}{210} = \frac{6 \cdot 6}{6 \cdot 35} = \frac{6}{35}$.

However, if we factor the numerator and denominator first, we can cancel factors before multiplying:

$\frac{4}{15} = \frac{2 \cdot 2}{3 \cdot 5}$ and $\frac{9}{14} = \frac{3 \cdot 3}{2 \cdot 7}$. Then a 2 in the numerator of the first fraction and the 2 in the denominator of the second would cancel, as would the 3 in the denominator of the first and a 3 in the numerator of the second. Then the product is $\frac{2}{5} \cdot \frac{3}{7} = \frac{6}{35}$. This method is much simpler than the first and thus leads to fewer errors.

When fractions are divided, the divisor is inverted and the operation changed to multiplication. For example, $\frac{2}{3} \div \frac{1}{2} = \frac{2}{3} \cdot \frac{2}{1} = \frac{4}{3}$ or $1\frac{1}{3}$.

Recall that a fraction whose numerator is larger than its denominator is called an *improper fraction* and can be changed to a mixed number.

Raising a fraction to a power (an exponent) is just multiplying it by itself the number of times indicated by the power:

$$\left(\frac{2}{3}\right)^3 = \frac{2}{3} \cdot \frac{2}{3} \cdot \frac{2}{3} = \frac{8}{27}$$

If the original fraction is in lowest terms (cannot be reduced), then the evaluated power fraction will also be in lowest terms.

Exercise 1.2: Evaluate the following, recalling the rules for operations with fractions and the rules for order of operations.

a. $\dfrac{2}{3} + \dfrac{1}{2} \div \dfrac{3}{4} - \left(\dfrac{1}{2}\right)^2$
   b. $\left(\dfrac{2}{3} + \dfrac{1}{2}\right) \div \left(\dfrac{3}{4} - \dfrac{1}{2}\right)^2$
   c. $\dfrac{2}{3} + \left(\dfrac{1}{2} \div \dfrac{3}{4} - \dfrac{1}{2}\right)^2$

Answers:

a. $\dfrac{2}{3} + \dfrac{1}{2} \div \dfrac{3}{4} - \left(\dfrac{1}{2}\right)^2 =$

$\dfrac{2}{3} + \dfrac{1}{2} \div \dfrac{3}{4} - \dfrac{1}{4} =$ Exponentiation.

$\dfrac{2}{3} + \dfrac{1}{2} \cdot \dfrac{4}{3} - \dfrac{1}{4} =$ Division.

$\dfrac{2}{3} + \dfrac{2}{3} - \dfrac{1}{4} =$ Multiplication.

$\dfrac{8}{12} + \dfrac{8}{12} - \dfrac{3}{12} =$ Common denominator.

$\dfrac{16}{12} - \dfrac{3}{12} =$ Addition and subtraction.

$\dfrac{13}{12} = 1\dfrac{1}{12}$ Addition and subtraction.

b. $\left(\dfrac{2}{3} + \dfrac{1}{2}\right) \div \left(\dfrac{3}{4} - \dfrac{1}{2}\right)^2 =$

$\left(\dfrac{4}{6} + \dfrac{3}{6}\right) \div \left(\dfrac{3}{4} - \dfrac{2}{4}\right)^2 =$ Parentheses work (common denominator).

$\dfrac{7}{6} \div \left(\dfrac{1}{4}\right)^2 =$ More parentheses.

$\dfrac{7}{6} \div \dfrac{1}{16} =$ Exponentiation.

$\dfrac{7}{6} \cdot \dfrac{16}{1} =$ Division.

$\dfrac{56}{3} = 18\dfrac{2}{3}$ Multiplication.

c. $\dfrac{2}{3} + \left(\dfrac{1}{2} \div \dfrac{3}{4} - \dfrac{1}{2}\right)^2 =$

$$\frac{2}{3} + \left(\frac{1}{2} \cdot \frac{4}{3} - \frac{1}{2}\right)^2 =$$
Division in parentheses.

$$\frac{2}{3} + \left(\frac{2}{3} - \frac{1}{2}\right)^2 =$$
Multiplication in parentheses.

$$\frac{2}{3} + \left(\frac{4}{6} - \frac{3}{6}\right)^2 =$$
Common denominator.

$$\frac{2}{3} + \left(\frac{1}{6}\right)^2 =$$
Subtraction in parentheses.

$$\frac{2}{3} + \frac{1}{36} =$$
Exponentiation.

$$\frac{24}{36} + \frac{1}{36} =$$
Common denominator.

$$\frac{25}{36}$$
Addition.

Changing Fractions to Decimals and Percents

Most calculators do not deal with fractions. If we use a calculator to evaluate a fraction by division, such as 1/4 or 1 ÷ 4 or $\frac{1}{4}$, the calculator gives us a result of .25. Thus, as a practical matter, when fractions are added, subtracted, multiplied, or divided on a calculator, the calculator changes the fractions to their decimal equivalents.

USING A CALCULATOR TO CHANGE FRACTIONS TO DECIMALS

Most fractions do not have a terminating decimal equivalent like .25. For example, if we try to convert the answer to (c) above, 25/36, to a decimal, we get 0.694444444 on a calculator that holds ten places. Actually, the correct decimal equivalent to 25/36 is .6944... with the 4s repeating forever.

As a practical matter, nonterminating decimals like .69444... are usually rounded off to the nearest hundredth or thousandth—two or three decimal places. If the number in the next decimal place is more than 5, increase the last number of the previous decimal place and drop the others. If the number in the next decimal place is less than 5, drop it and the later places. If the number in this place is exactly 5, see Chapter 2 for a rule concerning its rounding.

To say that 25/36 = .694 is not completely correct. Instead, the symbol ≈ should be used to indicate approximation: 25/36 ≈ .694.

Since much work in statistics makes use of a calculator, almost all answers will be rounded off. When possible, try to use fractions rather than rounded decimals in the body of the calculations to avoid errors caused by rounding.

CHANGING DECIMALS TO PERCENTS

Percent means part of 100. To change a decimal to a percent, just move the decimal point two places to the right. Thus, .694 becomes 69.4%, and .25 is 25%. The number 1 changes to 100%; numbers greater than 1 yield percent equivalents greater than 100%. Most of the work done in statistics is based on a whole of 100% and its parts: 1%, 5%, 68%, and 95% are some percentages that will be used again and again.

Exercise 1.3: Using your calculator, change the following fractions to decimals; round to the nearest thousandth if necessary and convert the decimals to percents.

a. 1/2 b. 2/3 c. 13/17

d. 3 1/10 e. 24/25 f. 477/1000

Answers:

a. 1/2 = .5 = 50% (terminating decimal)

b. 2/3 ≈ .667 = 66.7% (round off .6666... to .667)

c. 13/17 ≈ .765= 76.5% (round off .7647... to .765)

d. 3 1/10 = 3.1 = 310% (terminating decimal)

e. 24/25 = .96 = 96% (terminating decimal)

f. 477/1000 = .477 = 47.7% (terminating decimal)

Roots

Often in statistics a square root of a number must be found. The square root of a number is a number that, when multiplied by itself, equals the original number. For example, the square root of 9 is 3, since $3 \cdot 3 = 9$. Actually, positive numbers have two square roots, a positive and a negative, since $(-3)(-3) = 9$ also. However, in statistics the square roots requested will be the positive root, unless otherwise noted.

The notation for square root is $\sqrt{\ }$. Thus, $\sqrt{25} = 5$. Most calculators have a square root key, $\sqrt{\ }$, which is very useful for statistics, since most numbers do not have rational square roots. For example, $\sqrt{3}$ is 1.732050808, according to a ten-place calculator. If you multiply this number by itself, the result is close to, but not exactly, 3. The same rules for rounding decimals are used for square roots; in the above case, $3 \approx 1.732$, to three decimal places, or thousandths.

Exercise 1.4: Using your calculator, find the following square roots and round each to three decimal places.

a. $\sqrt{27}$ b. $\sqrt{7.5}$ c. $\sqrt{324}$ d. $\sqrt{.25}$

Answers:

a. $\sqrt{27} \approx 5.196$

b. $\sqrt{7.5} \approx 2.739$

c. $\sqrt{324} = 18$ (324 is a perfect square)

d. $\sqrt{.25} = .5$ (.25 is also a perfect square)

ALGEBRAIC CONCEPTS

This section highlights those topics from first year algebra that are needed for statistics.

Signed Numbers

Algebra introduces the concept of signed numbers. Negative numbers as well as positive numbers are used in computation and can be answers to some problems. A negative number results when subtracting a larger number from a smaller one. Signed numbers can be added, subtracted, multiplied, divided, and raised to powers.

Negative numbers have negative signs in front of them, like –9. Positive numbers are usually represented without a sign, like 9.

The square root of a negative number is not a real number and thus will not be part of the statistical processes in this course. If any of your calculations call for finding the square root of a negative number, like $\sqrt{-36}$, a mistake has been made.

Many calculators have a key marked +/– on it. To enter a negative number, say –8, enter 8 and push the +/– key. This will change 8 to –8. Then all calculations can be done as usual.

ABSOLUTE VALUE

The absolute value of a number represents the distance of that number from 0, denoted by the positive of that number. If the number is already positive, its absolute value is equal to the number. For example, $|6| = 6$, where $|6|$ is read "absolute value of 6."

If the number is negative, its absolute value is its positive. Therefore, $|-3| = 3$ — the absolute value of negative three is three. Absolute value bars act like parentheses for order of operation problems: all work inside the absolute value bars must be done before they are removed. When the final calculation inside the bars results in a single positive number, then the bars can be removed. If the resulting number is negative, then it must be changed to a positive number before the bars are removed.

Exercise 1.5: Find the following absolute values:

a. $|18|$ b. $|-12.7|$ c. $|0|$

Answers:

a. $|18| = 18$ b. $|-12.7| = 12.7$

c. $|0| = 0$ (0 is neither positive nor negative)

Operations with Signed Numbers

Here are some basic rules for working with signed numbers:

1. Addition of two signed numbers:
   a. If the numbers have the same sign, add the absolute values and give the common sign to the answer (sum).
   $3 + 7 = 10$ and $(-3) + (-7) = -10$.
   b. If the signs are different, subtract their absolute values and give the sum the sign of the number with the larger absolute value.
   $3 + (-7) = -4$ and $(-3) + 7 = 4$.

2. Addition of more than two signed numbers:
   To add more than two signed numbers, add all the positive numbers together (this sum is positive) and add all the negative numbers together (this sum is negative). Then proceed with the two sums as in 1(b) above.
   $2 + (-5) + (-8) + 9 + 7 + (-3) = ?$
   $2 + 9 + 7 = 18$
   $(-5) + (-8) + (-3) = -16$
   $18 + (-16) = 2$

3. Subtraction of two signed numbers:
   To subtract two signed numbers, change the problem to addition of two signed numbers by changing the sign of the second number to its opposite. Then proceed as in addition. The answer to a subtraction problem is called the *difference*.
   $2 - 7 = 2 + (-7) = -5$.
   $2 - (-7) = 2 + 7 = 9$.
   $-2 - 7 = -2 + (-7) = -9$.
   $-2 - (-7) = -2 + 7 = 5$.

4. Multiplication of signed numbers:
   a. To multiply two signed numbers, use the following rule: if the signs are the same (two negatives or two positives), the product (answer) has a positive sign; if the signs are different, the product has a negative sign:
   $(3)(5) = 15$ $(-3)(-5) = 15$ $(3)(-5) = -15$ $(-3)(5) = -15$

   b. To multiply more than two signed numbers, first multiply the numbers, ignoring the signs. If there is an even number of negative numbers, the product is positive. If there is an odd number of negative numbers, the product is negative.
   $(-7)(3)(5)(-1)(-2) = -210$.

c. To raise a negative number to a power, use the multiplication rule in (b) above. If the power is even, the answer is positive. If the power is odd, the result is negative.
$(-2)^3 = (-2)(-2)(-2) = -8$.

5. Division of signed numbers:

Division, like subtraction, involves two numbers only. If the signed numbers have the same sign, the result or quotient is positive. If the numbers to be divided have different signs, the quotient is negative.
$3 \div 5 = .6$
$(-3) \div (-5) = .6$
$3 \div (-5) = -.6$
$(-3) \div 5 = -.6$

Exercise 1.6:   Evaluate the following.

a. $32 + (-60) \div 4 + 2 - 2 \cdot (-3)^2$

b. $32 + (-60) \div (4 + 2) - [2 \cdot (-3)]^2$

c. $[32 + (-60)] \div 4 + (2 - 2) \cdot (-3)^2$

Answers:

a. $32 + (-60) \div 4 + 2 - 2 \cdot (-3)^2 =$

$32 + (-60) \div 4 + 2 - 2 \cdot 9 =$

$32 + (-15) + 2 - 18 =$

$32 + (-15) + 2 + (-18) = 34 + (-33) = 1.$

b. $32 + (-60) \div (4 + 2) - [2 \cdot (-3)]^2 =$

$32 + (-60) \div 6 - (-6)^2 =$

$32 + (-60) \div 6 - 36 =$

$32 + (-10) - 36 =$

$32 + (-10) + (-36) = 32 + (-46) = -14.$

c. $[32 + (-60)] \div 4 + (2 - 2) \cdot (-3)^2 =$

$(-28) \div 4 + 0 \cdot (-3)^2 =$

$(-28) \div 4 + 0 \cdot 9 = -7 + 0 = -7.]$

Solving Equations

An important idea behind algebra is representing unknown numbers by letters like x, called variables. Instead of asking "What number added to 7 is 9?", we write the equation $x + 7 = 9$. Finding the value of x that makes the expression $x + 7$ equal to 9 answers the above question.

The key to solving equations is to isolate the variable, in this case x. Remember that an equation is a balance: whatever is done to one side (of the equal sign) must be done to the other. If the left side of the equation is multiplied by 3, the right side must also be multiplied by 3.

For example, let's solve the equation $4x + 17 = 25$. To isolate the variable x, we begin by subtracting 17 from each side. This gives:

$$4x + 17 = 25$$

$$4x + 17 - 17 = 25 - 17$$

$$4x + 0 = 8$$

$$4x = 8$$

Then we divide each side by 4:

$$\frac{4x}{4} = \frac{8}{4}$$

$$1x = 2$$

$$x = 2$$

To check, substitute 2 for x in $4x + 17 = 25$. If $x = 2$, then $4(2) + 17$ should equal 25. Since $8 + 17 = 25$, this answer checks.

When writing a product of a number and a variable, it is not necessary to use the usual symbols for multiplication. Writing the number next to the variable, like $4x$, means that x is multiplied by 4. The number, called the *coefficient*, is always written before the variable. If we wrote $x4$, it might be confused with x^4.

Exercise 1.7: Solve the following equations for x. Check your solutions.

a. $3x + 7 = 10$ b. $3(x + 7) = 12$ c. $3x - 7 = 11$

Answers:

a. $3x + 7 = 10$

$$3x + 7 - 7 = 10 - 7$$

$$3x + 0 = 3$$

$$3x = 3$$

$$\frac{3x}{3} = \frac{3}{3}$$

$$1x = 1$$

$$x = 1$$

Check:

$$3x + 7 = 10$$

$$3(1) + 7 = 10$$

$$3 + 7 = 10$$

$$10 = 10$$

b. $\dfrac{3(x+7)}{3} = \dfrac{12}{3}$

$1(x+7) = 4$

$x + 7 = 4$

$x + 7 + (-7) = 4 + (-7)$

$x + 0 = -3$

$x = -3$

Check:

$3(x+7) = 12$

$3[(-3)+7] = 12$

$3(4) = 12$

$12 = 12$

c. $3x - 7 = 11$

$3x - 7 + 7 = 11 + 7$

$3x + 0 = 18$

$\dfrac{3x}{3} = \dfrac{18}{3}$

$1x = 6$

$x = 6$

Check:

$3x - 7 = 11$

$3(6) - 7 = 11$

$18 - 7 = 11$

$11 = 11$

SOLVING FRACTIONAL EQUATIONS

The same principles can be applied to solving equations that contain fractions; but the best way to begin solving a fractional equation is to change it to an equivalent equation with no fractions.

Multiplying or dividing both sides of an equation by the same value does not change the equation's solution, only the form of the equation. For example, in the above Exercise 1.8, dividing each of the equations by 3 did not change the solution; this process only changed the form of the equation to simplify solving it.

Suppose the equation to solve is $\dfrac{1}{5}x + 2 = 7$. To begin solving this, multiply both sides by the denominator of the fraction, 5. This yields

$$5\left(\frac{1}{5}x+2\right)=5\cdot 7$$

$$5\left(\frac{1}{5}\right)x+5(2)=5\cdot 7$$

$$1x+10=35$$

$$x+10-10=35-10$$

$$x+0=25$$

$$x=25$$

Suppose there are several fractions in the equation, like $\frac{1}{3}x-\frac{1}{2}x=1$. If we multiply both sides by 3, we will still have a fraction on the left side of the equation. Therefore, we need to multiply both sides by a larger number, 6:

$$6\left(\frac{1}{3}x-\frac{1}{2}x\right)=6(1)$$

$$6\left(\frac{1}{3}\right)x-6\left(\frac{1}{2}\right)x=6(1)$$

$$2x-3x=6$$

$$-1x=6$$

$$(-1)(-1x)=(-1)(6)$$

$$1x=-6$$

$$x=-6$$

Even if there is an x in the denominator, the equation can be solved. For example,

$$\frac{9}{x}+\frac{3}{x}=4$$

$$x\left(\frac{9}{x}+\frac{3}{x}\right)=x(4)$$

$$x\left(\frac{9}{x}\right)+x\left(\frac{3}{x}\right)=4x$$

$$9+3=4x$$

$$12=4x$$

$$\frac{12}{4}=\frac{4x}{4}$$

$3=x$, so $x=3$ is the solution.

Exercise 1.8: Solve each of the following equations:

a. $\frac{1}{5}x + 4 = 0$ b. $\frac{1}{x} = \frac{2}{3}$ c. $x - \frac{1}{3}x = 8$

Answers:

a. $\frac{1}{5}x + 4 = 0$

$5\left(\frac{1}{5}\right)x + 5(4) = 5(0)$

$1x + 20 = 0$

$x + 20 - 20 = 0 - 20$

$x + 0 = -20$

$x = -20$

b. $\frac{1}{x} = \frac{2}{3}$

$3x\left(\frac{1}{x}\right) = 3x\left(\frac{2}{3}\right)$

$3 = 2x$

$\frac{3}{2} = \frac{2x}{2}$

$\frac{3}{2} = 1x$

$x = \frac{3}{2}$

c. $x - \frac{1}{3}x = 8$

$3\left(x - \frac{1}{3}x\right) = 3\,(8)$

$3x - 3\left(\frac{1}{3}\right)x = 24$

$3x - x = 24$

$2x = 24$

$\frac{2x}{2} = \frac{24}{2}$

$1x = 12$

$x = 12$

COORDINATE GEOMETRY

Equations in Two Variables

An equation like $x + 7 = 10$ is an equation in one variable, x. It has only one solution, $x = 3$. However, equations in two variables, such as $y = 3x - 2$, are satisfied by many values of x and y. For example, $x = 1$, $y = 1$ satisfy this equation; $x = 2$, $y = 4$ also satisfy this equation.

In reality, there is an infinite set of ordered pairs of numbers of the form (x, y) that satisfy the equation $y = 3x - 2$. Pairs like $(1, 1)$ and $(2, 4)$ can be generated by choosing any real number for x (like $x = 0$) and substituting that number into $y = 3x - 2$ to arrive at a value for y ($y = -2$). Thus, $(0, -2)$ is a third ordered pair of solutions to $y = 3x - 2$.

$(0, -2)$ is called an *ordered pair* because it is different from $(-2, 0)$. You can see that whereas $(0, -2)$ satisfies $y = 3x - 2$, $(-2, 0)$ does not. Ordered pairs are always given in alphabetical order (x-value, y-value) or (x, y).

Exercise 1.9: Find six ordered pairs that satisfy the equation $y = 3x + 2$.

Answers: There are many different possible answers to this, including $(0, 2)$, $(1, 5)$, $(-1, -1)$, $(1/3, 3)$, $(-2/3, 0)$, $(10, 32)$.

Graphing in a Plane

Geometry and algebra have a very close relationship. A number can be represented as a point in geometry. The *number line* is a line of numbers with a starting point, 0, and a unit. All real numbers can be found on the number

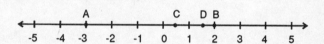

Figure 1.1:
Real Number Line

line. The number line is sketched in Figure 1.1.

To the right of 0 are the positive integers, 1, 2, 3, . . . , each a unit apart; to the left of 0 are the negative integers, $-1, -2, -3, \ldots$, also a unit apart. It is easy to locate numbers like -3 (Point A) and 2 (Point B) on this number line. All real numbers can be located on it, given that it can be extended infinitely in both directions. Notice that the fraction 1/2 is at Point C, while Point D represents the real number $\sqrt{3}$.

If a vertical number line and a horizontal number line are drawn with their 0s intersecting, any point on the plane containing these number lines can be located. When drawn this way, the horizontal number line is called the *x*-axis, the vertical number line is called the *y*-axis, and their point of intersection is called the origin.

These axes are usually drawn on a grid, with the units being squares or boxes, as in the diagram below. The *x*- and *y*-axes divide the plane into four quadrants numbered I, II, III, and IV, starting with the upper right quadrant and proceeding counterclockwise (Figure 1.2).

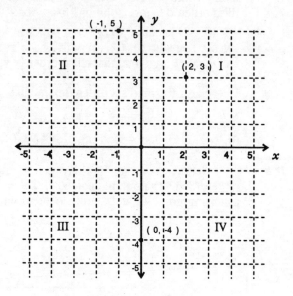

Figure 1.2:
Coordinate Graph

Points on the plane can be located by their coordinates, the ordered pairs that represent their *x*- and *y*- values. Every point in the plane is located either in a quadrant or on an axis. For example, the point (2, 3) is two units from the origin in the positive *x*-direction (to the right) and three units from the origin in the positive *y*-direction (up). It is in quadrant I.

The point (–1, 5) is located one unit from the origin in the negative *x*-direction (left) and 5 units in the positive *y*-direction. It is in quadrant II.

The point (0, –4) is located zero units in the *x*-direction and 4 units in the negative *y*-direction (down). It is on the *y*-axis.

The origin, being located zero units away from both axes, is at their intersection and has the coordinates (0, 0).

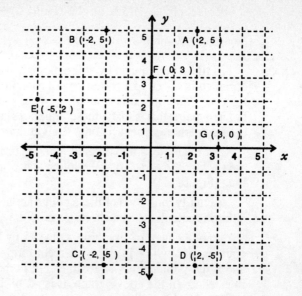

Figure 1.3:
Some Points on a Coordinate Graph

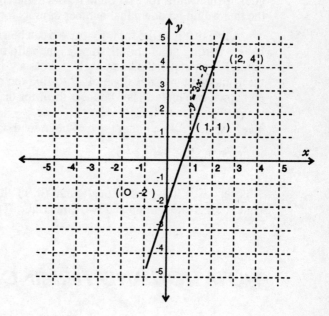

Figure 1.4:
Graph of the line $y = 3x - 2$

Exercise 1.10: Locate the following points on a coordinate graph: A(2, 5); B (–2, 5); C (–2, –5); D (2, –5); E (–5, 2); F (0, 3); G (3, 0).

Answers: See Figure 1.3.

Graphing Lines

A linear equation in two variables is an equation with two variables, neither of which is raised to a power or is a root, nor is either in the denominator of a fraction. The previous example, $y = 3x - 2$, is a linear equation. When the ordered pairs that satisfy these equations are graphed, the points that these ordered pairs represent lie on a straight line.

For example, some ordered pairs that satisfy the linear equation $y = 3x$ 2 are (1, 1), (2, 4), and (0, –2). Notice that when these are graphed, they lie on a line. (Figure 1.4)

Actually, only two of these points are needed to draw the line. Sometimes a third is calculated as a check to see if they are all on the same line.

Another way of graphing a line is by the slope-intercept method. The equation of any line in slope-intercept form is $y = mx + b$, where m is the slope and b the y-intercept. The y-intercept is the place on the y-axis that the line intersects. In the above graph, it is –2 because one point on the line has the coordinates (0, –2).

The slope of the line is the ratio of the number of units up (rise) to the number of units to the right (run) in going from one point to another. In the case of the line $y = 3x - 2$, the slope (the coefficient of the x term) is 3, so the line goes up three units for every unit it goes to the right. If the slope were negative, the line would go down that number of units for every unit it goes to the right.

A line that is in the form $y = mx + b$ can be graphed by using its y-intercept, b, as a starting point and its slope as the ratio of rise over run to get a second point. For example, the line $y = -2x + 3$ has a y-intercept of 3. Starting at (0, 3), the y-intercept, use the slope of –2 to find the next point one unit to the right and down two units. Then connect them for the line (Figure 1.5).

Exercise 1.11: Use either the two-point method or the slope-intercept method to graph the line $y = \frac{1}{2}x + 1$.

Answer: The line goes through point (0, 1), the y-intercept, since $b = 1$. The next point is one unit up and two units right. The graph is in Figure 1.6.

NOTATION AND TERMINOLOGY

There are some notations you will encounter in statistics and in later mathematics courses that you may not have seen before. They will be explained as they are introduced in subsequent chapters, but first we will discuss them here in a more general sense.

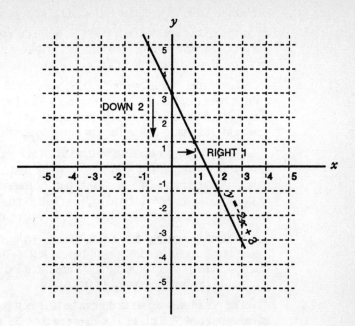

Figure 1.5:
Graph of the Line $y = -2x + 3$

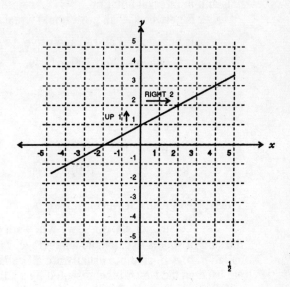

Figure 1.6:
Graph of $y = \frac{1}{2}x + 1$

Inequalities and Intervals

Sometimes, instead of indicating that x is equal to some number, we wish to write that x is greater than a certain number, say 5. This can be written using the greater than symbol, $>$. Thus, we write $x > 5$. If we want to write that x is less than 8, the reverse symbol, $<$, is used. Thus, $x < 8$.

To say that x is between 5 and 8, we write $5 < x < 8$. This means that x has a value between 5 and 8, excluding both 5 and 8. If instead we want to include 5 and 8, we use a slightly different notation. In this case we write $5 \leq x \leq 8$, which means that 5 is less than or equal to x, which is less than or equal to 8.

The real number line can be used as an alternate way to express inequalities. Instead of writing $5 < x < 8$, we can write that x is in the interval (5, 8). This means that the value of x is on that part of the number line from the number 5 to the number 8. The interval (5, 8) is called an *open interval*. Do not confuse this notation with the ordered pair (5, 8) where x is 5 and y is 8.

Instead of writing $5 \leq x \leq 8$, we can write that x is in the interval [5, 8]. These brackets (instead of parentheses) tell us that 5 and 8 are included in the interval. The points $x = 5$ and $x = 8$ are included in [5, 8] but not in (5, 8). The interval [5, 8] is called a *closed interval*.

The possibility exists that x can be between two numbers, 5 and 8, and might equal 5 but not 8. This can be expressed by $5 \leq x < 8$ or x is in the interval [5, 8). The interval [5, 8) is a *half-open interval*; (5, 8] is also a half-open interval, but in this case, x could equal 8 but not 5. The interval (5, 8] can also be expressed as an inequality: $5 < x \leq 8$.

Exercise 1.12: Write each of the following inequalities with the correct symbols and in interval notation.

  a. x is between –2 and 0; x could equal 0 but is greater than –2.

  b. x is between –3 and –1 inclusive.

  c. x is between –4 and 100 exlusive.

Answers:

  a. $-2 < x \leq 0$; (–2, 0]

  b. $-3 \leq x \leq -1$; [–3, –1]

  c. $-4 < x < 100$; (–4, 100)

SUBSCRIPTS AND SUMMATION

In the course of statistics, we will want to add a group of numbers, to find the sum of scores to calculate an average. These numbers, in general, could be called $a, b, c, d,$ etc., but usually are all called by the same letter, x. *Subscripts* are used so the first x is represented by x_1, the second x by x_2, etc. If there are 100 different scores, for example, the last score will be represented by x_{100}. These numbers are referred to as x-one, x-two, and x-one hundred. Subscripts provide an easy way of referring to numbers in general, counting them as we compute with them.

Suppose we want to find the sum of these 100 numbers. We could write the sum as $x_1 + x_2 + x_3 + \ldots + x_{100}$ but a shorter notation is provided by using the capital Greek letter sigma, $\sum$, along with i, an index. In the case in which we are summing from x_1 to x_{100}, the index goes from 1 to 100, through the whole numbers only. The above sum can be written as follows:

$$\sum_{i=1}^{100} x_i = x_1 + x_2 + x_3 + \ldots + x_{100}.$$

Often, the index is dropped, so the summation is symbolized just by $\sum x_i$ or even $\sum x$.

Suppose we want to find the sum of the first five counting numbers, $1 + 2 + 3 + 4 + 5$. We could write this in a summation notation as $\sum_{i=1}^{5} i$.

Exercise 1.13: Find $\sum_{i=1}^{5} i^2$.

Answer: In this case, the i is not a subscript but an actual number. The index goes from $i = 1$ to 5, so:

$$\sum_{i=1}^{5} i^2 = 1^2 + 2^2 + 3^2 + 4^2 + 5^2$$

$$= 1 + 4 + 9 + 16 + 25 = 55.$$

DOUBLE SUBSCRIPTS

Information in statistics is often displayed in a table. The following table displays numbers in rows and columns:

17	23	-6	14	81
-4	12	10	28	33
37	25	62	-5	19

This table has three rows and five columns. Each of these entries can be addressed in general by use of a double subscript. The first number in the subscript represents the row, and the second represents the column. For example, 81 is in the first row, fifth column, so it can be called x_{15}. 28 is in the second row, fourth column, so $x_{24} = 28$. In this way, the elements of a table, which is also called a *matrix,* can be easily named.

Exercise 1.14: Using the above matrix, find x_{25} and x_{32}.

Answers: $x_{25} = 33$ and $x_{32} = 25$.

*T*his chapter reviewed some basic arithmetic and algebraic skills you will need for statistics. It is assumed that you have a calculator available for work in statistics. Many inexpensive calculators have statistical functions, so you may want to have one with these functions. However, virtually all calculators have the functions used in this chapter, such as square roots, sign changing, and the four basic operations.

The arithmetic topics covered here were order of operations, operations with fractions, and converting from fractions to decimals and percents. The algebra needed for statistics includes working with signed numbers, solving simple equations, and graphing lines. Some notation used in this book includes inequality expressions, both symbols and intervals, summation signs, and single and double subscripts.

These topics and notation will be explained again as the need for them arises. If your calculations do not match the book's solutions, review this chapter; if this is not sufficient, you may need to review arithmetic and/or algebra more thoroughly. Statistics does require a working knowledge of mathematics; the more you know when you take statistics, the more secure you will feel in the course.

2

Organizing Data

*T*he study of statistics is divided into two parts: descriptive and inferential. "Descriptive statistics" describes number sets: how many numbers, the middle number, the spread of the numbers. "Inferential statistics" uses some of these descriptions to make inferences or guesses about an entire population based on a sample of the data. The next three chapters deal with descriptive statistics; our first task is to organize sets of numbers so we can describe them.

TYPES OF DATA

Qualitative and Quantitative Data

Two types of information can be collected in statistical studies: qualitative or named data and quantitative data. *Quantitative data* consists of measures or quantities that can be put into an order or ranked in some way. The set of ages of students in your statistics class is an example of quantitative data.

Qualitative data is not comparable by arithmetic relations. The eye color of the students in your statistics class is an example of qualitative data.

Exercise 2.1: One hundred people are selected at random from the telephone book and interviewed. Classify each of the following items that were asked of the people as qualitative (N for named) or quantitative (O for ordered).

1. Weight.
2. Salary.
3. Presidential candidate for whom they expect to vote.
4. Birth year.
5. Marital status.
6. Height.

7. Shoe size.
8. Number of children.
9. Gender.
10. Favorite television program.

Answers: Numbers 3, 5, 9, and 10 are qualitative (N).
Numbers 1, 2, 4, 6, 7, and 8 are quantitative (O).

Discrete and Continuous Data

Among the quantitative data sets a further distinction exists between discrete and continuous data. *Discrete data* is measured in exact, or discrete, numbers. Between two consecutive numbers there is no other number. For example, men's suit jackets are sold in sizes 38, 39, 40, etc., but not in size 39 1/2. Therefore, the set of men's suit jacket sizes consists of discrete data.

Data that can assume any value within an interval, or between two numbers, is an example of *continuous data*. One's height, when measured precisely, can be any number. Suppose Tom says his height is 70 inches. This really means that his height is between 69.5 and 70.5 inches: it is somewhere in the interval (69.5, 70.5). When Tom said his height is 70 inches, he rounded it to the nearest whole number of inches.

Suppose John says his height is 70.4 inches. This really means John's height is between 70.35 and 70.45 inches: it is somewhere in the interval (70.35, 70.45). When John said his height is 70.4 inches, he rounded his height to the nearest tenth of an inch. Because a height can really be any number within an interval, the set of people's heights is an example of continuous data.

Exercise 2.2: From the data in Exercise 2.1 that was identified as quantitative, identify each as discrete (D) or continuous (C).

Answers: Items 2 (salary), 4 (birth year), 7 (shoe size), and 8 (number of children) are examples of discrete data. Items 1 (weight) and 6 (height) are examples of continuous data.

Rounding Numbers

Calculations often result in numbers with more decimal places than are needed for the final answer or that contain an infinite number of decimal places. For example, the decimal equivalent of 1/3 is .3333..., and the decimal equivalent of 1/7 is .14285714.... These numbers need to be rounded to a manageable number of decimal places. If a calculator is used, rounding need only be done in presenting the final answer.

STEPS FOR ROUNDING NUMBERS

If the decimal place after the one to be rounded is more than 5, increase the number in the previous decimal place by 1 and drop the subsequent numbers. For example, let's round .142857... to three decimal places, or thousandths. Since the fourth decimal place is more than 5 (it is 8), increase the third decimal place by 1 (from 2 to 3), and drop the others. The resulting number, rounded to three decimal places, is .143.

If the decimal place after the one to be rounded is less than 5, it and all subsequent numbers are dropped. Let's round .142857... to two decimal places, or hundredths. Since the third decimal place is less than 5 (it is 2), it is dropped, along with the other numbers. The resulting number, rounded to two decimal places, is .14.

If the decimal place after the one to be rounded is exactly 5, use the next two places instead. For example, if .142857 is to be rounded to four decimal places, or ten thousandths, look at the 57 in the fifth and sixth places. Since it is greater than 50, round up; the number rounded to the nearest ten thousandth is thus .1429.

Suppose a number to be rounded terminates after a 5 and must be rounded to the decimal place one before the 5. For example, suppose 26.14500 is to be rounded to two decimal places. The rule generally followed is to drop the 5, along with the following 0s, if the number before the 5 is even, and round to the next higher one if it is odd. In the case of rounding 26.14500 to two decimal places, we would get 26.14 since 4 is even. On the other hand, 26.175 rounded to two decimal places is 26.18 since 7, being odd, must be rounded to the next higher (and thus even) number. The final decimal place in these cases will thus always be even.

Exercise 2.3:

a. Round each of the following to two decimal places.

1. 37.2650	2. 37.27500	3. 37.265001

b. Round each of the following to a whole number.

1. 373.4999	2. 87.5	3. 86.50

Answers:

a. 1. 37.26   2. 37.28   3. 37.27

b. 1. 373   2. 88   3. 86

SIGNIFICANT FIGURES

The number of significant figures in a number is simply the number of digits in it. For example, 26.145000 has eight significant figures while 26.145 has five. The trailing zeros in 26.145000 indicate that the actual measure is between 26.1449995 and 26.1450005; i.e., in the interval (26.1449995, 26.1450005). In the second case, the number 26.145 implies that the actual measure is between 26.1445 and 26.1455, or in the interval (26.1445, 26.1455).

Exercise 2.4: How many significant figures are there in each of the original numbers in the previous Exercise 2.3?

a.	1. 37.2650	b.	1. 373.4999
	2. 37.27500		2. 87.5
	3. 37.265001		3. 86.50

Answers: a. 1. 6; 2. 7; 3. 8   b. 1. 7; 2. 3; 3. 4

ORGANIZING DATA

Stem and Leaf Display

The first step in handling data is to organize it. One of the quickest ways to do this is a stem and leaf display. In this method, the first part of a number is the *stem*, and the rest of the number is the *leaf*. All possible stems are displayed in a column with each of the leaves in the same row. For example, below are recorded the prices in dollars of twenty randomly chosen new automobiles.

Data Set 1

8520	9274	8142	11298	10624
7987	11172	12899	10737	9198
13625	9462	11847	10178	12240
11690	10069	11240	12745	12995

If the number of thousands of dollars is used for the stem and the lesser place holders for the leaf, the stem and leaf display appears as follows:

Table 2.1

Stem	Leaf	Count
7	987	1
8	520, 142	2
9	274, 198, 462	3
10	624, 737, 178, 069	4
11	298, 172, 847, 690, 240	5
12	899, 240, 745, 995	4
13	625	1
		$\overline{20}$

It is a good idea to total the count to be sure no number was omitted.

Exercise 2.5: Construct a stem and leaf display for the expected miles per gallon for the twenty randomly chosen new cars, as listed below:

Data Set 2

27	25	31	19	40
20	17	24	25	32
47	34	26	31	22
26	28	30	31	41

Answer:

Table 2.2

Stem	Leaf	Count
1	9, 7	2
2	7, 5, 0, 4, 5, 6, 2, 6, 8	9
3	1, 2, 4, 1, 0, 1	6
4	0, 7, 1	3
		$\overline{20}$

Relative Frequency Distribution

Another method of organizing data is a relative frequency distribution. Numbers are grouped in classes whose size, or widths, are equal. For example, using Data Set 1, prices of new cars, notice that they range from 7987 to 13,625. One way to arrive at a proper width is to use the same organization as in the stem and leaf display. This means, for example, that the first class would go from $7000 to $7999, the second from $8000 to $8999, etc. All the classes would be exactly $1000 wide. However, this may result in too many or too few classes. The usual number of classes for a relative frequency distribution of a small data set (fifteen to thirty numbers or data points) is from five to seven classes.

Once the class boundaries have been decided upon, the number in each class is tabulated. The percentage or proportion of numbers in each class is also displayed. This proportion is called the *relative frequency* because it measures the part of the entire data set in each class. For example, suppose a class width of $1500 is used for the prices of new cars. Then this information can be tabulated in a relative frequency distribution table as follows:

Table 2.3

Price	Frequency	Relative Frequency
7000 – 8499	2	.10
8500 – 9999	4	.20
10000 – 11499	7	.35
11500 – 12999	6	.30
13000 – 14499	1	.05
		1.00

Notice that by making each class width 1500 rather than 1000, the number of classes is five. Usually, the number of classes is chosen first and then the width calculated from that number.

The relative frequency is calculated using the following formula: $r = c/t$ where r is relative frequency, c is class frequency, and t is total frequency. For example, to get the relative frequency of the third class, 10000–11499, divide 7 by 20 and round off to two decimal places. The relative frequency of this class is .35 or 35%. Since the relative frequencies are calculated as parts of 20, and all the frequencies add up to 20, the sum of the relative frequencies is 1.00 or 100%. Whereas the sum of the frequencies depends on the number of items in the data set, the sum of the relative frequencies will always be 1.00 or 100%.

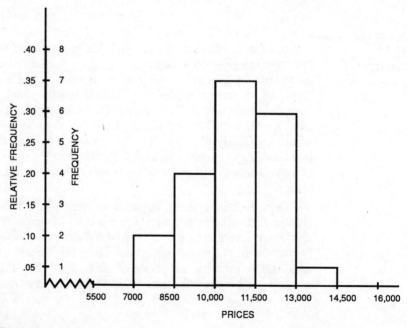

Figure 2.1:
Relative Frequency Histogram
Prices of New Cars

Histograms

Data organized in frequency distribution tables is often displayed in a histogram or bar graph. The classes, each the same width, are indicated on the horizontal axis. The vertical axis can display either the frequency or the relative frequency. Both frequencies and relative frequencies are indicated in the following histogram (Figure 2.1), which represents the prices of new cars; these prices were taken from Table 2.3.

Notice that unless the first class starts at 0, we compress the horizontal axis and begin the numeration a class width below our first class. It makes for a more accurate histogram if each class ends on the same number at which the next one begins. This will be done in subsequent histograms, though care must be taken that the endpoints of the classes not be in the data set, else the same number will fall in two different classes.

On the vertical axis is the percentage or proportion of the entire number set in each class—the relative frequency. The actual frequencies can also appear on the vertical axis. The horizontal and vertical axes will usually not use the same unit of measure: in this case, the unit on the horizontal axis is $1500, while the unit on the vertical axis is 1 (number of cars) or .05 (relative frequency) of that number.

FINDING THE CLASS BOUNDARIES FOR HISTOGRAMS

The number of data points determines the number of classes into which a data set should be divided for displaying the numbers in a relative frequency distribution and a histogram. The number of classes usually varies from five to twenty; the higher numbers might be used for data sets with several hundred elements. For the problems in this book, five to seven classes is sufficient.

The following are weights in pounds of twenty-four men:

Data Set 3

173	157	204	198	162	153
140	172	189	191	166	147
132	212	197	183	165	171
167	158	166	163	179	155

In order to divide these weights into classes, first determine their range. The difference between the largest and smallest numbers in a data set is the *range* of the data set. Subtract the lowest from the highest: $212 - 132 = 80$. Add 1 to this number to be sure the highest number falls within the last class.

Then decide upon the number of classes, say five (six or seven could also be used). Divide the range plus one, $80 + 1 = 81$, by the number of classes, 5, and round *up* for the class width: $81/5 = 16.2 \approx 17$. (If the number is not rounded up, or if 1 is not added to the range, the larger numbers can fall out of the last class.)

To be certain that none of the numbers fall on the boundaries and that the high boundary in class one is the same as the low one in class two (making for a nicer picture), start the lowest class boundary .5 below the lowest weight (132), at 131.5. Add 17 to 131.5, and 17 again and again until five classes are outlined. Notice that the highest weight (212) falls in the last class, 199.5–216.5.

Count the number of weights in each class and find the percentage in each class of the total number of weights (to the nearest whole percent or to two decimal places in proportion). See the frequency and relative frequency table (Table 2.4) and the histogram (Figure 2.2) for this problem.

Table 2.4

Weight (Class)	Frequency	Relative Frequency
131.5 – 148.5	3	.12
148.5 – 165.5	7	.29
165.5 – 182.5	7	.29
182.5 – 199.5	5	.21
199.5 – 216.5	2	.08
	$\overline{24}$	$\overline{.99^*}$

*Not quite equal to 1.00 due to rounding.

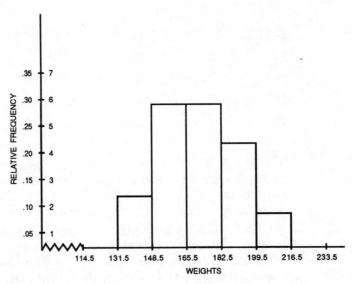

Figure 2.2:
Relative Frequency Histogram
Men's Weights

Relative Frequency Polygons

A relative frequency polygon is the set of line segments formed by plotting the class mark (midpoint of the class interval) against the class frequency or relative frequency. The relative frequency polygon for the data in Figure 2.2 is obtained by joining in order the midpoints of the tops of all rectangles (bars) on the histogram. The first connection is a segment from the midpoint of the class before the first class [middle of the interval (114.5, 131.5)] to the middle of the top of the first bar. The class mark can be found by averaging the endpoints: (114.5 + 131.5)/2 = 123. The last connection is a segment from the middle of the top of the last bar to the midpoint of the class after it [middle of the interval (216.5, 233.5)], which is 225.

We can think of the first and last points of the relative frequency polygon as being midpoints of bars with frequency 0, since none of the 24 weights is in either class. The frequency polygon for the histogram in Figure 2.2 is shown in Figure 2.3.

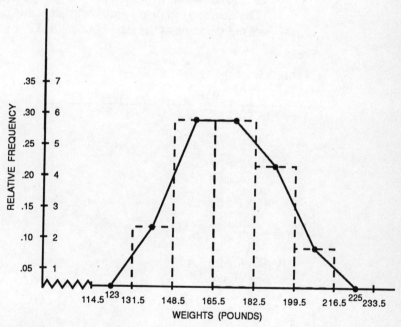

Figure 2.3:
Relative Frequency Polygon
Men's Weights

Exercise 2.6: Using the data from Exercise 2.5, miles per gallon of twenty new cars:
  a. Construct a relative frequency distribution table using five classes.
  b. Construct a relative frequency histogram.
  c. Draw a relative frequency polygon.

The mileage figures are repeated below.

Data Set 2

27	25	31	19	40
20	17	24	25	32
47	34	26	31	22
26	28	30	31	41

Answers:
  a. First calculate the range of the mileages: $47 - 17 = 30$; then add 1. Then, to find the width of each class for five classes, use $31/5 = 6.2$, rounded up to 7. Starting at 16.5 (0.5 less than 17, the lowest number in the table) and adding 7 for each interval will generate Table 2.5. (The stem and leaf display may help in counting, even though the stems are not the same as the class boundaries.)

Table 2.5

Miles per Gallon	Frequency	Relative Frequency
16.5 – 23.5	4	.20
23.5 – 30.5	8	.40
30.5 – 37.5	5	.25
37.5 – 44.5	2	.10
44.5 – 51.5	1	.05
	20	1.00

  b. See Figure 2.4.
  c. See Figure 2.5

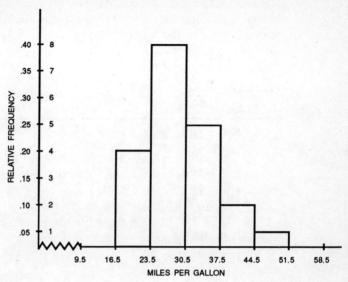

Figure 2.4:
Relative Frequency Histogram
Miles per Gallon

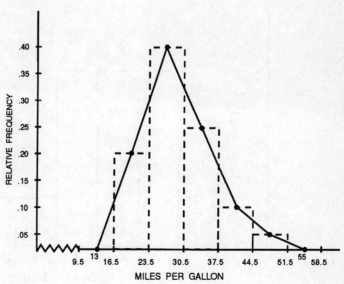

Figure 2.5:
Relative Frequency Polygon
Miles per Gallon

Exercise 2.7: Repeat Exercise 2.6 using seven rather than five classes.

Answers: The range of the mileages, plus 1, is still 31; 31 is now divided into 7 classes, yielding 4.42+, which rounds up to 5. Therefore, the width of each class is 5. Again, the smallest class starts at 16.5, but this time adding 5 will generate the table below:

Table 2.6

Miles per Gallon	Frequency	Relative Frequency
16.5 – 21.5	3	.15
21.5 – 26.5	6	.30
26.5 – 31.5	6	.30
31.5 – 36.5	2	.10
36.5 – 41.5	2	.10
41.5 – 46.5	0	.00
46.5 – 51.5	1	.05
	20	1.00

b. See Figure 2.6.

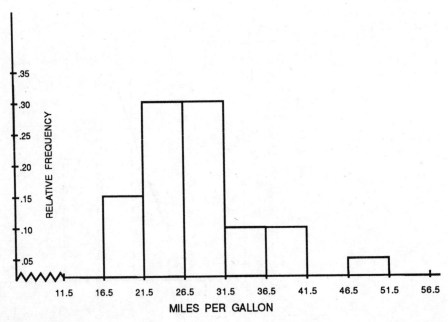

Figure 2.6:
Relative Frequency Histogram
Miles per Gallon

c. See Figure 2.7.

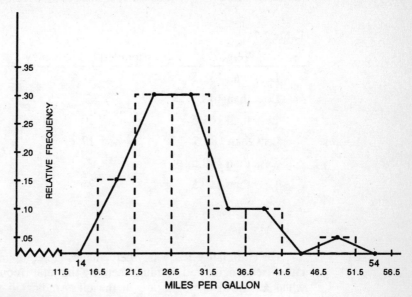

Figure 2.7:
Relative Frequency Polygon
Miles per Gallon

Cumulative Frequencies and Ogives

In addition to determining frequencies or relative frequencies in each class, we are sometimes asked to find cumulative frequencies. *Cumulative frequencies* are subtotals for each class boundary. For example, look at Table 2.4, which is reproduced below.

Table 2.4

Weight (Class)	Frequency	Relative Frequency
131.5 – 148.5	3	.12
148.5 – 165.5	7	.29
165.5 – 182.5	7	.29
182.5 – 199.5	5	.21
199.5 – 216.5	2	.08
	$\overline{24}$	$\overline{.99}$

Instead of finding the frequency in each class, accumulate the totals until all weights in the set are included. This is called a cumulative frequency table.

Instead of having upper and lower bounds for each class, only the upper class bound is considered. For example, there are seventeen weights in this data set that are less than 182.5 lbs.: 17 is the sum of the frequencies in the first three weight classes and thus includes all the weights in Data Set 3 that are less than 182.5 lbs. The cumulative frequency table, which also indicates the cumulative frequency percentage, is shown in Table 2.7.

Table 2.7

Weight	Cumulative Frequency	Cumul. Freq. Percent
Less than 131.5	0	.00
Less than 148.5	3	.12
Less than 165.5	10	.42
Less than 182.5	17	.71
Less than 199.5	22	.92
Less than 216.5	24	1.00

The cumulative frequency percentages are computed by taking the cumulative frequencies and dividing them by the total frequency, 24. At the point when all the data points are in the class indicated at the left, cumulative frequency percentage is 100%.

Histograms are rarely used to picture cumulative frequencies; ogives are used instead. *Ogives* are cumulative frequency polygons with the cumulative frequencies and/or cumulative frequency percentages on the vertical axis. On the horizontal axis are indicated the original class marks or midpoints, beginning with the class mark of the class below the first one from the data set. The class marks are the midpoints of the intervals (Figure 2.8).

Notice the numbers on the horizontal axis. Recall that the frequency polygon for this same data set (Figure 2.3) used as its first point on the horizontal axis the midpoint of the class below 131.5–148.5, which is the interval (114.5, 131.5).

The midpoint of (114.5, 131.5) can be calculated by adding the endpoints (114.5 + 131.5 = 246) and then dividing by 2: 246/2 = 123. For subsequent class marks (midpoints) just add the class width from the relative frequency table. The ogive is horizontal after 208, the class mark of the last class.

Exercise 2.8: Using the relative frequency Table 2.5 from Exercise 2.6, construct both the cumulative frequency percentage table and its ogive.

Answers: To make this problem easier, the original table of relative frequencies is reproduced below.

The next table is changed to a cumulative frequency table by summing the frequencies cumulatively and using the upper bounds for each class as indicated below.

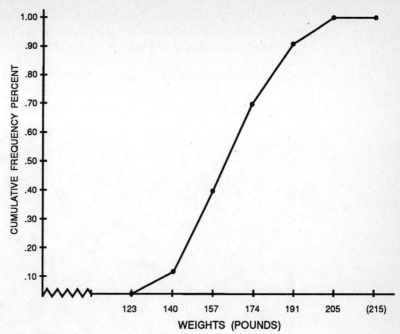

Figure 2.8:
Ogive (Cululative Frequency Polygon)
Men's Weights

Table 2.5

Miles per Gallon	Frequency	Relative Frequency
16.5 – 23.5	4	.20
23.5 – 30.5	8	.40
30.5 – 37.5	5	.25
37.5 – 44.5	2	.10
44.5 – 51.5	1	.05
	$\overline{20}$	$\overline{1.00}$

Table 2.8

Miles per Gallon	Cumulative Frequency	Cumul. Freq. Percent
Less than 16.5	0	.00
Less than 23.5	4	.20
Less than 30.5	12	.60
Less than 37.5	17	.85
Less than 44.5	19	.95
Less than 51.5	20	1.00

(Refer to Figure 2.9.) Notice how the class marks for the above ogive were found. First, find the class below 16.5–23.5, which is the interval (9.5, 16,5). Then find the midpoint of this interval by adding the endpoints and dividing by 2: $9.5 + 16.5 = 26$ and $26/2 = 13$. Next add the class width, 7, to each successive midpoint (13, 20, etc.) until the last class mark, 48, is reached. These numbers (13, 20, . . . 48) are plotted against the cumulative frequencies. The ogive is horizontal after 48, since 100% of the class marks are less than or equal to 48.

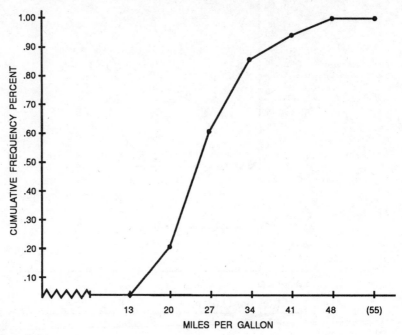

Figure 2.9:
Ogive (Cumulative Frequency Polygon)
Miles per Gallon

Smoothing Curves

Often frequency polygons and ogives are presented by approximating their shapes with a smooth curve. Some examples are shown below. The smooth curve, represented by a solid line, is close to the original frequency polygon or ogive represented by a dashed line. The first example is a smooth curve whose ogive appears in Figure 2.9 above (Figures 2.10a and 2.10b).

Exercise 2.9: Data set 4 represents I.Q.s of thirty students in a statistics course.

    a.   Organize the data in a stem and leaf display.
    b.   Organize the data in a relative frequency table with five classes.
    c.   Construct a histogram and a relative frequency polygon for the data. Smooth the polygon.
    d.   Organize the data in a cumulative frequency percentage table.
    e.   Construct an ogive for the above and smooth it.

Data Set 4

97	100	109	122	118	124
127	105	112	128	107	114
115	121	135	98	111	117
120	130	123	141	107	113
116	119	121	131	129	139

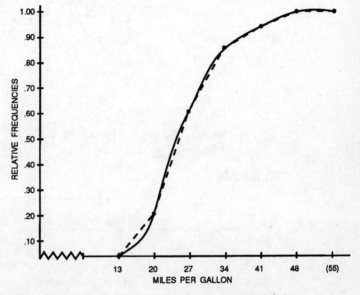

Figure 2.10a: Dashed Line – Ogive; Solid Line – Smoothed Ogive

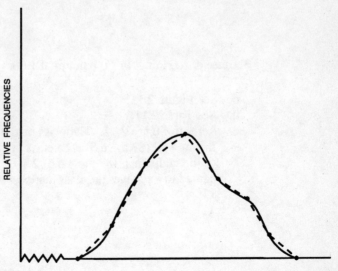

Figure 2.10b: Dashed Line – Relative Frequency Polygon; Solid Line – Smoothed Relative Frequency Polygon

Answers:

a. Table 2.9—Stem and Leaf Display

Stem	Leaf	Count
9	7, 8	2
10	0, 9, 5, 7, 7	5
11	8, 2, 4, 5, 1, 7, 3, 6, 9	9
12	2, 4, 7, 8, 1, 0, 3, 1, 9	9
13	5, 0, 1, 9	4
14	1	1
		$\overline{30}$

b.   The range is $141 - 97 = 44$, $44 + 1 = 45$; $45/5 = 9$, which is the class width.

Table 2.10

Relative Frequency Distribution

I.Q.s	Frequency	Relative Frequency
96.5–105.5	4	.13
105.5–114.5	7	.23
114.5–123.5	10	.33
123.5–132.5	6	.20
132.5–141.5	3	.10
	$\overline{30}$	$\overline{.99}$*

*Because of rounding, this did not total 1.00.

c.   See Figure 2.11.

d.   See Table 2.11

e.   Refer to Figure 2.12. The class below the first class in Table 2.10 is the interval (87.5, 96.5). The class mark of this interval is the average of the endpoints, $(87.5 + 96.5)/2 = 92$. Adding 9 to the class marks consecutively gives the class marks of 92, 101, 110, 119, 128, 137, and 146.

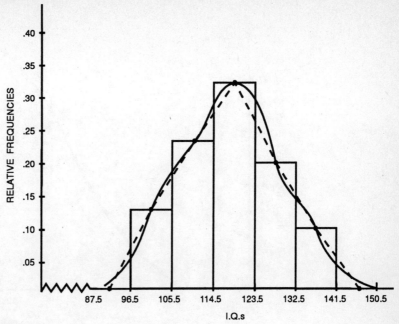

Figure 2.11:
Boxes – Relative Frequency Histogram;
Dashed Lines – Relative Frenquency Polygon;

d. Table 2.11

Cumulative Frequency Percentages

I.Q.s	Cumulative Freq.	Cumul. Freq. Percent
Less than 96.5	0	.00
Less than 105.5	4	.13
Less than 114.5	11	.37
Less than 123.5	21	.70
Less than 132.5	27	.90
Less than 141.5	30	1.00

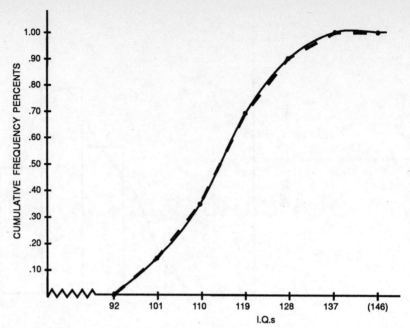

Figure 2.12:
I.Q.s
Dashed Line – Ogive
Solid Line – Smoothed Ogive

*T*his chapter has discussed organizing data. Data is classified as qualitative (named) data or quantitative (ordered) data. Examples of qualitative data include marital status and eye color; examples of quantitative data include age and test grades.

Quantitative data can be further classified as discrete or continuous. Discrete data are exact numbers; for example, glove sizes include 6, 6 1/2, 7, and 7 1/2, but not 6.247 or 7.3781. Continuous data, when presented, are usually rounded off: e.g., a person's height is given to the nearest inch.

Data must be organized and displayed to be used effectively. Data can be organized using a stem and leaf diagram, a relative frequency distribution table, or a cumulative frequency distribution table. Data can be displayed by a histogram, a relative frequency polygon, or an ogive. The last two can be smoothed into curves that approximate their shape, presenting a different picture of the data distribution.

3

Measures of Central Tendency

In continuing to describe data sets—the part of statistics known as descriptive statistics—the next task is to find a middle number for the data that has been described by relative frequency tables, histograms, and polygons. There are several middle numbers we will consider: these are called measures of central tendency. Loosely defined, the "central tendency" of a set of numbers is the tendency of the data to cluster around certain numerical values.

AVERAGE

A dictionary definition of *average* is a quantity intermediate to a set of numbers. But what is meant by intermediate? Is this the sum of all the numbers in the data set divided by the number in the set? Is it the number in the middle when all the numbers in the data set are ranked? Or is it the number most often represented in the data set? Each of these three ideas leads to a different measure of central tendency: the mean, the median, and the mode.

Arithmetic Mean

The *arithmetic mean* of a data set, usually called just the mean, is the sum of the measures in the data set divided by the number of measures in the set. This results in an average value of the data set. For example, if Bob's grades on his four statistics tests are 74, 83, 69, and 78, the average value of his grades—the mean of this data set—is obtained by adding these four measures and dividing by 4: $\bar{x} = (74 + 83 + 69 + 78) \div 4 = 304/4 = 76$. Notice that the symbol for mean of a data set is $\bar{x}$, pronounced *x* bar.

The formula for finding the mean of a set of measurements, or data set, is

$$\bar{x} = \sum_{i=1}^{n} \frac{x_i}{n} = \frac{x_1 + x_2 + x_3 + \dots + x_n}{n}$$

where n is the number of data points and $\sum x_i$ is the sum of the n data points. In the previous chapter an example listed the prices of twenty randomly selected new automobiles. These prices in dollars are reproduced below:

Data Set 1

8520	9274	8142	11298	10624
7987	11172	12899	10737	9198
13625	9462	11847	10178	12240
11690	10069	11240	12745	12995

To find the mean price for a new automobile, add the prices and divide the sum by 20, the number of prices or data points in the data set. Using a calculator to add these is simple: just enter each number, and hit the "+" button. If you have statistics functions on your calculator, the method of entering numbers is different. After you enter all the numbers using the statistics function, press the button marked $\bar{x}$ (this is usually a second function) to get the mean.

Using the calculator without its statistics function, the sum of the prices of these new cars is 215942. Dividing this sum by the number of prices, 20, gives the mean price of the twenty cars listed above: $\bar{x} = \$10,797.10$. Notice that none of the prices is $10,797.10, but the mean is this number. If this mean were subtracted from each car price and these differences added, they would total 0: the mean is exactly in the middle of the data set.

Exercise 3.1: John's scores on five statistics tests were 85, 74, 92, 68, 86. Find the mean of John's statistics scores.

Answer:

$$\sum_{i=1}^{n} \frac{x_i}{n} = \frac{x_1 + x_2 + x_3 + x_4 + x_5}{n}$$

$$\bar{x} = \frac{(85 + 74 + 92 + 68 + 86)}{5} = \frac{405}{5} = 81$$

Exercise 3.2: John must take a sixth and last test in statistics. In order to get a B for the course, he needs to have an 80 average or better. Assuming his first five scores were those listed in Exercise 3.1, what is the lowest grade he can receive on his last test to earn a B for the course (that is, the mean of all six grades should be at least 80)?

Answer: A little algebra is needed here. John needs to determine what sixth grade, x_6, he would need so that the average of the five tests he has already taken plus x_6 would be at least 80. Therefore, letting $x = x_6$:

$$\frac{85 + 74 + 92 + 86 + x}{6} = 80 \ (minimum\ mean)$$

$$\frac{405 + x}{6} = 80$$

$$405 + x = 80\,(6) = 480$$

$$x = 75$$

John needs at least 75% on the last test to earn a B.

Exercise 3.3: In Exercise 2.9 in the previous chapter, I.Q.s of thirty students in a statistics class were given. These are reproduced below. Find, to the nearest point, the mean I.Q. of students in this class.

Data Set 4

97	100	109	122	118	124
127	105	112	128	107	114
115	121	135	98	111	117
120	130	123	141	107	113
116	119	121	131	129	139

Answer:

$$\bar{x} = \frac{97 + 100 + 109 + \dots 129 + 139}{30} = \frac{3549}{30} = 118.3 \approx 118$$

Median

Another measure of central tendency, another "middle" of a data set, is the median. This number, which is sometimes denoted $\tilde{x}$, is the middle value in a set of numbers that has been arranged lowest to highest. The data set consisting of the numbers 1, 3, 5, 6, 100 has already been arranged in order, lowest to highest: the lowest number is 1, the next is 3, and so on. The median would therefore be the third number in this set of measures, i.e., 5.

The arithmetic mean of the data set {1, 3, 5, 6, 100} is 23. In this case, the median presents a better measure of central tendency than the mean because most of the numbers are low. The median is a good central tendency measure in a set in which the data is *skewed*. A skewed data set is one in which one or more numbers is much larger or much smaller than the rest.

The median is calculated by arranging the numbers in rank order from smallest to largest (1st, 2d, 3d, etc.) and labeling the number in the middle rank. If the data set has an even number of data points, the median is defined as the mean of the numbers in the middle two ranks. For example, the set of numbers {1, 3, 5, 6, 100, 101} is already arranged in order from lowest to highest, in this case 1st, 2d, 3d, 4th, 5th, 6th. Since there is an even number of data points in this set, the median is calculated by taking the mean of the *two* middle ranked numbers, in this case the 3d and 4th numbers, which are 5 and 6: $(5 + 6) \div 2 = 5.5$, so $\tilde{x} = 5.5$.

A data set in the previous section listed the prices of new cars. This set is reproduced below:

Data Set 1

8520	9274	8142	11298	10624
7987	11172	12899	10737	9198
13625	9462	11847	10178	12240
11690	10069	11240	12745	12995

There are twenty numbers in this data set. To find its median, $\tilde{x}$, the twenty prices must first be arranged in rank order from smallest to largest. The median will be the mean of the middle two ranked numbers. In this case, the 10th– and 11th–ranked numbers are the middle two.

To rearrange these numbers in rank order, first find the smallest for the first rank, then the next smallest for the second, etc. The data set arranged in rank order looks like this:

Rank	Price	Rank	Price	Rank	Price	Rank	Price
1	7987	6	9462	11	11172	16	12240
2	8142	7	10069	12	11240	17	12745
3	8520	8	10178	13	11298	18	12899
4	9198	9	10624	14	11690	19	12995
5	9274	10	10737	15	11847	20	13625

This tabulation can be done most easily using a stem and leaf display or a relative frequency table. The numbers that are of interest are the two middle ones, the 10th-ranked price, $10,737, and the 11th-ranked price, $11,172. The mean of these two prices is $(10,737 + 11,172)/2 = \$10,954.50$. Note that this is slightly higher than the mean of this set, $10,797.10, which was calculated in the section on arithmetic means.

Exercise 3.4: Data Set 2 for Exercise 2.5, mileage for twenty new cars, is reproduced below.

Data Set 2

27	25	31	19	40
20	17	24	25	32
47	34	26	31	22
26	28	30	31	41

    a. Find the mean number of miles per gallon for the twenty cars.
    b. Find the median number of miles per gallon for the same data set.

Answers:

a. $\bar{x} = \sum_{i=1}^{20} \dfrac{x_i}{20} = \dfrac{576}{20} = 28.8$

b. Ranking the miles per gallon figures from smallest to largest, there are again twenty ranks. The two middle ranks are the 10th and 11th, as in the car price example above. Table 2.2, the stem and leaf display, is reproduced below.

Table 2.2

Stem	Leaf	Count
1	9, 7	2
2	7, 5, 0, 4, 5, 6, 2, 6, 8	9
3	1, 2, 4, 1, 0, 1	6
4	0, 7, 1	$\dfrac{3}{20}$

    The 11th–ranked number is the highest number in Stem 2, or 28, since there are 11 (cumulative) numbers in Stems 1 and 2. The 10th–ranked number is the next-to-highest number in Stem 2, or 27. Therefore, the median, $\tilde{x} = (27 + 28)/2 = 27.5$.

Exercise 3.5: In Exercise 3.3, I.Q.s of thirty students were listed as below. Find the median I.Q. of the thirty students.

Data Set 4

97	100	109	122	118	124
127	105	112	128	107	114
115	121	135	98	111	117
120	130	123	141	107	113
116	119	121	131	129	139

Answer: This problem can also be done using a stem and leaf display, but instead we will rank them from 1st to 30th as in the next table shown.

Rank	I.Q.	Rank	I.Q.	Rank	I.Q.	Rank	I.Q.
1	97	9	112	16	119	23	127
2	98	10	113	17	120	24	128
3	100	11	114	18	121	25	129
4	105	12	115	19	121	26	130
5	107	13	116	20	122	27	131
6	107	14	117	21	123	28	135
7	109	15	118	22	124	29	139
8	111					30	141

This set also has an even number of numbers. The middle two numbers are the 15th-ranked number, 118, and the 16th-ranked number, 119. The median is $\tilde{x} = (118 + 119)/2 = 118.5$. Notice that the median of the data set, 118.5, is very close to its mean of 118.3

Mode

The *mode* of a data set is a third measure of central tendency. It is the number that appears most frequently in the set. The set $\{1, 1, 1, 2, 3, 7, 7, 9\}$ has a mode of 1 since that number appears three times, more than any other. If a set has two numbers that appear the same number of times and more than any other numbers in the set, then the set is called *bimodal*. The set $\{1, 1, 2, 3, 7, 7, 9\}$ is bimodal since there are two numbers, 1 and 7, that are represented twice, while the others appear only once. For larger data sets, a stem and leaf diagram can help to identify the mode or modes.

Data Set 1, the prices of new cars, has no mode since each price appears only once.

MODAL CLASS

Modal *class* is another measure of central tendency. It is defined as the class in the relative frequency distribution table, or histogram, that has the most data points in it. For example, in Chapter 2, a frequency distribution and a histogram summarized the data on car prices (Table 2.3 and Figure 2.1), using five classes. The highest frequency (7) occurred in the class whose boundaries were 10,000 and 11,499. Therefore, this is the modal class for this data when five classes are used.

Exercise 3.6: Find the mode of the data set of mileage per gallon for twenty new cars, as listed in Exercise 3.4 above. This set is reproduced below.

Data Set 2

27	25	31	19	40
20	17	24	25	32
47	34	26	31	22
26	28	30	31	41

Answer: The stem and leaf display is reproduced in the next table:

Table 2.2

Stem	Leaf	Count
1	9, 7	2
2	7, 5, 0, 4, 5, 6, 2, 6, 8	9
3	1, 2, 4, 1, 0, 1	6
4	0, 7, 1	3
		$\overline{20}$

It is clear from this table that there are three cars that get 31 miles per gallon. Since there are no other miles per gallon figures that are represented three times, 31 is the mode of the data set.

Look at the three measures of central tendency of Data Set 2. The mean, $\bar{x} = 28.8$, the median, $\tilde{x} = 27.5$, and the mode is 31. Each "middle" is a different number.

Exercise 3.7: Find the mode of the data set consisting of the I.Q.s of thirty students. See Data Set 4, used in Exercise 3.5.

Answer: The rank order of these I.Q.s was used for the median in Exercise 3.5; this can help us spot the two I.Q. measures that occur the most, 107 and 121, which are represented twice each in the data set (frequency for each is 2). Therefore, 107 and 121 are the modes of this bimodal distribution.

Exercise 3.8: Using the relative frequency distribution of the above data set in Table 2.10, what is the modal class of this data set?

Data Set 4

97	100	109	122	118	124
127	105	112	128	107	114
115	121	135	98	111	117
120	130	123	141	107	113
116	119	121	131	129	139

Answer: Referring to Table 2.10 in Chapter 2, the class that consists of I.Q.s between 114.5 and 123.5 has the highest frequency of all five classes, 10. Therefore, the modal class for a five-class frequency distribution is 114.5–123.5.

FREQUENCY DISTRIBUTIONS

If a frequency polygon is smoothed, the resulting curve can take one of several shapes. Three of these are indicated by the figures below.

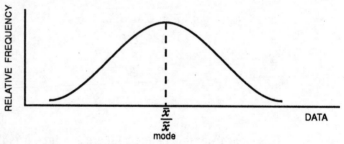

Figure 3.1:
Symmetric Distribution

Symmetric Distribution

The distribution in Figure 3.1 is called *symmetric* because both sides are exactly the same. If this curve meets certain other criteria (which will be discussed in Chapters 4 and 6), it is called a *normal* or *bell-shaped* distribution. In this symmetric distribution, the mean, median, and mode (or modal class) are identical (in the same place) as shown by the dashed line.

Skewed Distributions

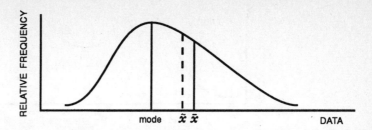

Figure 3.2:
Right-Skewed Distribution

The curve in Figure 3.2 is skewed to the right. It illustrates that there are a few very high values in the data set this curve represents. Since there are only a few of these high numbers, the mean is higher than (to the right of) the median in a right-skewed distribution.

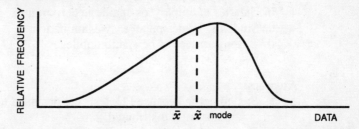

Figure 3.3:
Left-Skewed Distribution

The curve in Figure 3.3 is skewed to the left. It shows a data set containing a few numbers that are much lower than most of the other numbers. The mean is lower than (to the left of) the median in a left-skewed distribution.

In all three cases, the mode is at the highest point of the curve. Recalling that this is a smoothed frequency polygon, this highest point of the curve is the midpoint of the top of the rectangle that represents the modal class, which is the class with the highest frequency.

Bimodal Distribution

The curve in Figure 3.4 represents a bimodal distribution, one in which there are two modes or in which two relative frequency classes have the same, or nearly the same, frequency.

An example of a bimodal distribution might be heights of people in a set that contains both men and women. The set would have two modes: one, perhaps 64 inches, representing the height of the largest number of women in the set, and one, perhaps 70 inches, representing the height of the largest number of men in the data set.

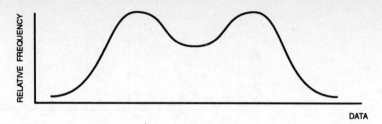

Figure 3.4:
Bimodal Distribution

Exercise 3.9: Consider the following data sets. For each, decide whether the smoothed curve of the frequency polygon would be (S) symmetric, (R) skewed right, or (L) skewed left. Why?

    a. I.Q.s of a large sample of people chosen at random.
    b. Salaries of employees at a large corporation.
    c. Students' grades on an easy examination.
    d. Base list prices of new automobiles.

Answers:

    a. S: symmetric because I.Q. tests are designed to produce measures that are normally distributed.
    b. R: skewed right because there are a few very high salaries, like the salaries of the president and CEO.
    c. L: skewed left because there will be a few low grades, but many high ones.
    d. R: skewed right because there are a few very high priced cars, like Rolls Royce.

*T*his chapter discussed measures of central tendency in a set of numbers. Three of these are the arithmetic mean (denoted $\bar{x}$), the median or middle number in a ranked data set (denoted $\tilde{x}$), and the mode or most frequently occurring number in a set. The modal class is the relative frequency or histogram class with the highest number.

    Data sets that are represented by smoothed frequency polygons can be symmetric, skewed right, or skewed left. The shape depends on whether the distribution of numbers in the set is approximately the same on either side of the mean, or whether a very few of the numbers are much higher or lower than most of the others. The relative positions of the mean and median in these sets depends on the shape of the smoothed polygon. In a symmetric data set, the mean and the median are approximately the same number; if the distribution is skewed right, the mean is higher than the median; if it is skewed left, the median is higher than the mean.

Exercise 3.10: The following data set represents the ages, to the nearest year, of 27 students in a statistics class.

Data Set 5

17	21	23	19	27	18
20	21	28	31	18	21
24	30	25	19	22	27
35	18	29	22	20	30
28	21	23			

    a.   Make a stem and leaf display for these ages.

    b.   Using five classes, construct a relative frequency table and a histogram for this data. Then construct a frequency polygon and smooth it.

    c.   Describe the shape of the frequency polygon. What relationship would you expect to find between the location of the median and the location of the mean? Why?

    d.   Find the mean, median, mode, and modal class for the data.

Answers:

    a.   See Table 3.1.

Table 3.1

Stem and Leaf Display

Stem	Leaf	Count
1	7, 9, 8, 8, 9, 8	6
2	1, 3, 7, 0, 1, 8, 1, 4, 5, 2,	17
	7, 9, 2, 0, 8, 1, 3	
3	1, 0, 5, 0	4
		$\overline{27}$

Table 3.2

Relative Frequency Distribution

Ages	Frequency	Relative Frequency
16.5–20.5	8	.30
20.5–24.5	9	.33
24.5–28.5	5	.19
28.5–32.5	4	.15
32.5–36.5	1	.04
	$\overline{27}$	1.01*

*Not exactly 1.00 due to rounding

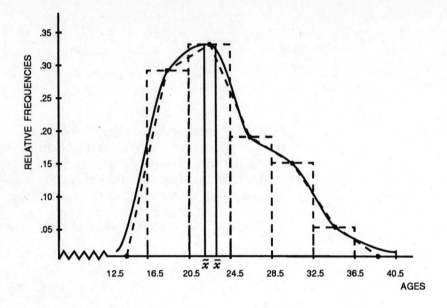

Figure 3.5:
Relative Frequency Histogram – Boxes
Relative Frequency Polygon – Dashed Line
Smoothed Relative Frequency Polygon –Solid Line

b.   Range: $35 - 17 = 18$; $18 + 1 = 19$, $19/5 = 3.8 \approx 4$. Five classes, each of width 4, starting at 16.5. See Table 3.2

c.   See Fig 3.5. The distribution curve in Figure 3.5 is skewed right. Therefore, the median should be lower than the mean (there are a small number of higher ages).

d.   Mean:

$$\bar{x} = \frac{\sum x_i}{27} = \frac{637}{27} = 23.59$$

Median:
The median is the 14th ranked (middle) number, since 27 is an odd number. In the stem and leaf display above, notice that the 14th ranked number is in Stem 2, since the 7th through 23rd ranked numbers are in that stem.

Counting up:
the 7th number is 20, 8th is also 20, 9th is 21, 10th is 21, 11th is 21, 12th is 21, 13th is 22, and 14th is 22. Therefore, the median, $\tilde{x} = 22$. Note, as predicted in (c), the median is smaller than the mean.

Mode:
    The most frequent age, the mode, is 21. There are four 21s.
Modal class:
The class with the highest frequency is the second class, 20.5–24.5. This answer will differ if more than five classes are used.

4

Measures of Dispersion

In the previous chapter we discussed measures of central tendency, focusing on the fact that numbers in a data set tend to cluster around such middle numbers as the mean, median, and mode. In this chapter we look at the opposite tendency, that of numbers to spread, vary, or disperse from the middle number.

One dispersion measure we have already discussed and used in calculations for class width in relative frequency distribution tables is the "range." It is simply the difference between the largest and smallest numbers in a data set. For example, in the set {1, 2, 50, 98, 99}, the mean is 50 and the range is 99 – 1 = 98. In the set {40, 45, 50, 55, 60} the mean is also 50, but the range is 60 – 40 = 20. Although the two sets have the same mean, the variability or spread of the first is much greater than that of the second.

VARIANCE

For some pairs of data sets, the range does not differentiate variability. For example, consider two sets: A = {40, 40, 50, 60, 60} and B = {40, 49, 50, 51, 60}. Notice that both A and B have the same mean, $\bar{x} = 50$, and the same range, $R = 20$. But in which set are the numbers more spread out, further away from the mean? The answer is set A, in which four of the numbers are ten units away from the mean. Only two in set B are ten units from 50; two others are only one unit away. The measure of dispersion that distinguishes these differences is called the *variance* of data sets.

Calculating Variance

To determine the variance of a data set, we must find a number that indicates how far the data points vary or deviate from the mean. In calculating the variance, first we subtract the mean of the data set from each of the numbers in the data set.

For example, using set A = {40, 40, 50, 60, 60}, subtract the mean of A, $\bar{x}$ = 50, from each number in the data set. The results are –10, –10, 0, 10, and 10. Using set B = {40, 49, 50, 51, 60}, subtract the mean of B, $\bar{x}$ = 50, from each number in the data set. These differences are –10, –1, 0, 1, and 10.

The differences are called *deviations from the mean*. To check the subtraction, add all the deviations in a single set together: for set A, (-10) + (-10) + 0 + 10 + 10 = 0. The sum of the deviations itself cannot be used to calculate variance, since this sum is always 0.

The next step in calculating the variance is to square each of the deviations and sum these squared deviations. The squared sum is the number that distinguishes between data sets whose values are all clustered around the mean and data sets whose values are dispersed more.

For example, for set A, the sum of the squared differences is $(-10)^2 + (-10)^2 + 0^2 + 10^2 + 10^2 = 100 + 100 + 0 + 100 + 100 = 400$. For set B, this sum of squared differences is $(-10)^2 + (-1)^2 + 0^2 + 1^2 + 10^2 = 100 + 1 + 0 + 1 + 100 = 202$. Notice this sum is much larger for set A than for set B.

The last step in calculating variance is to divide the sum of the squared deviations by a number that is one less than the number of data points. For set A, therefore, the variance is $400 \div 4 = 100$, and for set B it is $202 \div 4 = 50.5$. Notice that the variance of set A is much greater than the variance of set B, which indicates that set A is more disperse, that its data points have a larger spread from its mean.

The formula for the variance of a data set is

$$v = \frac{\sum(x_i - \bar{x})^2}{n-1}$$

where $(x_i - \bar{x})$ is the difference between each number x_i in the data set and the mean of the data set, $\sum(x_i - \bar{x})^2$ is the sum of each of the squared differences, and $(n - 1)$ is one less than the number of data points in the set.

Exercise 4.1: Calculate the variance for the set {1, 2, 50, 98, 99}.

Answer: The mean of this set is 50. To use the formula above, subtract the mean from all the data points: 1 – 50 = –49; 2 – 50 = –48; 50 – 50 = 0; 98 – 50 = 48; 99 – 50 = 49.
Square each and add to find the sum of the squared differences:
$(-49)^2 + (-48)^2 + 0^2 + 48^2 + 49^2 = 2401 + 2304 + 0 + 2304 + 2401 = 9410$. Dividing 9410 by 4 (since there are $n = 5$ data points, $n - 1 = 4$) results in a variance of 2352.5.

Exercise 4.2: Calculate the variance for the set {40, 45, 50, 55, 60}.

Answer: These results will be displayed in a column form to make the calculations a little clearer. The mean of the data set is 50.

$(x_i - \bar{x})$	$(x_i - \bar{x})^2$	$(x_i - \bar{x})^2$
$(40 - 50)$	$(-10)^2$	100
$(45 - 50)$	$(-5)^2$	25
$(50 - 50)$	0^2	0
$(55 - 50)$	5^2	25
$(60 - 50)$	10^2	100
		$\overline{250}$

The variance is the sum of the squared deviations divided by $(n - 1)$, one less than the number of data points: $250 \div 4 = 62.5$, so $v = 62.5$.

Note that the data sets in Exercises 4.1 and 4.2 have the same number of points and the same mean, but their variances are much different.

STANDARD DEVIATION

The most common measure of dispersion is called the *standard deviation*. It is simply the square root of the variance and is represented in statistics by the letter s. As a matter of fact, the usual symbol for variance is s^2.

One advantage to using the standard deviation as a measure of dispersion instead of the variance is that the units of standard deviation are the same units as those of the data set and of the mean. For example, if the data in a set is given in dollars, then the mean is also measured in dollars, as is the standard deviation. The standard deviation, like the variance, can be used to contrast the dispersion in different data sets. But it can also be used to provide a measure of variability within a single data set. This use of the standard deviation will be discussed later in this chapter.

Using Calculators with Statistics Functions

Calculators with statistics functions have both the mean and standard deviation, usually as second or inverse operations. The mean is represented by $\bar{x}$, our usual symbol, and the standard deviation by either s or σ_{n-1}. The Greek letter σ (sigma) is used to represent standard deviation of a population (this will be discussed more fully later). Be sure you use the σ_{n-1} button rather than the σ_n button if both appear on your calculator. The σ_{n-1} button yields the sum of the squared deviations divided by $(n-1)$ whereas the σ_n button divides the sum of the squared deviations by n.

You must put your calculator into the statistics mode to calculate the mean and standard deviation. These calculations are done simultaneously: you need enter the data set only once and then press the appropriate button. The calculator presents the answers to as many decimal places as it can hold, but you will usually round off means and standard deviations to two or three decimal places when the calculations are completed.

Exercise 4.3: Find the standard deviations for the two sets of data points in Exercises 4.1 and 4.2.

Answers: In Exercise 4.1, the variance $s^2 = 2352.5$. The square root of this number, $s = 48.503$ to the nearest thousandth. The square root function appears on every calculator. In Exercise 4.2, the variance, $s^2 = 62.5$. The square root of this number, $s = 7.906$ to the nearest thousandth.

Formulas for Standard Deviation

When a calculator has no statistics functions, it is necessary to use a formula to calculate the standard deviation of a data set. Since the standard deviation is just the square root of the variance, $s = \sqrt{v}$, and

$$s = \sqrt{\frac{\sum(x_1 - \overline{x})^2}{n-1}}$$

This formula is fairly easy to work with as long as n is small (not too many data points in the set) and the mean, $\overline{x}$, is an integer. But if x is not an integer, the calculation of subtracting it from each of the numbers in the data set, which usually are whole numbers, is cumbersome. There is a shortcut formula that, while not actually very short, is a little easier to use and is exactly equal to the formula above. It is

$$s = \sqrt{\frac{\left[\sum x_i^2 - \frac{(\sum x_i)^2}{n}\right]}{(n-1)}}$$

where $\sum x_i^2$ is the sum of the squares of each of the data points, and $(\sum x_i)^2$ is the square of the sum of the data points.

Exercise 4.4: Given the data set D = {2, 7, 5, 3, 4, 1}, calculate the mean and standard deviation without using the statistics functions on a calculator.

Answers:
$$\overline{x} = \frac{\sum x_i}{n} = \frac{(2 + 7 + 5 + 3 + 4 + 1)}{6} = \frac{22}{6} \approx 3.67.$$
Since the mean is not an integer, the second formula for the standard deviation is simpler to use.

$$s = \sqrt{\frac{\left[\sum x_i^2 - \frac{(\sum x_i)^2}{n}\right]}{(n-1)}}$$

$$\sum x_i^2 = 2^2 + 7^2 + 5^2 + 3^2 + 4^2 + 1^2 = 4 + 49 + 25 + 9 + 16 + 1 = 104$$

$$\sum x_{i}=22; \; (\sum x_{i})^{2} = 22^{2} = 484;$$

$$\frac{(\sum x_{i})^{2}}{n} = \frac{484}{6} \approx 80.67$$

$$s = \sqrt{\frac{(104-80.67)}{(6-1)}} = \sqrt{\frac{23.33}{5}} = \sqrt{4.666} \approx 2.16$$

to the nearest hundredth. Therefore, the standard deviation of the data set D is 2.16.

Exercise 4.5: The data set for Exercise 3.4, mileage for twenty new cars, is reproduced below.

Data Set 2

27	25	31	19	40
20	17	24	25	32
47	34	26	31	22
26	28	30	31	41

Find the standard deviation of this data set.

Answer: Using the calculator in statistics mode, the standard deviation s = 7.57 to the nearest hundredth.

To do this problem without the statistics functions on your calculator, recall from Exercise 3.4 that the mean $\bar{x}$ = 28.8. Use the alternate formula to compute the standard deviation:

$$s = \sqrt{\frac{\left[\sum x_{i}^{2} - \frac{(\sum x_{i})^{2}}{n}\right]}{(n-1)}}$$

Following are the results of some preliminary calculations:

$$\sum x_{i}^{2} = 17678; \; \sum x_{i} = 576;$$

$$(\sum x_{i})^{2} = (576)^{2} = 331776;$$

$$\frac{(\sum x_{i})^{2}}{n} = \frac{331776}{20} = 16588.8;$$

$$s = \sqrt{\frac{(17678-16588.8)}{19}} = \sqrt{\frac{1089.2}{19}} \approx \sqrt{57.326} = 7.57$$

The standard deviation of the above set is 7.57.

Using the Standard Deviation

The standard deviation, taken along with the mean, can be used to provide a measure of variability within a single data set, as well as a contrast between two data sets. We can use the standard deviation in a single data set by finding intervals of one, two, and three standard deviations around the mean and counting the number and percentage of data points within those intervals.

A one standard deviation interval from the mean is the set of numbers ranging from one standard deviation to the left of the mean, $\bar{x} - s$, to one standard deviation to the right of the mean, $\bar{x} + s$. This interval may be written in two ways: $(\bar{x} - s, \ \bar{x} + s)$ or $\bar{x} \pm s$.

In the data set from Exercise 4.4, D = {2, 7, 5, 3, 4, 1}, $\bar{x} = 3.67$, and $s = 2.16$, to the nearest hundredth. A one standard deviation interval from the mean is 3.67 ± 2.16 or $(1.51, 5.83)$. Notice that the data points 2, 3, 4, and 5 from D are within one standard deviation of the mean. Four of the six points, approximately 67% of the data points in D, are within one standard deviation of the mean.

A two standard deviation interval is the set of numbers between the mean minus two standard deviations, $\bar{x} - 2s$ and the mean plus two standard deviations, $\bar{x} + 2s$. Its notation is $(\bar{x} - 2s, \ \bar{x} + 2s)$ or $\bar{x} + 2s$. In the above set, {2, 7, 5, 3, 4, 1}, the two standard deviation interval is $3.67 \pm 2(2.16) = 3.67 \pm 4.32$ or $(-.65, 7.99)$. Notice that 1, 2, 3, 4, 5, and 7, all the numbers in D or 100% of the data points, are within two standard deviations of the mean.

Similarly, a three standard deviation from the mean is the interval $(\bar{x} - 3s, \ \bar{x} + 3s)$ or $\bar{x} \pm 3s$.

Exercise 4.6:   Using the miles per gallon figures below, the mean ($\bar{x} = 28.8$) calculated in Exercise 3.4, and the standard deviation ($s = 7.57$) calculated in Exercise 4.5:

   a. Find the one standard deviation interval for the data set. Indicate which points and what percentage of the entire data set fall in this interval.

   b. Repeat (a) for the two standard deviation interval.

   c. Repeat (b) for the three standard deviation interval.

Data Set 2

27	25	31	19	40
20	17	24	25	32
47	34	26	31	22
26	28	30	31	41

Answers:

   a. $\bar{x} \pm s = 28.8 \pm 7.57 = (21.23, 36.37)$. From the data set above, the following numbers are in the one standard deviation interval: {27, 26, 25, 34, 28, 31, 24, 26, 30, 25, 31, 31, 32, 22}. Since fourteen of the twenty numbers in the data set are in the $(\bar{x} \pm s)$ interval, 70% of the numbers in Data Set 2 are within one standard deviation of the mean.

b. $x \pm 2s = 28.8 \pm 2(7.57) = 28.8 \pm 15.14 = (13.66, 43.94)$. From the data set above, in addition to the fourteen numbers that are in the one standard deviation interval, the numbers {20, 17, 19, 40, 41} are in the two standard deviation interval, making a total of nineteen of the twenty numbers or 95% of the numbers in Data Set 2 that are in the $\bar{x} \pm 2s$ interval.

c. $x \pm 3s = 28.8 \pm 3(7.57) = 28.8 \pm 22.71 = (6.09, 51.51)$. All of the miles per gallon figures from Data Set 2, or 100% of the numbers in the set, are within three standard deviations of the mean.

EMPIRICAL AND CHEBYSHEV'S RULES

The Empirical Rule

A certain smoothed frequency polygon is called a *normal* or *bell-shaped* curve. This normal frequency distribution has certain properties that taken together are called the *Empirical Rule*. The Empirical Rule states that if a frequency distribution is normal, then:

a. Approximately 68% of the data points will have a value within one standard deviation of the mean, $\bar{x} \pm s$.

b. Approximately 95% of the data points will have a value within two standard deviations of the mean, $\bar{x} \pm 2s$.

c. Almost all of the data points ($\approx 99.7\%$) will have a value within three standard deviations of the mean, $\bar{x} \pm 3s$.

Notice in Exercise 4.6 above that 70% of the data points fell within one standard deviation of the mean, 95% within two standard deviations, and 100% within three standard deviations. Since these percentages are very close to those given by the Empirical Rule, the distribution of the miles per gallon figures for these cars is approximately a normal distribution. Another way to say this is that the set of items in Data Set 2 seems to be normally distributed.

Chebyshev's Rule

Even if the frequency distribution is not normal, *Chebyshev's Rule* applies. It states that for any frequency distribution:

a. Possibly very few data points are within one standard deviation of the mean, $\bar{x} \pm s$, but

b. At least 3/4 of the data points are within two standard deviations of the mean, $\bar{x} \pm 2s$, and

c. At least 8/9 of the data points are within three standard deviations of the mean, $\bar{x} \pm 3s$.

d. Generally, at least $1 - 1/k^2$ of the measurements in the data set have a value within k standard deviations of the mean, in the interval $\bar{x} \pm ks$, for any number $k > 1$.

Chebyshev's Rule holds for any frequency distribution. Even one shaped like a U would still produce the "at least" fraction of data points within two, three, and up to k standard deviations of the mean.

The Empirical Rule is a subrule of Chebyshev's. For example, approximately 95% of the data points in a normal frequency distribution are within two standard deviations of the mean; however, at least 3/4 or 75% of the data points in any frequency distribution are within two standard deviations of the mean. Therefore, in a normal distribution, at least 75% (namely 95%, which is at least 75% and a lot more) of the points are within two standard deviations of the mean. Part (d) of Chebyshev's Rule says that for any distribution we can find the least fraction of the set of points that are within any number of standard deviations (above 1) from the mean. For example, the fraction of the set of data points of any distribution that are within five standard deviations of the mean is $(1 - 1/5^2) = 1 - 1/25 = 1 - .04 = .96$ or 96%. Therefore, 96% of the data points in any distribution are within five standard deviations of the mean. Of course, if the distribution is normal, more than 99% of the data points are within only three standard deviations of the mean.

Exercise 4.7: In Exercise 2.9, the I.Q.s of thirty students in a statistics class were given. The data is reproduced below:

Data Set 4

97	100	109	122	118	124
127	105	112	128	107	114
115	121	135	98	111	117
120	130	123	141	107	113
116	119	121	131	129	139

a. Find the mean and standard deviation for the data set.
b. Find the one, two, and three standard deviation intervals.
c. What actual percentages of the above I.Q.s are within one, two, and three standard deviations of the mean?
d. As prescribed by Chebyshev's Rule, do at least $(1 - 1/k2)$ of the measures fall within $(x - ks, x + ks)$ for $k = 2$?
e. Is the distribution of I.Q.s in Data Set 4 approximately normal?

Answers:
a. In Exercise 3.3, the mean was calculated: $\bar{x} = 118.3$. To calculate s, use the shortcut formula:

$$s = \sqrt{\frac{\left[\sum x_i^2 - \frac{(\sum x_i)^2}{n}\right]}{(n-1)}}$$

$$\sum x_i^2 = 423,615$$

$$\sum x_i = 3549$$

$n = 30$ so

$$s = \sqrt{\frac{(423,615) - \dfrac{3549^2}{30}}{(30 - 1)}}$$

$$= \sqrt{\frac{423,615 - \dfrac{12,595,401}{30}}{29}} = \sqrt{\frac{3768.3}{29}}$$

$$= \sqrt{129.94} \approx 11.4 \text{ to the nearest tenth.}$$

The standard deviation of Data Set 4 is 11.4 to the nearest tenth.

b. $\bar{x} \pm s = 118.3 \pm 11.4 = (106.9, 129.7)$
    $\bar{x} \pm 2s = 118.3 \pm 2(11.4) = 118.3 \pm 22.8 = (95.5, 141.1)$
    $\bar{x} \pm 3s = 118.3 \pm 3(11.4) = 118.3 \pm 34.2 = (84.1, 152.5)$

c. Twenty-one of the thirty scores are within one standard deviation of the mean, i.e., in the interval (106.9, 129.7); 21/30 = 70%. Nine more of the thirty scores are within two standard deviations of the mean, i.e., in the interval (95.5, 141.1); 30/30 = 1 = 100%.

    Since all of the scores are within two standard deviations of the mean, they are also all within three standard deviations of the mean, i.e., in the interval (84.1, 152.5): 100%.

d. For $k = 2$, $1 - 1/k^2 = 1 - (1/2)^2 = 3/4$. At least 75% of the measures should be within two standard deviations of the mean. In reality, 100% of the numbers in Data Set 4 are within two standard deviations of the mean.

e. According to part (c), 70% of the I.Q. measures from Data Set 4 are within one standard deviation of the mean and 100% of these I.Q. measures are within two standard deviations of the mean.

    The Empirical Rule, which is true for all normal curves, says that about 68% of the data points from a normal distribution will be within one standard deviation, and 95% will be within two standard deviations. The 70% and 100% actual percentages in this example are usually considered to be close enough to the 68% and 95% from the Empirical Rule to say that this data set is *approximately* normally distributed.

Z-SCORES

In order to get a general idea of how a certain data point is related to the mean, the standard deviation, and other data points, it is useful to look at that data point on a smoothed frequency polygon whose mean and standard deviation have been indicated. This smoothed frequency polygon is called a *distribution curve*.

Suppose the set of car prices, Data Set 1, and the set of miles per gallon, Data Set 2, are really different measures on the same cars. Look at these two sets again:

Data Set 1 (Prices of New Cars)

8520	9274	8142	11298	10624
7987	11172	12899	10737	9198
13625	9462	11847	10178	12240
11690	10069	11240	12745	12995

The mean of this set is $10,797.10. The standard deviation turns out to be $1675.63: $\bar{x} = 10797.10$ and $s = 1675.63$.

Data Set 2 (Miles per Gallon of New Cars)

27	25	31	19	40
20	17	24	25	32
47	34	26	31	22
26	28	30	31	41

The mean of this set is 28.8, and the standard deviation is 7.57: $\bar{x} = 28.8$ and $s = 7.57$.

These two data sets represent the same cars in the order they appear on the grid. As discussed in Chapter 1, these tables are really matrices, so the cars can be named by their matrix position.

For example, suppose the car in the (1,1) position, first row, first column, is called Car A, and Car B is in the (1,2) position, first row, second column, in both data sets. Car H, the one we will be discussing here, is in the (2,3) position, second row, third column.

In the price data set, Data Set 1, the one standard deviation interval is $\bar{x} \pm s = 10797.10 \pm 1675.63 = (9121.47, 12472.73)$. Car H, which costs $12,899, is more than one standard deviation to the right of the mean of its Data Set 1.

In Data Set 2, the miles per gallon data set, the one standard deviation interval is $\bar{x} \pm s = 28.8 \pm 7.57 = (21.23, 36.37)$. Car H, which averages 24 miles per gallon, is less than one standard deviation to the left of the mean of its Data Set 2. Car H thus costs over one standard deviation more than the mean price per car in Data Set 1, but gets less than one standard deviation fewer miles per gallon than the mean miles per gallon per car in Data Set 2.

What is needed here is a better way to compare a particular data set item to others in its data set, and then to be able to say something meaningful about that comparison relative to other measures in the same or other data sets. These data sets have different means and different standard deviations and contain different data. Their *z-scores* (discussed below) can put data points from these sets on the same curve.

Standard Unit Normal

The standard unit normal is a normal distribution with mean equal to zero and standard deviation equal to one ($\bar{x} = 0$ and $s = 1$). This curve is sketched in Figure 4.1.

As in all normal curves, the Empirical Rule holds. So 68% of the area under the curve is within one standard deviation of the mean. In ordinary curves, this would be represented by the interval ($\bar{x} - s$, $\bar{x} + s$), but in the standard unit

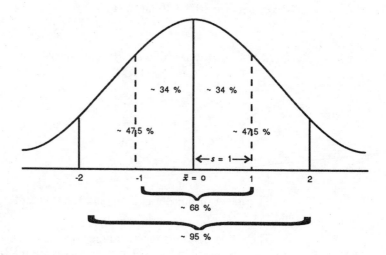

Figure 4.1:
Standard Unit Normal

normal, this one standard deviation interval is $(0 - 1, 0 + 1) = (-1, 1)$. Similarly, 95% of the area under the curve is in the two-standard deviation interval $(-2, 2)$.

Each data point has a *z-score* on this standard unit normal curve. If a data point in the original set were exactly two standard deviations above the mean, its z-score would equal 2. If a data point were exactly one standard deviation below the mean, its z-score would be –1.

The mean of Data Set 2 is $\bar{x} = 28.8$, and its standard deviation $s = 7.57$. Again, look at the miles per gallon for Car H, 24. How far is the data point 24 from the mean 28.8, in terms of the number of standard deviations? The rough estimate was that 24 is less than one standard deviation to the left of the mean, 28.8. But the z-score can be calculated for a more accurate answer.

Calculating Z-Scores

The formula for calculating a z-score is

$$z = \left(\frac{x_i - \bar{x}}{s}\right)$$

where x_i is the data point whose z-score is to be calculated, $\bar{x}$ is the mean, and s the standard deviation of the data set containing x_i.

To calculate the z-score for 24, the mileage for Car H, use the above formula:

$$z = \frac{24 - 28.8}{7.57} = -\frac{4.8}{7.57} = -.63.$$

Car H's z-score for miles per gallons (mpg) is −.63, so its mpg is .63 standard deviations below (to the left of) the mean in its data set (2). (Fig 4.2)

To calculate the z-score for Car H's price, $12,899, use the mean (10797.10) and standard deviation (1675.63) of Data Set 1 in the formula for z-score:

$$z = \frac{12899 - 10797.10}{1675.63} = \frac{2101.90}{1675.63} = 1.25.$$

Car H's z-score for price is 1.25, so its price is 1.25 standard deviations above (to the right of) the mean in its data set. This is pictured in Figure 4.3.

Now we can be more precise in our analysis of the worth of Car H. The z-score of its price is $z = 1.25$, and the z-score of its mpg is $z = -.63$. If miles per gallon is the only criterion you use, Car H is not a good buy, since the z-score for its price is far above the mean and the z-score for its mpg is only a little bit below the mean. However, most people look at other features in addition to mileage figures when purchasing a car.

Exercise 4.8: Using the mean and standard deviation of the set of I.Q.s from Data Set 4 in Exercise 4.7 ($\bar{x} = 118.3$, $s = 11.4$), find z-scores for the following data points: a. 123   b. 139   c. 118   d. 97

Answers: The formula for calculating z-scores is:

$$z = \frac{x_i - \bar{x}}{s}$$

a. $z = (123 - 118.3) \div 11.4 = 4.7 \div 11.4 = .41$
b. $z = (139 - 118.3) \div 11.4 = 20.7 \div 11.4 = 1.82$
c. $z = (118 - 118.3) \div 11.4 = -.3 \div 11.4 = -.03$
d. $z = (97 - 118.3) \div 11.4 = -21.3 \div 11.4 = -1.87$

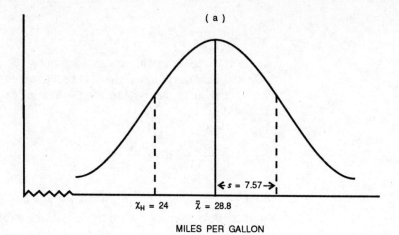

(a)

$x_H = 24$ $\bar{x} = 28.8$ $s = 7.57$

MILES PER GALLON

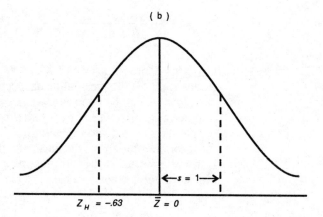

(b)

$Z_H = -.63$ $\bar{Z} = 0$ $s = 1$

Figure 4.2:
Standard Unit Normal

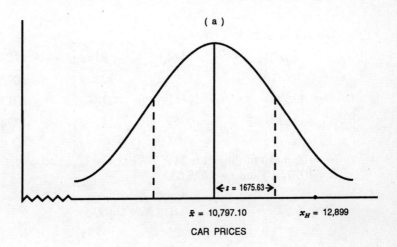

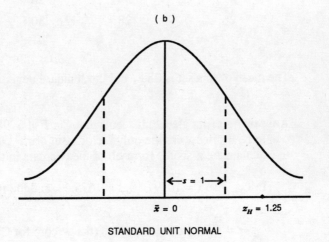

Figure 4.3:
Standard Unit Normal

Exercise 4.9: A car buyer has narrowed his choices to two new cars, Car E and Car F. Recall that Car E is in the (1,5) position in both the price (Data Set 1) and the miles per gallon (Data Set 2) matrices, and Car F is in the (2,1) position. If mileage and price are the chief criteria in choosing a car, which one should he choose and why?

Data Set 1 (Prices of New Cars)

8520	9274	8142	11298	10624(E)
7987(F)	11172	12899	10737	9198
13625	9462	11847	10178	12240
11690	10069	11240	12745	12995

The mean of this set is $10,797.10. The standard deviation is $1675.63: $\bar{x} = 10797.10$ and $s = 1675.63$.

Data Set 2 (Miles per Gallon of New Cars)

27	25	31	19	40(E)
20(F)	17	24	25	32
47	34	26	31	22
26	28	30	31	41

The mean of this set is 28.8, and the standard deviation is 7.57: $\bar{x} = 28.8$ and $s = 7.57$.

Answer: At first glance, it seems that Car F at $7987 is the better buy, and it would be if price were the only factor. But Car F gets only 20 mpg. We need to calculate the z-scores for each of the two cars in their respective data sets:

Price: Use $\bar{x} = 10797.10$, $s = 1675.63$, and the formula

$z = \dfrac{x_i - \bar{x}}{s}$ to calculate z_{EP} (the z-score for Car E's price):

$z_{EP} = (10624 - 10797.10) \div 1675.63$

$\qquad = -173.1/1675.63 = -.10$

Calculating z_{FP} (the z-score for Car F's price):

$z_{FP} = (7987 - 10797.10) \div 1675.63$

$$= -2810.1/1675.63 = -1.68.$$

MPG: Using $\bar{x} = 28.8$ and $s = 7.57$, calculate z_{EM} (the z-score for Car E's mileage):

$$z_{EM} = (40 - 28.8) \div 7.57 = 1.48 \text{ . Then}$$
$$z_{FM} = (20 - 28.8) \div 7.57 = -1.16$$

Car E has a price z-score of -0.10 and a mileage z-score of 1.48. Car F has a price z-score of -1.68 and a mileage z-score of -1.16. Recall that the car buyer is looking for the best (lowest) price and the best (highest) mileage. Although Car F has the lower price, it has the higher mileage figure. Car E is below the mean (has a negative z-score) for price and above the mean (has a positive z-score) for mileage. Car E may be the better purchase for this consumer if mileage and price are the chief criteria.

MEDIAN-BASED MEASURES: PERCENTILES, DECILES, AND QUARTILES

As mentioned in Chapter 3, sometimes the median is a better measure of central tendency than is the mean. In particular, if the data is skewed, i.e., if a very few measures are much higher or much lower than the others in the data set, then the median is a better middle number than the mean. If the median is used to describe the middle of a data set, then data points are placed in median-based dispersion measures rather than a mean-based dispersion measure (the standard deviation). These dispersion measures are known as percentiles.

Percentiles

For a set of measures arranged in rank order, the pth *percentile* is a number such that $p\%$ of the measures are below the pth percentile and $(1 - p)\%$ of the measures are above the pth percentile.

For example, suppose Meg received a 75 on her statistics test. To find what percentile her grade is in, all the grades are arranged in rank order. There must be a large number of grades in order for the percentile to be meaningful. Suppose there were 100 grades in this test, and 80% of them were below the 75 that Meg received. Then Meg's test score is in the 80th percentile.

In order to use the median and its percentiles, all measures in a data set must be placed in rank order. For example, suppose the numbers in a certain ordered set are $\{1, 2, 3, 4, 5, 7\}$. The median of this set is 3.5 and can be renamed as the 50th percentile. This means that 50% of the numbers in the set are *below* 3.5. In a similar manner, the number 3 is the 33rd percentile since 1/3 of the data points fall below 3.

If a number is in the 99th percentile, 99% of the data points in the set are below this number. Scores on standardized tests such as achievement tests are often reported in percentiles. If your score in mathematics is in the 60th percentile, 60% of the people taking the examinations scored lower than you in math; the remainder, $(100 - 60)\% = 40\%$, scored higher. In large sets of data, any one score is negligible. However, no one's grade is in the 100th or 0th percentile: 100% or 0% of everyone taking the examination cannot score higher or lower than you because your score is one of the grades counted and you can not score higher or lower than yourself.

Deciles and Quartiles

Deciles are ten percentile divisions. For example, if a score is in the fourth decile, it is the same as the 40th percentile. Colleges often ask in which decile of a graduating class an applicant's grade point average (G.P.A.) lies. A grade point average in the fourth decile is in the 31st to 40th percentile of the class.

A *quartile* is a division of scores into quarters or fourths. Q_1 is the first quartile or the 25th percentile; Q_2 is the second quartile or 50th percentile (or the median); Q_3 is the third quartile or 75th percentile. A student whose G.P.A. is in the third quartile has a rank between the 50th and 75th percentiles of the class.

Recall that to compute the median, all the numbers in the data set are arranged in rank order; the median is the number in the middle rank. If the data set contains an even number of numbers, then the two middle-ranked numbers are averaged. To divide a data set into quartiles, this same idea is extended by taking the 1/4 and 3/4 divisions of the ranks. The formulas that are used to find the ranks of Q_1 and Q_3 are:

Rank of $Q_1 = (n + 1) \div 4$ and Rank of $Q_3 = 3(n + 1) \div 4$, where n is the number of data points.

Usually, when calculated, these ranks will not be whole numbers. If they are not, round off to the nearest whole number and take the number at that rank for the quartile division.

Recall the set of new car prices discussed earlier.

Data Set 1 (Prices of New Cars)

8520	9274	8142	11298	10624
7987	11172	12899	10737	9198
13625	9462	11847	10178	12240
11690	10069	11240	12745	12995

To find the quartiles, first arrange these numbers in rank order:

Rank	Price	Rank	Price
1	7987	11	11172
2	8142	12	11240
3	8520	13	11298
4	9198	14	11690
5	9274	15	11847
6	9462	16	12240
7	10069	17	12745
8	10178	18	12899
9	10624	19	12995
10	10737	20	13625

The median, which was found earlier, is the average of the 10th- and 11th-ranked numbers, $(10737 + 11172) \div 2 = 10954.50$.

To find the rank of Q_1, take $(n + 1) \div 4 = 21 \div 4 = 5.25 \approx 5$ to the nearest whole number. Therefore, the fifth number, 9274, is Q_1. To find the rank of Q_3, take $3(n + 1) \div 4 = 3(21) \div 4 = 63 \div 4 = 15.75 \approx 16$ to the nearest whole number. Therefore, the sixteenth number, 12240, is Q_3.

Exercise 4.10: Given the twenty mileage figures as used in previous exercises:

Data Set 2

27	25	31	19	40
20	17	24	25	32
47	34	26	31	22
26	28	30	31	41

a. Find the median of Data Set 2.
b. Find its quartiles: Q_1, Q_2, and Q_3.

Answers: In order to find the median and the quartiles, all numbers should be in rank order:

Rank	Number	Rank	Number
1	17	11	28
2	19	12	30
3	20	13	31
4	22	14	31
5	24	15	31
6	25	16	32
7	25	17	34
8	26	18	40
9	26	19	41
10	27	20	47

a. The median is the average of the 10th- and 11th-ranked numbers: $\tilde{x} = 27.5$.

b. The rank of Q_1 is $(n + 1)/4 = 21/4 = 5.25$ or 5. Therefore, the number 24, which is in the 5th rank, represents Q_1. Q_2 is the median, $\tilde{x} = 27.5$. The rank of Q_3 is $3(n + 1)/4 = 3(21)/4 = 63/4 = 15.75$ or 16. Therefore, the number 32, which is in the 16th rank, represents Q_3.

BOX PLOTS

A *box plot* is a graph whose elements are based on quartiles. It is a succinct way of describing the relationship of the data set to its median and quartiles, rather than to its mean and standard deviation. Box plots are a recent introduction to descriptive statistics methodology, and computer software has been designed to sketch the box and the other components of the plot.

We have already discussed the computations we must do to begin a box plot. Three of these are finding the median of the data set and computing the lower and upper quartiles, Q_1 and Q_3. Another necessary element to a box plot is called the *interquartile range*, IQR: $IQR = Q_3 - Q_1$.

In Exercise 4.10 above, $\tilde{x} = 27.5$, $Q_1 = 24$, and $Q_3 = 32$. Therefore, IQR = $32 - 24 = 8$.

Drawing the Box

To plot the box part of the box plot, a horizontal axis is sketched and the values of Q_1 and Q_3 are noted on the axis. In the case of the gas mileages noted earlier, the points 24 (Q_1) and 32 (Q_3) are noted on the axis (Figure 4.4).

A box is then drawn with vertical line segments at the first and third quartiles as two of its sides. Its base is the horizontal axis, and its top is the segment joining the two sides. The median is placed in the box at the appropriate number

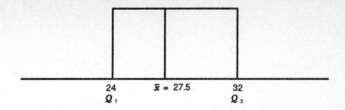

Figure 4.4:
Miles per Gallon
(Partial Box Plot)

on the horizontal axis. The median is always in this box, since the ends of the box are the quartiles.

Inner Fences

The *inner fences* are then placed. Inner fences usually define the limits of approximately 95% of the data, much the way the two standard deviations from the mean encompass the same percentage.

The inner fences are found by first multiplying the IQR by 1.5. In this case, IQR = 8 so 1.5(8) = 12. This number is subtracted from Q_1 for the lower inner fence and added to Q_3 for the upper inner fence. In this example the inner fence will be at the point on the horizontal axis given by $Q_1 - 1.5(\text{IQR}) = 24 - 12 = 12$; the outer fence will be at a point on the horizontal axis given by $Q_3 + 1.5(\text{IQR}) = 32 + 12 = 44$. Vertical lines (the inner fences) are drawn at these points, 12 and 44 (Figure 4.5).

Whiskers

The lowest and highest numbers from the original data set that are still within the inner fences are put on the box plot with asterisks (*). These asterisks are connected to the sides of the box with dotted horizontal lines. These lowest and highest data points within the inner fences, along with the connections to the box, are called *whiskers*. The length of these whiskers indicates the manner and extent to which the data set is skewed, in the direction of the longer whisker.

In the case of our present example, 17 is the lowest and 47 the highest data point. However, although 17 is within the inner fence, the highest data point within the inner fence is 41, so the whiskers are at 17 and 41, as shown in Figure 4.5. Data point 47 is higher than the inner fences.

Outer Fences

Sometimes the lowest or the highest number in the data set falls outside the inner fences. If this is the case, as with the highest number in the set being used here, 47, the outer fences must also be placed. The *outer fences* are limits between which virtually all data points fall. They are found by multiplying the IQR by 3; this product is then subtracted from Q_1 and added to Q_3.

In our present example, the outer fences are located at $Q_1 - 3(\text{IQR}) = 24 - 3(8) = 0$ and $Q_3 + 3(\text{IQR}) = 32 + 3(8) = 56$ on the horizontal axis. The outer fences are also sketched as vertical lines at their marks, 0 and 56, and the highest

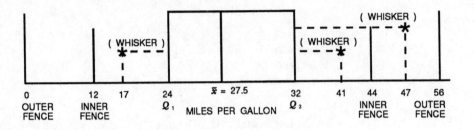

Figure 4.5:
Completed Box Plot

(and lowest) data points between the inner and outer fences are also represented by asterisks joined to the box. Figure 4.5 represents a completed box plot.

Outliers

Very rarely, some numbers in a data set fall outside the outer fence. If they do, they must also be indicated on a box plot. Sometimes an "o" is used to represent the position of these data points, which are called *outliers* or *suspect outliers*. The presence of outliers usually indicates problems with the data, either an incorrect measure or a data point that comes from a different set than the others.

Exercise 4.11: Draw a box plot for the data in Exercise 4.7, which is reproduced below. Data Set 4 contains I.Q.s of thirty statistics students.

Data Set 4

97	100	109	122	118	124
127	105	112	128	107	114
115	121	135	98	111	117
120	130	123	141	107	113
116	119	121	131	129	139

Answer: With the help of the stem and leaf display in Table 2.8, the thirty numbers are ranked as follows:

Rank	Number	Rank	Number	Rank	Number
1	97	11	114	21	123
2	98	12	115	22	124
3	101	13	116	23	127
4	105	14	117	24	128
5	107	15	118	25	129
6	107	16	119	26	130
7	109	17	120	27	131
8	111	18	121	28	135
9	112	19	121	29	139
10	113	20	122	30	141

The median is the average of the 15th- and 16th-ranked numbers, which is 118.5. The rank of $Q_1 = 31/4 = 7.75 \approx 8$, so $Q_1 = 111$, the 8th-ranked number.

The rank of $Q_3 = 3(31)/4 = 23.25 \approx 23$, so $Q_3 = 127$, the 23d-ranked number. The sides of the box are erected at 111 and 127, with the median drawn at 118.5.

The interquartile range (IQR) is $127 - 111 = 16$; $(1.5)(IQR) = 1.5(16) = 24$, so the inner fences are erected at $111 - 24 = 87$ and $127 + 24 = 151$. Since there are no data points outside these values, it is not necessary to erect the outer fences. Whiskers are at the data points 97, the smallest value inside the inner fences, and 141, the largest value inside the inner fences (Figure 4.6).

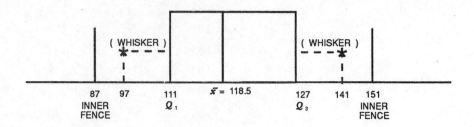

Figure 4.6:
Box Plot
I.Q. Scores

*I*n this chapter we have discussed measures of dispersion of data away from the central tendency numbers of the data set. The most useful of these measures is the standard deviation, which is the square root of the variance. The variance is calculated by taking the distances of each data point from the mean, squaring this distance, and dividing the sum of these squared distances by one less than the number of data points.

The Empirical Rule states that under a normal frequency distribution curve, approximately 68% of the data is within one standard deviation of the mean and about 95% is within two standard deviations of the mean. To find the relationship between a number in a data set and the mean of the data set, its z-score is calculated. A data point with a z-score of 1.5 is 1.5 standard deviations to the right of the mean of the data set. A data point whose z-score is −.3 is .3 standard deviations to the left of the mean of its data set.

Numbers in a data set can also be placed in relation to the median of the data set. These measures of relative standing to the median are called percentiles, deciles, and quartiles. To graphically illustrate the relationship between numbers in a data set to its quartiles, a box plot is drawn. This plot locates extreme values of data points in the set and suspect outliers, data that does not seem to belong to the data set plotted.

Exercise 4.12: In an example from Chapter Two, the weights of twenty-four men were given. This data is reproduced below.

Data Set 3

173	157	204	198	162	153
140	172	189	191	166	147
132	212	197	183	165	171
167	158	166	163	179	155

a. Find the mean and standard deviation of this data set.
b. Find the percentage of the weights within one, two, and three standard deviations of the mean. Do you think this relative frequency distribution is approximately normal? Explain.
c. Find the z-scores of the highest and lowest weights.
d. Rank these weights; find the median and the quartiles and draw a box plot for the data.

Rank	Number	Rank	Number	Rank	Number
1	132	9	163	17	179
2	140	10	165	18	183
3	147	11	166	19	189
4	153	12	166	20	191
5	155	13	167	21	197
6	157	14	171	22	198
7	158	15	172	23	204
8	162	16	173	24	212

Answers: a. The mean of the data set is calculated using the formula

$$\bar{x} = \frac{\sum x_i}{n}$$

Since $\sum x_i = 4100$, $\bar{x} = 4100 \div 24 = 170.83$. The standard deviation of the data set is calculated using the formula

$$s = \sqrt{\frac{\left[\sum x_i^2 - \frac{(\sum x_i)^2}{n}\right]}{(n-1)}}$$

$$\sum x_i{}^2 = 709{,}778; \quad \sum x_i = 4100; \quad n = 24$$

$$\left(\sum x_i\right)^2 = 16{,}810{,}000; \quad \frac{16{,}810{,}000}{24} = 700{,}416.67;$$

$$s = \frac{709{,}778 - 700{,}416.67}{23} = \frac{9361.33}{23} = 407.01 = 20.17.$$

b. $(\bar{x} \pm s)$ is (170.83 ± 20.17) or the interval $(150.66, 191)$; 16/24 or 67% of the weights are within this interval. Notice that the interval is an open interval, so 191 is not included in it.

$(\bar{x} \pm 2s)$ is (170.83 ± 40.34) or the interval $(130.49, 211.17)$; 23/24 or 96% of the weights are within this interval.

$(\bar{x} \pm 3s)$ is (170.83 ± 60.51) or the interval $(110.32, 231.34)$: all (100%) of the twenty-four weights are within this interval. The one, two, and three standard deviation percentages are 67%, 96%, and 100%; these are very close to the percentages found under the normal curve. Since the Empirical Rule states that the one, two, and three standard deviation percentages under a normal curve are 68%, 95%, and 97.4%, respectively. Therefore, the frequency distribution of these weights is approximately normal.

c. The highest weight is 212 lbs. Its z-score is given by the formula $z = (x_i - \bar{x}) / s = (212 - 170.83)/20.17 = 41.17 - 20.17 = 2.04$. Notice that this weight is more than two standard deviations from the mean, which is why it was not in the $\bar{x} \pm 2s$ interval above. The lowest weight is 132 lbs. Its z-score is given by
$z = (132 - 170.83)/20.17 = -38.83/20.17 = -1.93$.
Notice that this score is within two standard deviations less than the mean.

d. Ranking the above weights in order yields the following:

The median of this set is 166.5, the average of the 12th- and 13th-ranked weights. Q_1 is the weight at the $(24 + 1)/4 = 25/4 = 6.25$ or 6th rank, so $Q_1 = 157$. Q_3 is the weight at the $3(24 + 1)/4 = 75/4 = 18.75$ or 19th rank, so $Q_3 = 189$.

The box for the box plot should be drawn between 157 and 189.

The interquartile range is the difference between the two quartiles or IQR $= 189 - 157 = 32$. The inner fences are erected at $1.5(\text{IQR}) = 1.5(32)$ or 48 less than 157 and 48 more than 189. Therefore, the inner fences go up at $157 - 48 = 109$ and $189 + 48 = 237$. All the weights are within the inner fences; the whiskers are at 132 and 212 (Figure 4.7).

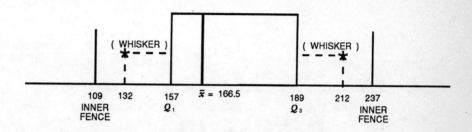

Figure 4.7:
Box Plot: Men's Weights

5

Probability

This chapter introduces elementary probability theory. Understanding probability is essential for further work in sampling and inferential statistics. Recall that inferential statistics makes inferences or guesses about an entire population based on a sample of the population. These guesses are qualified by assigning a probability to them: for example, one can be 95% sure that a certain statement is true.

SIMPLE PROBABILITIES

An *experiment* is a process leading to a result that cannot be predicted all the time. A *simple event* is the outcome or result of an experiment. For example, consider the experiment of picking a card from an ordinary deck of fifty-two cards. The event is the choice of the eight of hearts. The *sample space* of an experiment is the total number of possible *outcomes* of the experiment. The sample space of the example of choosing a card from a deck of fifty-two cards is a list of all fifty-two possible outcomes: two of clubs, nine of diamonds, king of spades, etc.

The *probability* of an event is the ratio of the number of favorable outcomes (simple events) of an experiment to the total number of outcomes in the sample space. The probability of picking an eight of clubs from a deck of cards is 1/52, since only one (the eight of clubs) of the fifty-two (total number in the sample space) is favorable. The probability ratio can be expressed as a fraction (1/52), a decimal (.01923) or a percent (1.9%). This particular probability is best expressed as a fraction, since its decimal equivalent does not terminate. All probabilities can be expressed in these three ways.

Formula for Simple Probability

The formula for a simple probability is:

$$p(x) = \frac{n(f)}{n(s)}$$

where $n(f)$ is number of favorable outcomes and $n(s)$ is total number of events in the sample space.

For our first simple probability examples, it will be helpful to list the sample space of an experiment. For example, the sample space of the experiment of tossing a coin is {H, T}, heads or tails. Set notation is used to list the possible outcomes in the sample space. If the only favorable outcome is getting heads (H) on the toss of the coin, then the set of favorable outcomes is {H}.

The number of possible outcomes in the sample space is the denominator of the probability fraction, $n(s)$. In the coin toss example, $n(s) = 2$, since there are only two outcomes in the sample space, namely H and T. The numerator of the probability fraction is the number of events in the sample space that have favorable outcomes, $n(f)$. In the coin toss example, $n(f) = 1$, since only one outcome, H, is favorable. By the formula, $p(x) = 1/2$; the probability of tossing heads on one coin toss is 1/2. This probability can also be expressed as a decimal, .5, or as a percent, 50%.

THE NUMERIC RANGE OF PROBABILITIES

If none of the events in the sample space is favorable, the probability fraction will have a numerator of 0, $n(f) = 0$; therefore, the value of the entire fraction, $p(x)$ is 0. This means that the probability of a favorable event in this sample space is 0 or, expressed as a percent, $p(x) = 0\%$.

If all of the events in the sample space are favorable, the numerator of the probability fraction will be equal to the denominator; the value of the probability fraction will then be 1, $p(x) = 1$. This means that the probability of a favorable event in that sample space is 1 or, expressed as a percent, $p(x) = 100\%$.

All probabilities, and therefore all responses to the question "what is the probability of . . . ?", are between zero and one inclusive (including 0 and 1). When probabilities are expressed as percents, all probabilities are between 0% and 100%. In formula terms, if $p(x)$ is the probability of event x, $0 \leq p(x) \leq 1$ or $0\% \leq p(x) \leq 100\%$.

Applications with a Single Outcome

Reviewing the coin toss problem, suppose a coin is tossed once. There are two outcomes in the sample space: {H, T}; $n(s)$, the denominator of the probability fraction, is 2. Suppose a favorable outcome is heads.

Of the two possible outcomes in the sample space, H and T, only one, H, is favorable; $n(f)$, the numerator of the probability fraction, is 1. Therefore $p(x)$, the probability fraction, is 1/2. Giving a value of H to x, $p(H) = 1/2$: the probability of tossing heads on a single coin toss is 1/2.

Suppose a single die (one of a pair of dice) is tossed. The events in the sample space are {1, 2, 3, 4, 5, 6}, which represent the number of dots or pips on the "up" face of the tossed die. There are six events in the sample space; $n(s) = 6$. Suppose a favorable outcome is a number less than 3. The question is, "What is the probability of tossing a number less than 3 with a die?". This question can be written symbolically as $p(x < 3)$.

Only $\{1, 2\}$, the tosses of either a 1 or a 2, are favorable events, so $n(f) =$ 2. Two of six possible outcomes are favorable. The probability of tossing a number less than 3, $p(x < 3) = n(f)/n(s) = 2/6$, which can be reduced to 1/3. Thus, $p(x < 3) = 1/3$.

Exercise 5.1: A single card is picked from an ordinary fifty-two card deck. Recall that a card deck consists of four suits, spades (S), hearts (H), diamonds (D), and clubs (C)–and thirteen denominations–2, 3, 4, 5, 6, 7, 8, 9, 10, jack, queen, king, and ace. All the cards are different. To symbolize each, a shorthand is used: for example, 3D is the three of diamonds and KH is the king of hearts. What is the probability of picking a queen from this deck in one pick?

Answer: The sample space is: $\{2S, 2H, 2D, 2C, 3S, \ldots AD, AC\}$, and $n(s) = 52$. The set of favorable outcomes is $\{QS, QH, QD, QC\}$, so $n(f) = 4$. Therefore, the probability of picking a queen from a deck of cards is $p(Q) = n(f)/n(s) = 4/52 = 1/13$.

Applications with More than One Outcome

Each of the above examples had only one outcome (tossing heads, tossing a number less than three, picking a queen). This section will discuss probabilities when more than one event in the sample space is favorable. For example, what is the probability of tossing *at most* one heads in a toss of two coins?

At most one means tossing either no heads or one heads in the two coin tosses. The sample space for a toss of two coins is $\{TT, TH, HT, HH\}$. This is the set of outcomes from tossing two coins. If the first coin lands tails, the second can land either heads or tails; if the first coin lands heads, the second can land either heads or tails. Notice that TH is a different outcome from HT. In TH, the first coin lands tails and the second one heads, whereas in HT, the first coin lands heads and the second tails. You can visualize this by pretending the two coins are different denominations, like a nickel and a dime.

Even if the coins are both pennies, for example, they are still different coins, so TH and HT are different events. TH and HT are called ordered pairs: that is, the order is important so the pairs are different.

The number of events in the sample space is four, $n(s) = 4$. Favorable outcomes include only those with no heads or one heads. From the set above, TT, TH, and HT include one or no heads. Therefore, $n(f) = 3$. Therefore, p(at most one heads) $= n(f)/n(s) = 3/4$.

Exercise 5.2: Two dice are tossed. What is the probability that their sum totals 7?

Answer: Recall that a die is a cube on each face or side of which is a different number of dots, or pips, from one to six. The sum of a pair of dice consists of the sum of the dots on the up faces. Notice that, just as with the coins, the dice are different. They can be thought of as two different colors, red and green for example, so that a green 2 and a red 6 differ from a green 6 and a red 2. The first can be represented as the ordered pair (2, 6) and the second as the ordered pair (6, 2).

The sample space for the toss of two dice is the following set of ordered pairs:

{(1, 1)   (1, 2)   (1, 3)   (1, 4)   (1, 5)   (1, 6)

(2, 1)   (2, 2)   (2, 3)   (2, 4)   (2, 5)   (2, 6)

(3, 1)   (3, 2)   (3, 3)   (3, 4)   (3, 5)   (3, 6)

(4, 1)   (4, 2)   (4, 3)   (4, 4)   (4, 5)   (4, 6)

(5, 1)   (5, 2)   (5, 3)   (5, 4)   (5, 5)   (5, 6)

(6, 1)   (6, 2)   (6, 3)   (6, 4)   (6, 5)   (6, 6)}

There are thirty-six ordered pairs in the sample space, so $n(s) = 36$.

Notice that the sums of these numbers are all between 2 and 12. The favorable outcomes are only those in which the sum of the two dice totals 7. The pairs from the sample space that are favorable are (1, 6), (2, 5), (3, 4), (4, 3), (5, 2), and (6, 1). Since there are six of these favorable ordered pairs, $n(f) = 6$. Therefore, the probability that the sum of the two dice is 7 is $n(f)/n(s) = 6/36$ or $p(7) = 1/6$.

Applications Without Replacement

When two or more cards are dealt from a deck of playing cards, as in a card game in which each person is dealt a hand of two or five or thirteen cards, the number of events in the sample space is calculated in a much different manner than in the above problems involving dice or coins. One difference comes from the fact that these cards are not replaceable. If the king of hearts is one of three cards dealt or chosen, then the king of hearts cannot appear in another hand or in the original hand again. Cards are not replaceable, unless each card is chosen, observed, and replaced in the deck. With coins or dice, it is easy to see that the toss of the first one has no influence on the toss of the second. If the first coin falls heads, what does this mean for the second coin? Or for the second toss of that coin? One difference in using cards is that you are not replacing. and thus not reusing the card chosen on the first pick.

UNORDERED PAIRS

Another difference in using cards rather than coins or dice is that the order of the deal is not material to the final outcome, or hand, that is dealt. For example, suppose two cards are picked or dealt from a deck of fifty-two cards. After the cards are dealt, they are observed. Suppose the two cards dealt are the ace of diamonds and the three of clubs; it makes no difference if they were dealt AD, 3C or 3C, AD. The outcome—which cards are in the hand—is the same in either case for all card games. We can extend this concept to poker (five-card hands) or bridge (thirteen-card hands). It is immaterial in what order the thirteen cards are dealt; the important feature for probability or, indeed, the game is which thirteen cards they are.

Suppose two cards are drawn from an ordinary fifty-two card deck. What is the probability that at least one of them is an ace?

Up until now, the sample space has been listed and counted. Given enough time and space, the sample space for two card draws from the deck can be listed, but it is a large space. In this problem, instead of listing the entire sample space, we will use a more sophisticated means for counting the number of pairs in this sample space.

There are fifty-two possible different picks for the first card (see Exercise 5.1). Once the first card is picked, however, the second card pick has fifty-one possibilities, since there are only fifty-one cards left. This would result in a sample space numbering $52 \cdot 51 = 2652$. But consider the sample space carefully: among the 2652 pairs would be {AD, 3C} and {3C, AD}. As mentioned before, these are considered the same hand in most card games. The final sample space thus consists of *unordered* pairs of cards. Since the sample space of 2652 contains ordered pairs, half of these are repeats. The sample space for picks of two cards from the fifty-two has one-half of 2652, or 1326, events in it. Therefore, $n(s) = 1326$.

To list the favorable outcomes, those with at least one ace in the pair, first look at those pairs containing exactly one ace, like AD, 4S and AC, JH. How many pairs are there that have exactly one ace? There are four possible aces that can be the "exactly one" ace. Then another card must be picked, but that card cannot be an ace. There are forty-eight nonaces in the deck of fifty-two cards. For each of the four aces, there are forty-eight ways to complete the pair with a nonace. Therefore, there are $4 \cdot 48 = 192$ picks of two cards that include a single ace. Notice that the order was not considered in this: the ace was chosen first, but if the nonace were chosen before the ace, the total number (which would be twice 192) would then have to be halved.

There are also six picks that include two aces. They are {AD, AH}, {AD, AC}, {AD, AS}, {AH, AC}, {AH, AS}, and {AS, AC}. Since there are $192 + 6 = 198$ favorable outcomes, $n(f) = 198$. The probability that there will be at least one ace in a pick of two cards from an ordinary deck is $p(x) = n(f)/n(s) = 198/1326$. This probability might be best expressed as a decimal, .149, or even an approximate percent, 15%, which says that approximately fifteen of every hundred picks of two cards from an ordinary deck of cards will contain at least one ace.

Exercise 5.3: Two cards are drawn from an ordinary fifty-two card deck. What is the probability that at least one of them is a diamond?

Answer: Again the sample space consists of all picks of two cards from the fifty-two card deck. As above, this can be done in $52 \cdot 51/2 = 1326$ ways. Therefore, $n(s) = 1326$.

A list of favorable outcomes, at least one diamond, can be divided into those pairs having one diamond and those pairs with two diamonds. For the latter, there are thirteen possible picks for the first diamond and twelve for the second. However, a pick of {3D, JD} is the same hand as {JD, 3D}, so the number of pairs with two diamonds is $(13 \cdot 12)/2 = 78$. So seventy-eight pairs of cards consist of two diamonds.

Now, consider the pairs with only one diamond; there are thirteen diamonds in the deck, along with thirty-nine other cards. For each of the thirteen diamonds, thirty-nine other cards may be chosen to make a unique pair. Therefore, there are $13 \cdot 39 = 507$ pairs that consist of only one diamond. The total number of pairs having either one or both diamonds is thus $78 + 507 = 585$, so $n(f) = 585$.

The probability of a pick of two cards from an ordinary deck containing at least one diamond is $p(D) = n(f)/n(s) = 585/1326$. Expressed as a percent, this fraction is approximately 44%. Therefore, approximately 44% of all picks of two cards will contain at least one diamond.

COMPOUND EVENTS

Often probabilities must be determined for the outcomes of several different events that may or may not be dependent upon each other. For example, consider two kinds of problems we have already discussed: tossing a pair of dice and choosing two cards from a deck. In the first case, the number that lands face up on the toss of the first die has no impact upon the outcome of the toss of the second die. However, in the case of picking two cards, the deck is reduced to fifty-one cards after the first pick, so the first card pick does influence the outcome of the second pick.

Suppose one coin is tossed twice. One favorable outcome is heads on the first toss and another favorable outcome is heads on the second toss. These outcomes can be described by the following symbols:

A: First toss of the coin is heads. A is the event symbolized by $\{HH, HT\}$.

B: Second toss of the coin is heads. B is the event symbolized by $\{TH, HH\}$.

Two different questions come to mind. One, what is the outcome set of either A or B happening, either the first toss being heads or the second toss being heads or both? Two, what is the outcome set of both A and B happening, both the first and second tosses of the coin being heads?

Venn Diagrams

Questions involving compound events, either A or B happening or both A and B happening, can be answered more easily by using diagrams called *Venn diagrams*. In these diagrams, the universal set or sample space is represented by a rectangle, whose entire interior is referred to as "S." The various simple events of interest in the sample space are represented by circles labeled A and B. An example is given in Figure 5.1.

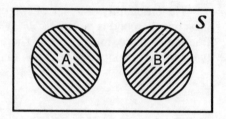

Figure 5.1:
Venn Diagram
Sets A, B Shaded

SET UNION

The *union* of two sets A and B, symbolized A∪B, is the set consisting of the events in A, the events in B, *or* the events in both A and B. Recall that in the coin toss, the events in A were {HH, HT} and those in B were {TH, HH}. Therefore, A∪B = {HT, TH, HH}. Figure 5.2 is a Venn diagram representing A∪B.

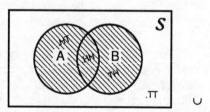

Figure 5.2:
Venn Diagram
Toss of Two Coins

SET INTERSECTION

The *intersection* of two sets A and B, symbolized A∩B, is the set consisting only of the events in *both* A and B. In the coin toss example, the set A∩B = {HH}. Figure 5.3 is a Venn diagram representing A∩B.

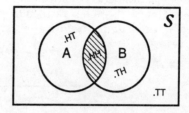

Figure 5.3:
Venn Diagram
Toss of Two Coins
A ∩ B Shaded

SUBSETS

The previous two Venn diagrams illustrate two sets with some, but not all, elements in common. Other configurations are also possible. For example, suppose G is the set of all outcomes less than 6 on a single die toss. Therefore, G = {1, 2, 3, 4, 5}. D is the set of all outcomes that are odd numbers on a single die toss, so D = {1, 3, 5}. The relationship between G and D is not the same as between A and B above. Every element in D is also in G; D is a *subset* of G, symbolized D⊂G. Figure 5.4 is the Venn diagram illustrating this relationship.

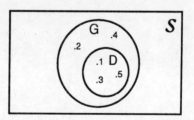

Figure 5.4:
Venn Diagram
D ⊂ G (Subset)

It would be helpful to find the union and intersection of G and D, G∪D and G∩D.

G∪D = {1, 2, 3, 4, 5} so G∪D = G; G∩D = {1, 3, 5} so G∩D = D. In the case of subsets, the union of the two is always equal to the larger set, and the intersection of the two is always equal to the smaller one.

DISJOINT SETS

Another possible configuration for two sets is that they have no elements in common. A Venn diagram of this general case is Figure 5.1. Let E be the set of all even numbers possible from summing two dice and let F be the set of all odd numbers possible. Thus, E = {2, 4, 6, 8, 10, 12} and F = {3, 5, 7, 9, 11}. Notice that there are no numbers which are in both E and F. Figure 5.5 illustrates this relationship, which is called disjoint or mutually exclusive. Two sets are *disjoint* (or *mutually exclusive*) if they have no elements in common.

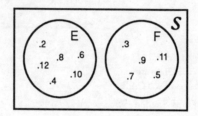

Figure 5.5:
 Venn Diagram
E ∩ F = ∅
Disjoint Sets

E∪F = {2, 3, 4, 5, 6, 7, 8, 9, 10, 11, 12} and E∩F = { } or ∅. The symbol ∅ is the Greek letter phi and is read either as the *null* or the *empty* set: the set with no elements. If the intersection of two sets is empty, the sets are disjoint and their union consists of the elements in one and the elements in the other. There are no elements common to both.

SET COMPLEMENT

Sometimes we are interested in the events of the sample space that are not favorable outcomes. In Venn diagrams, the set of unfavorable outcomes is represented by the part of the rectangular area that lies outside the set of favorable outcomes. If A is the set of favorable outcomes, then the *complement* of A, denoted A′ and read "A prime," is the set of outcomes not in A. For example, if the sample space is the set of cards that can be chosen in one pick from a deck, and A is the outcome that the card is an ace, then A′ is the outcome that the card is not an ace. Figure 5.6 is the Venn diagram for this example.

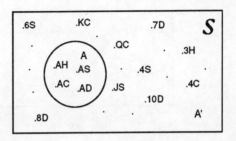

Figure 5.6:
Venn Diagram
A ∪ A′ = S
Complementary Sets

Notice that A∪A′ = S (the entire sample space) and A∩A′ = { } or ∅. Therefore, the union of a set and its complement is the entire sample space, and the intersection of a set and its complement is the null set.

An earlier example involved the outcomes of tosses of two dice. These were classified in sets of even sums, E = {2, 4, 6, 8, 10, 12}, and odd sums, F = {3, 5, 7, 9, 11}. Since the entire sample space S = {2, 3, 4, 5, 6, 7, 8, 9, 10, 11, 12}, E and F are complements of each other. Therefore, E′ = F and F′ = E.

Exercise 5.4: Six chips marked 0, 1, 2, 3, 4, 5 are in a box. Two chips are chosen from the box. Event A is the event that the first chip chosen is odd; event B is the event that the second chip is odd.

    a.   Find S, the sample space of ordered pairs of chips that can be drawn from the box if the chip is replaced after the first drawing.

    b.   Find the ordered pairs in the outcomes A and B if A and B are subsets of S.

    c.   Find the ordered pairs in the compound outcomes A∪B and A∩B.

d.   Draw a Venn diagram of the above experiment.

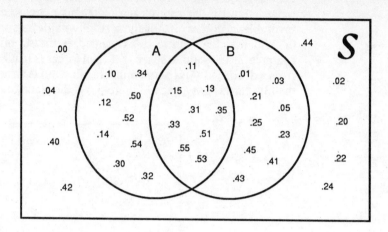

Figure 5.7:
Venn Diagram
Two Chips Chosen with Replacement

Answers:
    a.   S is the set of all outcomes of choosing two chips from the set {0, 1, 2, 3, 4, 5} when the first chip is replaced before drawing the second chip. Thus, S = {00, 01, 02, 03, 04, 05, 10, 11, 12, 13, 14, 15, 20, 21, 22, 23, 24, 25, 30, 31, 32, 33, 34, 35, 40, 41, 42, 43, 44, 45, 50, 51, 52, 53, 54, 55}
    b.   A is the event that the first chip chosen is odd. A = {10, 11, 12, 13, 14, 15, 30, 31, 32, 33, 34, 35, 50, 51, 52, 53, 54, 55}
    B is the event that the second chip chosen is odd. B = {01, 03, 05, 11, 13, 15, 21, 23, 25, 31, 33, 35, 41, 43, 45, 51, 53, 55}
    c.   A∪B is the event that the pair of chips chosen is in A or in B or in both. A∪B = {10, 11, 12, 13, 14, 15, 30, 31, 32, 33, 34, 35, 50, 51, 52, 53, 54, 55, 01, 03, 05, 21, 23, 25, 41, 43, 45}
    A∩B is the event that the pair of chips chosen is both A and B. A∩B = {11, 13, 15, 31, 33, 35, 51, 53, 55}
    d.   See Figure 5.7.

Exercise 5.5: Six chips marked 0, 1, 2, 3, 4, 5 are in a box. Two chips are chosen from the box. Event A is the event that the first chip chosen is odd; event B is the event that the second chip is odd.

    a. Find T, the sample space of ordered pairs of chips that can be drawn from the box, if the chip is *not* replaced after the first drawing.

    b. Find the ordered pairs in the outcomes A and B if A and B are subsets of T.

    c. Find the ordered pairs in the compound outcomes A $\cup$ B and A$\cap$B.

    d. Draw a Venn diagram of the above.

Answers:

    a. T is the set of all outcomes when two chips are drawn from the box without replacement. T = {01, 02, 03, 04, 05, 10, 12, 13, 14, 15, 20, 21, 23, 24, 25, 30, 31, 32, 34, 35, 40, 41, 42, 43, 45, 50, 51, 52, 53, 54}

    b. A is the set of ordered pairs of chips in T in which the first chip chosen is odd. A = {10, 12, 13, 14, 15, 30, 31, 32, 34, 35, 50, 51, 52, 53, 54} B is the set of ordered pairs of chips in T in which the second chip chosen is odd. B = {01, 03, 05, 13, 15, 21, 23, 25, 31, 35, 41, 43, 45, 51, 53}

    c. A$\cup$B is the set of ordered pairs of chips in A or B or both (first odd, second odd or both odd). A$\cup$B = {10, 12, 13, 14, 15, 30, 31, 32, 34, 35, 50, 51, 52, 53, 54, 01, 03, 05, 21, 23, 25, 41, 43, 45} A$\cap$B is the set of ordered pairs of chips in both A and B (both odd). A$\cap$B = {13, 15, 31, 35, 51, 53}

    d. See Figure 5.8.

Numbers of Elements in Compound Events

Before calculating the probability of favorable outcomes for compound events, the numbers of events in the unions and intersections must be counted. For example, the number of events in A∪B is not always the number of events in A plus the number of events in B.

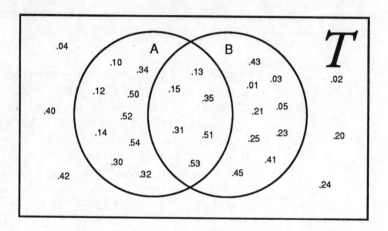

Figure 5.8:
Venn Diagram
Two Chips Chosen Without Replacement

If A and B intersect (see Figures 5.2, 5.3, 5.7, 5.8), then the events in A∩B would be counted twice if the number of events in A were simply added to those in B. In order to compensate for counting the elements in A∩B twice, that number can be subtracted from the number in A plus the number in B. The formula used for counting the number of elements in the union of two sets is

$$n(A \cup B) = n(A) + n(B) - n(A \cap B)$$

Recall an example from one of the previous sections that involved the toss of a coin twice and where:
A is the event that the first toss of the coin is heads.
B is the event that the second toss of the coin is heads.

Remember that the events in A are HT, HH and those in B are HH, TH. Therefore, $n(A) = 2$ and $n(B) = 2$; thus, $n(A \cap B) = 1$ since HH is in both. Thus $n(A \cup B) = n(A) + n(B) - n(A \cap B) = 2 + 2 - 1 = 3$. This agrees with our count, since A∪B = {HH, TH, HT} and $n(A \cup B) = 3$. (A∪B is a set with three elements.)

Recall another example of a previous section in which G = {1, 2, 3, 4, 5} and D = {1, 3, 5}. Since D is a subset of G, G∩D = D = {1, 3, 5} and G∪D = G = {1, 2, 3, 4, 5}. Thus, $n(G) = 5$; $n(D) = 3$; $n(G ∪ D) = 5$; $n(G∩D) = 3$. By the formula, $n(G∪D) = n(G) + n(D) - n(G ∩ D)$. Substituting: $5 = 5 + 3 - 3$ which is an identity (always true). The formula for counting numbers of events in unions and intersections holds even when one set is a subset of the other.

Recall a third example of a previous section in which E = {2, 4, 6, 8, 10, 12} and F = {3, 5, 7, 9, 11}. E∩F = ∅ or { }. $n(E) = 6$ and $n(F) = 5$. Since E and F are disjoint, $n(E ∩ F) = 0$ (zero).

Substituting in $n(E∪F) = n(E) + n(F) - n(E ∩ F) = 6 + 5 - 0 = 11$. To check, count the number in E ∪ F = {2, 3, 4, 5, 6, 7, 8, 9, 10 11, 12}: $n(E∪F) = 11$. Therefore, the counting formula holds even if the sets are disjoint. It is only in this case, where A and B are disjoint, that $n(A∪B) = n(A) + n(B)$.

Exercise 5.6: In Exercise 5.4, two chips marked {0, 1, 2, 3, 4, 5} were drawn from a box. Event A was the event that the first chip was odd, and Event B was the event that the second chip was odd. Unions and intersections were formed based on the following sets, with the first chip being replaced before the second chip was drawn.

A = {10, 11, 12, 13, 14, 15, 30, 31, 32, 33, 34, 35, 50, 51, 52, 53, 54, 55}

B = {01, 03, 05, 11, 13, 15, 21, 23, 25, 31, 33, 35, 41, 43; 45, 51, 53, 55}

Verify the counting formula for A∪B.

Answer:

A∪B = {10, 11, 12, 13, 14, 15, 30, 31, 32, 33, 34, 35, 50, 51, 52, 53, 54, 55, 01, 03, 05, 21, 23, 25, 41, 43, 45}
A∩B = {11, 13, 15, 31, 33, 35, 51, 53, 55}

$n(A) = 18$; $n(B) = 18$;

$n(A∪B) = 27$; $n (A∩B) = 9$.

$n(A∪B) = n(A) + n(B) - n(A∩B)$;

$27 = 18 + 18 - 9 = 27$.

Exercise 5.7: In Exercise 5.5 two chips marked from 0 to 5 were drawn from a box. A was the event that the first chip was odd, and B was the event that the second chip was odd. Unions and intersections were formed based on the following sets, where the first chip was not replaced before the second chip was drawn.

A = {10, 12, 13, 14, 15, 30, 31, 32, 34, 35, 50, 51, 52, 53, 54}

B = {01, 03, 05, 13, 15, 21, 23, 25, 31, 35, 41, 43, 45, 51, 53}

Verify the counting formula for A∪B.

Answer:

A∪B = {10, 12, 13, 14, 15, 30, 31, 32, 34, 35, 50, 51, 52, 53, 54, 01,
03, 05, 21, 23, 25, 41, 43, 45}

A∩B = {13, 15, 31, 35, 51, 53}

$n(A) = 15; n(B) = 15; n(A∪B) = 24; n(A∩B) = 6$

$n(A∪B) = n(A) + n(B) - n(A∩B);$

$24 = 15 + 15 - 6 = 24.$

Probability of Compound Events

The formula for the probability of A∪B is just a variation of the formula for the number of elements in A∪B:

$$p(A \cup B) = p(A) + p(B) - p(A \cap B)$$

If the probability of any three of the four events in the formula, A, B, A∪B, or A∩B, is known, the probability of the fourth event can be found. For example, suppose $p(A) = 1/2, p(B) = 1/3$, and $p(A∩B) = 1/6$. Since $p(A∪B) = p(A) + p(B) - p(A∩B), p(A∪B) = 1/2 + 1/3 - 1/6 = 3/6 + 2/6 - 1/6 = 4/6$ or 2/3. Therefore, $p(A∪B) = 2/3$.

Suppose a coin is tossed twice: A is the event that the first toss of the coin is heads, and B is the event that the second toss of the coin is heads. In this problem, what is the probability that either the first or second toss (or both) falls heads?

The formula for this is $p(A∪B) = p(A) + p(B) - p(A∩B); p(A) = 1/2$ and $p(B) = 1/2; p(A∩B)$ can be derived by looking first at the sample space of tossing a coin twice. This sample space has four elements: {HH, HT, TH, TT}.

The favorable outcome for A∩B, A and B both, has only one element: {HH}. Therefore, $p(A∩B) = 1/4$. Substituting in:

$p(A∪B) = p(A) + p(B) - p(A∩B)$

$p(A∪B) = 1/2 + 1/2 - 1/4 = 3/4$

Therefore, the probability that the first or second or both tosses of a coin will fall heads is 3/4.

INDEPENDENT EVENTS

If two events are independent, the occurrence of one does not affect the occurrence of the other. Sometimes it is intuitively obvious that two events are independent; sometimes it is not. But there is a test to assure that two events are independent. Two events A and B are *independent* if and only if $p(A∩B) = p(A) \cdot p(B)$. The phrase "if and only if" means that the statement can be read both ways: if the events are independent, the formula holds, and if the formula holds, then the events are independent.

In the coin problem above, $p(A∩B) = 1/4$. But notice that $p(A) \cdot p(B) = (1/2)(1/2) = 1/4$. Therefore, the two events, the first and the second tosses of the coin, are independent. This is a good way to test for independence, particularly if it is not obvious that the events are, indeed, independent.

In a previous example, $p(A \cup B) = 2/3$, $p(A) = 1/2$, $p(B) = 1/3$ and $p(A \cap B)$ turned out to be 1/6. Events A and B are independent since $p(A \cap B) = 1/6$ and $p(A) \cdot p(B) = (1/2) \cdot (1/3) = 1/6$.

Another previous example involved the toss of one die. G is the event of tossing a number less than 6 with a single die, and D is the event of tossing an odd number with a single die. Therefore, $G = \{1, 2, 3, 4, 5\}$ and $D = \{1, 3, 5\}$. The sample space for the experiment is $S = \{1, 2, 3, 4, 5, 6\}$; $p(G) = 5/6$ and $p(D) = 3/6$, since $n(G) = 5$, $n(D) = 3$, and $n(S) = 6$. The event $G \cap D$ has a probability $p(G \cap D) = 3/6$ also, since D is a subset of G.

Are G and D independent? To answer this, test to see if $p(G \cap D) = p(C) \cdot p(D)$. Substituting, the question becomes does $3/6 = (5/6) \cdot (3/6)$? Since $3/6 \neq 15/36$, G and D are not independent.

It should also be intuitively obvious that G and D are not independent events, since if G occurs, D is more likely than if G had not happened. This concept will be discussed further in the section on conditional probability.

INDEPENDENCE AND MUTUALLY EXCLUSIVE EVENTS

Earlier we discussed E and F as two mutually exclusive sets of numbers, E consisting of the even number sums of a toss of two dice ($E = \{2, 4, 6, 8, 10, 12\}$) and F the odd number sums of the toss of two dice ($F = \{3, 5, 7, 9, 11\}$).

Although we never calculated the probability of E and the probability of F, we can easily calculate $p(E \cap F)$: since $E \cap F$ is empty, the numerator of $p(E \cap F)$ is 0, so its probability is also 0. Therefore, E and F are not independent since the product of their probabilities can never be zero. (If the product of two numbers is 0, at least one of the numbers must be 0.) As long as each event has a nonzero probability, mutually exclusive or disjoint events can never be independent. By definition, the occurrence of one affects the occurrence of the other (causes it not to happen). Events that are independent, like two tosses of a coin, do not affect each other.

ODDS

The odds in favor of an event happening are the ratio of the probability of its occurring to the probability of its not occurring. For example, in tossing two coins, the probability of getting two heads, $p(HH) = 1/4$. Therefore, $p(HH)'$ (complement of HH) = 3/4. The odds in favor of two heads are $(1/4) \div (3/4) = 1/3$; in the case of odds, this is usually written 1:3. If the denominators are the same (and they should be), then the odds of an event happening are expressed by the ratio of the numerators, a/b or more commonly, $a:b$. The odds against an event happening are the reverse, or $b:a$.

Exercise 5.8: Six chips marked 0, 1, 2, 3, 4, 5 are in a box. Two chips are chosen from the box. Event A is the event that the first chip chosen is odd; event B is the event that the second chip is odd. The chip from the first pick is replaced before the second chip is chosen.
   a. Find $p(A)$, $p(B)$, $p(A \cup B)$, $p(A \cap B)$.
   b. Are A and B independent? Explain.
   c. Find the odds in favor of both choices being odd numbers ($A \cap B$).

Answers:
a. The total number of picks of two chips with replacement from the set {0, 1, 2, 3, 4, 5} is 36, since the first place can be filled by any one of the six chips and, after that, the second place can be filled by any one of the six chips. Therefore, the denominator of any single probability is 36. List all pairs in the sample space if you do not arrive at 36: {00, 01, 02, 03, 04, 05, 10, . . . }.

In order to find $p(A)$, the probability that the first chip is odd, find the number of two pairs of two chips in which the first chip is either 1, 3, or 5. For each of these three first chips, the second chip can be any one of the six chips given. Therefore, the numerator of the probability of A, or $n(A)$, is $3 \cdot 6 = 18$. Note that n(A) in Exercise 5.6 using these chips is also 18. So the probability of A is 18/36 or $p(A) = 1/2$.

In a similar manner, $p(B) = 18/36 = 1/2$ also.

$p(A \cap B) = n(A \cap B)/n(S)$. $n(S) = 36$. $A \cap B$ is the set in which both chip are odd. There are three possibilities for the first chip and three in the second, so there are $3 \cdot 3 = 9$ events in $A \cap B$. Therefore, $n(A \cap B) = 9$ and $p(A \cap B) = 9/36 = 1/4$.

$p(A \cup B) = p(A) + p(B) - p(A \cap B)$, so $p(A \cup B) = 1/2 + 1/2 - 1/4 = 3/4$.

b. Intuitively, it seems A and B should be independent events, since with replacement, the event that the first chip is odd does not affect the event that the second is odd. The formula test is to check if $p(A \cap B) = p(A) \cdot p(B)$. Since $p(A) = 1/2$, $p(B) = 1/2$, and $p(A \cap B) = 1/4$, the formula holds and A and B are independent events.

c. The probability of both A and B occurring is $p(A \cap B) = 1/4$. Since for any set J, $p(J) + p(J') = 1$, $p(A \cap B) + p(A \cap B)' = 1$. Therefore, $p(A \cap B)' = 3/4$. The odds in favor of $A \cap B$ are given by the ratio of 1/4 to 3/4. Therefore, the odds in favor of $A \cap B$ are 1:3.

Exercise 5.9: Six chips marked 0, 1, 2, 3, 4, 5 are in a box. Two chips are chosen from the box. Event A is the event that the first chip chosen is odd; event B is the event that the second chip is odd. The chip from the first pick is not replaced before the second chip is chosen.
a. Find $p(A)$, $p(B)$, $p(A \cup B)$, $p(A \cap B)$.
b. Are A and B independent? Explain.
c. Find the odds in favor of both choices being odd numbers, $A \cap B$.

Answers:
a. The total number of picks of two chips from the set {0, 1, 2, 3, 4, 5} with replacement is 30, since the first place can be filled by any one of the six chips and, after that, the second place can be filled by any one of the five remaining chips. Therefore, the denominator of any single probability is 30. List all pairs in the sample space if you do not arrive at 30: {01, 02, 03, 04, 05, 10, 12, . . .}.

In order to find p(A), the probability that the first chip is odd, find the number of two pairs of two chips in which the first chip is either 1, 3, or 5. For each of these three chips, the second chip can be any one of the six chips given except the one already picked. Therefore, the numerator of the probability of A, or $n(A)$, is $3 \cdot 5 = 15$. Note that $n(A)$ in the previous exercise using these chips without replacement was also 15. So the probability of A is 15/30, or $p(A) = 1/2$.

In a similar manner, $p(B) = 15/30 = 1/2$ also.

$p(A \cap B) = n(A \cap B)/n(S)$; $n(S) = 30$. $A \cap B$ is the set in which both chips are odd. There are three possibilities for the first chip but only two in the second, since the first is not replaced. So there are $3 \cdot 2 = 6$ events in $A \cap B$. They are $\{13, 15, 31, 35, 51, 53\}$. Therefore, $n(A \cap B) = 6$ and $p(A \cap B) = 6/30 = 1/5$.

$p(A \cup B) = p(A) + p(B) - p(A \cap B)$, so $p(A \cup B) = 1/2 + 1/2 - 1/5 = 8/10 = 4/5$.

b. Intuitively it seems that A and B should not be independent events since without replacement, the event that the first chip is odd does affect the event that the second is odd. The formula test is whether $p(A \cap B) = p(A) \cdot p(B)$. Since $p(A) = 1/2$, $p(B) = 1/2$, and $p(A \cap B) = 1/5$, the formula does not hold: $(1/2)(1/2) \neq 1/5$, so A and B are not independent events.

c. The probability of both A and B occurring is $p(A \cap B) = 1/5$. It follows that $p(A \cap B)' = 4/5$. The odds in favor of $A \cap B$ are given by the ratio of 1/5 to 4/5. Therefore, the odds in favor of $A \cap B$ are 1:4.

CONDITIONAL PROBABILITY

Sometimes, if additional information about an event is available, the probability of the event changes. For example, the probability of picking the five of diamonds from an ordinary deck of cards is 1/52; the numerator $n(f) = 1$ since there is only one 5D in the deck, and the denominator $n(s) = 52$ since there are fifty-two possible picks of a single card. Suppose an additional piece of information is available: the card chosen is a five. Then the probability of picking the 5D knowing that the pick is a five becomes 1/4 since $n(f) = 1$ and $n(s) = 4$ (there are only four fives in the deck). This is a much higher probability.

What has happened to change the probability? In the original problem, the sample space contained fifty-two cards. In the second case, with the additional knowledge that the card picked is a five, the sample space contains only four cards, since there are only four fives in the deck. This problem is an example of *conditional probability* .

Formula for Calculating Conditional Probability

The formula for conditional probability answers the following question: Knowing that event B has already occurred, what is the probability of event A occurring? Conditional probability is calculated using the formula

$$p(A\mid B) = \frac{p(A\cap B)}{p(B)}$$

In words, the probability of A happening knowing that B has already happened is the probability of both A and B occurring divided by the probability of B occurring.

Consider the above example of the probability of picking the five of diamonds from a deck of cards knowing, in the second instance, that a five has been chosen. In that case, $p(A\cap B)$ is the probability (A) of picking the five of diamonds and (B) of picking a five.

The event "picking the five of diamonds" is a subset of the event "picking a five." Recall that the probability of both these events is the same as the probability of the smaller (subset) or $p(A)$, picking the five of diamonds. Therefore, the numerator of the conditional probability fraction, $p(A\cap B) = p(A)$ = 1/52. The denominator of the conditional probability formula, $p(B)$, is the probability of picking a five from a deck of cards, so $p(B)$ = 4/52.

Thus, $p(A\mid B) = p(A\cap B)/p(B)$ = 1/52 ÷ 4/52 = 1/4, the same answer as that obtained by reducing the sample space.

Conditional Probability and Independent Events

Independent events can be redefined in terms of conditional probabilities. Two events A and B are independent if $p(A\cap B) = p(A)$. This means that the probability of A given B is the same as the probability of A not knowing anything about B. A happens with the same probability whether B happens or not. Recall the formula for conditional probability:

$$p(A\mid B) = \frac{p(A\cap B)}{p(B)}$$

If the events A and B are independent, $p(A\mid B) = p(A)$. Substituting:

$$p(A\mid B) = p(A) = \frac{P(A\cap B)}{p(B)};$$ multiplying both sides by $p(B)$ leads to $p(A\cap B)$

$= p(A)\cdot p(B)$. This was the definition of independent events given in an earlier section.

Exercise 5.10: Two dice are tossed. Event A is the toss of a five on at least one die. Event B is the toss of a seven on both dice. Find the following:
- a. $p(A)$
- b. $p(B)$
- c. $p(A\mid B)$
- d. $p(B\mid A)$
- e. Are A and B independent events? Explain.

Answers: It may help to write out the sample space for the entire experiment in addition to the ordered pairs in the favorable events. The sample space for the event of tossing two dice is listed in Exercise 5.2; $n(S)$ = 36. The ordered pairs for event A, a five on at least one die, are {15, 25, 35, 45, 55, 65, 56, 54,

53, 52, 51}. The ordered pairs for event B, a total of seven on two dice, are {16, 25, 34, 43, 52, 61}.

  a. $p(A) = n(A)/n(S) = 11/36$. The probability that there is a five on at least one die is 11/36.

  b. $p(B) = n(B)/n(S) = 6/36$ or 1/6. The probability that there is a total of seven on both dice is 6/36.

  c. $p(A|B) = p(A \cap B)/p(B)$; to get $p(A \cap B)$, list the ordered pairs in $A \cap B$. They are all those pairs in both A and B, which are only {25, 52}. Therefore, $n(A \cap B) = 2$, and $n(S) = 36$. So $p(A \cap B) = 2/36$.
      $p(A|B) = p(A \cap B)/p(B) = 2/36 \div 6/36 = 2/6$, so $p(A|B) = 1/3$.

      The probability of tossing a five on at least one die, knowing that a seven has been tossed on both dice, is 1/3. Notice that the probability of tossing a five on at least one dice, not knowing anything else, is 11/36.

  d. $p(B|A) = p(A \cap B)/p(A)$. $p(A \cap B) = 2/36$, as shown in (c) above; $p(A) = 11/36$. Therefore, $p(B|A) = 2/36 \div 11/36 = 2/11$. The probability of tossing a seven with two dice knowing that at least one of them is a five is 2/11. Notice that the probability of tossing a seven with two dice, not knowing anything else, is 1/6.

  e. If A and B were independent events, $p(B|A) = p(B)$ and $p(A|B) = p(A)$. However, $p(B|A) = 2/11$ while $p(B) = 1/6$, and $2/11 \neq 1/6$.
      $p(A|B) = 1/3$ while $p(A) = 11/36$, and $1/3 \neq 11/36$. Therefore, A and B are *not* independent events. (It is not necessary to use both $p(A|B)$ and $p(B|A)$ to do this problem; either one would be sufficient to prove that A and B are not independent.)

COUNTING

Often it is very difficult to list all the events in a sample space and all the favorable outcomes when computing the probability of an event. But it is not necessary to know which events are in the sample space or favorable outcome, just how many events there are. That is why we now discuss counting.

Tree Diagrams

Suppose an event can happen in five different ways and a second, subsequent event can happen in three ways. In how many ways can both events occur? For each of the five ways the first event can occur, the second event can happen in three ways. Therefore, the total number of ways that both events can occur is $5 \cdot 3 = 15$ ways. If you can choose any one of five restaurants for lunch and after lunch any one of three movies, then you have fifteen different choices of the day's activities.

Sometimes counting is made easier by using a tree diagram. In it are listed all the first choices and, after each, the second choices. The total number is counted. A tree diagram for the lunch and movie problem is shown in Figure 5.9.

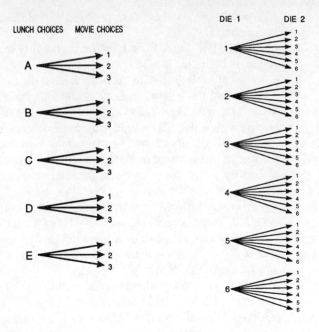

Figure 5.9:
Tree Diagram
Lunch and Movie

Figure 5.10:
Tree Diagram:
Tossing Two Dice

Notice that the fifteen choices are A1, A2, A3, B1, B2, B3, C1, C2, C3, D1, D2, D3, E1, E2, and E3. But, again, we are not interested in what the choices are, just how many of them we have.

Exercise 5.11: A die can fall any one of six ways, with 1, 2, 3, 4, 5, or 6 showing. A second die can also fall any one of six ways with the same numbers possible. By use of a tree diagram, show the number of ways that a pair of dice can fall.

Answer: Refer to Figure 5.10. Notice that the dice can fall thirty-six different ways. We know this is correct because earlier in the chapter those thirty-six ways were enumerated.

This way of counting can be extended to any number of consecutive events. If event X (or choice X) can occur in x number of ways, and event Y can occur in y number of ways, and event Z can occur in z number of ways, then events X, Y, and Z can occur in $x \cdot y \cdot z$ ways. At the restaurant mentioned above, if the menu lists six choices of appetizers, five choices of entrees, and seven choices of dessert, then there are $6 \cdot 5 \cdot 7$ or 210 different dinners that can be chosen from the menu. This too could be represented by a (very large) tree diagram.

Suppose a certain state has a license plate that consists of two letters of the alphabet, A to Z, and three digits chosen from 0, 1, 2, . . ., 9. Also suppose that no other license plate configurations are allowed. How many cars can be licensed in that state?

There are twenty-six letters of the alphabet, and these might be repeated, such as BB. Therefore, there are $26 \cdot 26 = 676$ different combinations of two letters to start the plates. Then there are ten digits, each of which can be repeated or not, so there are $10 \cdot 10 \cdot 10 = 1000$ different numerical parts (the numbers range from 000 to 999). There are $676 \cdot 1000 = 676,000$ different license plates that are possible in that state.

Exercise 5.12: In some large cities or local calling areas, the advent of car telephones and fax machines has led to a great increase in the number of telephones, and thus in the number of telephone numbers. This, in turn, has required the introduction of new area codes to make available new telephone numbers. For example, the two telephone numbers (212) 555–1212 and (718) 555–1212 were a single number when New York City had but a single area code, 212. Now that there are two area codes, 212 and 718, these are two different numbers. Given a new area code, how many new telephone numbers can be assigned?

Answer: Assuming any exchange (first three numbers after the area code) is possible, then there are seven digit places, each of which can be filled in ten ways, by the digits {0, 1, 2, 3, 4, 5, 6, 7, 8, 9}. Therefore, there are 10^7 or 10,000,000 new telephone numbers possible.

As a practical matter, however, no new exchange begins with 0 or 1. So the first number can be one of only eight numbers (2, 3, 4, 5, 6, 7, 8, 9), while the rest can be any of the ten digits above. So there are only 8,000,000 new numbers possible. Also, there are exchanges that are reserved for other uses, like 911 and 555. In reality, there are fewer than 8,000,000 new telephone numbers released by designating a new area code.

Permutations

From a club of fifteen people, officers are to be elected: president, vice president, secretary, and treasurer. In how many ways can this be done? That is, how many different choices are possible?

The president can be chosen from fifteen people, so there are fifteen ways that this can occur. Afterwards, the vice president is chosen, but there are no longer fifteen, but only fourteen people available to be vice president since one has already assumed the presidency. In the same way, there are thirteen people available for secretary and twelve people for treasurer.

Therefore, there are $15 \cdot 14 \cdot 13 \cdot 12$ or 32,760 different possible choices for these four positions. For example, consider two possible choices: (1), Ann, president; Bob, vice president; Carl, secretary; Dot, treasurer (one complete choice); and (2) Ann, president; Bob, vice president; Dot, secretary; Carl, treasurer (another complete choice). This second choice includes the same people but in different positions; it is a different configuration. One of those configurations could be called an ordered quadruple, which is like an ordered pair only with four items.

The above example is called a *permutation*. A permutation involves *picking* r things (i.e., people, food, numbers) from n (total available) and *arranging* those r in a certain order (president, vice president, secretary, treasurer).

FACTORIALS

The formula for permutations depends on a mathematical idea known as factorials, symbolized !. When the factorial sign follows a positive integer, it means that integer should be multiplied by one less than itself, two less than itself, and so on all the way down to 1.

$n! = n(n-1)(n-2)(n-3) \ldots 3 \cdot 2 \cdot 1$ and

$5! = 5(5-1)(5-2)(5-3)(5-4) = 5 \cdot 4 \cdot 3 \cdot 2 \cdot 1 = 120$. Some calculators have an $n!$ key; if yours does, do use it.

By the way, 0! is not equal to 0, but by definition equals 1; 1! = 1 as well.

One advantage to writing factorials is that at any point in writing one, we can stop subtracting one from the previous number and just write another factorial. For example, $5! = 5 \cdot 4! = 5 \cdot 4 \cdot 3! = 5 \cdot 4 \cdot 3 \cdot 2!$ We often do write these factorials in different ways, depending upon how they will be evaluated. For example, if we have the division 6!/4!, this can be written as the division $6 \cdot 5 \cdot 4!/4!$ The 4!s cancel and we are left with $6 \cdot 5 = 30$.

PERMUTATION FORMULA

When there are n items to choose from and r of these n items to be chosen and arranged, we have a *permutation* of n things taken r at a time. The symbol for permutation is usually written $_nP_r$ where n is the total items available and r is the number of items picked and arranged.

$_nP_r$ is calculated by using the following formula:

$$_nP_r = n! \div (n-r)!$$

(Some calculators have this permutation key also. Be sure to look for it on yours.)

Consider again the earlier problem of choosing from fifteen people four to take the offices of president, vice president, secretary, and treasurer. This example is a permutation, because we are picking four people from the available fifteen and arranging them in a particular order: president, vice president, secretary, and treasurer.

This problem is solved using the permutation formula $_nP_r$, where n = 15 (total number of people available) and r = 4 (number of people to be picked and arranged). $_nP_r = n!/(n-r)!$ so $_{15}P_4 = 15!/(15-4)! = 15!/11! = 15 \cdot 14 \cdot 13 \cdot 12 \cdot 11!/11$. The two 11!s in the numerator and denominator cancel. This leaves $_{15}P_4 = 15 \cdot 14 \cdot 13 \cdot 12 = 32,760$, the same result as when the permutation formula was not used.

Exercise 5.13: There are twenty cats competing for "best in show" at a cat show. Three ribbons are to be awarded: first, second, and third best in show. In how many different ways, assuming each cat is equally qualified, can these ribbons be awarded?

Answer: This is a permutation since three cats will be picked from twenty and awarded first, second, and third prizes (i.e., arranged in order). If Alfie gets first prize, Bubbles second, and Chloe third, it is a different arrangement than if Alfie gets first, Chloe second, and Bubbles third. The formula for this permutation is $_nP_r = {}_{20}P_3 = 20!/(20 - 3)! = 20!/17! = 20 \cdot 19 \cdot 18 \cdot 17!/17! = 20 \cdot 19 \cdot 18 = 6840$. There are 6840 different ways to pick three cats from twenty and give them the three prizes for "best in show."

Combinations

When r things (i.e., people, food, numbers) are picked from n things and arranged in some order, it is called a permutation. But when r things are picked from n and not arranged, it is called a *combination* .

For example, consider the group of fifteen people discussed previously. Suppose again a committee of four is to be chosen from the fifteen, but the officers of this committee are not to be assigned. In how many ways can a committee of four be chosen (and not arranged in any order) from the fifteen available?

If they were to be picked and arranged, there would be $_nP_r$ or $_{15}P_4$ arrangements, as shown before. Among those arrangements would be the two listed above: Ann for president, Bob for vice president, Carl for secretary, Dot for treasurer; and Ann for president, Bob for vice president, Dot for secretary, and Carl for treasurer. Let's abbreviate these as ABCD and ABDC.

For the purposes of combinations, these two choices, ABCD and ABDC, are the same, since we are only concerned with which four people are chosen from the fifteen, not in what order they are chosen. As a matter of fact, there are many other permutations that repeat the same people (letters) in different order: for example, BADC and DCBA. It turns out that there are $_4P_4$ of these "repeats," the number of ways of arranging all four people of one choice. Recall that $_4P_4 = 4!/(4 - 4)! = 4!/0! = 4!/1 = 4 \cdot 3 \cdot 2 \cdot 1 = 24$. So every choice of four from the fifteen using a permutation gives us twenty-four arrangements of the four (ABCD). Try listing these to be sure you get twenty-four.

Therefore, the number of permutations of fifteen people taken four at a time, $_{15}P_4$, includes 4! arrangements for each choice of four people. To calculate the number of ways to pick four people from fifteen and not the number of ways to pick four people from fifteen and arrange them in order, we divide the permutation $_{15}P_4$ by 4! or, in general, we divide $_nP_r$ by $r!$ to find the number of nonarranged choices of r items from n, the number of combinations of n things taken r at a time.

In general, the number of combinations (picking without arranging) is calculated by dividing the number of permutations by the permutations of the r picks or $_nC_r = {}_nP_r/{}_rP_r = {}_nP_r/r!$

COMBINATION FORMULA

The actual formula for combinations is:

$$_nC_r = \frac{n!}{(n-r)!r!}$$

Notice that $n!$ is divided not only by $(n-r)!$ as in permutations, but also by $r!$. Calculators that have $_nP_r$ buttons also have nCr buttons.

Suppose three letters from RSTUV are chosen and not ordered. The number of ways in which they can be picked is $_nC_r = n!/(n-r)!r! = 5!/(5-3)!3! = 5!/2!3! = 5 \cdot 4 \cdot 3!/2! \cdot 3! = 5 \cdot 4/2 \cdot 1 = 20/2 = 10$ ways. These are, choosing but not arranging: RST, RSU, RSV, RTU, RTV, RUV, STU, STV, SUV, and TUV.

Most card games involve combinations because, as mentioned earlier in this chapter, it is not important in which order the cards are dealt, just which cards are dealt.

For example, poker starts with a five card hand. How many different five card hands can be dealt from a fifty-two card deck, without regard to order? There are $_{52}C_5$ ways (different hands) of picking five cards from fifty-two. There are $52!/(52-5)!5! = 52!/47!5! = 52 \cdot 51 \cdot 50 \cdot 49 \cdot 48 \cdot 47!/47!5! = 2,598,960$ different five-card hands possible from an ordinary deck of cards.

Exercise 5.14: There are twenty cats competing for "best in show" at a cat show. Three ribbons are to be awarded as honorable mentions, in no particular order. In how many different ways, assuming each cat is equally qualified, can these ribbons be awarded?

Answer: This is a combination since three cats will be picked from twenty and awarded three honorable mentions in no particular order. If Alfie, Bubbles, and Chloe are picked, this will be one of the combinations possible: another combination will have at least one different cat (Alfie, Bubbles, and Donald, for example).

The formula for this combination, is $_nC_r = {_{20}C_3} = 20!/(20-3)!3! = 20!/17!3! = 20 \cdot 19 \cdot 18 \cdot 17!/17!3! = 20 \cdot 19 \cdot 18/3!$ since the 17!s cancel. $20 \cdot 19 \cdot 18/3 \cdot 2 \cdot 1 = 6840/6 = 1140$. Thus, there are 1140 different ways to pick three cats from twenty and give them the three honorable mentions for "best in show."

Probabilities Using Combinations

Probability questions can often be answered by using combinations. For example, if three letters are chosen from RSTUV, what is the probability that one of the three letters is an R?

The number of ways to pick but not arrange three items from five is $_nC_r = {_5C_3} = 10$ ways, as shown above. Therefore, the denominator of the probability fraction $n(s) = 10$, the number of events in the sample space. How many of those ten choices contain an R?

An R can be picked from RSTUV in $_1C_1$ or one way, since there is only one R. Recall that there will be three letters chosen and only one of them is R. From the four other letters, STUV, choose two to go along with the R. Picking two letters from four can be done in $_4C_2 = 4!/2!2! = 6$ ways. So $1 \cdot 6$ of the 10 choices contain the letter R.

Since $n(R) = 6$ and $n(s) = 10$, $p(R) = n(R)/n(s) = 6/10 = 3/5$. The probability that a choice of three letters from RSTUV contains an R is $3/5$.

Notice that six of the ten actual sets of three letters listed above (RST, RSU, RSV, RTU, RTV, RUV, STU, STV, SUV, and TUV) *do* contain the letter R.

Combinations are used more frequently than are permutations, particularly in probability problems. To do these, first calculate the total number of combinations possible with no restrictions (as above, the total number of ways of choosing three letters from RSTUV). This number will be the denominator, $n(s)$, of the probability fraction, the number of elements in the sample space.

The numerator, $n(f)$, is the number of favorable combinations (as above, the number of these combinations that contain the letter R). This fraction will be the probability of the favorable combination appearing in the choice.

Exercise 5.15: From a group of four men and five women, a committee of three is chosen.
   a. How many different committees of three are possible among the nine people?
   b. How many of these committees will have all men on them?
   c. How many of these committees will consist of all women?
   d. How many will contain both men and women?
   e. What is the probability that the committee of three will consist of:
      (i) all men (ii) all women (iii) both men and women?

Answers:
   a. The number of committees of three people that can be chosen from nine people is $_nC_r = n!/(n-r)!r! = {}_9C_3 = 9!/6!3! = 84$. Therefore, there are eighty-four different committees of three possible.
   b. The number of committees consisting of men only is the number of committees that have three men and no women on them. Therefore, the three men must be chosen from the group of four men and zero women from the group of five women. The combination formula for this is $_4C_3 \cdot {}_5C_0$ which represents, first, the number of ways to choose three men from four, $_4C_3$. This factor is followed by the number of ways to choose zero women from five, $_5C_0$.
      Evaluating the first factor, $_4C_3 = 4!/1!3! = 4$. The second is $_5C_0 = 5!/5!0! = 1$ (remembering that $0! = 1$). Thus, the number of those eighty-four committees that consist only of men is just $4 \cdot 1 = 4$.
   c. In a similar manner, the number of committees all of whose members are women is $_5C_3 \cdot {}_4C_0 = 10.1 = 10$. Therefore, ten of the eighty-four committees will consist of women only.
   d. If there are to be both men and women on the committee, it can happen in one of two different configurations.
      One way is that there will be one man and two women on the committee, which can occur in $_4C_1 \cdot {}_5C_2$ (the number of ways one man can be chosen from the four men, followed by the number of ways two

women can be chosen from the five women). The combination product is $_4C_1 \cdot {}_5C_2 = 4 \cdot 10 = 40$, so there are forty committees consisting of one man and two women.

Similarly, the other configuration, two men and one woman, can be chosen in $_4C_2 \cdot {}_5C_1 = 6 \cdot 5 = 30$ ways. Therefore, there are $40 + 30 = 70$ mixed committees.

Notice that the number of all men committees (4) plus the number of all women committees (10) plus the number of mixed committees (70) equals the total number of committees of three that can be chosen from the nine people (84 different committees).

e. (i)   The probability that the committee chosen will consist of men only is $n(m)/n(s)$, the ratio of the number of committees of men only divided by the total number of committees possible. From (b), $n(m) = 4$ and from (a), $n(s) = 84$. Therefore, $p(m) = 4/84 = 1/21$. The probability that the committee chosen will be all men is 1/21.

(ii)   The probability that the committee chosen will consist of women only is $n(w)/n(s)$. From (c), $n(w) = 10$. Therefore, $p(w) = 10/84 = 5/42$. The probability that the committee chosen will consist of women only is 5/42.

(iii)   The probability of the committee consisting of both men and women is $n(b)/n(s)$. From (d), $n(b) = 70$. Therefore, $p(b) = 70/84 = 5/6$. Notice that if the three probabilities for (i), (ii), and (iii) are added, $4/84 + 10/84 + 70/84$, the result is certainty, 1.

*I*n this chapter we have discussed elementary probability theory and counting methods. The probability of an event is the ratio of the number of favorable outcomes of an experiment to the total number of events in the sample space: $p(x) = n(f)/n(s)$.

The probability of simple and compound (more than one) events was discussed. Venn diagrams help picture unions and intersections of sets, which assists in calculating the probabilities of unions and intersections of events.

The probability of the union of two events, A and B, is given by the formula $p(A \cup B) = p(A) + p(B) - p(A \cap B)$, where $A \cup B$ is the event that A or B or both occur and $A \cap B$ is the event that both A and B occur. If A and B cannot happen at the same time, they are called mutually exclusive events. If A and B are mutually exclusive, $A \cap B = 0$ and $p(A \cap B) = 0$.

Conditional probability, $p(A|B)$, was given by the formula $p(A|B) = p(A \cap B)/p(B)$. In the case in which A and B are independent, the fact that B happens does not affect the probability of A happening. In that case, $p(A|B) = p(A)$ and for independent events only, $p(A \cap B) = p(A) \cdot p(B)$.

In order to solve more complicated probability problems with large sample spaces, counting methods were introduced. Tree diagrams help visualize sequential counting, but the main focus was on permutations and combinations. A permutation is a formula for finding the number of possible picks and arrangements of r things from a total of n. The formula for a permutation is $_nP_r = n!/(n - r)!$

The number of choices of r items from a total of n without arranging those r things is called a combination. The formula for a combination is

$_nC_r = n!/(n-r)!r!$

Combinations are often used in connection with probability calculations, since using the combination formula will give the number of the elements in a sample space as well as the number of favorable elements in the space. These counting methods provide a way to calculate probabilities without listing the entire sample space for the problem.

Exercise 5.16: The game of poker illustrates how probability is the foundation of card games. For example, in poker certain hands (combinations of cards) beat (are higher than) other hands. Remembering that poker involves dealing five cards from a deck of fifty-two, how many of these $_{52}C_5 = 2,598,960$ hands will consist of the following good combinations?

 a. Four of a kind (four of one denomination, such as four jacks).

 b. A full house (three of one denomination and two of another, such as three kings and two fives).

 c. A flush (all five cards from the same suit, such as five hearts).

 d. A straight (all five cards in order, with ace high only, such as 3H, 4S, 5D, 6H, 7S). Ace high means that the ace can only be used in sequence after the king, not before the 2 as a 1, which is permissible in some card games.

 e. A straight flush (all five cards in order, ace high only, of the same suit, such as 8D, 9D, 10D, JD, QD).

 f. A royal flush (a straight flush starting with a ten).

 g. Find the probabilities for each of the above and then order the hands as to which combination beats which on the basis of which is least probable (has the smallest probability), second to least probable, etc.

Answers:

 a. First, for four of a kind, in how many ways can the "kind" be chosen? There are thirteen different denominations $(2, 3, 4, \ldots J, Q, K, A)$. One denomination can be chosen from the thirteen in $_{13}C_1 = 13$ ways.

  Then, from the four cards in this denomination (S, H, D, C), all must be chosen, which can be done in $_4C_4 = 1$ way.

  The fifth card (to fill out the five card hand) must be chosen from the remaining forty-eight cards, which can be done in $_{48}C_1 = 48$ ways. Therefore, there are $13 \cdot 1 \cdot 48 = 624$ different hands that contain four of a kind.

 b. From the thirteen different denominations, one denomination is chosen for the three of a kind, which can happen in thirteen ways, as above.

  From the four cards available in the chosen denomination, three must be chosen to get three of a kind. This can be done in $_4C_3 = 4$ ways.

  Then a second denomination, for the two of a kind part of this hand, is chosen from the twelve remaining denominations in $_{12}C_1 = 12$ ways.

  From the four cards available in the chosen denomination, two cards can be chosen in $_4C_2 = 6$ ways.

Therefore, the number of different poker hands consisting of a full house is $13 \cdot 4 \cdot 12 \cdot 6 = 3744$.

c. For a flush, first, in how many ways can the suit be chosen? There are four suits (spades, hearts, diamonds, clubs), so they can be chosen in $_4C_1 = 4$ different ways. Then, there are thirteen cards in the suit, so the five for the poker hand can be chosen in $_{13}C_5 = 1287$ ways. Therefore, the number of different poker hands consisting of a Flush is $4 \cdot 1287 = 5148$.

d. The first question to consider for a straight is which cards can be the lowest (or highest) in the sequence? For example, a king cannot be the lowest card of a straight because there would have to be four higher ones and ace is the only denomination higher than king. Only two, three, four, five, six, seven, eight, nine, or ten can be the lowest card in a straight, so the first card choice is one of these from the nine listed above, or $_9C_1 = 9$.

Once the lead card is found, that and each of the subsequent four cards can be chosen in $_4C_1 = 4$ ways, since to start a straight with a seven, for example, there are four possibilities, 7S, 7H, 7D, 7C. The next card, which is an eight, can also be any one of four cards, 8S, 8H, 8D, 8C.

Once the lead card is chosen, the five cards can each be chosen in four ways: thus, the five cards can be chosen in 4^5 ways. The hand can be filled in $9 \cdot 4^5 = 9216$ ways. Therefore, there are 9216 possible poker hands consisting of straights.

e. For a straight flush, again only nine different first cards are possible (the straight part of the straight flush). All cards are of the same suit, so for each of the nine lowest cards, the only other choice is which suit, four choices in all.

All cards are determined once the first card is chosen. The lowest card is chosen in $9 \cdot 4 = 36$ ways, where nine is the number of denominations possible and four is the number of suits. For example, if the first card is 8H, then the others must be 9H, 10H, JH, QH. Therefore, the total number of straight flushes possible is thirty-six.

f. There are only four royal flushes possible (count them).

g. For each of the probabilities, divide the number of ways of filling the hand (number of hands possible) by total possible number of poker hands. Recall that the total number of poker hands is given by the combination $_{52}C_5$, the number of ways of choosing five cards from a fifty-two card deck. Recall also that we calculated $_{52}C_5 = 2,598,960$ so the number of poker hands in the sample space, $n(s) = 2,598,960$.

$p(a) = 624/2,598,960 = .000240$, where (a) is four of a kind.
$p(b) = 3744/2,598,960 = .001441$, where (b) is a full house.
$p(c) = 5148/2,598,960 = .001981$, where (c) is a flush.
$p(d) = 9216/2,598,960 = .003546$, where (d) is a straight.
$p(e) = 36/2,598,960 = .0000139$, where (e) is a straight flush.
$p(f) = 4/2,598,960 = .00000154$, where (f) is a royal flush.

The least probable hand is the royal flush. Of the others listed, the next least probable are, in order, the straight flush, four of a kind, full house, flush and, finally, straight. These probabilities dictate the rules for which poker hand beats which: the hand with the lower probability beats hands with higher probabilities.

Be aware that there are other good hands in poker whose probabilities were not calculated here, including two pairs, three of a kind, and one pair. In the case in which more than one player has the same kind of hand, the ranking of denominations (ace high, two low) is included in the game outcome.

6

Probability Distributions

At the beginning of Chapter Two, different types of data were discussed. Quantitative data, which consists of meaures or quantities, was divided into two distinct types, discrete and continuous. Discrete data is measured in exact numbers, like glove sizes. Continuous data is measured over an interval; for example, a person's height is not exactly 71 inches, but may be 71 to the nearest inch, or the upper inch. This chapter will discuss probabilities of both discrete and continuous variables.

DISCRETE RANDOM VARIABLES

A random variable is a number assigned to an outcome of an experiment. For example, suppose a coin is tossed. The results, as have been discussed previously, are either H (heads) or T (tails). Instead of using H and T, the outcome of the coin toss can be quantified (given a value) as follows: let x be the number of heads in one toss of the coin.

The outcome H gives the random variable x the value 1, while outcome T gives x the value 0. The toss has probabilities associated with it: $p(1) = .5$ and $p(0) = .5$. This information can be displayed in a table (Table 6.1).

Table 6.1

x	0	1
$p(x)$	.5	.5

Notice that x is a discrete, not a continuous, random variable; it can only take on the value 0 or 1.

Graphing Probability Distributions

Another method of displaying this data is to graph the probability distribution. The graph resembles a histogram, but the numbers are placed in the centers of the bases of the rectangles. The graph of the probability distribution in Table 6.1 is shown in Figure 6.1.

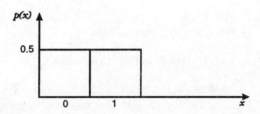

Figure 6.1:
Probability Distribution Graph
Table 6.1
x = No. of Heads in One Coin Toss

The total area of the graph is 1. Each rectangle has a width of 1 and a height of .5; thus each rectangle has an area of $A = hw = .5(1) = .5$. An important characteristic of all probability distributions is that their total area is 1, representing the sum of the probabilities for the sample space.

Suppose a coin is tossed three times and x, the random variable, is the number of heads in the three tosses. The problem is to find and graph the probability distribution of x.

If a coin is tossed three times, there can be zero, one, two, or three heads. There are eight outcomes to the three tosses: each toss is independent, and after each toss there are two outcomes for the next toss. The sample space is {TTT, TTH, THT, HTT, THH, HTH, HHT, HHH} and all are equally probable ($p = 1/8$ for each of the eight possibilities).

Only one of the tosses, TTT, has zero heads, so its probability, $p(0) = 1/8$. Three of the tosses, TTH, THT, HTT, have one head, so $p(1) = 3/8$. Three other tosses, THH, HTH, and HHT, have two heads, so $p(2) = 3/8$, and one toss has three heads, so $p(3) = 1/8$. These results are summarized in Table 6.2 and in Figure 6.2.

Note that the total area of the graph is the sum of the areas of the rectangles:

Table 6.2

x	0	1	2	3
$p(x)$	1/8	3/8	3/8	1/8

$A = 1/8 + 3/8 + 3/8 + 1/8 = 1.$

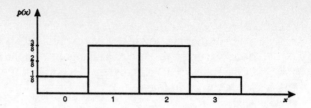

Figure 6.2:
Probability Distribution Graph
Table 6.2
x = No. of Heads in Three Coin Tosses

Exercise 6.1: Exercise 5.15 discussed a committee of three people chosen from a group of four men and five women. For this problem, let x, the random variable, represent the number of women on the committee. Find and graph the probability distribution of x.

Answer: Since the committee will have three people on it, and there are more than three women to choose from, the random variable x has the values 0, 1, 2, and 3, denoting committees with zero women, one woman, two women, and three women. The probability of some of these combinations was calculated in Chapter Five, but let's work them out again.

The denominator is the total number of committees of three people that can be chosen from nine. From nine possible members, choose three: the denominator is $_9C_3 = 84$.

The numerator for $x = 0$ is the number of committees that can be formed with no women. This is found by choosing zero women from five followed by three men from four: $_5C_0 \cdot _4C_3 = 1 \cdot 4 = 4$. Therefore, the probability of a committee with zero women is $p(0) = 4/84$.

The numerator for $x = 1$ is the number of committees that can be formed with one woman and two men to fill out the committee of three. This is $_5C_1 \cdot _4C_2 = 5 \cdot 6 = 30$, so $p(1) = 30/84$.

The numerator for $x = 2$ gives the number of committees that can be formed with two women and one man: $_5C_2 \cdot _4C_1 = 10 \cdot 4 = 40$; therefore, $p(2) = 40/84$.

Finally, the numerator for a committee of all women, three women and no men, is found by $_5C_3 \cdot _4C_0 = 10 \cdot 1 = 10$, so $p(3) = 10/84$.

All the above is summarized in this table and in Figure 6.3.

Table 6.3

x	0	1	2	3
$p(x)$	4/84	30/84	40/84	10/84

(Notice that the sum of the probabilities is 1.)

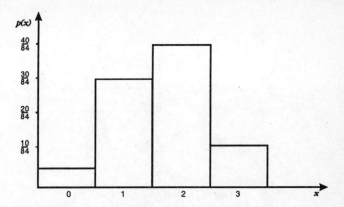

Figure 6.3:
Probability Distribution Graph
Table 6.3
x = No. of Women on Committee

EXPECTATION

One advantage of assigning a random variable to the outcome of an experiment is that the mean of the probability distribution of the random variable can be calculated. Recall that the mean of a data set is represented by $\bar{x}$. The mean of a population is represented by the Greek letter μ (mu).

In the case of a probability distribution of discrete variables (i.e., x can take on only certain values, usually, but not always, whole numbers as illustrated above), this mean, μ, can also be referred to as expectation, $E(x)$. In short, $E(x)$ is the number you expect to be the average when the experiment is done many times.

Table 6.4

x	0	1	2
$p(x)$	1/4	2/4	1/4
$p(x)$ (decimal form)	.25	.50	.25

For example, suppose two coins are tossed, and x, the random variable, represents the number of heads. Table 6.4 and Figure 6.4 show the probability distribution table and graph.

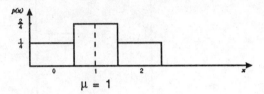

Figure 6.4 :
Probability Distribtuion Graph
x = Number of Heads in Toss of Two Coins
$\mu = 1$

To find the mean, or the expected number, use the formula

$$\mu = E(x) = \Sigma x \cdot p(x)$$

This means that the expectation is calculated by taking the sum of the products of the random variable and its probability. In this problem, $E(x) = \Sigma x \cdot p(x) = (0 \cdot .25) + (1 \cdot .5) + (2 \cdot .25) = 1$. Therefore, the mean of this probability distribution is 1. The average number of heads we expect to get (in the long run) is 1.

Most of the time, the expectation is not a possible value of the random variable. For example, suppose three coins are tossed, x being the random variable representing the number of heads. The table is reproduced as Table 6.5.

Table 6.5

x	0	1	2	3
$p(x)$	1/8	3/8	3/8	1/8
$p(x)$ decimal	.125	.375	.375	.125

The mean of this distribution is given by

$$\mu = E(x) = \Sigma x \cdot p(x)$$
$$= (0 \cdot .125) + (1 \cdot .375) + (2 \cdot .375) + (3 \cdot .125)$$
$$= 0 + .375 + .750 + .375$$
$$= 1.5.$$

Therefore, we expect, in the long run, an average of 1.5 heads in three tosses of a coin, even though 1.5 heads is not a possible outcome of the toss of three coins.

Insurance Premiums

The formula for expectation can be used to calculate premiums or profits in insurance policies. For example, suppose Jim is thirty years old and wishes to purchase a $100,000 one-year life insurance policy. From actuarial tables, suppose the probability of his dying in the next year is .0003. If he pays $400 for the policy, what is the insurance company's profit (expectation)?

The random variable x represents the insurance company's profit or loss. The two values that x can take are +400 and –99,600. If Jim lives, the company takes his $400. If he dies, the company must pay his heirs $100,000, but Jim has already paid $400 of this, so the net payout from the insurance company is $99,600. The probability that they will pay out this money is .0003. The probability that they will keep the $400 is $(1 - .0003) = .9997$, the probability that Jim lives. This information is summarized in Table 6.6.

Table 6.6

x	+ 400	– 99,600
$p(x)$	.9997	.0003

The insurance company's expectation is:

$$E(x) = \Sigma x \cdot p(x) = 400\,(.9997) - 99{,}600\,(.0003) = \$370.$$

Jim's expectation is –$370, which is what he is expecting to lose. Naturally, neither of these numbers is possible in this one case, but in the long run, if the insurance company sells policies to thousands of thirty-year-olds (which they do), $370 is their expected gain per policy, and each of the thirty-year-olds is expected to lose $370.

Exercise 6.2: Two dice are tossed once. Let the random variable be the sum of the up faces on the dice.

a. Find and graph the probability distribution of the random variable.

b. Calculate the mean (or expectation) of this distribution.

Answers: The possible values of x, the random variable, are 2, 3, 4, 5, 6, 7, 8, 9, 10, 11 and 12. In Exercise 5.2, all the ordered pairs (thirty-six total) were listed.

For example, the sum 2 can appear only by tossing (1, 1), 1 on each up face of the dice: there is only one way to arrive at the sum 2. The sum 5 can be made by the pairs (2, 3), (3, 2), (4, 1), and (1, 4). So there are four ways to arrive at the sum 5 when tossing a pair of dice. We need to find the count of favorable outcomes [e.g., $n(2) = 1$, $n(5) = 4$] for each of the random variables, 2 to 12, which represent all the possible values of the sum of the two dice. The probabilities of each can be found by dividing each of the numbers of favorable events for the random variable by 36.

a. Each random number, along with its probability, is listed in Table 6.7.

Table 6.7

x	2	3	4	5	6	7	8	9	10	11	12
$p(x)$	1/36	2/36	3/36	4/36	5/36	6/36	5/36	4/36	3/36	2/36	1/36

The probability distribution is also graphed in Figure 6.5.

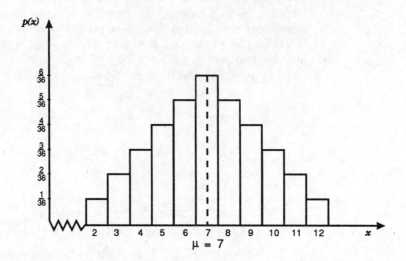

Figure 6.5:
Probability Distribution Graph
Table 6.7
x = Sum of Pips on Two Dice
$\mu = 7$

b. $E(x) = \sum x \cdot p(x) = 2(1/36) + 3(2/36) + 4(3/36) + 5(4/36) + 6(5/36) +$
7(6/36) + 8(5/36) + 9(4/36) + 10(3/36) + 11(2/36) + 12(1/36)
= 2/36 + 6/36 + 12/36 + 20/36 + 30/36 + 42/36 + 40/36 + 36/36 + 30/36
+ 22/36 + 12/36 = 252/36 = 7.
Notice that the graph of the probability distribution is symmetric and has a
mean of 7.

**Variance of
Probability
Distributions**

Along with the calculation of the mean of random variable probability
distribution μ, the variance and thus the standard deviation can also be calculated. Recall that the variance of a data set is denoted s^2. The variance of a

population, or probability distribution, is denoted by the Greek letter σ^2, sigma (squared). Capital sigma, Σ, is used to represent summation, but small sigma, σ, is the symbol for the standard deviation of a probability distribution.

The formula for the variance, σ^2, of a random variable distribution is $\sigma^2 = \Sigma(x - \mu)^2 \cdot p(x)$, where x is the random variable and μ is the mean or expectation.

To calculate the variance, the mean (μ) must be subtracted from each value of the random variable. That quantity is squared and then multiplied by the probability of that value for the random variable. The sum of all these products (as many as there are values for the random variable) is the variance of the random variable probability distribution.

Table 6.8

x	0	1	2	3
$p(x)$	.125	.375	.375	.125

Table 6.8 is similar to Table 6.5: the random variable is the number of heads in three coin tosses. The mean, which was calculated above, is 1.5. Sometimes in calculating the variance it is quickest to add a row above the x, designated $(x - \mu)^2$, which can be found once μ is calculated. Then the table looks like Table 6.9.

Table 6.9

$(x - \mu)^2$	2.25	.25	.25	2.25
x	0	1	2	3
$p(x)$	.125	.375	.375	.125

Then $\sigma^2 = \Sigma(x - \mu)^2 \cdot p(x) = 2.25(.125) + .25(.375) + .25(.375) + 2.25(.125)$ = .75.

Since $\sigma^2 = .75$, the standard deviation of the probability distribution is $\sigma = \sqrt{.75} \approx .866$.

Exercise 6.3: Using the experiment in Exercise 6.2 of tossing two dice:
  a. determine the variance and standard deviation of the probability distribution;
  b. find what percentage of the probability distribution is within one, two, and three standard deviations of the mean.

Answers: First we reproduce Table 6.7 as Table 6.10 and add the top line. This represents the difference between each of the random variable values (2, 3, . . . , 12) and the mean, $\mu = 7$, as found in Exercise 6.2.

Table 6.10

$(x-\mu)^2$	25	16	9	4	1	0	1	4	9	16	25
x	2	3	4	5	6	7	8	9	10	11	12
$p(x)$	1/36	2/36	3/36	4/36	5/36	6/36	5/36	4/36	3/36	2/36	1/36

a. Then $\sigma^2 = 25(1/36) + 16(2/36) + 9(3/36) + 4(4/36) + 1(5/36) + 0(6/36)$
   $+ 1(5/36) + 4(4/36) + 9(3/36) + 16(2/36) + 25(1/36)$

   $= 25/36 + 32/36 + 27/36 + 16/36 + 5/36 + 0/36 + 5/36 + 16/36 + 27/36$
   $+ 32/36 + 25/36$

   $= 210/36 \approx 5.83.$
   (Since a denominator of 36 produces nonterminating decimals, it is more accurate to work with <u>fractions</u> until the last calculation.)
   The standard deviation $\sigma \approx \sqrt{5.83} \approx 2.4$.

b. The one standard deviation interval around the mean is $7 \pm 2.4 = (4.6, 9.4)$. The values in this interval are 5, 6, 7, 8, and 9. Their probabilities total $4/36 + 5/36 + 6/36 + 5/36 + 4/36 = 24/36$, or 2/3. Approximately 67% of probability distribution of the random variable values is within one standard deviation of the mean.

   Two standard deviations from the mean, $7 \pm 2(2.4)$, is the interval $(2.2, 11.8)$. The numbers in this interval are 3, 4, 5, 6, 7, 8, 9, 10, and 11, whose probabilities total 34/36. The percentage of the probability distribution of the random variable values within two standard deviations of the mean is approximately 94%.

   All the numbers, 100% of the random variable values, are within three standard deviations of the mean, $7 \pm 3(2.4) = (-.2, 14.2)$.

   These percentages are very close to those of the normal distribution, 68%, 95%, and 99.7%. Recall that these represent the percentages of numbers in the normal distribution that are within one, two, and three standard deviations from the mean, respectively.

BINOMIAL RANDOM VARIABLES

Many experiments, including some we have already discussed, consist of a number of identical trials in which one result is considered "success" and all others are considered "failures." The probability of success is the same for each of the trials.

Examples of this type of experiment include tossing a coin many times, calling the outcome heads success and the outcome tails failure, or throwing a pair of dice a number of times, calling the outcomes 7 and 11 success and any other outcome a failure.

When these conditions have been met (i.e., numbers of identical trials; two outcomes, success or failure; and the same probability of success for each trial), then x, the random variable representing the number of successes in the entire experiment, is called a *binomial random variable*.

. Suppose two coins are tossed one hundred times. Success is defined as both coins landing heads. The binomial random variable x is the number of successes. Since the coins are tossed 100 times, the number of successes (both heads) can be any number from 0 to 100: x can equal $0, 1, 2, \ldots, 100$. The binomial random variable formula will show how to calculate the probability of that number of successes: $p(x = 0)$, $p(x = 1)$, $\ldots$, $p(x = 100)$. The binomial probability distribution will also have a mean, μ, and a variance, σ^2, just as with the random variable probability distribution in the previous sections.

FORMULA FOR BINOMIAL RANDOM VARIABLES

The probability of x can be calculated using the binomial random variable formula, which relies on some of the concepts we developed earlier.

$$p(x) = {}_nC_x \cdot p^x q^{n-x} \text{ , where}$$

p = probability of success on a single trial;

$q = 1 - p$ = probability of failure on a single trial;

n = number of trials;

x = number of successes in n trials (the random variable)

For example, toss a coin six times. What is the probability of tossing exactly four heads in the six tosses? Some possible sets of successful tosses are {HHHHTT}, {HHTTHH}, {TTHHHH}.

One way to answer this question is to list all possible results of six tosses of a coin (which is the same as a toss of six coins), the sample space. Then we can count how many have four heads, as do the three listed above. However, this would be tedious since there are $2^6 = 64$ different sets of tosses in the sample space. So we will use the above formula for this problem.

$$p(x) = {}_nC_x \cdot p^x q^{n-x};$$

$p = 1/2$, the probability of heads (success) in a single toss of one coin;

$q = 1 - p = 1 - 1/2 = 1/2$, the probability of tails (failure) in a single toss of one coin;

$n = 6$, the number of trials (tosses);

$x = 4$, the number of successes in the six trials.

Substituting in the formula above,

$$p(4) = {}_6C_4 \cdot \left(\frac{1}{2}\right)^4 \left(\frac{1}{2}\right)^{(6-4)}$$

$$= \frac{6!}{2!4!} \left(\frac{1}{2}\right)^4 \left(\frac{1}{2}\right)^2$$

$$= 15 \cdot \left(\frac{1}{16}\right)\left(\frac{1}{4}\right) = 15/64.$$

If we listed all sixty-four of the outcomes in the sample space for tossing one coin six times, fifteen of them would contain four heads.

Consider now the question of the probability of four *or more* heads ($x > 4$) in six tosses of the coin. To the result for p (4) would have to be added p (5) and p (6).

$$p(5) = {}_6C_5 \cdot \left(\frac{1}{2}\right)^5 \left(\frac{1}{2}\right)^{(6-5)}$$

$$= \frac{6!}{1!5!} \left(\frac{1}{2}\right)^5 \left(\frac{1}{2}\right)^1 = 6 \cdot \left(\frac{1}{32}\right)\left(\frac{1}{2}\right) = 6/64.$$

$$p(6) = {}_6C_6 \cdot \left(\frac{1}{2}\right)^6 \left(\frac{1}{2}\right)^{(6-6)}$$

$$= \frac{6!}{0!6!} \left(\frac{1}{2}\right)^6 \left(\frac{1}{2}\right)^0$$

(Recall that $x^0 = 1$ for $x \neq 0$, and $0! = 1$)

$$= 1! \cdot \left(\frac{1}{64}\right) = 1/64.$$

$$p(x \geq 4) = p(4) + p(5) + p(6) = 15/64 + 6/64 + 1/64 = 22/64 \text{ or } 11/32$$

Therefore, the probability that four or more heads appear in six tosses of a coin is 11/32.

Exercise 6.4:   A pair of dice is tossed five times. Success is a sum of either 7 or 11 on the pair; failure is any other result. Find the probability of exactly two successes in the five trials.

Answer: From previous examples, including the table from Exercise 6.2, the probability of tossing a sum of 7 with a pair of dice is 6/36, and the probability of 11 is 2/36.

Therefore, $p(7 \text{ or } 11) = 6/36 + 2/36 = 8/36 = 2/9$ (these are mutually exclusive events, so the probability of either occurring is the sum of each occurring).

Therefore, $p = 2/9$; $q = 1 - p = 1 - 2/9 = 7/9$; $n = 5$; and $x = 2$.

$$p(x) = {}_nC_x \cdot p^x q^{n-x}.$$

Thus, $p\,(2) = {}_5C_2 \cdot (2/9)^2 (7/9)^3 = 10(4/81)(343/729) \approx .23$.

The probability of tossing 7 or 11 twice in five tosses of a pair of dice is approximately .23.

Binomial Probability Distribution

If the binomial random variables are computed for the entire sample space of a single experiment, these probabilities together form a binomial probability distribution.

For example, recall in the previous section the experiment of tossing a coin six times. The random variable was the number of heads (successes) in those six tosses. This variable takes on the values 0, 1, 2, 3, 4, 5, or 6. Each of these has a probability associated with it, three of which were computed in the previous section: $p(4) = 15/64$; $p(5) = 6/64$; $p(6) = 1/64$. Using the same formula, $p(0) = 1/64$, $p(1) = 6/64$, $p(2) = 15/64$ (these are symmetric since $p = q$) and $p(3) = {}_6C_3 \cdot (1/2)^3 (1/2)^3 = 20/64$. Table 6.11 displays these probabilities.

Table 6.11

x	0	1	2	3	4	5	6
$p(x)$	1/64	6/64	15/64	20/64	15/64	6/64	1/64

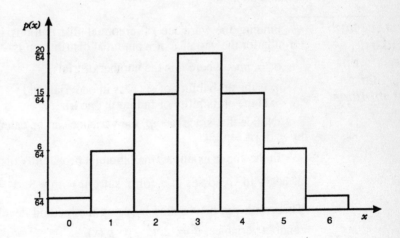

Figure 6.6:
Binomial Probability Distribution Graph[x]
Table 6.11
x = No. of Heads (Successes) in Six Coin Tosses

This can also be graphed as in Figure 6.6.

Mean of Binomial Distributions

The binomial random variable distribution is a special type of random variable distribution. Recall that we can find the mean (μ) of a random variable distribution by the formula

$$\mu = \Sigma x \cdot p(x)$$

Using this formula on the binomial distribution in Table 6.11 we have

$$\mu = \Sigma x \cdot p(x)$$

$$= 0\left(\frac{1}{64}\right) + 1\left(\frac{6}{64}\right) + 2\left(\frac{15}{64}\right) + 3\left(\frac{20}{64}\right) + 4\left(\frac{15}{64}\right) + 5\left(\frac{6}{64}\right) + 6\left(\frac{1}{64}\right) + 0\left(\frac{1}{64}\right)$$

$$= \frac{0 + 6 + 30 + 60 + 60 + 30 + 6}{64} = \frac{192}{64} = 3.$$

When the random variable is a binomial random variable, computing the mean is much simpler. The mean is calculated by multiplying the number of trials by the probability of success in any one trial: $\mu = np$. Since p in the above problem is 1/2 (probability of success, heads) and $n = 6$ (there are six trials—tosses of a coin), $\mu = np = 6\left(\frac{1}{2}\right) = 3$, the same result obtained by the random variable method.

Variance and Standard Deviation of Binomial Distributions

Finding the variance of binomial distributions is equally simple. The formula for the variance of a binomial distribution is

$\sigma^2 = npq$, where n is the number of trials,

p is the probability of success in one trial, and
q is the probability of failure in one trial.

Notice that since $\mu = np$, the variance can be calculated by multiplying μ by q, or $\sigma^2 = \mu q$.

In the above example (the binomial probability distribution of the number of heads in six tosses of a coin), since $\mu = np = 3$, $\sigma^2 = npq = 6\left(\frac{1}{2}\right)\left(\frac{1}{2}\right) = 1.5$.

This result can be checked by using the method developed in the section on random variables, $\sigma^2 = \Sigma(x - \mu)^2 p(x)$.

The standard deviation σ of the binomial probability distribution is calculated by taking the square root of the variance. The formula for the standard deviation of a binomial probability distribution is thus $\sigma = \sqrt{npq}$.

In the above problem, since $\sigma^2 = 1.5$, $\sigma = \sqrt{1.5} \approx 1.22$.

Exercise 6.5: David is late to statistics class 1/5 of the time.
   a. Find the probabilities that he is late to the next five statistics classes zero, one, two, three, four, and five times.

b. Graph the binomial probability distribution of the random variable x for the next five statistic classes.

c. Find the mean, variance, and standard deviation of that distribution.

Answers:

a. For the next five classes, David can be late zero, one, two, three, four, or five times. The switch in this problem is that success is defined as being *late*. Therefore, $p = 1/5 = .2$ and $q = 1 - .2 = .8$; $n = 5$ (next five classes).

These probabilities for $x = 0, 1, 2, 3, 4, 5$ can be computed using the binomial random variable formula:

$$p(x) = {_n}C_x \cdot p^x q^{(n-x)}.$$
$$p(0) = {_5}C_0 \, (.2)^0 (.8)^5 = .8^5 = .32768$$

The probability that David will not be late to any of his next five statistics classes is .32768.

$$p(1) = {_5}C_1 (.2)^1 (.8)^4 = 5 \cdot (2)(.4096) = .4096$$

The probability that he will be late to exactly one of his next five statistics classes is .4096.

$$p(2) = {_5}C_2 (.2)^2 (.8)^3 = 10 \cdot (.04)(.512) = .2048$$

The probability that he will be late to exactly two of his next five statistics classes is .2048.

$$p(3) = {_5}C_3 (.2)^3 (.8)^2 = 10 \cdot (.008)(.64) = .0512$$

The probability that he will be late to exactly three of his next five statistics classes is .0512.

$$p(4) = {_5}C_4 (.2)^4 (.8)^1 = 5 \cdot (.0016)(.8) = .0064$$

The probability that he will be late to exactly four of his next five statistics classes is .0064.

$$p(5) = {_5}C_5 (.2)^5 (.8)^0 = .2^5 = .00032$$

The probability that he will be late to all of his next five statistics classes is .0064.

(Note that $\sum\limits_{i=0}^{5} p(i) = 1$.)

These probabilities are recorded in Table 6.12.

Table 6.12

x	0	1	2	3	4	5
$p(x)$	.32768	.4096	.2048	.0512	.0064	.00032

b. The graph of the binomial probability distribution for the problem is shown in Figure 6.7.

c. $\mu = np = 5(.2) = 1$;

$$\sigma^2 = npq = 5(.2)(.8) = .8;$$

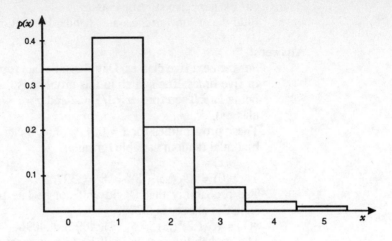

Figure 6.7 :
Binomial Probability Distribution Graph
Table 6.12
x = Number of Times David Is Late to Next Five Statistics Classes

$$\sigma = \sqrt{npq} = \sqrt{.8} \approx .89.$$

NORMAL DISTRIBUTION

The random variables in the preceding sections have all been discrete random variables: they have referred to the number of times an event can occur, the number of women who can be chosen for a committee, or the numbers representing the sum on a pair of dice.

Continuous Variables

Most of the numbers we use every day are continuous random variables: men's heights or miles per gallon of gas (not rounded off). Many of these continuous random variables are normally distributed. This means that, when plotted, the curve is symmetric and has the properties described in the Empirical Rule, which states: If the frequency distribution is normal, then:

a. Approximately 68% of the data points will fall within one standard deviation of the mean: $\bar{x} \pm s$.

b. Approximately 95% of the data points will fall within two standard deviations of the mean: $\bar{x} \pm 2s$.

c. Almost all of the data points ($\approx$99.7%) will fall within three standard deviations of the mean: $\bar{x} \pm 3s$.

Z-Scores

In Chapter Four, z-scores were calculated in order to change scores into a standard unit normal distribution. Z-scores are translations of the x-values (in this case, continuous random variables) into common units on the horizontal axis of a standard normal distribution. The mean of the standard normal distribution is 0, and the standard deviation is 1; the distribution is symmetric and satisfies the Empirical Rule, and the total area under the curve is 1.

The formula used was $z = (x - \bar{x})/s$, where $\bar{x}$ was the sample mean and s the sample standard deviation. To place population scores on a standard unit normal curve, the formula is the same: $z = (x - \mu)/\sigma$, where μ is the population mean and σ the population standard deviation. Using these formulas, we usually calculate z-scores between -2 and 2. By "usually," we mean approximately 95% of the time. This range $[-2, 2]$ represents two standard deviations to the left of the mean and two standard deviations to the right, given that the mean $\mu = 0$.

The reason for calculating z-scores is that the area under a normal curve is usually available in standard unit normal tables. Remember that the normal distribution is a probability distribution, so the total area under the normal curve is one. In calculus, we learn a set of techniques (called integration) to determine areas under a curve; areas can be found by integrating the function that produces the curve.

However, the function that produces the normal curve is difficult to integrate, even for those who have had calculus courses. Therefore, the areas under

Table 6.13

z	.00	.01	.02	.03	.04	.05. . .
.						
.						
.						
0.9	.3159	.3186	.3212	.3238	.3264	.3289. . .
1.0	.3413	.3438	.3461	.3485	.3508	.3531. . .
1.1	.3643	.3665	.3686	.3708	.3729	.3749. . .
.						
.						
2.0	.4772	.4778	.4783	.4788	.4793	.4798. . .
.						
.						

the normal curve (within approximately three standard deviations of the mean) will be found in the table in Appendix A. Part of this table and the diagram are reproduced in Figure 6.8 and in Table 6.13.

Standard Unit Normal (Z) Table

To use Table 6.13, suppose a certain variable x has a z-score of .93. This table will help you find, directly, the area under the normal curve between 0 and .93, the shaded part of Figure 6.8.

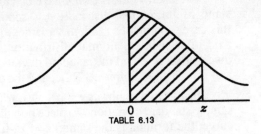

TABLE 6.13

Figure 6.8:
Areas Under Normal Curve between 0 and z (Table 6.13)

To find this number, locate the first decimal place (tenths) in the first (z) column. The .9 row gives the areas under the normal curve for all two-place decimals that begin with .9, or that are the sum of .9 and the column headings, .00, .01, etc. To find the z-score of .93 we look across the top row for .03, since .9 + .03 = .93; .93 is represented by the fourth column, headed .03. The number in the table that represents the area under the curve between 0 and .93 is .3238.

The probability that numbers in a normally distributed data set have z-scores between 0 and .93 is .3238. The percent of numbers in a data set that have z-scores between 0 and .93 is thus 32.38%. These numbers, which represent areas, are rounded off to four decimal places in the table.

Suppose instead the z-score was –.93. Since the normal curve is symmetric, the area between 0 and –.93 is identical to the area between 0 and .93, which is .3238. Therefore, there is no need to have an additional table of negative z-scores: just find the area under the curve for the positive z-scores.

Standard Normal Table and the Empirical Rule

Notice that the area under the unit normal curve between 0 and 1.00 is .3413. Therefore, the area between –1 and 1, which represents on any normal curve the area within one standard deviation of the mean, is 2(.3413) = .6826. This is the "approximately 68%" given in the first part of the Empirical Rule.

Also notice that for a z-score of 2.00, representing the area under the unit normal between 0 and 2, the number in the table is .4772. Doubling that to include the area between –2 and 0, the area under a normal curve within two standard deviations of the mean is 2(.4772) = .9544. Remember that the Empirical Rule states that the area within two standard deviations of the mean is "approximately 95%."

Exercise 6.6:
a. Find the areas under the normal curve between 0 and the following z-scores.

1. 1.03   2. –2.04   3. 0.95

b. Find the positive *z*-scores that yield the following areas under the normal curve between 0 and *z*.

1. .3186   2. .4788   3. .3665

Use Table 6.13 or Appendix A for this exercise.

Answers:

a. 1. For *z* = 1.03, the area under the normal curve between 0 and *z* is .3485.
2. For *z* = –2.04, the area under the normal curve is the same as for *z* = 2.04. This area is .4793.
3. For *z* = .95, the area under the normal curve between 0 and *z* is .3289.
b. 1. The positive *z*-score that yields an area of .3186 under the normal curve is .91. Therefore, the area under the normal curve between 0 and *z* = .91 is .3186.
2. The positive *z*-score that yields an area of .4788 is 2.03.
3. The positive *z*-score that yields an area of .3665 is 1.11.

TAIL PROBABILITIES

Many problems call for probabilities and percentages in what is called the tail of the normal curve, the part of the normal curve that comes after the *z*-score, not between 0 and *z*.

For example, instead of asking for the percentage of numbers with *z*-scores between 0 and .93, a more typical question might ask the percentage of numbers with *z*-scores greater than .93. Again the symmetric property of the normal distribution is used. The total area under the curve is 1, so each half has an area of .5. The area from 0 to .93 is .3238; the total area to the right of 0 is .5. Therefore, the area under the curve to the right of .93 is given by (.5 – .3238) = .1762: 17.62% of the numbers in the normally distributed data set have *z*-scores greater than .93.

Exercise 6.7:   I.Q.s of the population are normally distributed with a mean equal to 100 and a standard deviation of 15.
a. Find the *z*-score for an I.Q. of 120.
b. What percentage of the population have I.Q.s greater than 120?
c. What percentage of the population have I.Q.s between 115 and 120?
d. An organization for people with high I.Q.s wants to limit its membership to people whose I.Q.s are in the top 1% of the population. What I.Q. score would one have to achieve in order to become a member of this organization?

Answers:
a. $z = (x - \mu)/\sigma = (120 - 100)/15 = 20/15 = 1.33$. Round off *z*-scores to two decimal places, since those in the table have two decimal places.
b. A diagram of the I.Q. distribution and the standard unit normal will help (see Figure 6.9).

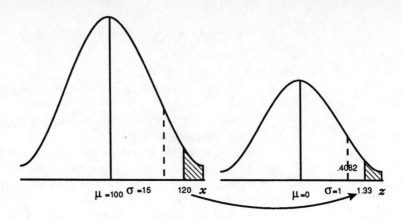

Figure 6.9:
I.Q. Distribution
Normal Curve Shaded : I.Q.s > 120
Standard Unit Normal Shaded > 1.33

The z-score shows that the area that represents the percentage of people having I.Q.s more than 120 is to the right of the mean. A score of 120 is 1.33 standard deviations to the right of 0. I.Q.s greater than 120 will be found in the tail, starting at 1.33. Referring to the table in Appendix A, the area between 0 and 1.33 is .4082. Therefore, the area in the tail (represented by scores >1.33) is .5 – .4082 = .0918.

Approximately 9.18% of the population have I.Q.s greater than 120.

c. A set of diagrams for this problem is in Figure 6.10. The z-score for 120 has already been calculated in part (a) at 1.33. The z-score for 115 is (115 – 100)/15 = 1.

The area under the normal curve between 0 and 1.33 is .4082. Checking the table in Appendix A indicates that the area under the normal curve between 0 and 1 is .3413. Therefore, the area under the normal curve between z-scores of 1 and 1.33 is: (.4082 – .3413) = .0669. This means that the percentage of people who have I.Q.s between 115 and 120 is 6.69%.

d. Another diagram will help in this last part (see Figure 6.11). In this problem, the percentage under the curve in the tail is known. The high I.Q. club wants only the top 1%.

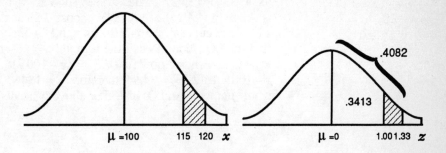

Figure 6.10
I.Q. Distribution Normal Curve Shaded 115 < I.Q. < 120

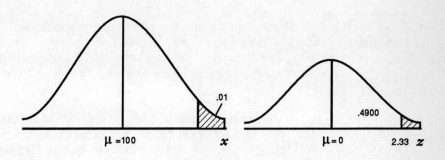

Figure 6.11:
I.Q. Distribution
Upper 1% Shaded Standard Unit Normal

The first step is to find, using the table, the z-score that leaves only .01 in the tail. The area under the curve between 0 and that z-score is $.5 - .01 = .4900$. The z-score that yields an area of .4900 between 0 and itself is between 2.32 (area .4898) and 2.33 (area .4901). Since .4900 is closer to .4901 than to .4898, choose 2.33 as the z-score that leaves 1% of the curve in the tail (to its right). A little algebra is needed to find the I.Q. score. Recall the formula $z = (x - \mu)/\sigma$. By substituting what is known, we now find $2.33 = (x - 100)/15$. Cross-multiplying, $x - 100 = 15(2.33) = 34.95$; therefore, $x = 134.95$, or 135 to the nearest whole number. An I.Q. of 135 or above is needed to join this club.

NORMAL DISTRIBUTION AND BINOMIAL DISTRIBUTION

When an experiment fulfills the conditions of a binomial probability distribution, and when n, the number of trials, is very large, the binomial distribution looks like the normal distribution, except it is discrete instead of continuous. If p, the probability of success, is close to .5 (in which case q, the probability of failure, would also be close to .5), then even for a small number of trials the binomial distribution resembles a normal distribution (see Figure 6.6 and the accompanying binomial distribution shown in Table 6.11, which display the number of heads in six tosses of a coin, along with their probabilities).

Approximating the Binomial with the Normal

Often when one or both of these two conditions exist (either n, the number of trials, is very large or p, the probability of success in a single trial, is close to .5), then the area of the rectangles can be closely approximated by the area under a normal curve whose mean $\mu = np$ and whose standard deviation

$$\sigma = \sqrt{npq}\,.$$

Suppose David is late to statistics class 1/5 of the time, as in Exercise 6.5. The probability graph in Figure 6.7, in which each rectangle represents the probability that he will be late x times in the next five classes, doesn't look at all normal. But if David has fifty more statistics classes, and those rectangles were graphed, this binomial probability distribution would more closely resemble the normal distribution, as in Figure 6.12.

The mean of the binomial probability distribution is $\mu = np = 50\left(\dfrac{1}{5}\right) = 10$. The standard deviation is $\sigma = \sqrt{npq} = \sqrt{50\,(1/5)(4/5)} = \sqrt{8} \approx 2.83$.

Suppose our problem is to find the probability that David will be late to fewer than five of the next fifty classes. By the binomial random variable calculation, we need the sum of the five boxes $p(0) + p(1) + p(2) + p(3) + p(4)$. Notice that the next box, $p(5)$, is not included because the problem is to find the

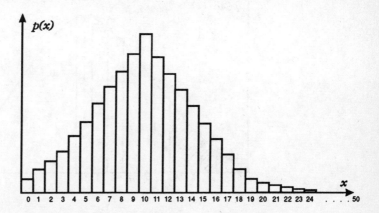

Figure 6.12:
Probability of David Being Late to 0, 1, 2, . . . , 49, 50 of the Next 50 Statistics Classes

probability that David will be late fewer than five, or zero, one, two, three, or four times. We could sum each of the binomial probabilities,

$$[_{50}C_0 \cdot \left(\frac{1}{5}\right)^0 \cdot \left(\frac{4}{5}\right)^{50}] + [_{50}C_1 \cdot \left(\frac{1}{5}\right)^1 \cdot \left(\frac{4}{5}\right)^{49}] + \ldots + [_{50}C_4 \cdot \left(\frac{1}{5}\right)^4 \cdot \left(\frac{4}{5}\right)^{46}],$$

but it is very difficult to calculate this sum.

However, a normal curve may possibly be a good approximation for this area. Instead of summing the boxes, the task now is to find the area under the part of the curve in Figure 6.13 that closely matches the area of the rectangles from 0 to 4 in Figure 6.12. Basically, we are converting the discrete (binomial probability distribution) to a continuous (normal) distribution because we have tables to determine quickly the areas under normal distribution curves.

Notice that the 4 at the base of the 4 rectangle is in the center of the box. In order to include the entire area of the rectangle in the calculation, the z-score for the normal curve is for the x-value of 4.5, the number at the right edge of the box. In that way, the entire shaded area under the normal curve will be found.

Then $z = (x - \mu)/\sigma = (4.5 - 10)/2.83 \approx -1.94$. The area of the unit normal (table in Appendix A) between 0 and 1.94 is .4738, so the area between 0 and -1.94 is also .4738. The area up to -1.94, or the left tail of the curve, is equal to $.5 - .4738 = .0262$.

Therefore, the probability that David will be late to class fewer than five of the next fifty times is approximately .0262 or 2.62%.

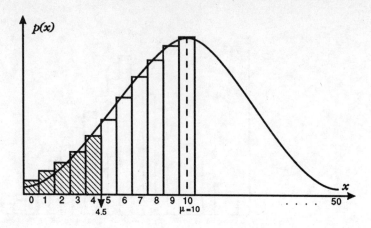

Figure 6.13:
Normal Approximation to Binomial Distribution in Figure 6.12
Shaded Area: Probability that David Is Late Fewer than Five Times

Testing for Good Approximation

Recall that criteria for binomial distributions to be closely approximated by the normal distribution include a large number of trials (n large) and/or p close to .5. But how large is large or how close is close? This section will outline a numerical test to decide whether a particular binomial distribution can be approximated well by the corresponding (same μ, same σ) normal distribution.

The total interval covered by a binomial distribution is $[0, n]$. That is, the total number of favorable outcomes in a binomial experiment with n trials is between 0 and n. The mean of this distribution will be somewhere between the 0 rectangle and the n rectangle.

Suppose we put a three-standard deviation interval around the mean of the binomial distribution, μ. Then we have the interval $\mu \pm 3\sigma$ or $(\mu - 3\sigma, \mu + 3\sigma)$. If the normal distribution is to closely approximate a binomial distribution with the same mean and standard deviation, this three standard deviation interval $(\mu - 3\sigma, \mu + 3\sigma)$ must be a subinterval of $[0, n]$; that is, the three-standard deviation interval around the mean is a subset of the total interval covered by the binomial probability distribution.

This test, whether the $(\mu - 3\sigma, \mu + 3\sigma) \subset [0, n]$, indicates whether the normal is a good approximation of that particular binomial distribution. The three-standard deviations should cover most, but not all, of the rectangles in the binomial interval $[0, n]$ since approximately 99.7% of the area under a normal curve is in the three-standard deviation interval around the mean.

The test checks whether $(\mu \pm 3\sigma) \subset [0, n]$. In this case, is $10 \pm 3(2.83)$ a subset of $[0, 50]$? $10 \pm 3(2.83) = 10 \pm 8.49 = (1.51, 18.49) \subset [0, 50]$. Therefore, normal distribution is considered a good approximation for this binomial probability distribution. This check should be performed whenever this approximation is going to be used.

Exercise 6.8: Four aces from an ordinary deck of cards are put into a hat. An experiment consists of drawing one card at random from the hat and replacing it. This is done 432 times. Success is the drawing of the ace of clubs.

    a. Find the probability of success in each trial.

    b. Find the expected number of successes (mean of the probability distribution).

    c. Find the standard deviation of this probability distribution.

    d. Show that the normal probability distribution can be used to approximate this binomial probability distribution.

    e. Using the normal curve approximation, find the approximate probability that the ace of clubs will be drawn 150 times or more in this experiment.

    f. Find the approximate probability that the ace of clubs will be drawn exactly 108 times in this experiment.

Answers:

    a. $p = \dfrac{1}{4}$ since one of the four aces is the ace of clubs.

    b. $E(x) = \mu = np$ where $n = 432$ and $p = \dfrac{1}{4}$. $\mu = np = 432\left(\dfrac{1}{4}\right) = 108$. The mean of the binomial distribution is 108.

    c. $\sigma = \sqrt{npq}$ where $q = 1 - p = 1 - \dfrac{1}{4} = \dfrac{3}{4}$.

        $\sigma = \sqrt{npq} = \sqrt{432(1/4)(3/4)} = \sqrt{81} = 9$. The standard deviation of the binomial distribution is 9.

    d. The normal curve can be used to approximate the binomial distribution if $\mu \pm 3\sigma \subset [0, n]$. In this case, $108 \pm 3 \cdot 9 \subset [0, 432]$ or $(81, 135) \subset [0, 432]$.

        Therefore, a good approximation to the binomial probability distribution can be obtained using the normal curve.

    e. Refer to Figure 6.14.

        To convert the discrete (binomial probability) distribution to a continuous (normal) distribution, we need to determine if the rectangle whose base is indicated by the 150 should be included in the area to be determined.

        Since the problem asks for the probability that the ace of clubs will be drawn 150 times or more, the rectangle whose base is indicated as 150 should be included in the area to be determined. This rectangle's base begins at 149.5 on the horizontal axis, so the z-score we must find is for $x = 149.5$. This score is given by $z = (x - \mu)/\sigma = (149.5 - 108)/27 = 1.54$.

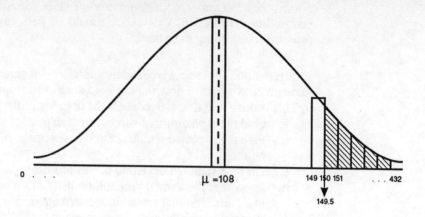

Figure 6.14:
Normal Approximation to Binomial Distribution
Shaded Area: Probability of Picking the Ace of Clubs 150 Times or More out of 432 Picks

e. The area under the unit normal between 0 and 1.54, according to the table in Appendix A, is .4382. Therefore, the area in the tail greater than $z = 1.54$, and thus greater than 149.5 on the normal approximation of this binomial distribution, is $(.5 - .4382) = .0618$. Thus, the probability of drawing the ace of clubs 150 times or more is .0618 or 6.18%.

f. The task here is to find the area of the rectangle at 108, as shown in Figure 6.15. Since the normal curve can be used to approximate the binomial, z-scores must be found for each end of the rectangle, 107.5 and 108.5.

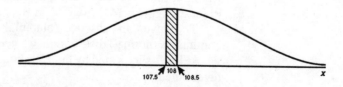

Figure 6.15:
Normal Approximation to Binomial Distribution
Shaded Area: Probability of Picking the Ace of Clubs 108 Times

These are symmetric points, since the area between 107.5 and the mean 108 is equal to the area between 108.5 and 108. The z-score for 108.5 is given by the formula $z = (108.5 - 108)/27 \approx .02$; for 107.5, the z-score is approximately $-.02$.

According to the normal curve table, the area under the curve between 0 and .02 is .0080. This area is the same on both sides of 108, so the total area of the normal curve between z-scores of $-.02$ and .02 is 2(.0080) or .0160.

The probability of getting exactly 108 aces of clubs during this experiment is .016 or 1.6%.

Exercise 6.9: Jim and Judy have four children. Judy's parents have made them the following proposal: if all four children go to college, Judy's parents will give Jim and Judy $10,000.

If three of the children go to college, Jim and Judy will get $5000 from Judy's parents; if two go to college, Jim and Judy will get $2000; if one goes, they will get $1000.

If none of the children goes to college, Jim and Judy will get no money from Judy's parents. Assuming the probability of each child going to college is .5, what is Jim and Judy's monetary expectation?

Answers: This problem is an expectation problem, so the probability distribution table should be set up. Let x be the amount of money the couple is to receive and $p(x)$ the probability they will receive it. These probabilities are binomial since p, the probability of going to college, is the same for each child, .5.

The random variable x is the money Jim and Judy will receive from Judy's parents.

So first calculate the probability for each number of children going to college. This will be paired with the amount of money in a table.

$$p(10000) = {}_4C_4\left(\frac{1}{2}\right)^4\left(\frac{1}{2}\right)^0 = 1 \cdot \left(\frac{1}{16}\right) \cdot (1) = \frac{1}{16}.$$

($10,000 will be given only if all four children go to college.)

$$p(5000) = {}_4C_3\left(\frac{1}{2}\right)^3\left(\frac{1}{2}\right)^1 = 4 \cdot \left(\frac{1}{8}\right) \cdot \left(\frac{1}{2}\right) = \frac{4}{16}.$$

($5000 will be given if any three of the four children go to college.)

$$p(2000) = {}_4C_2\left(\frac{1}{2}\right)^2\left(\frac{1}{2}\right)^2 = 6 \cdot \left(\frac{1}{4}\right) \cdot \left(\frac{1}{4}\right) = \frac{6}{16}.$$

($2000 will be given if any two of the four children go to college.)

$$p(1000) = {}_4C_1\left(\frac{1}{2}\right)^1\left(\frac{1}{2}\right)^3 = 4 \cdot \left(\frac{1}{2}\right) \cdot \left(\frac{1}{8}\right) = \frac{4}{16}.$$

($1000 will be given if any one of the four children goes to college.)

$$p(0) = {}_4C_0\left(\frac{1}{2}\right)^0\left(\frac{1}{2}\right)^4 = 1 \cdot (1) \cdot \left(\frac{1}{16}\right) = \frac{1}{16}.$$

(No money will be given if none of the four children goes to college.)

This information is summarized, along with each monetary gift, in Table 6.14.

Table 6.14

x	10,000	5,000	2,000	1,000	0
$p(x)$	1/16	4/16	6/16	4/16	1/16

$$\mu = E(x) = \Sigma x \cdot p(x)$$

$$= 10{,}000\left(\frac{1}{16}\right) + 5000\left(\frac{4}{16}\right) + 2000\left(\frac{6}{16}\right) + 1000\left(\frac{4}{16}\right) + 0\left(\frac{1}{16}\right)$$

$\mu = 625 + 1250 + 750 + 250 + 0 = 2875$. Jim and Judy thus have a monetary expectation of $2875.

Exercise 6.10:   The lengths of babies at birth is a continuous random variable, normally distributed with a mean of 19" and a standard deviation of 1.3". Out of 10,000 babies born, how many will be:

a.   Over 22" long?
b.   Between 19" and 21.5" long?
c.   Exactly 20" long, to the nearest whole inch?

Answers:

a.   Find the z-score for 22 and place as in Figure 6.16.
    $z = (22 - 19)/1.3 = 2.31$.
    The area between 19" and 22" is the same as the area between 0 and 2.31 on the unit normal curve, which is .4896 (see table in Appendix A). Therefore, the percentage of babies whose length is more than 22" is .5 − .4896 = .0104 or 1.04%. Out of 10,000 babies, 1.04% or 104 will be over 22" long.

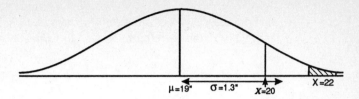

Figure 6.16:
Lengths of Babies at Birth
Normal Distribution

b. The z-score for 19" is 0, since 19 is the mean. The z-score for 21.5" is $z = (21.5 - 19)/1.3 \approx 1.92$. The area under the normal curve between the z-scores of 0 and 1.92 is .4726. The number of babies whose length is between 19" and 21.5" out of 10,000 is 4726.

c. Babies between 19.5" and 20.5 inches are measured at 20" to the nearest inch. Both z-scores must be calculated.
    $z_1 = (19.5 - 19)/1.3 \approx .5/1.3 = .38$ and
    $z_2 = (20.5 - 19)/1.3 = 1.5/1.3 \approx 1.15$. The area under the unit normal probability distribution between 0 and .38 is .1480 and between 0 and 1.15 is .3749. To find the area between .38 and 1.15, subtract: $(.3749 - .1480) = .2269$. Therefore, 2269 out of 10,000 babies have lengths between 19.5" and 20.5", or 20" to the nearest inch.

In this chapter we have discussed probability distributions of both discrete and continuous random variables. The mean of the probability distribution of a discrete random variable can be calculated using the formula

$$\mu = E(x) = \Sigma x \cdot p(x);$$

the variance can be found by the formula $\sigma^2 = \Sigma(x - \mu)^2 p(x)$.

When a discrete probability distribution has the characteristics of a binomial distribution (i.e., n identical trials, two results that are termed success and failure, and the same probability p for success in each trial), the mean and variance are even easier to calculate: $\mu = np$ *and* $\sigma^2 = npq$. *The probabilities of each of the individual binomial random variable values (from x = 0 to x = n) can be found using the formula* $p(x) = {}_nC_x \cdot p^x q^{(n-x)}$. *The normal distribution, a continuous random variable distribution, can be used to calculate probabilities involving areas between two numbers or in the tails of the curve. In order to do this, the raw scores or x-values must be changed to z-scores. The table in Appendix A is used to find these areas. These areas can be thought of as probabilities that the value we are seeking is between two numbers or in the tails of the curve, or as percentages of the data set that have values between two numbers or greater or less than a number.*

The normal distribution can often be used to approximate areas under the rectangles of a binomial probability distribution. This can be done if n is large enough, if p and q are close enough in value, or if both are true.

7

Sampling Theory

A set of data that comes from all members of an entire group is called a "population." For example, I.Q. scores from everybody in your college is a population. A set of data that comes from a small part of the group is called a "sample." The I.Q. scores of thirty people in your statistics class is a sample of the population.

It is possible that a very large population, like the I.Q.s of all students in your college, could be a sample of an even larger population, the I.Q.s of all college students in the country. But the samples discussed in this book will generally be smaller than the I.Q.s of all students in your college. Similarly, the U.S. Census sent extensive questionnaires to a very small percentage of all U.S. residences, but that small percentage represented a sample of over a million out of a population in the hundred millions.

When a sample of a population is chosen, the sample will be tested to see what it says about the population from which it comes. So it will be very important to identify the sample and the population in all problems. This chapter deals with sampling theory.

SAMPLES AND POPULATIONS

Sample Notation

Chapters 2, 3, and 4 discussed various aspects of descriptive statistics: relative frequency tables, histograms and frequency polygons, measures of central tendency, and measures of variability. The data sets that were used to illustrate components of descriptive statistics were really samples of other, larger data sets: Data Set 1 (prices of twenty randomly chosen new cars) is a sampling of the larger set, or population, of the prices of all new cars.

Data Set 3 (weights of twenty-four men) is a random sampling of twenty-four men out of an entire population of men, perhaps all the men living in a large city. The mean of these sets has been represented by the symbol $\bar{x}$, while the standard deviation by the notation s. These numbers are called *sample statistics*: they are measures of a sample.

Population Notation

When other data sets were discussed in Chapter 6, different symbols for mean and standard deviation were used. For example, in the probability distribution of the random variable that represents the number of heads in a toss of two coins, the mean was represented by the Greek letter mu (μ) and the standard deviation by the Greek letter sigma (σ). Again, do not confuse this with the capital letter sigma (Σ) used in the summation signs.

Sample Statistics vs. Population Parameters

The distinction between using Arabic (our alphabet) and Greek letters to represent the same concept is the following. If the set involved is a sample or part of a larger set or population, then the symbols $\bar{x}$ and s are used to represent the mean and standard deviation respectively. If the set involved is a population, such as all possible values of the random variable (number of heads when two coins are tossed), then the symbols μ and σ are used to represent the mean and standard deviation respectively. These numbers are called *parameters*: they are measures of a population.

In this chapter, the relationship between the sample statistic and the population parameter will be derived. This will be done by finding all samples possible from special populations.

Exercise 7.1: Identify each of the following data sets, as a sample or a population. Then give the symbol for its mean and standard deviation.
  a. The ages of all college students.
  b. The ages of students in your statistics class.
  c. The lengths of babies born today in the local hospital.
  d. The lengths of all babies born this year in your state.

Answers:
  a. Population: mean is μ; standard deviation is σ.
  b. Sample: mean is $\bar{x}$; standard deviation is s.
  c. Sample: mean is $\bar{x}$; standard deviation is s.
  d. Population: mean is μ; standard deviation is σ.

SAMPLING DISTRIBUTIONS

Suppose the population of interest is the ages of all students at your college. To estimate the mean of this population, take a random sample of twenty students and find its mean. How does that mean relate to the mean of the population? Is it the same?

Take a second random sample of twenty students (since the samples are random, some students' ages might be in both) and compute its mean. Repeat the experiment by taking additional samples and finding their means.

Then draw a histogram, a relative frequency polygon, and the smoothed curve using the means of the various random samples as the data set. This distribution is called the *sampling distribution of the means*. The histogram representing the sampling distribution of the means is the probability distribution of a statistic. The same process can be repeated to graph the sampling distribution of the median, the variance, or the standard deviation.

Since these sampling distributions are really probability distributions, their means and standard deviations can be calculated as in Chapter 6. Therefore, the mean and variance of a sampling distribution of the mean can be found. The mean and variance of a sampling distribution of the median can also be found, although it turns out these are not as interesting.

How do the mean and variance of the sampling distribution of the mean compare to the mean and variance of the original population? How about the shape of the sampling distribution of the mean? Is it approximately normal? These are the questions whose answers will be explored in this chapter.

Sampling Distribution of Means

One of the populations mentioned above is the number of heads when two coins are tossed. The probability distribution of the random variable (number of heads) and the probability distribution of the means of samples of that population will now be discussed.

Two coins are tossed; x is the random variable representing the number of heads in a toss of the coins.

Population Distribution and Parameters

The distribution of the random variable is given in Table 7.1 (Table 6.4 from the previous chapter). Recall that the diagram representing this table was given in Figure 6.4. It is repeated in Figure 7.1.

Table 7.1

x	0	1	2
p(x)	.25	.50	.25

The mean of this distribution is given by

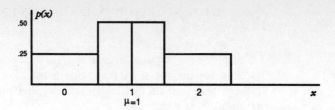

Figure 7.1: — Probability Distribution of x Where x is number of Heads in Two Coin Tosses (See Table 7.1)

$$\mu = E(x) = \Sigma x \cdot p\,(x) = 0(.25) + 1(.50) + 2(.25) = 1.$$

Since x is a binomial random variable, the mean also could have been calculated by $\mu = np = 2(.5) = 1$.

The variance of this distribution can be calculated by

$$\sigma^2 = \Sigma\,(x-\mu)^2 \cdot p\,(x) = (-1)^2(.25) + 0^2(.50) + 1^2(.25) = .25 + 0 + .25 = .50.$$

Since x is a binomial random variable, the variance can also be calculated by $\sigma^2 = npq = 2(.5)(.5) = .5$. No matter how it is calculated, $\mu = 1$ and $\sigma^2 = .5$.

Sampling Distribution and Statistics

The next step is to take samples of the population listed above. These can be samples of two tosses of the two coins, three tosses of the two coins, 1000 tosses of the two coins, or any other number of tosses of the two coins. For example, four tosses of the two coins might yield the following sample (0, 2, 1, 1), which means that there were zero heads on the first toss, two heads on the second toss, and one head each on the third and last tosses. There are many different samples of four tosses of the two coins.

Let's list the samples of two tosses of the two coins. The first toss can yield zero, one, or two heads, three values of the random variable. The second toss can also yield three values of the random variable. By the counting rule, there are $3 \cdot 3 = 9$ different samples. These are (0, 0), (0, 1), (1, 0), (0, 2), (2, 0), (1, 1), (1, 2), (2, 1), (2, 2).

For the three values of each random variable (zero heads, one head, two heads), there are $3 \cdot 3 = 9$ different samples when samples of two are chosen. If the two coins are being tossed three times instead of twice, there are $3 \cdot 3 \cdot 3 = 27$ different samples when samples of three are picked. If four coins are tossed, there are $3^4 = 81$ different samples of four, of which (0, 2, 1, 1) mentioned above is one.

MEANS OF THE SAMPLES

After listing all possible different samples, find the mean of each sample. Using the samples of two coins tossed twice, the mean is obtained by adding the numbers of heads on each toss and dividing by 2, the number of tosses. For example, the mean of the sample (2, 1) is calculated as follows: $2 + 1 = 3$; $3 +$

2 = 1.5. The list of the samples and their calculated means is shown in Table 7.2.

Table 7.2

Sample	(0, 0)	(0, 1)	(1, 0)	(0, 2)	(2, 0)	(1, 1)	(1, 2)	(2, 1)	(2, 2)
Mean	0	.5	.5	1	1	1	1.5	1.5	1.5

PROBABILITIES OF THE SAMPLES

The next step is to find the probability of each sample. Since the outcome of the first toss of two coins does not affect the outcome of the second toss of two coins, these events are independent. Therefore, their probabilities can be multiplied to arrive at the probability for any configuration of tosses.

Table 7.3

Sample	(0, 0)	(0, 1)	(1, 0)	(0, 2)	(2, 0)	(1, 1)	(1, 2)	(2, 1)	(2, 2)
$\bar{x}$	0	.5	.5	1	1	1	1.5	1.5	2
$p(\bar{x})$	.0625	.125	.125	.0625	.0625	.25	.125	.125	.0625

For example, the probability of the sample (2, 1) is calculated in the following way: the probability of 2 according to Table 7.1 is .25, and the probability of 1 is .50. Since the events are independent (in this case, tossing two heads on a toss of two coins, followed by one head on a toss of two coins), the probability that both will occur (2 on first toss and 1 on second) is the product of the two independent probabilities: p (2, 1) = (.25)(.5) = .125. In a similar way, Table 7.3, consisting of Table 7.2 plus an extra line for the probabilities, can be completed as shown.

Note that the sum of the probabilities is 1. This tells us that these samples are exhaustive (they have all been listed).

Probability Distribution of the Means

Now, a new probability distribution will be formed. In this new distribution, called the *probability distribution of the mean*, the random variable is the value of the *mean* in this experiment. Thus the random variable takes on values 0, .5, 1, 1.5, or 2 with certain probabilities.

For example, the mean 1 comes from three samples: (2, 0), (0, 2), and (1, 1). In each of these samples, $\bar{x}$ = 1. The probabilities of these samples are .0625, .0625, and .25, respectively. Therefore, the probability of $\bar{x}$ = 1 is .0625 + .0625 + .25 = .375.

All these calculations are summarized in Table 7.4, which represents the sampling distribution of the means of samples of two from the coin toss problem. It represents a probability distribution; note that the sum of all the

Table 7.4

$\overline{x}$	0	.5	1	1.5	2
$p(\overline{x})$	.0625	.25	.375	.25	.0625

probabilities is $.0625 + .25 + .375 + .25 + .0625 = 1$. The graph of this sampling distribution of the mean is shown in Figure 7.2.

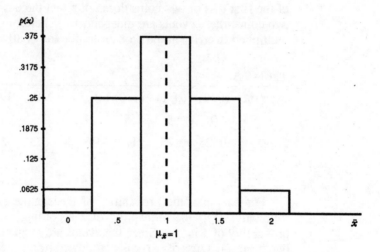

Figure 7.2: — Sampling Distribution of $\overline{x}$ Where $\overline{x}$ Is Mean of Samples of Two from Two Coin Tosses (See Table 7.4)

MEAN OF THE SAMPLING DISTRIBUTION OF THE MEANS

The table and figure just presented represent a probability distribution, but a special one — the sampling distribution of the means of samples of two from the coin toss problem. Each of the rectangles in the graph represents the probability of a certain mean occurring. The rectangle at 1, .375, tells us that $p(1) = .375$. This distribution has a mean itself, and it is calculated like any other mean of a probability distribution, using the formula:

$$\mu = E(x) = \sum x \cdot p(x)$$

Because the calculation involves the mean of the sampling distribution of means the formula's notation is slightly modified:

$$\mu_{\overline{x}} = E(\overline{x}) = \sum \overline{x} \cdot p(\overline{x})$$

To calculate the mean of the sampling distribution of the mean (Table 7.4 and Figure 7.2), take the sum of the products of the means $\bar{x}$ with their respective probabilities $p(\bar{x})$. The calculation looks like this:

$$\mu_{\bar{x}} = E(\bar{x}) = \Sigma\bar{x} \cdot p(\bar{x})$$

$$= 0(.0625) + .5(.25) + 1(.375) + 1.5(.25) + 2(.0625)$$

$$= 0 + .125 + .375 + .375 + .125 = 1.$$

Notice that the mean of the sampling distribution of the means (Table 7.4 and Figure 7.2) is the same as the mean of the original probability distribution (Table 7.1 and Figure 7.1) from which the sample of two was chosen.

If the mean of the sampling distribution of the means is the same as the mean of the population distribution, then the statistic $(\bar{x})$ is said to be an unbiased estimator of the mean of the population distribution, the parameter μ. In the above sample, $\bar{x}$ is an unbiased estimator of μ.

Exercise 7.2:   A population is described by the probability distribution shown in Table 7.5. In this population, .4 of the values of x are 0 and .6 of the values of x are 3.

Table 7.5

x	0	3
$p(x)$	.4	.6

a.   Graph the probability distribution in Table 7.5. Then calculate the mean of the distribution, $E(x)$.

b.   Find all samples of three elements from the above distribution. Find the mean of each sample.

c.   Calculate the probability of each sample mean. Find and graph the sampling distribution of the sample means $\bar{x}$.

d.   Find $E(\bar{x})$. Is $\bar{x}$ a biased or an unbiased estimator of μ? Explain.

Answers:

a.   Refer to Figure 7.3.

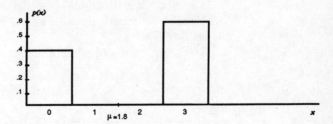

Figure 7.3: — Probability Distribution of x from Table 7.5

$E(x) = \mu = 0(.4) + 3(.6) = 1.8.$

b. Samples of three elements from the above distribution are called ordered triples, of the form (a, b, c).

First, find out how many different ordered triples can be formed with only two elements, 0 or 3. For filling the first place in the ordered triple (a), there are two possibilities, 0 or 3. Similarly, for the second place (b) there are the same two possibilities, as is true for the third place (c).

Therefore there will be $2^3 = 8$ ordered triples. They are $(0, 0, 0)$, $(0, 0, 3)$, $(0, 3, 0)$, $(3, 0, 0)$, $(0, 3, 3)$, $(3, 0, 3)$, $(3, 3, 0)$, $(3, 3, 3)$.

The mean of each sample can be calculated by adding the three numbers together and dividing by 3. For example, the mean x of $(3, 0, 3)$ is $(3 + 0 + 3)/3 = 6/3 = 2$. The samples and their means are tabulated in Table 7.6.

Table 7.6

Sample	(0,0,0)	(0,0,3)	(0,3,0)	(3 ,0,0)	(0,3,3)	(3,0,3)	(3,3,0)	(3,3,3)
$\bar{x}$	0	1	1	1	2	2	2	3

c. The probabilities for each sample can be calculated by multiplying the probabilities attached to either 0 or 3 (three times). For example, the probability of the sample $(3, 0, 3)$ equals $p(3) \cdot p(0) \cdot p(3)$ (from Table 7.5), which is $(.6)(.4)(.6) = .144$. So the probability of the ordered triple $(3, 0, 3) = .144$.

Table 7.7

Sample	(0, 0,0)	(0,0,3)	(0,3,0)	(3 ,0,0)	(0,3,3)	(3,0,3)	(3,3,0)	(3,3,3)
$\bar{x}$	0	1	1	1	2	2	2	3
$p(\bar{x})$	.064	.096	.096	.096	.144	.144	.144	.216

The sampling distribution of the mean is found by adding the probabilities for each possible mean. For example, $p(\bar{x} = 1) = .096 + .096 + .096 = .288$.

The sampling distribution of the means is summarized in Table 7.8.

Table 7.8

$\bar{x}$	0	1	2	3
$p(\bar{x})$	.064	.288	.432	.216

The graph of the sampling distribution of the means is pictured in Figure 7.4.

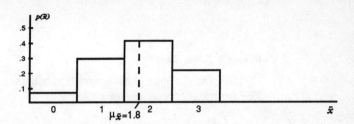

Figure 7.4: — Sampling Distribution of $\bar{x}$ from Table 7.8

d. The mean of the sampling distribution of the means, $E(\bar{x})$, is calculated below:

$$E(\bar{x}) = \mu_{\bar{x}} = \Sigma \bar{x} \cdot p(\bar{x})$$
$$E(\bar{x}) = 0(.064) + 1(.288) + 2(.432) + 3(.216)$$
$$= 0 + .288 + .864 + .648 = 1.8.$$

Since $\mu = 1.8$ and $E(\bar{x}) = 1.8$, $\bar{x}$ is an unbiased estimator of μ.

Sampling Distributions of Variances

Consider again the population formed by tossing two coins discussed at the beginning of this chapter. Table 7.1, the probability distribution of the random variable x that represents the number of heads in two tosses, is reproduced below..

Table 7.1

x	0	1	2
$p(x)$	.25	.50	.25

Recall that the mean of this population is 1 ($\mu = 1$). The variance of this population is given by

$$\sigma^2 = \Sigma (x - \mu)^2 \cdot p(x)$$

$$= (-1)^2(.25) + 0^2(.50) + 1^2(.25)$$

$$= .25 + 0 + .25 = .50,$$

so the variance, $\sigma^2 = .5$.

Again, choose samples of two from this distribution, but now find both the mean and the variance of each sample. Recall the means of samples of two were given in Table 7.2 which is reproduced here.

Table 7.2

Sample	(0, 0)	(0, 1)	(1, 0)	(0, 2)	(2, 0)	(1, 1)	(1, 2)	(2, 1)	(2, 2)
Mean	0	.5	.5	1	1	1	1.5	1.5	2

VARIANCE OF A SAMPLE

To find the variance of each sample, use the variance formula from Chapter 3. The formula for variance of a sample is

$$s^2 = \frac{\Sigma (x - \bar{x})^2}{(n - 1)}$$

To calculate the variance of (0, 1) from its mean, .5, take each number in the sample, subtract the mean .5 from it, and square. Then add all the squared sample differences and divide by $n - 1$. For the variance of (0, 1),

$$s^2 = [(0 - .5)^2 + (1 - .5)^2] \div (2 - 1) = [(-.5)^2 + .5^2] \div 1 = .25 + .25 = .5.$$

In a similar manner, all the variances can be calculated.

The variances of (0, 0) from its mean of 0, (1, 1) from its mean of 1, and (2, 2) from its mean of 2 are all 0, since the numerator of the variance formula for each is 0.

Recall also Table 7.3, which gave the probability of each sample's mean. It is reproduced here.

Table 7.3

Sample	(0, 0)	(0, 1)	(1, 0)	(0, 2)	(2, 0)	(1, 1)	(1, 2)	(2, 1)	(2, 2)
$\bar{x}$	0	.5	.5	1	1	1	1.5	1.5	2
$p(\bar{x})$	.0625	.125	.125	.0625	.0625	.25	.125	.125	.0625

Instead of listing probabilities of the mean, these same probabilities can be thought of as probabilities of the variance of each pair from its mean. This is illustrated in Table 7.9.

Table 7.9

Sample	(0, 0)	(0, 1)	(1, 0)	(0, 2)	(2, 0)	(1, 1)	(1, 2)	(2, 1)	(2, 2)
s^2	0	.5	.5	2	2	0	.5	.5	0
$p(s^2)$	.0625	.125	.125	.0625	.0625	.25	.125	.125	.0625

Notice that there are only three different possible variances in the samples: 0, .5, and 2. Collecting probabilities for each of these different variances leads to a probability distribution of the sample variances table. For example, the probability of a variance of .5 is calculated by adding the probabilities of each .5 together, or $4(.125) = .5$.

These results are summarized in a table of the sampling distribution of the variances, Table 7.10.

Table 7.10

s^2	0	.5	2
$p(s^2)$	.375	.5	.125

MEAN OF THE SAMPLING DISTRIBUTION OF THE VARIANCES

As in any probability distribution, the sampling distribution of the variances has a mean that is calculated using the formula

$$E(s^2) = \mu_s{}^2 = \Sigma s^2 \cdot p(s^2).$$

Calculating this mean:

$$E(s^2) = 0(.375) + .5(.5) + 2(.125) = 0 + .25 + .25 = .5.$$

Notice that the mean of the sampling distribution of the variances, $\mu_s{}^2 = .5$ is the same as the variance of the original population, $\sigma^2 = .5$. This means that s^2 is an unbiased estimator of σ^2.

If a statistic is an unbiased estimator of the parameter, the statistic can be used in place of the parameter in certain formulas. This substitution will be discussed in future chapters.

Exercise 7.3: Recall from Exercise 7.2 the following population distribution:

Table 7.5

x	0	3
$p(x)$	.4	.6

Eight samples of three random numbers were chosen. These samples, their probabilities, and their means are reproduced here.

Table 7.7

Sample	(0,0,0)	(0,0,3)	(0,3,0)	(3,0,0)	(0,3,3)	(3,0,3)	(3,3,0)	(3,3,3)
$\bar{x}$	0	1	1	1	2	2	2	3
$p(\bar{x})$	.064	.096	.096	.096	.144	.144	.144	.216

    a. Find the variances of each of the samples.

    b. Summarize the variances and their probabilities in a table showing the sampling distribution of the variances. Find the mean of this distribution.

    c. Is s^2 a biased or an unbiased estimator of σ^2? Explain.

Answers:

    a. To find the variances of the samples, use the formula for variances given below on each sample:

$$s^2 = \frac{\Sigma (x - \bar{x})^2}{(n-1)}$$

For example, the mean of the sample (0, 3, 3) is $\bar{x} = 2$, so the variance calculation for this sample is

$$s^2 = \frac{(0-2)^2 + (3-2)^2 + (3-2)^2}{(3-1)} = [(-2)^2 + 1^2 + 1^2] \div 2 = 6 \div 2 = 3$$

The variance of the sample (0, 3, 3) from its mean 2 is 3 ($s^2 = 3$). In a similar manner, the other variances are calculated and listed in Table 7.11.

Table 7.11

Sample	(0,0,0)	(0,0,3)	(0,3,0)	(3,0,0)	(0,3,3)	(3,0,3)	(3,3,0)	(3,3,3)
s	0	3	3	3	3	3	3	0
$p(s)$	.064	.096	.096	.096	.144	.144	.144	.216

    b. Notice that there are only two values of the variance in these samples: 0 and 3. Summarizing the above in a distribution of the sample variances leads to Table 7.12.

Table 7.12

s^2	0	3
$p(s^2)$	.28	.72

Finding the mean of the above distribution:

$$E(s^2) = \mu_s{}^2 = \Sigma s^2 \cdot p(s^2)$$
$$= 0(.28) + 3(.72) = 2.16.$$

    c. To determine whether $s^2 = 2.16$ is a biased or an unbiased estimate of σ^2, we must find σ^2. To find σ^2, use the original population probability distribution table.

Recall that $\mu = 1.8$. The variance is calculated using the population variance formula:

Table 7.5

x	0	3
p(x)	.4	.6

$$\sigma^2 = \Sigma \, (x - \mu)^2 \cdot p \, (x)$$
$$= (0 - 1.8)^2 \cdot (.4) + (3 - 1.8)^2 (.6)$$
$$= (-1.8)^2 (.4) + (1.2)^2 (.6)$$
$$= (3.24)(.4) + (1.44)(.6)$$
$$= 1.296 + .864 = 2.16.$$

Since $E(s^2) = 2.16$ and $\sigma^2 = 2.16$, s^2 is an unbiased estimator of σ^2.

Variance of Sampling Distribution of Means

In the above sections, the mean of a sampling distribution of means and the mean of a sampling distribution of variances were calculated. The main reason for calculating these is to be able to use the sample mean and the sample variance as an estimator for the population mean and the population variance, in cases in which we know or can calculate the sample statistics but not the population parameters.

Every distribution has a mean and a variance. It has been noted that the mean of a sampling distribution of means is an unbiased estimator of the mean of the population from which the samples for the sampling distribution were drawn.

In addition to finding the mean of a sampling distribution of means, we also need to calculate the variance of a sampling distribution of means. We do this to answer the question, "How does the variance of a sampling distribution of means relate to the variance of the population?" The answer to this will provide a link between the variance of a sample and the variance of the population from which the sample is drawn.

Consider Table 7.4, repeated here, which represents the sampling distribution of the means of samples of two taken from the set {0, 1, 2}, for which the probabilities are .25, .50, .25 respectively. Recall that these were the results of tossing two coins twice and recording the number of heads from each toss. There were nine ordered pairs with elements 0, 1, 2 indicating the number of heads

Table 7.4

$\bar{x}$	0	.5	1	1.5	2
$p \, (\bar{x})$	.0625	.25	.375	.25	.0625

on the first toss of two coins in the first place, and the number of heads on the second toss of two coins in the second place in the ordered pairs. The means and probabilities were summarized in Table 7.4.

The mean of this distribution, which was calculated earlier by using the same formula as for the mean of a population distribution, is

$$\mu_{\bar{x}} = E(\bar{x}) = \sum \bar{x} \cdot p(\bar{x})$$

$$= 0(.0625) + .5(.25) + 1(.375) + 1.5(.25) + 2(.0625)$$

$$= 0 + .125 + .375 + .375 + .125 = 1.$$

Therefore, $\mu_{\bar{x}} = 1$.

To calculate the variance of the sampling distribution of the means, add a line above the $\bar{x}$ line of the table above to represent $(\bar{x} - \mu_{\bar{x}})^2$, as below. Recall that the general formula for variance of a population is

$$\sigma^2 = \sum (\bar{x} - \mu_x)^2 \cdot p(x)$$

Table 7.13

$(\bar{x} - \mu_{\bar{x}})^2$	1	.25	0	.25	1
$\bar{x}$	0	.5	1	1.5	2
$p(\bar{x})$	.0625	.25	.375	.25	.0625

The variance of this distribution is

$$\sigma_{\bar{x}}^2 = \sum (\bar{x} - \mu_{\bar{x}})^2 p(\bar{x}) = 1(.0625) + .25(.25) + 0(.375) + .25(.25) + 1(.0625) = .0625 + .0625 + .0625 + .0625 = .25.$$

Recall that the variance of the original population distribution from which these samples were taken is .5.

FORMULA FOR VARIANCE OF SAMPLING DISTRIBUTION OF MEANS

It turns out that the variance of the sampling distribution of the means is related to the variance of the population from which the samples were drawn. The variance of the sample distribution of the means is the same as the variance of the population divided by the number in each sample. The formula is

$$\sigma_{\bar{x}}^2 = \frac{\sigma^2}{n}$$ where $\sigma_{\bar{x}}^2$ is the variance of the sampling distribution of the

means; σ^2 is the population variance; and n is the sample size.

The variance of the sampling distribution of the means in the example above is .25. The variance of the original population distribution is .5. Notice that .25 = .5/2, where 2 is the sample size.

STANDARD DEVIATION OF SAMPLING DISTRIBUTION OF MEANS

Since $\sigma_{\bar{x}}^2 = \dfrac{\sigma^2}{n}$, it follows that $\sigma_{\bar{x}} = \dfrac{\sigma}{\sqrt{n}}$; i.e., the standard deviation of the sampling distribution of the means, $\sigma_{\bar{x}}$ is equal to the standard deviation of the population divided by the square root of the sample size.

For example, since $\sigma^2 = .5, \sigma = \sqrt{.5} \approx .71$.

Since $\sigma_{\bar{x}} = \sigma/\sqrt{n}$, $\sigma_{\bar{x}} = .71/\sqrt{2} \approx .71/1.4 = .5$.

A common statistics problem involves finding the standard deviation of the sampling distribution of the means. This can be found by taking the standard deviation of the population, or an unbiased estimator of the population, and dividing it by the square root of the number in the sample.

Exercise 7.4: Recall from Exercise 7.2 that we found the sampling distribution of the means of samples of three from a population with two values, 0 and 3, with probabilities .4 and .6. That table, Table 7.8, is reproduced here.

Table 7.8

$\bar{x}$	0	1	2	3
$p(\bar{x})$	.064	.288	.432	.216

a. Find the variance of the sampling distribution of the means above.

b. The variance of the original population distribution was 2.16. How does the variance of the sampling distribution of the means relate to 2.16? Explain.

Answers:

a. To find the variance of the above distribution, recall that the mean of this distribution is 1.8. Add a line in this table above the line $\bar{x}$ to

Table 7.14

$(\bar{x} - \mu_{\bar{x}})^2$	3.24	.64	.04	1.44
$\bar{x}$	0	1	2	3
$p(\bar{x})$	.064	.288	.432	.216

represent $(\bar{x} - \mu_{\bar{x}})^2$:

The variance of this distribution is calculated by the formula

$$\sigma_{\bar{x}}^2 = \Sigma(\bar{x} - \mu_{\bar{x}})^2 p(\bar{x})$$

$$= 3.24(.064) + .64(.288) + .04(.432) + 1.44(.216)$$
$$= .20736 + .18432 + .01728 + .31104 = .72.$$

b. The variance of the sampling distribution of the means of samples of three is given by

$$\sigma_{\bar{x}}^{2} = \frac{\sigma^{2}}{n} = \frac{2.16}{3} = .72.$$

But the answer in (a), computed directly from the samples of three, is also .72. Therefore, the formula holds and the variance of the sampling distribution is equal to the variance of the population divided by the sample size.

CENTRAL LIMIT THEOREM

From a population of very large or even infinite size, samples of a certain number n are randomly chosen. Each of these samples has a mean, $\bar{x}$. If there are 500 samples of, for example, seven scores, then there are 500 means, each obtained by adding the seven scores and dividing by 7. These 500 means form a sampling distribution of the means.

Mean and Standard Deviation of the Sampling Distribution

The mean of the sampling distribution of the means is identical to the mean of the original population ($\mu_{\bar{x}} = \mu$), which was shown in the work in the preceding sections. This relationship was demonstrated by using all subsets of sizes two or three, subsets whose means were easily determined, along with the probability of those particular pairs or triples.

The standard deviation of the sampling distribution of the means is equal to the standard deviation of the population divided by the square root of the number in the sample. In the case above, 500 samples of 7 each, $\sigma_{\bar{x}} = \sigma/\sqrt{7}$. This too was demonstrated by using all subsets of a small size from a known probability distribution.

Notice that the standard deviation of the sampling distribution of the means is much smaller than that of the original population. The larger the number in the sample, the smaller will be the standard deviation, since it is obtained by dividing the population standard deviation by the square root of the number in the sample.

Table 7.5

x	0	3
$p(x)$	.4	.6

$\sigma_{\bar{x}} = \dfrac{\sigma}{\sqrt{16}} = \dfrac{\sigma}{4}$. If two fractions have the same numerator, the fraction with

the greater denominator is smaller, so $\dfrac{\sigma}{10} < \dfrac{\sigma}{4}$, and the standard deviation of the

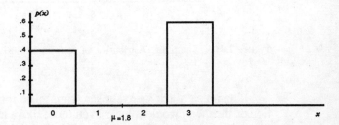

Figure 7.3: — Probability Distribution of x from Table 7.5

sampling distribution of samples of 100 is smaller than that of the sampling distribution of samples of 16, both samplings coming from the same population.

Shape of the Sampling Distribution of the Means

Another important part of sampling theory is the shape of the distribution of sample means. It turns out that for very large samples, the shape of the sampling distribution of the means is approximately normal. Even if the original distribution is not shaped like a normal distribution at all, the sampling distribution of the means will be normal for large *n*. This will be illustrated below.

Consider the sampling distribution of the population given in Exercises 7.2, 7.3, and 7.4. The original distribution was not normal in shape (see Table 7.5 and Figure 7.3).

Recall that the mean of the population is $\mu = 1.8$ and the variance of the population is $\sigma^2 = 2.16$.

Notice the table and distribution graph for the sampling distribution of the means (Table 7.8 and Figure 7.4, reproduced here).

Table 7.8

$\bar{x}$	0	1	2	3
$p(\bar{x})$	.064	.288	.432	.216

Even though samples of three cannot be considered large samples, the graph appears to be close to normal in shape, a lot closer than the probability distribution pictured in Figure 7.3.

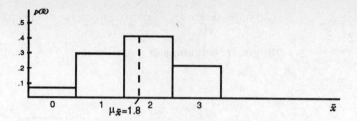

Figure 7.4: — Sampling Distribution of $\bar{x}$ from Table 7.8

If samples of ten were chosen from this population, the sampling distribution of the mean would appear even more like a normal distribution. There are 2^{10} or 1024 samples of ten where each number in the ordered ten-tuple is either 0 or 3. For example, (0, 0, 3, 0, 3, 3, 3, 0, 0, 3) is one of the 1024 samples of 10.

The mean of each of the samples of ten would then be calculated, a table of means and their probabilities set up, and the sampling distribution then graphed, according to the probability distribution of each possible mean. The sampling distribution of the mean would be approximately normal in shape. Its mean would be $\mu_{\bar{x}} = \mu = 1.8$ and its standard deviation would be

$$\sigma_{\bar{x}} = \frac{\sigma}{\sqrt{n}} = \frac{\sqrt{2.16}}{\sqrt{10}} = \sqrt{2.16} \text{ (divide under the square root sign)} = .465.$$

The Central Limit Theorem

The Central Limit Theorem summarizes the results in this chapter so far. It states:

a. The mean of a sampling distribution of the means is equal to the mean of the population: $\mu_{\bar{x}} = \mu$.

b. The standard deviation of a sampling distribution of the means is equal to the standard deviation of the population divided by the square root of the number in each sample: $\sigma_{\bar{x}} = \frac{\sigma}{\sqrt{n}}$.

c. For large sample sizes, the sampling distribution of the means is approximately normal in shape. Large sample sizes are those where $n > 30$.

USING THE CENTRAL LIMIT THEOREM

The Central Limit Theorem has many important applications. For example, what is the probability that a sample purportedly taken from a known population (i.e., the mean and standard deviation is known, even if the shape is not) really is from that population? That is, is it likely that the sample came from the population, or has it more likely been drawn from a different population? The following problem is an example:

At a certain college, the mean grade point average is 2.93 with a standard deviation of .32. A sample of forty-nine grade point averages is chosen from students in a statistics class. What is the probability that the sample will have a mean greater than 3.0?

Look at the sampling distribution of the means, which is described by the Central Limit Theorem.

Since forty-nine is a large sample ($n \geq 30$), the shape of the sampling distribution of the means is approximately normal.

The mean of the sampling distribution of the means is 2.93, since it is the same as the population mean, which was given as 2.93.

The standard deviation of the sampling distribution of the means is equal to the standard deviation of the population divided by the square root of the number in the sample. Therefore, the standard deviation of the sampling distribution is $\dfrac{.32}{\sqrt{49}} = \dfrac{.32}{7} \approx .0457$.

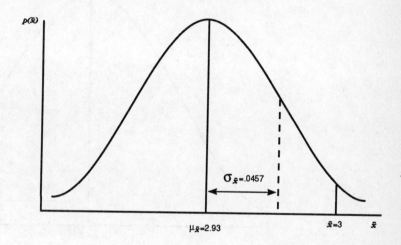

Figure 7.5: — Sampling Distribution of $\overline{x}$: Samples of Size $n = 49$ from Population with $\mu = 2.93$; $\sigma = .32$ (G.P.A. s)

This information is summarized in Figure 7.5, which is a graph of the sampling distribution of the means for this problem. Notice that the mean of the sampling distribution of the means is 2.93, but the standard deviation is .0457.

The original question asked the probability that the sample of forty-nine chosen from a statistics class has a mean greater than 3.0. In order to calculate this probability, we must find the z-score for 3.0 so we can use the standard unit table, which gives probabilities for areas between 0 and a given z-score.

To calculate the z-score for 3.0, use the formula

$$z = \frac{(\bar{x} - \mu_{\bar{x}})}{\sigma_{\bar{x}}}$$ where $\bar{x}$ is the observed mean,

$\mu_{\bar{x}}$ is the mean of the sampling distribution of the means, and

$\sigma_{\bar{x}}$ is the standard deviation of the sampling distribution of the means.

For this problem, $z = (3.0 - 2.93) \div .0457 \approx 1.53$.

Now go to the Standard Unit Normal (z) table in Appendix A to find the area associated with a z-score of 1.53. The standard unit normal is pictured in Figure 7.6.

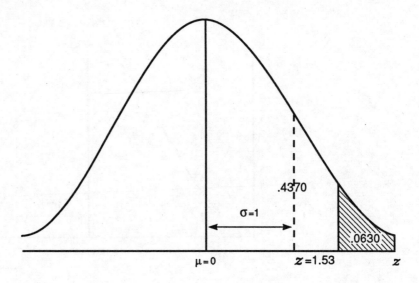

Figure 7.6: — Standard Unit Normal for Figure 7.5; Shaded Area: z-Scores > 1.53

The area between a z-score of 0 and 1.53, as found using a standard unit normal table, is .4370. However, the problem asked for the probability (area under the curve) that the sample has a mean greater than 3.0 (whose z-score is 1.53). Since the standard unit normal is symmetric, and the area under the entire curve is 1, the area to the right of the mean is .5.

Subtracting .4370 from .5 yields .5 − .437 = .063, the area in the tail of the curve. Therefore, the probability that a sample of forty-nine will have a mean greater than 3.0 is .063.

Another way of interpreting this answer is to note that 63 out of 1000 samples of forty-nine chosen from the given population (grade point averages in the entire college) will have a mean (grade point average) of 3.0 or greater.

Exercise 7.5:   The lengths of babies at birth has a mean $\mu = 19"$ and a standard deviation $\sigma = 1.3"$. Samples of one hundred babies are chosen.
- a.   Find the mean and standard deviation of the sampling distribution of the means of the chosen samples.
- b.   What is the shape of the sampling distribution of the means?
- c.   What is the probability that one of the samples of 100 babies will have a mean less than 18.7"?

Answers:
- a.   The mean of the sampling distribution of the means is given by the formula $\mu_{\bar{x}} = \mu$. Therefore, the mean of the sampling distribution is also 19".

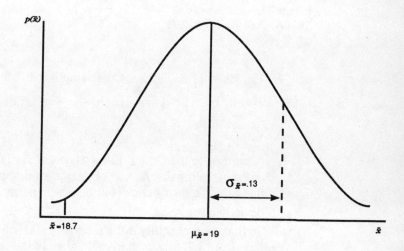

Figure 7.7: — Sampling Distribution of $\bar{x}$: Samples of Size $n = 100$ from Population with $\mu = 19$ Inches, $\sigma = 1.3$ Inches (Length of Babies at Birth)

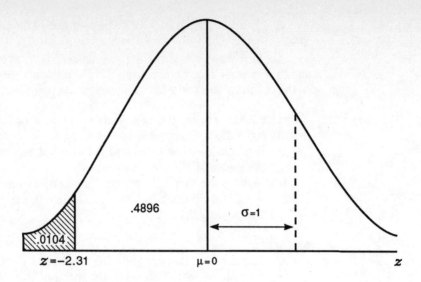

.4896

σ=1

.0104

z=−2.31

μ=0

z

Figure 7.8: — Standard Unit Normal for Figure 7.7,
Shaded Area: z-Scores < −2.31

The standard deviation of the sampling distribution of the means is given by the formula: $\sigma_{\bar{x}} = \dfrac{\sigma}{\sqrt{n}}$. Therefore, $\sigma_{\bar{x}} = 1.3 \div$

$\sqrt{100} = \dfrac{1.3}{10} = .13.$

b. According to the Central Limit Theorem, for large samples the shape of the sampling distribution of the means is approximately normal. In this case, the distribution is normal with mean, $\mu_{\bar{x}} = 19$ and standard deviation, $\sigma_{\bar{x}} = .13.$

c. To find the probability that a sample of 100 babies would have a mean less than 18.7, first examine a diagram of the sampling distribution of the means (Figure 7.7).

The score of 18.7 in Figure 7.7 must now be translated into an equivalent z-score. To calculate the z-score for 18.7:

$$z = \frac{\bar{x} - \mu_{\bar{x}}}{\sigma_{\bar{x}}}$$

$z = (18.7 - 19)/.13 \approx - 2.31.$ Look at
$z = - 2.31$ on a standard unit normal (Figure 7.8).

In the standard unit normal table, the area under the curve between 0 and 2.31 is .4896. Because the normal curve is symmetric, the area under the curve between 0 and −2.31 is also .4896. The area in the left tail, before −2.31, is equal to .5 − .4896 = .0104. Therefore, the

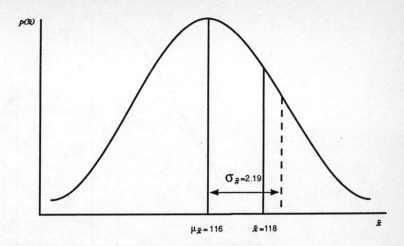

Figure 7.9: — Sampling Distribution of $\bar{x}$: Samples of Size $n = 30$ from Population with $\mu = 116$, $\sigma = 12$ (I.Q.s of Students in ABC College)

probability that the mean of a sample of 100 babies' lengths is less than 18.7" is .0104.

Exercise 7.6: The I.Q.s of students at ABC College have a mean of 116 and a standard deviation of 12. In a statistics class at the college, thirty students were sampled and the mean of their I.Q.s was 118. What is the probability that a sample of thirty students at that college will have a mean I.Q. greater than 118?

Answer: Consider the sampling distribution of the means. The mean of this sampling distribution is the same as the population mean, so $\mu_{\bar{x}} = 116$. The standard deviation of this sampling distribution is equal to the population standard deviation divided by the square root of the number in the sample. Therefore, $\sigma_{\bar{x}} = 12 \div \sqrt{30} \approx \dfrac{12}{5.48} \approx 2.19$.

Thirty or more in a sample is considered a large sample for our purposes. According to the Central Limit Theorem, the shape of the sampling distribution of the means is approximately normal. The diagram in Figure 7.9 locates 118 on the normal curve.

The z-score for 118, the mean of the thirty I.Q.s in a statistics class, is calculated by the formula

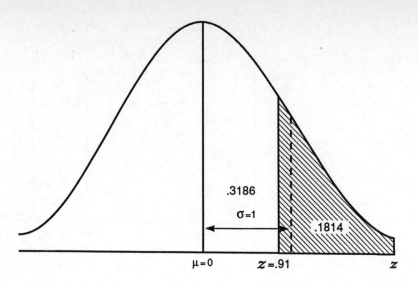

Figure 7.10: — Standard Unit Normal for Figure 7.10; Shaded Area: z-Scores > 0.91

$$z = \frac{\bar{x} - \mu_{\bar{x}}}{\sigma_{\bar{x}}}$$

$z = (118 - 116)/2.19 = 2/2.19 = .91$. I.Q.s 118 and above have z-scores of .91 and above (Figure 7.10).

The area under the normal curve from 0 to .91 is .3186. The area in the upper tail of the normal curve above .91 is .5 −.3186 = .1814. The probability that a sample of thirty students from ABC College will have a mean I.Q. score greater than 118 is .1814.

T his chapter has dealt with sampling theory. Samples, populations, and the numbers associated with them were defined. A parameter is a number associated with a population: for example, μ is the mean of a population and σ is the standard deviation of the population. A sample statistic is a number associated with a sample: for example, $\bar{x}$ is the mean of a sample, $\tilde{x}$ is the median of a sample, and s is the standard deviation of a sample.

There is a relationship between a population mean and the mean of a sampling distribution consisting of the means of samples of the same size drawn from the population: they are equal. Similarly, the variance of a population and the mean of a sampling distribution of variances are also equal. Therefore, we say that $\bar{x}$ is an unbiased estimator of μ and s^2 is an unbiased estimator of

σ^2. *These relationships were found by examining probability distributions and all possible samples of n drawn from these distributions.*

Focusing on the sampling distribution of the means, two more ideas were introduced. First, as stated above, it was shown that the mean of the sampling distribution of the means equals the mean of the population from which it was drawn, $\mu_{\bar{x}} = \mu$.

It was also shown that the standard deviation of the sampling distribution of the means equals the standard deviation of the population divided by the square root of the number in the sample, $\sigma_{\bar{x}} = \dfrac{\sigma}{\sqrt{n}}$. *These two facts, together with a third statement, constitute the Central Limit Theorem. The third statement is that for large samples of a population, the sampling distribution of the means is approximately normal.*

The Central Limit Theorem allows one to calculate the probability of the mean of a sample being greater or less than a certain number. The calculation is performed by finding the z-score of the sample mean and using the standard unit normal table to find areas under the normal curve.

8

Large Sample Inferential Statistics

*T*he first few chapters of this book discussed descriptive statistics, ways of organizing and describing data sets. Then, after probability was covered, discrete and continuous probability distributions were also discussed. The chapter on the Central Limit Theorem concerns the relationship of the shape, mean, and standard deviation of the sampling distribution of the means to the mean and standard deviation of the population from which the samples come.

This chapter concerns the reverse: if a random sample is drawn from a population and certain statistics associated with it are calculated (e.g., its mean, standard deviation, etc.), what do these statistics say about the parameters of the population, and with how much certainty? If, for example, the I.Q.s of a random sample of students in your college were collected and some statistics on them computed, what and with how much certainty could be said about the mean I.Q. of all students at your college?

ESTIMATION OF THE POPULATION MEAN

As stated in the Central Limit Theorem, the mean of the sampling distribution of means is equal to the mean of the population, $\mu_{\bar{x}} = \mu$. But very rarely does the statistician know the population parameter and seek to find the sample statistic. Most often, the sample is all the statistician has to work with, and he or she must make some estimates or guesses of the population parameters from these sample statistics. For example, suppose the set of I.Q.s of a random sample of thirty students at a certain college has a mean of 118.3 and a standard deviation of 11.4. What is the mean I.Q. of the entire population of students at this college?

This question cannot be answered with 100% certainty. The best that can be done is to provide an interval around the sample mean, 118.3, in which it is quite certain (99% or 95% or 90%) that the population mean also lies.

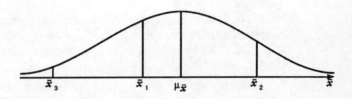

Figure 8.1:
Sampling Distribution of $\bar{x}$ Possible Sample Means $\bar{x}_1$, $\bar{x}_2$, $\bar{x}_3$

Figure 8.1 represents the sampling distribution of the means of the I.Q.s in samples of thirty students drawn at random from the I.Q.s of the population of students at a college. For some $\bar{x}$, $\bar{x}$ is an unbiased estimator of μ; $\bar{x}$ will be an unbiased estimator of μ if $\bar{x}$ is equal to $\mu_{\bar{x}}$. Most of the time this will not happen, so for most samples, $\bar{x} \neq \mu$. However, chances are that the mean of the sample of thirty I.Q.s will be fairly close to $\mu_{\bar{x}}$, the mean of the sampling distribution of $\bar{x}$.

As a matter of fact, chances are approximately 68% that $\bar{x}$ will be within one standard deviation of $\mu_{\bar{x}}$, as is $\bar{x}_1$ in Figure 8.1. Chances are approximately 95% that $\bar{x}$ will be within two standard deviations of $\mu_{\bar{x}}$, as is $\bar{x}_2$ in Figure 8.1. Recall from the Central Limit Theorem that the sampling distribution of the means of large samples (greater than or equal to thirty) is approximately normally distributed. Also recall that in a normal distribution, 68% of the area under the curve is within one standard deviation of the mean, and 95% of the area under the curve is within two standard deviations of the mean.

Of course, the random sample might not have its mean within one or two standard deviations of $\mu_{\bar{x}}$. For example, if $\bar{x}_3$ is the mean of the sample, then μ, the population mean, is not within two standard deviations of $\bar{x}_3$. But the probability of that is very small since in that case x_3 would be way out in a tail of the normal distribution. If this were the case, then a two standard deviation interval around $\bar{x}_3$ would not include the population mean. We can never be entirely certain that the population mean is included in an interval around the sample mean. However, we can be 90% or 95% or 99% certain of this by finding the interval around the sample mean in which the population mean probably lies, the confidence interval of the mean.

Confidence Interval for the Population Mean

Suppose, as above, a random sample of thirty student I.Q.s is chosen from the I.Q.s of all students at a certain college. The task is to estimate the mean I.Q. of all the students at the college.

The question to be asked before this estimation is attempted is "with what degree of certainty should this estimation be given?". That is, the problem is to find an interval around the sample mean (118.3 in this case) such that the statistician is, for example, 95% certain that the population mean is in this interval.

The interval on either side of the sample mean is called the *confidence interval of the mean*, because one is 95% confident that, when the confidence interval is computed, the population mean will be somewhere within it.

If 95% of the normal curve is within the confidence interval, then 5% is outside the interval or in the tails of the curve. The symbol for the probability that a value is in a tail or in one of two tails of a normal distribution curve is α (Greek letter alpha).

Formula for the Confidence Interval

The confidence interval of the population mean, written in the form (a, b), is given by the following formula:

$(a, b) = \bar{x} \pm z_{/2} \cdot \sigma_{\bar{x}}$ where $\bar{x}$ is the sample mean,

$\sigma_{\bar{x}}$ is the standard deviation of the sampling distribution, and

$z_{\alpha_{/2}}$ is the z-score that leaves $\dfrac{\alpha}{2}$ in each tail of the normal curve.

Recall that (a, b) is an open interval on the real number line with $a < b$.

If, for example, $\bar{x} = 25$ and $z\alpha_{/2} \cdot \sigma_{\bar{x}} = 3$, then the confidence interval would be $25 \pm 3 = (22, 28)$. This means that we would be a certain percent confident that the mean of the population from which the sample mean 25 was taken is between 22 and 28. The number 3, the number that is subtracted from and added to the sample mean, is called the *bound* of the interval.

Suppose we are asked to find the interval around the sample mean that would include the population mean with a 95% confidence level. That is, we want to be 95% certain that the population mean is in the interval.

Finding the Z-Score for Confidence Intervals

Part of the formula for confidence intervals makes use of the z-score $z_{\alpha_{/2}}$. The alpha or tail area for confidence intervals is calculated by using the formula $\alpha = 1 - c.l.$, where α is the area in the tails and $c.l.$ is the confidence level. When a 95% confidence level is required, $\alpha = 1 - .95 = .05$. This .05 is divided between the two tails of the standard normal curve as shown in Figure 8.2. This means that each tail's area is $.05/2 = .025$, so the z-scores to be calculated must leave .025 or 2.5% of the distribution in each tail. By symmetry, the z-score is that which leaves $.5 - .025 = .4750$ of the curve between 0 and the z-score itself.

Up until now, we have assumed that this z-score would be ± 2, since the Empirical Rule states that in a normal distribution, approximately 95%, of the curve is within two standard deviations of the mean. However, in checking the standard unit normal table, we find that the z-score that puts half of 95% or .4750, of the curve between 0 and itself, according to the table in Appendix A,

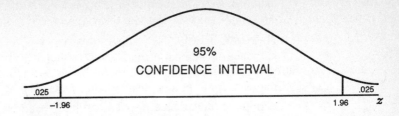

Figure 8.2:
Standard Unit Normal: 95% Confidence Interval
.025 in Each Tail; .95 in Body of Normal Curve

is 1.96, not 2. This number is found by locating .4750 in the body of the table and going back to find the corresponding z-score ($z = 1.96$).

Therefore, the z-score for a confidence interval of 95%, or one whose tail area is equal to $.05/2 = .025$, is 1.96. The formula for a 95% confidence interval for the population mean is:

$$(a, b) = \overline{x} + z_{\alpha/2} \cdot \sigma_{\overline{x}}$$
$$= \overline{x} \pm z_{.025} (\sigma_{\overline{x}}) = \overline{x} \pm 1.96 (\sigma_{\overline{x}})$$

Z-SCORES OF OTHER COMMON CONFIDENCE INTERVALS

We are not always trying to find a 95% confidence interval for the mean; other common confidence levels are 90% and 99%. As a matter of fact, these three confidence levels (90%, 95%, and 99%) are so often the levels required, both for confidence intervals and for hypothesis testing (which will be discussed later in this chapter), that it is useful to memorize the z-scores, $z_{\alpha/2}$, for these.

When $\alpha = 10\%$, $z_{\alpha/2} = z_{.10/2} = z_{.05} = 1.645$. So when a 90% confidence interval is required, the appropriate z-score is $z_{.05} = 1.645$.

When $\alpha = 1\%$, $z_{\alpha/2} = z_{.01/2} = z_{.005} = 2.58$. So when a 99% confidence interval for the mean is requested, the z-score is $z_{.005} = 2.58$.

Of course, these scores can always be found in the standard normal table, just as the $z_{.025}$ score was found to be 1.96, but it is a good idea to remember some of these scores since they are used so often. It is not usual to ask for a 75% confidence interval or a 68% confidence interval because these are such small confidence levels. It is very common to require a 90%, 95%, or 99% confidence interval in order to have a high degree of confidence in the answer.

STANDARD DEVIATION OF THE CONFIDENCE INTERVAL

By the Central Limit Theorem, the standard deviation of the sampling distribution, $\sigma_{\overline{x}}$, equals $\frac{\sigma}{\sqrt{n}}$; the standard deviation of the population, σ, is divided by $\sqrt{n}$, the square root of the sample size. The standard deviation of the sampling distribution of the means, $\sigma_{\overline{x}}$, is part of the formula for the confidence interval of the mean.

However, it would be unlikely that the population standard deviation is known, since the population mean, which is what is to be estimated by obtaining the confidence interval, is not known. Recalling the work with sampling theory in Chapter 7, for large samples the sample variance, s^2, is an unbiased estimator of the population variance, σ^2. Therefore, the sample standard deviation, s, is an unbiased estimator of the population standard deviation, σ.

In any large sample, therefore, the sample standard deviation s can be substituted for σ, the population standard deviation. In the confidence interval of the mean formula, $\sigma_{\overline{x}} = \dfrac{\sigma}{\sqrt{n}} = \dfrac{s}{\sqrt{n}}$; the working formula that is used to find the confidence interval for the population mean is

$$(a, b) = \overline{x} \pm z_{\alpha/2} \cdot \sigma_{\overline{x}} = \overline{x} \pm z_{\alpha/2} \cdot \left(\frac{s}{\sqrt{n}} \right)$$

Finding a Confidence Interval for the Mean

Consider again the problem concerning I.Q.s at a certain college. A random sample of thirty I.Q.s is chosen. In this sample, the mean $\overline{x} = 118.3$ and the standard deviation $s = 11.4$. We want to find a 95% confidence interval for the population mean; that is, an interval around the sample mean I.Q. $\overline{x} = 118.3$ such that we are 95% confident that the population mean is within that interval.

For a 95% level of confidence, $\alpha = 1 - .95 = .05$. Therefore, $\dfrac{\alpha}{2} = .025$ and $z_{\alpha/2} = z_{.025} = 1.96$.

Since the population standard deviation, σ, is not given, s is used as an unbiased estimator of σ: $\dfrac{s}{\sqrt{n}} = \dfrac{11.4}{\sqrt{30}} \approx 2.08$.

Therefore,

$$(a, b) = \overline{x} \pm z_{\alpha/2} \cdot \frac{s}{\sqrt{n}} = 118.3 \pm 1.96 \cdot 2.08 = 118.3 \pm 4.1 = (114.2, 122.4).$$

With 95% confidence we can say that the mean I.Q. of the students at the college is between 114.2 and 122.4.

Instead of the 95% confidence interval, suppose the problem asked us to find a 99% confidence interval for the mean I.Q. score at the college. Will this 99% confidence interval be larger or smaller than the 95% confidence interval, (114.2, 122.4), found above?

For a 99% level of confidence, $\alpha = 1 - .99 = .01$. Therefore, $\dfrac{\alpha}{2} = .005$ and $z_{\alpha/2} = z_{.005} = 2.58$.

$$(a, b) = \overline{x} \pm z_{\alpha/2} \cdot \frac{s}{\sqrt{n}} = 118.3 \pm 2.58 \left(\frac{11.4}{\sqrt{30}} \right) = 118.3 \pm 2.58(2.08) = 118.3 \pm 5.4$$
$$= (112.9, 123.7).$$

Note that the width of the 95% confidence interval (114.2, 122.4) is 8.2 (W = 2B or width equals twice the bound of 4.1), and the width of the 99% confidence interval (112.9, 123.7) is 10.8 (twice the bound of 5.4). The 99% confidence interval for the population mean is larger than the 95% confidence interval for the population mean, which makes sense because the wider the interval the more confident we can be that the mean is in it; the narrower the interval, the less confident we can be about the inclusion of the population mean.

Exercise 8.1: The mean of a random sample of 100 employees' salaries in Company ABC is $18,500 per year with a standard deviation of $2000. Find:
   a. the 90% confidence interval for the mean salary of all the employees in Company ABC.
   b. the 99% confidence interval for the mean salary of all the employees in Company ABC.
   c. Which interval is larger? Explain why.

Answers:
   a. The formula for confidence interval is

$$(a, b) = \bar{x} \pm z_{\alpha/2} \cdot \frac{s}{\sqrt{n}}.$$ In this problem, $\bar{x} = 18,500$, $s = 2000$, and $n = 100$.

Since $\alpha = 1 - .90 = .10$, $\frac{\alpha}{2} = .05$ and $z_{\alpha/2} = z_{.05} = 1.645$.

Substituting, $(a, b) = 18,500 \pm 1.645 \left(\frac{2000}{\sqrt{100}} \right) = 18,500 \pm 1.645(200)$

$= 18,500 \pm 329 = (18,171, 18,829)$.

The 90% confidence interval for the mean salary of all the employees in Company ABC is (18,171, 18,829). With a confidence level of 90%, we can say that the mean salary of all the employees in Company ABC is between $18,171 and $18,829.
   b. $\bar{x} = 18,500$, $s = 2000$, and $n = 100$.

Since $\alpha = 1 - .99 = .01$, $\frac{\alpha}{2} = .005$ and $z_{\alpha/2} = z_{.005} = 2.58$. Substituting, $(a, b) = 18,500 \pm 2.58(2000/\sqrt{100}) = 18,500 \pm 2.58(200) = 18,500 \pm 516 = (17,984, 19.016)$.

The 99% confidence interval for the mean salary of all the employees in Company ABC is (17,984, 19,016). With a confidence level of 99%, we can say that the mean salary of all the employees in Company ABC is between $17,984 and $19,016.
   c. The 99% confidence interval (17,984, 19,016) is larger than the 90% confidence interval (18,171, 18,829).

The tails of the curve in Part b ($\alpha = .01$) are smaller than the tails of the curve in Part a ($\alpha = .10$). These tails represent the area of uncertainty (lack of confidence) since they are outside the confidence interval.

The more confident (99%) we are that the population mean is in the interval, the larger the interval must be to justify the confidence.

Determining Sample Size

Before beginning an experiment, that is, before drawing a sample from a population, it is important to know how large the sample should be. Drawing large samples costs money and time. For example, if an experiment is performed to determine the mean I.Q. of a certain population, each person in the sample must take an I.Q. test; administering each I.Q. test requires time and money. Therefore, before drawing the sample, how does the statistician know how many to choose?

The answer to this question is another question: how large a confidence interval does the statistician want? Suppose a 95% confidence interval for the population mean is desired. In the problem dealing with I.Q.s above (a sample of thirty, $\bar{x} = 118.3$, and $s = 11.4$, and a 95% confidence interval,) the width of the confidence interval was 8.2. The bound of the confidence interval was $8.2/2 = 4.1$. (In general, $B = W/2$, where B is the bound and W the width of the confidence interval.)

The bound of 4.1 means that the sample mean was 4.1 units (I.Q. points) from the endpoints of the 95% confidence interval: 118.3 is 4.1 units from each end, 114.2 and 122.4, of the interval in which it is expected (with 95% certainty) that the population mean would be found.

CALCULATING THE SAMPLE SIZE

In the same problem, assume the bound was too large. The statistician still wants a 95% confidence interval, but this time he or she wants the entire confidence interval to be only 4 units wide, giving a bound of 2. This means that the formula $\bar{x} \pm z_{\alpha/2}\left(\dfrac{s}{\sqrt{n}}\right) = \bar{x} \pm 2$, rather than $\bar{x} \pm z_{\alpha/2}\left(\dfrac{s}{\sqrt{n}}\right) = \bar{x} \pm 4.1$, which it was when the bound was 4.1. Since $\bar{x}$, s, and $z_{\alpha/2}$ are the same, the new bound will be achieved by changing the sample size n.

We need to solve $\bar{x} \pm 1.96\left(\dfrac{s}{\sqrt{n}}\right) = \bar{x} \pm 2$ for n. Subtracting $\bar{x}$ from each side

of the equation gives $\pm 1.96\left(\dfrac{s}{\sqrt{n}}\right) = \pm 2$. Recall $s = 11.4$ from the sample of thirty.

$$\frac{\pm 1.96\,(11.4)}{\sqrt{n}} = \pm 2$$

Cross multiplying, $\pm 2(\sqrt{n}) = (\pm 1.96)(11.4)$. Dividing each side by 2 yields $\sqrt{n} = (\pm 1.96)(11.4)/(\pm 2) = \pm 11.172$. Squaring both sides gives $n = (\pm 11.172)^2 \approx 124.8$.

Since n represents the number in the sample to be drawn, it must always be rounded up, so the answer is 125. Thus, 125 people must be sampled to be 95% certain that the population I.Q. mean is within 2 points of the sample I.Q. mean.

If n were rounded down, the number would result in a sample that is *not* within the correct number of points of the bound. So even if n turned out to be 124.1 instead of 124.8, n would still have to be rounded up to 125.

Recall the calculations we made to find n. The formula for the confidence interval can be set equal to a general confidence interval, which can be thought of as the sample mean ± the bound, B. At this point, the general equation looks like this:

$$\bar{x} \pm z_{\alpha/2}\left(\frac{s}{\sqrt{n}}\right) = \bar{x} \pm B$$

Subtracting $\bar{x}$ from each side and cross multiplying, the above formula becomes

$$\pm B(\sqrt{n}) = z_{\alpha/2} \cdot s$$

Solving for $\sqrt{n}$, the formula now becomes

$$\sqrt{n} = \frac{z_{\alpha/2} \cdot s}{\pm B}$$

And squaring each side yields

$$n = \frac{(z_{\alpha/2})^2 \cdot s^2}{(\pm B^2)}$$, where $z_{\alpha/2}$ is the z-score that puts $\frac{\alpha}{2}$ % in each tail, s^2 is the variance of the large sample, and B is the bound of the confidence interval.

This formula makes it simple to calculate the sample size needed given a particular confidence level and bound. All we have to do is put in the z-score for the confidence interval, the desired bound, and the variance of the sample.

Exercise 8.2: A random sample of the salaries of employees at Company ABC is to be drawn in order to determine the mean salary of all the employees. If it is required that the population mean be in a 99% confidence interval whose width is $1000, how many employees must be sampled if the standard deviation of a previous large sample was $2000?

Answer: The formula for determining the number to be sampled is

$$n = \frac{(z_{\alpha/2})^2 \cdot s^2}{B^2}$$

$\alpha = 1 - .99 = .01$ so $\frac{\alpha}{2} = .01/2 = .005$. $z_{.005} = 2.58$.

$s = 2000$; $B = W/2$, where W (the width of confidence interval) = 1000, so $B = 1000/2 = 500$. Substituting in the formula, $n = (2.58)^2(2000)^2/500^2 = 6.6564(4,000,000)/250,000 = 106.5024 \approx 107$.

Therefore, 107 employees' salaries must be sampled to be 99% sure that the mean of all the salaries will be in an interval whose width is $1000.

HYPOTHESIS TESTING

At the beginning of Chapter 2, the two types of statistics, descriptive and inferential, were illustrated. Recall that inferential statistics makes guesses about the parameters of a population based on statistics of a sample of the population. Some of these inferential statistics have already been discussed in Chapter 8. For example, an interval on either side of the mean of a sample was found. The mean of the population is probably (with, say, 95% certainty) in this interval. Based on the sample statistics (sample mean and standard deviation), the confidence interval for the population mean was found.

The essence of inferential statistics is *hypothesis testing*, making a statement about some parameter of the population and testing sample statistics to see if the statement is true.

For example, assume that it has been common knowledge that the mean age of students at XYZ College is 21. A researcher believes that the mean age is not 21. Both of these two differing statements are called *hypotheses* (guesses). The first one, which represents what has been thought to be true, is called the *null hypothesis* and is symbolized H_o. The second statement is called the research or *alternative hypothesis* and is symbolized H_a. Since H_a says that $\mu \neq 21$, H_o says that $\mu = 21$.

Preliminaries for Hypothesis Testing

The first step in testing a null vs. an alternative hypothesis is outlining the two possibilities. In the case of the mean ages, they are written as follows

H_o: $\mu = 21$
H_a: $\mu \neq 21$

In order to test to see which of these hypotheses seems true, a random sample must be drawn. In this chapter, all samples will be large (n is greater than or equal to 30, $n \geq 30$).

Assume, in the case whose null and alternative hypotheses are outlined above, a random sample of $n = 100$ students has a mean age $\bar{x} = 22$ years and a standard deviation $s = 4$ years. It is possible that a sample drawn from the student population will have a different mean, $\bar{x} = 30$ or $\bar{x} = 16$, or any number in between depending on which students happened to be chosen.

But the likelihood is that the mean of a random sample will be fairly close to the population mean. Recall that by the Central Limit Theorem, the mean of the sampling distribution of means is the same as the mean of the population, $\mu_{\bar{x}} = \mu$; for large samples the distribution is approximately normal. Also recall that the standard deviation of the sampling distribution of the means, $\sigma_{\bar{x}}$, equals the standard deviation of the population divided by the square root of the number sampled, $\sigma_{\bar{x}} = \dfrac{\sigma}{\sqrt{n}}$.

Figure 8.3 is a sketch of the sampling distribution of the means for the age problem, assuming the null hypothesis is true. Notice that the mean $\mu_{\bar{x}} = 21$. Notice that the shape of the distribution is approximately normal since a sample of $n = 100$ was chosen. The standard deviation of the sampling distribution of

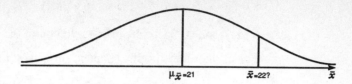

Figure 8.3:
Sampling Distribution of $\bar{x}$
Mean Ages of Samples of 100 Students at XYZ College
Assuming the Population Mean $\mu = 21$

the means $\sigma_{\bar{x}} = \dfrac{\sigma}{\sqrt{n}}$. For this problem, $s = 4$ can be used as an unbiased estimator of σ. Therefore, the standard deviation of the sampling distribution of the means $\sigma_{\bar{x}} = \dfrac{4}{\sqrt{100}} = \dfrac{4}{10} = .4$.

While it is possible that 30 and 16 could be the means of two of the samples included in this distribution, it is very unlikely: 30 and 16 are many standard deviations away from the assumed mean since the standard deviation of the sampling distribution of the means is only .4 years.

Where is $\bar{x} = 22$ (the value of the mean of the sample we did draw) on the sampling distribution of the means in Figure 8.3? When its place on this sampling distribution of the means is found, will it turn out to be close to $\mu = 21$ or far away from $\mu = 21$, the mean of the null hypothesis, the presumed mean of the population of ages of students at XYZ College?

Test Statistic

In order to answer these questions, we need to find the *test statistic*, a number that will place the mean of the sample drawn, $\bar{x} = 22$, on the standard unit normal in relation to the sampling distribution of the means. This test statistic is the z-score of the sample mean $\bar{x}$ and is also set up as part of the preliminaries of the hypothesis test. Now the hypothesis test looks like this:

$H_o: \mu = 21$

$H_a: \mu \neq 21$

Test Statistic: $z = \dfrac{\bar{x} - \mu}{\sigma_{\bar{x}}}$

CALCULATING THE TEST STATISTIC

After all the preliminaries are set up, the next step in hypothesis testing is to calculate the test statistic for the particular sample drawn. For this example, the test statistic is

$$z = \frac{\bar{x} - \mu}{\sigma_{\bar{x}}},$$ where $\bar{x}$ is the sample mean (22), μ is the assumed population

mean (21), and $\sigma_{\bar{x}}$ is the standard deviation of the sampling distribution.

For all problems in this chapter, since they involve large samples, $\sigma_{\bar{x}} = \frac{s}{\sqrt{n}}$ since s is an unbiased estimator of σ. Calculating z:

$$z = \frac{(22-21)}{4 / \sqrt{100}} = \frac{1}{.4} = 2.5.$$

Therefore, the z-score for 22 is 2.50.

REGION OF REJECTION

The last element of the hypothesis test preliminaries is setting the *region of rejection*, an area of the tail or tails of the standard unit normal that is set prior to calculating the test statistic. The most common regions of rejection comprise 1% or 5% or 10% of the standard unit normal, areas in the tails. If the test statistic z-score is larger than the positive z-score or smaller than the negative z-score preset in this part of the hypothesis test, then the null hypothesis is rejected; the z-score from the sample mean falls in the region of rejection. If the z-score calculated from the test statistic does not fall in the rejection region, then the null hypothesis is not rejected, it is accepted.

Specifically, if $\bar{x} = 22$ is too far away from μ, then it is unlikely that $\mu = 21$, as previously believed. Since many values of $\bar{x}$ are possible, even if μ is 21, a confidence level must be preset, which means it must be set before the sample mean is used to calculate the test statistic. Actually, an alpha-level or area in the tails of the standard unit normal is given for the region of rejection in the statement of the problem. This area is also referred to as the *significance level*. The most common value for this significance level is $\alpha = .05$.

The alternative hypothesis is two sided or nondirectional—it states that $\mu \neq 21$—rather than directional, which would state $\mu > 21$ or $\mu < 21$. Therefore, the tail area must be divided into two parts: since $\alpha = .05$, .025 is the probability in each tail. The z-score for this number is then found: in this example,

$$z_{.025} = 1.96 \text{ or } z_{.025} = -1.96.$$

If the z-score of $\bar{x}$, calculated from the test statistic, is greater than 1.96 or less than −1.96, then $\bar{x}$ will fall in a tail of the normal curve. This is the region of rejection, and it completes the preliminaries for the hypothesis test. Now the hypothesis test begins like this:

$H_o: \mu = 21$

$H_a: \mu \neq 21$

Test Statistic: $z = \dfrac{\bar{x} - \mu}{\sigma_{\bar{x}}}$

Region of Rejection (see Figure 8.4).

The region of rejection is usually given as a sketch of the distribution and its regions of acceptance and rejection, with the z-scores indicated.

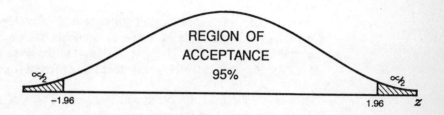

Figure 8.4:
Region of Rejection (Shaded)
$\alpha = .05$; $\alpha/2 = .025$
Two-tailed, Nondirectional Hypothesis Test

It is better to set up this entire hypothesis test before calculating the test statistic. Setting up the parts of the hypothesis test focuses on the general problem rather than the particulars. Once a statistician knows the value of the test statistic, he or she may be tempted to change the region of rejection or the alternative hypothesis in order to influence the results of the hypothesis test. In real life, the hypothesis test is set up even before the random sample is taken.

REJECTING OR ACCEPTING THE NULL HYPOTHESIS

If the z-score of $\bar{x}$, the calculated test statistic, falls in the rejection (shaded) region, then the conclusion is to reject the null hypothesis. That rejection means that the alternative hypothesis is accepted as true. In this example, there is a 5% probability that rejecting the null hypothesis is incorrect: 5% is the probability that even though our sample mean falls in the rejection region, it could still come from a population whose mean is 21.

On the other hand, if the z-score of $\bar{x}$ falls in the acceptance (nonshaded) region, the conclusion will be to accept the null hypothesis. To hedge their bets, statisticians usually use the phrase "fail to reject" rather than "accept" the null hypothesis. There is also a probability that failing to reject the null hypothesis will be an error. These errors will be discussed later in this chapter.

In this particular example, it was decided to reject the null hypothesis if the z-score of the mean of the sample was either less than –1.96 or greater than 1.96, which are the z-scores separating the region of rejection from the region of acceptance. The calculated z-score was 2.50. Since 2.50 > 1.96, the null hypothesis is rejected. Therefore, the conclusion is that the mean age of students at XYZ College is not equal to 21.

Exercise 8.3:   The mean age of students at XYZ college is thought to be 21 years. A random sample of forty-nine students has a mean age $\bar{x} = 22$ and a standard deviation $s = 4$. Using $\alpha = .10$, test to see if the mean age of students at XYZ college is really 21, or whether it is different from 21.

Answers: First set up the hypothesis test. Three of the elements will be identical to the one in the previous section.

$H_o: \mu = 21$

$H_a: \mu \neq 21$

Test Statistic: $z = \dfrac{\bar{x} - \mu}{\sigma_{\bar{x}}}$

Region of Rejection (Figure 8.5):

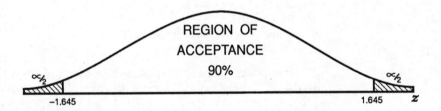

Figure 8.5
Region of Rejection (Shaded)
$\alpha = .10; \alpha/2 = .05$ Two-tailed,
Nondirectional Hypothesis Test

Calculating $\sigma_{\bar{x}} = \dfrac{s}{\sqrt{n}} = \dfrac{4}{\sqrt{49}} = \dfrac{4}{7} \approx .57, z = \dfrac{(22-21)}{.57} = 1.75.$

Since 1.75 > 1.645, the beginning of the right side region of rejection, reject H_o and conclude that the mean age of students at XYZ college is different from ($\neq$) 21.

Directional Hypothesis Testing

The problems above were examples of nondirectional hypothesis tests. That is, with the null hypothesis that the population mean $\mu = 21$, the alternative was that $\mu \neq 21$. Often, however, the alternative hypothesis has a direction, either $\mu >$ or $\mu <$ the value of μ in the null hypothesis.

For example, it is now known, through the previous hypothesis test, that the mean age of students at XYZ College is not 21 as had been previously suspected. Two hypothesis tests, using two different samples and two different α values, led to rejection of the null hypothesis. The next hypothesis to test should be a stronger one, a *directional hypothesis*.

Suppose a new sample of 64 students is chosen and their mean age is found. From the previous problems, one would suspect that the mean age is actually higher than (rather than just different from) the original guess, $\mu = 21$. This is because the z-scores for both the previous examples were positive, stemming from the fact that in both previous samples the mean of the sample $\overline{x} = 22$ was higher than the supposed mean.

Test the hypothesis that $\mu = 21$ against the alternative that $\mu > 21$. Use $\alpha = .05$. The new sample of 64 students has a mean $\overline{x} = 22.5$.

Since the alternative hypothesis says that $\mu > 21$, the null hypothesis should state that $\mu \leq 21$. However, in most hypothesis tests, it is sufficient to write the null hypothesis as an equality only, $\mu = 21$. It is very rare that the alternative

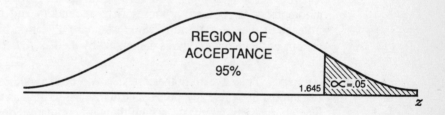

Figure 8.6:
Region of Rejection (Shaded)
$\alpha = .05$
One -Tailed (Upper), Directional Hypothesis Test

hypothesis yields a test statistic on the other side of the mean, such as a negative z-score for this problem.

The hypothesis test preliminaries are as follows:

$H_o: \mu = 21$

$H_a: \mu > 21$

Test Statistic: $z = \dfrac{\overline{x} - \mu}{\sigma_{\overline{x}}}$

Region of Rejection (Figure 8.6):

Notice that the region of rejection is in only one tail: the entire $\alpha = .05$ is in the upper tail because the null hypothesis will only be rejected if the z-score from the test statistic is greater than $z_{.05} = 1.645$, the z-score that leaves .05 in the upper tail of the standard unit normal.

The previous $s = 4$ is still an unbiased estimator of the standard deviation of the population. Therefore, the test statistic $z = \dfrac{22.5 - 21}{4/\sqrt{64}} = \dfrac{1.5}{.5} = 3.$

Since $3 > 1.645$, the null hypothesis is rejected. Therefore, the conclusion is that the mean age of college students at XYZ College is greater than 21. This conclusion is stronger than the previous one because it actually states that the age is *higher* than previously supposed, rather than just *different* than previously supposed.

Exercise 8.4: The E.P.A. (Environmental Protection Agency) has decreed that the mean miles per gallon yielded by all the automobiles manufactured by a particular company must be 26 mpg or greater. Rather than test all their automobiles, a company chooses fifty at random and finds that the mean mileage of these is 25.5 mpg with a standard deviation of 3 mpg. Will these cars meet the mileage figures demanded by the E.P.A.? Test using $\alpha = .05$.

Answer: This is a hypothesis test. The null hypothesis in this case is a directional one ($\mu \geq 26$), but H_o is usually just written as an equality ($\mu = 26$). The alternative hypothesis, which the auto company hopes is not the case, is $\mu < 26$ (the mean mileage of their cars is less than 26). The test statistic for hypothesis testing of a sample mean against a presumed population mean is always the same:

$z = \dfrac{\overline{x} - \mu}{\sigma_{\overline{x}}}$

Since the alternative hypothesis is directional, $\mu < 26$, the region of rejection is in only one tail of the curve. The entire $\alpha = .05$ is in a single left (negative) tail. $z_{.05} = 1.645$, but since the alternative hypothesis is "less than," $z_{.05} = -1.645$.

The region of rejection will comprise that part of the standard unit normal where the calculated z is less than -1.645. The preliminaries for the hypothesis test are summarized below:

$H_o: \mu = 26$

$H_a: \mu < 26$

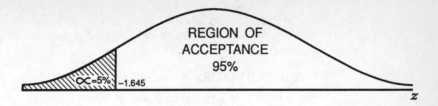

Figure 8.7:
Region of Rejection (Shaded)
$\alpha = .05$
One-tailed (Lower), Directional Hypothesis Test

Test Statistic: $z = \dfrac{\overline{x} - \mu}{\sigma_{\overline{x}}}$

Region of Rejection (see Figure 8.7).

$$z = \frac{25.5 - 26}{3/\sqrt{50}} = \frac{-.5}{.424} = -1.18.$$

Since the value of the test statistic, $z = -1.18$, is not less than the upper value of z on the region of rejection, $z = -1.645$, the null hypothesis is not rejected. The conclusion is that the mileage figures for cars by this manufacturer are in compliance with the E.P.A.'s demands.

Type I and Type II Errors

Just because there has been evidence to accept or reject the null hypothesis does not mean that the null hypothesis is true or false. There are, in fact, four outcomes of a hypothesis testing situation. These outcomes are:

1. H_o is true, and its truth is substantiated by the hypothesis test. (The null hypothesis is true, and it is accepted.)
2. H_o is true, but its truth is not substantiated by the hypothesis test. (The null hypothesis is true, but it is rejected.)
3. H_o is false, but the hypothesis test concludes it is true. (The null hypothesis is false, but it is accepted.)
4. H_o is false, and the hypothesis test concludes it is false. (The null hypothesis is false, and it is rejected.)

If either number 1 or 4 occurs, then the decision to accept or reject the null hypothesis is correct. However, if either number 2 or 3 occurs, an error has been made. These errors are distinguishable.

TYPE I OR α ERRORS

A Type I or α (alpha) error occurs when the null hypothesis is really true, but it is rejected. It is possible that a Type I error occurred in any of the above examples in which the null hypothesis was rejected. In the problems involving the mean age of students at XYZ College, all of which resulted in the the null hypothesis being rejected, a Type I error may have occurred.

The probability of a Type I error is equal to α, exactly the alpha-level or the value previously set for alpha. If a problem in which the null hypothesis was rejected had the alpha-level at .05, the probability of a Type I error having occurred is .05.

TYPE II OR β ERRORS

A Type II or β (beta) error occurs when the null hypothesis is not true, but it is not rejected. A Type II error could have occurred in Exercise 8.4, the problem concerning the mean miles per gallon in a line of automobiles, since the null hypothesis was not rejected. The probability of a Type II error, β, can also be calculated, but its calculation is beyond the scope of this book. Either a Type I or a Type II error can occur with every hypothesis test, if the decision made to reject or not to reject the null hypothesis is incorrect.

Exercise 8.5: The following are the grade point averages (G.P.A.s) of forty-two students chosen at random from XYZ College. Use them to test the hypothesis that the mean G.P.A. of all the students at XYZ College is 2.5 or less (the null hypothesis) against a claim that the mean G.P.A. of the students is higher than 2.5. Use .05 level of significance. If an error was committed in solving this problem, which type error was it?

Data Set 5

2.23	3.14	4.00	2.53	3.56	2.81
1.79	2.03	3.25	2.66	1.98	2.19
3.72	2.22	2.58	2.92	3.01	2.75
3.91	2.52	1.48	3.02	3.33	1.97
2.54	3.48	1.82	2.85	1.01	3.65
2.10	3.04	3.86	2.18	2.95	3.57
1.76	3.26	2.09	3.81	2.34	2.48

Answers: This exercise is set up the same as previous problems in hypothesis testing:

$H_o: \mu = 2.5$

$H_a: \mu > 2.5$

Test Statistic: $z = \dfrac{\bar{x} - \mu}{\sigma_{\bar{x}}}$

Region of Rejection: (See Figure 8.6).

Since the alternative hypothesis is directional (>), the region of rejection is one-tailed and the entire 5% level of significance is put in a single, upper (positive) tail.

If the calculated value of z is greater than $z_{.05} = 1.645$, then H_o will be rejected.

Calculating z, the test statistic, is not as easy at it has been in the previous problems because the data given is the raw data of forty-two students' G.P.A.s. Recall the formulas for the mean and standard deviation of a data set:

$$\bar{x} = \frac{\sum \bar{x_i}}{n} \text{ and } s = \frac{\sqrt{\sum x_i{}^2 - (\sum x_i)^2/n}}{n-1}$$

Some preliminary calculations are:

$$\sum x_i = 114.39; \bar{x} = 114.39/42 = 2.72$$

Therefore, the numerator of the test statistic is $2.72 - 2.5 = .22$.

To calculate the denominator, find s.

$$\sum x_i{}^2 = 333.299. \text{ Therefore,}$$

$$s = \frac{\sqrt{[(333.299) - (114.39)^2/42]}}{41} = \frac{\sqrt{(333.299 - 311.549)}}{41} = \frac{\sqrt{21.75}}{41}$$

Therefore, $s = \sqrt{.53} \approx .728$.

Calculating the z-score for 2.72,

$$z = \frac{\bar{x} - \mu}{s/\sqrt{n}} = \frac{(2.72 - 2.5)}{.728/\sqrt{42}}$$

$z = .22/.112 = 1.96$. Since $1.96 > 1.645$, reject H_o and conclude that the G.P.A.s of students at XYZ College are greater than 2.5. If an error was made, it was a Type I error, since the null hypothesis was rejected.

Observed Significance Level

Once an experiment has been completed and the test statistic has been calculated, more is known about the probability that the mean from the sample chosen could have come from the population of interest.

Before the test statistic is calculated, an alpha-level (α) is chosen for the region of rejection. This level is usually 10%, 5%, or 1%, reflecting the area in the tail or tails of the normal distribution. If the calculated z-score of the sample mean (the test statistic) is greater than the positive or less than the negative z-score, which leaves 10%, 5%, or 1% of the curve in the tails, then the null hypothesis is rejected.

P-VALUES

Up until now, it hasn't made any difference whether the calculated z-score of the sample mean is a little larger than the z-score that delineates the rejection region or whether it is a lot larger: the null hypothesis is rejected in either case. But this calculated z-score for the sample mean can be used to find another number, the observed significance level or p-value of the z-score of the sample mean. This *p-level* indicates the probability that the calculated z-score could have come from the sampling distribution, assuming the mean is that of the null hypothesis.

For example, in the problem concerning G.P.A.s in Exercise 8.5, after a one-tailed test (H_a: $\mu > 2.5$), the z-score for the mean was calculated to be 1.96. Since $1.96 > 1.645$, the z-score for the alpha-level, the null hypothesis was rejected.

Assume, instead, that the null hypothesis is true. Then the probability of getting a sample mean whose z-score is 1.645 or greater is .05, or 5%. But the calculated z-score for the test statistic, the z-score for the mean of the sample given (2.72), was 1.96. What is the probability that if H_o is true ($\mu = 2.5$), a sample mean could be 2.72 (with z-score = 1.96) or more? What is p ($z > 1.96$)?

Refer to Figure 8.8.

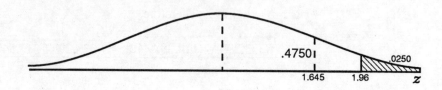

Figure 8.8:
Observed Significance (P-) Level (Shaded)
$p(z \geq 1.96) = .0250$
(1.96 is z-score of 2.72)

What is the probability—p-value—that, for a sample from a population whose mean is 2.5, the sample mean could be 2.72 or more, given that the sample has forty-two data points and that its standard deviation is .728? In other words, what is the area in the tail of the normal distribution starting at 1.96?

Looking up 1.96 in the standard normal table (Appendix A), we find the area under the curve from 0 to 1.96 is .4750. By subtracting .4750 from .5, we find the area under the normal curve after 1.96 to be .025. Therefore, the observed significance level or p-value of 1.96 is .025. The probability that a sample of forty-two with a mean of 2.72 or more (and a standard deviation of .728) could have come from a population whose mean is 2.5 is .025; p ($z > 1.96$) = .025.

Observed significance or p-values are useful for following up experiments. For example, if instead of setting $\alpha = .05$, we could set $\alpha = .01$ and still get the same result (i.e., rejecting the null hypothesis), our statement would be stronger. We could say we are 99% sure that the null hypothesis should be rejected (our α-level is .01). Of course, in the above example, if α had been set at .01, the null hypothesis would not have been rejected. Sometimes observed significance levels are even calculated before a hypothesis test is set up, to see which to pick. This method is not considered to be good statistical procedure.

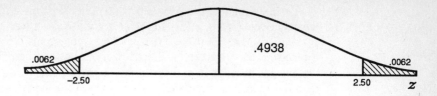

Figure 8.9:
Observed Significance (*P*-) Level (Shaded)
$p (z \leq -2.5$ or $z \geq 2.5) = .0062 + .0062 = .0124$ ± Is ± z- Score of 22 in Two-tailed Test

P-VALUES FROM TWO-TAILED TESTS

A two-tailed hypothesis test produces a slightly different *p*-value. In the first problem involving the ages of college students, the hypothesis test was nondirectional. That is, H_a: $\mu \neq 21$, rather than μ greater or less than 21. The calculated test statistic of $z = 2.50$ led to rejection of the null hypothesis, but two tails had to be searched to make sure that the calculated z-score for the sample mean was not in the acceptance region.

To calculate the *p*-value, therefore, one must look at the area under *both* the $z \leq -2.50$ and the $z \geq 2.50$ tails and find $p (z \leq -2.50$ or $z \geq 2.50)$. The "or" here is used in the same sense as in Chapter 5, or union of two sets:

$$p (z \leq -2.50 \text{ or } z \geq 2.50) = p (z \leq -2.50) + p (z \geq 2.50).$$

According to the standard normal table (Appendix A), the area under the curve between 0 and 2.5 is .4938 (Figure 8.9). The area in the upper tail where $z \geq 2.5$ is $.5 - .4938 = .0062$. But since the original hypothesis test set up two tails, the area in the lower tail, $z \leq -2.5$, must also be included in the *p*-value. Therefore, the *p*-value or observed significance level is $2(.0062) = .0124$ or 1.24%. The probability that a sample of 100 with a mean of 22 or more (or 20 or less, since the lower tail had to be searched also, and the *z*-score for 20 is

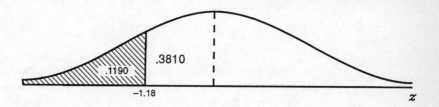

Figure 8.10:
Observed Significance (P-) Level (Shaded)
$p(z < -1.18) = .1190$
(−1.18 is *z*-score of 25.5)

−2.50) and a standard deviation of .4 could have come from a population whose mean is 21 is .0124: $p\,(z \leq -2.50 \text{ or } z \geq 2.50) = .0124$.

Exercise 8.6:   In Exercise 8.3, a lower one-tailed test of a hypothesis revealed that the gas mileage in a certain manufacturer's line was in agreement with that required by E.P.A. standards. The z-score of the mean was -1.18, which meant that the null hypothesis was not rejected. What is the probability that a sample mean has a z-score less than or equal to -1.18?

Answer: In Figure 8.10, the area under the curve between a z-score of 0 and z-score of -1.18 is .3810. The area in the tail, where $z < -1.18$ is $.5 - .3810 = .119$.

The probability that a sample mean from this population has a z-score less than or equal to -1.18, as the one from this sample has, is .119 or 11.9%. The observed significance level or p-value of -1.18 is .119: $p\,(z \leq -1.18) = .119$.

DIFFERENCE BETWEEN POPULATION MEANS—LARGE SAMPLES

A common statistical procedure compares the means of two samples to make inferences about the populations from which the samples are drawn. For example, suppose information exists about the I.Q.s of two samples drawn from what may or may not be two different populations. In this case, assume random samples of fifty students' I.Q.s are drawn from XYZ College's business majors and fifty from XYZ College's English majors. The results of this sampling are summarized in Table 8.1:

Table 8.1	Business Majors	English Majors
Sample Size	50	50
Sample Mean I.Q.	113	116
Sample standard Deviation	12.5	10.3

To distinguish between the populations these sample statistics come from, use subscripts. For example, the sample sizes of the two groups can be called n_B (number of business majors) and n_E (number of English majors). In a similar way, we will label the sample means $\bar{x}_B$ and $\bar{x}_E$ and the sample standard deviations s_B and s_E.

The question is whether the mean of the population of business majors' I.Q.s is the same as the mean of the population of English majors' I.Q.s. To answer this question, form the sampling distribution of $(\bar{x}_B - \bar{x}_E)$ as in Figure 8.11.

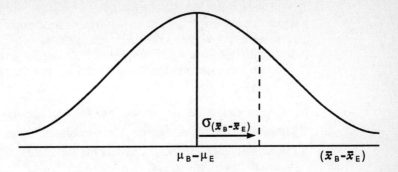

Figure 8.11:

Sampling Distribution of the Difference of Two Means

Mean of Distribution = $\mu_B - \mu_E$

Standard Deviation = $= \sqrt{\dfrac{\sigma_B{}^2}{n_B} + \dfrac{\sigma_E{}^2}{n_E}}$

Shape of Disrribution: Approximately Normal When $n_B \geq 30$ and $n_E \geq 30$

Sampling Distribution of the Difference of Means

Figure 8.11, the sampling distribution of the difference of means has the following properties:

1. It is approximately normal for large samples (each sample greater than or equal to thirty).

2. The mean of the sampling distribution of $(\bar{x}_B - \bar{x}_E)$ is $(\mu_B - \mu_E)$.

3. The standard deviation of the sampling distribution of $(\bar{x}_B - \bar{x}_E)$ is:

$$\sigma_{(\bar{x}_B - \bar{x}_E)} = \sqrt{\frac{\sigma_B{}^2}{n_B} + \frac{\sigma_E{}^2}{n_E}} \ ,$$

where $\sigma_B{}^2$ and $\sigma_E{}^2$ are the variances of the two populations being sampled and n_B and n_E are the sample sizes.

This standard deviation formula assumes that the two samples are independent; i.e., the populations from which they are drawn do not have any elements in common.

STANDARD DEVIATION OF DIFFERENCE OF MEANS DISTRIBUTION

Because this problem deals with business and English majors, we have been using the subscripts $_B$ and $_E$ to distinguish the sample statistics and parameters from each population. However, the general formula uses just numbers to differentiate between the samples. Therefore, in general the sample sizes are n_1 and n_2, the sample means are $\bar{x}_1$ and $\bar{x}_2$, and the populatition variances are σ_1^2 and σ_2^2.

Very rarely are the variances of the two populations known. Since large samples are used, s_1^2 and s_2^2 are unbiased estimators of σ_1^2 and σ_2^2, respectively. The working formula for the standard deviation of the sampling distribution of $(\bar{x}_1 - \bar{x}_2)$ is

$$\sigma_{(\bar{x}_1 - \bar{x}_2)} = \sqrt{\frac{s_1^2}{n_1} + \frac{s_2^2}{n_2}}$$

Hypothesis Testing of Difference Between Means

Suppose we want to see if the population of business majors and that of English majors at XYZ College have different mean I.Q.s. This is the same question as: Is $\mu_B - \mu_E = 0$, or not? Thus, the null and alternative hypotheses can be set up as follows:

$H_o: \mu_B - \mu_E = 0$ or $\mu_B = \mu_E$
$H_a: \mu_B - \mu_E \neq 0$ or $\mu_B \neq \mu_E$

The test statistic is z because these are large samples. The numerator of the test statistic is the difference between the sample means. The denominator is

Table 8.1	Business Majors	English Majors
Sample Size	50	50
Sample Mean I.Q.	113	116
Sample Standard Deviation	12.5	10.3

the standard deviation of the distribution of $(\bar{x}_B - \bar{x}_E)$, which is represented as $\sigma_{(\bar{x}_B - \bar{x}_E)}$ and is given by the formula

$$\sigma_{(\bar{x}_B - \bar{x}_E)} \sqrt{\frac{s_B^2}{n_B} + \frac{s_E^2}{n_E}}$$

The test statistic for testing whether the two populations have the same mean is:

$$\text{Test Statistic: } z = \frac{\bar{x}_B - \bar{x}_E}{\sigma_{(\bar{x}_B - \bar{x}_E)}}$$

Since our question was "is there a difference between . . . ?", this is a two-tailed or nondirectional hypothesis test. The region of rejection is indicated below. Assume $\alpha = .05$.

Region of Rejection: (See Figure 8.4)

To solve this problem, calculate the z-score from the information in Table 8.1 reproduced above.

Calculating the z-score for the difference between the means, the test statistic is used.

$$z = \frac{\bar{x}_B - \bar{x}_E}{\sigma_{\bar{x}_B - \bar{x}_E}}$$

The numerator of the z-score is $113 - 116 = -3$. The denominator is given by the formula for the standard deviation of the sampling distribution:

$$\sigma_{(\bar{x}_B - \bar{x}_E)} = \sqrt{\frac{s_B^2}{n_B} + \frac{s_E^2}{n_E}} = \sqrt{\frac{12.5^2}{50} + \frac{10.3^2}{50}} = \sqrt{3.125 + 2.1218} = 2.29.$$

$$z = \frac{-3}{2.29} = -1.31$$

Since -1.31 does not fall in the rejection region but falls between -1.96 and 1.96, which is the acceptance region, we do not reject H_o. The I.Q.s of the business majors and the English majors at XYZ College do not differ.

DIRECTIONAL HYPOTHESIS TESTING OF DIFFERENCE BETWEEN MEANS

Just as there was directional (greater than or less than) hypothesis testing involving the presumed population mean and the sample mean, so there can be directional hypothesis testing involving the difference between means. For example, in the previous problem concerning the difference in I.Q. scores between business and English majors, suppose instead of asking, "is there a diffence between . . . ?", we had asked, "Is the mean I.Q. of business majors lower than that of English majors?"

The null hypothesis would be the same, but the alternative hypothesis would be directional:

$H_o: \mu_B - \mu_E = 0 \qquad$ or $\mu_B = \mu_E$

$H_a: \mu_B - \mu_E < 0 \qquad$ or $\mu_B < \mu_E$

(The null hypothesis could read $\mu_B \geq \mu_E$.)

The test statistic would be the same:

$$z = \frac{\bar{x}_B - \bar{x}_E}{\sigma_{\bar{x}_B - \bar{x}_E}};$$

but the Region of Rejection is different, since the entire $\alpha = .05$ is in one, lower tail (the alternative hypothesis says "less than" rather than "greater than"). Therefore, the rejection region looks like the one in Figure 8.7.

Since the test statistic is the same, its value is also the same, $z = -1.31$. Since -1.31 is not less than -1.645, the null hypothesis is again not rejected. This means that the I.Q.s of business majors are not lower than those of English majors.

OBSERVED SIGNIFICANCE LEVEL

Notice that the p-value for the one-tailed, directional test (the probability that a z-score from these samples is less than or equal to -1.31) is $p\,(z < -1.31)$ $= .5 - .4049 = .0951$.

However, in the two-tailed, nondirectional test, two areas were searched to place -1.31, the value or the test statistic. Therefore, the probability that the z-score is less than -1.31 *or* more than 1.31 is $p\,(z \le -1.31$ or $z \ge 1.31) = .0951$ $+ .0951 = .1902$.

Notice that the observed significance level is much greater when we use a two-tailed test, given the same data.

Exercise 8.7: Random samples of students' G.P.A.s are gathered from two colleges, XYZ College and JKL College. The statistics are listed in Table 8.2.

Table 8.2	College XYZ	College JKL
Sample Size	42	35
Sample Mean G.P.A.	2.72	2.35
Sample Standard Deviation	.728	.819

Test the hypothesis that the mean G.P.A. of students at XYZ College is higher than the mean G.P.A. of students at JKL College. Use $\alpha = .05$.

Answer:

$H_o: \mu_X - \mu_J = 0$ or $\mu_X = \mu_J$

$H_a: \mu_X - \mu_J > 0$ or $\mu_X > \mu_J$

Test Statistic: $z = \dfrac{\bar{x}_x - \bar{x}_J}{\sigma_{(\bar{x}_x - \bar{x}_J)}}$

Region of Rejection: (See Figure 8.6)

Notice the use of subscripts on the statistics and parameters here; the subscript $_x$ indicates the numbers concerning College XYZ and the subscript $_J$ indicates the numbers connected with College JKL.

This is a one-tailed, positive (or upper) tail test because of the alternative hypothesis. Therefore, the entire $\alpha = .05$ goes in one (upper) tail. A z-score of 1.645 begins the region of rejection.

The numerator of the test statistic, $\bar{x}_X - \bar{x}_J = 2.72 - 2.35 = .37$.

The denominator is given by the formula:

$$\sigma_{(\bar{x}_X - \bar{x}_S)} = \sqrt{\frac{s_X^{\,2}}{n_X} + \frac{s_J^{\,2}}{n_J}} = \sqrt{\frac{.728^2}{42} + \frac{.819^2}{35}} = \sqrt{.0126 + .0192} \approx .178;$$

$$z = \frac{.37}{.178} \approx 2.08$$

Since $2.08 > 1.645$, reject H_o and conclude the mean G.P.A. of students at XYZ College is higher than that of students at JKL College.

Confidence Interval for the Difference Between Means

At the beginning of this chapter, we found a confidence interval for the population mean. This was an interval around the sample mean in which one could be, for example, 95% confident that the population mean resided. Sometimes we seek a confidence interval for the difference between two population means. Finding this confidence interval is important, not only to see how large it is, but also as an easy way to see if the hypothesis test was or will be done correctly.

Suppose a 95% confidence interval for the difference of the population means is sought with the data from Table 8.1 (the I.Q.s of business and English majors at XYZ College). The data for the samples is reproduced here.

Table 8.1	Business Majors	English Majors
Sample Size	50	50
Sample Mean I.Q.	113	116
Sample Standard Deviation	12.5	10.3

The confidence interval for the difference of the population means is given by the formula

$$(a, b) = (\bar{x}_B - \bar{x}_E) \pm z_{\alpha/2} \cdot \sigma_{(\bar{x}_B - \bar{x}_E)}, \text{ where}$$

$$\sigma_{(\bar{x}_B - \bar{x}_E)} = \sqrt{\frac{s_B^{\,2}}{n_B} + \frac{s_E^{\,2}}{n_E}}$$

Recall that the z-score for a confidence interval is always halved since the areas outside the interval are in both tails of the curve:

$$z_{\alpha/2} = z_{.05/2} = z_{.025} = 1.96 \, .$$

Substituting the numbers from the table to form the confidence interval:

$$(a, b) = (113 - 116) \pm 1.96 \sqrt{\frac{(12.5)^2}{50} + \frac{(10.3)^2}{50}} = -3 \pm 1.96(2.29)$$

(as above in the hypothesis testing) $= -3 \pm 4.49$, which results in the 95% confidence interval $(-7.49, 1.49)$. We are 95% confidence that the difference of the population mean I.Q.s between business and English majors at XYZ college is in this interval.

Notice that the number 0 is in this interval, since there is a negative number at one end and a positive number at the other. The presence of 0 in the confidence interval for the difference between means implies that it is possible that there is no difference between the two sample I.Q. means. That, in turn, implies that in a hypothesis testing situation, the null hypothesis will not be rejected. Notice that the null hypothesis was not rejected when we performed the hypothesis test.

Exercise 8.8: Random samples of students' G.P.A.s are gathered from two colleges, XYZ College and JKL College. The statistics are reproduced here.

Table 8.2	College XYZ	College JKL
Sample Size	42	35
Sample Mean G.P.A.	2.72	2.35
Sample Standard Deviation	.728	.819

a. Find a 90% confidence interval for the difference of the means of the population G.P.A.s.
b. Is 0 in the interval? Explain the significance of this.

Answers: a. The formula for the confidence interval for the difference of the means of the G.P.A.s at XYZ and JKL colleges is

$$(a, b) = (\bar{x}_x - \bar{x}_J) \pm z_{\alpha/2} \cdot \sigma(\bar{x}_x - \bar{x}_J),$$

where $\sigma_{(\bar{x}_x - 0\bar{x}_J)} = \sqrt{\dfrac{s_x^2}{n_x} + \dfrac{s_J^2}{n_J}}$, and $z_{\alpha/2} = z_{.10/2} = z_{.05} = 1.645$

Thus, the 90% confidence interval for the above problem is

$$(a, b) = (2.72 - 2.35) \pm 1.645 \sqrt{\dfrac{(.728)^2}{42} + \dfrac{(.819)^2}{35}} = .37 \pm 1.645 \, (.178)$$

$$= .37 \pm .293 = (.077, .663).$$

The 90% confidence interval for the difference between the mean G.P.A.s of students in XYZ and JKL Colleges is (.077, .663).

b. Since 0 is not in the interval, a hypothesis test would lead to rejection of the null hypothesis that the G.P.A. means at the two colleges are the same: $(\mu_x - \mu_J) \neq 0$.

*T*his chapter has been a long one, and rightly so: it is the first chapter on inferential statistics. First discussed was estimating the population mean from a large sample (greater than or equal to thirty is usually considered a large sample). This led to the idea of finding the confidence interval for the mean of the population; i.e., an interval around the sample mean in which one is reasonably (90%, 95%, 99%) certain that the population mean lies.

Formulas were derived to find how large a sample is needed to be almost certain that the population mean is within a certain interval bound or width.

Then followed a discussion of hypothesis testing of the mean. The preliminary setup for hypothesis tests must include the null (H_o) and alternative (H_a) hypotheses; also to be included is the test statistic, which in large sample hypothesis testing of means is a z-score, and the predetermined region of rejection, a sketch of the region of the standard unit normal curve that includes the z-score associated with the α-level.

The presence or absence of the calculated test statistic in the region of rejection will determine whether to accept (if the test statistic is in the acceptance region) or reject (if it is in the rejection region) the null hypothesis.

Acceptance and rejection each have connected with them a possible error, called Type I and Type II errors. Also discussed was the observed significance level or p-value of the calculated z-score.

Another topic of discussion in this chapter was sampling from two populations to find if the means of samples from the two populations were different, thus implying that the populations themselves were different. That is, instead of looking at the sampling distribution of the mean, $\bar{x}$, we graphed the sampling distribution of the differences of two means and the shape of the distribution, and formulas for its mean and standard deviation were derived. Hypothesis testing and confidence intervals for these differences were also covered.

The study of inferential statistics that we have begun in this chapter will continue throughout the remainder of the book.

Exercise 8.9: The E.P.A. has mandated that the mean miles per gallon required of all new cars by any manufacturer this year is thirty miles per gallon or more. The following figures are sample statistics in cars from two different automobile manufacturers, Companies C and F.

	C	F
Number Sampled	97	78
Mean M.P.G.	27.3	28.6
Standard Deviation	8.1	6.3

   a. Test C's cars to see if they meet the E.P.A. guidelines. Use $\alpha = .05$.
   b. Test F's cars to see if they meet the E.P.A. guidelines. Use $\alpha = .05$.
   c. Do F's cars have a higher mean m.p.g. than C's do? Test using $\alpha = .05$.

Answers:
a. $H_o: \mu = 30$
    $H_a: \mu < 30$

Test Statistic: $z = \dfrac{\overline{x}_C - \mu}{\sigma_{\overline{x}_C}}$

Region of Rejection: (See Figure 8.7)

$$z = \frac{(27.3 - 30)}{8.1/\sqrt{97}} = \frac{-2.7}{.822} \approx -3.28.$$

Since $-3.28 < -1.645$, reject H_o and conclude that Company C's mileages are below (do not meet) the E.P.A. guidelines.

b. H_o: $\mu = 30$

H_a: $\mu < 30$

Test Statistic: $z = \dfrac{\overline{x}_F - \mu}{\sigma_{\overline{x}_F}}$

Region of Rejection: (See Figure 8.7)

$$z = \frac{(28.6 - 30)}{6.3/\sqrt{78}} = \frac{-1.4}{.713} = -1.96.$$

Since $-1.96 < -1.645$, reject H_o and conclude that Company F's mileages are below (do not meet) the E.P.A. guidelines.

c. H_o: $\mu_C = \mu_F$

H_a: $\mu_C < \mu_F$

Test Statistic: $z = \dfrac{\overline{x}_C - \overline{x}_F}{\sigma(\overline{x}_C - \overline{x}_F)}$

Region of Rejection: (See Figure 8.7)

The numerator of the z-score is $27.3 - 28.6 = -1.3$. For the denominator, use the formula

$$\sigma_{(\overline{x}_c - \overline{x}_f)} = \sqrt{\frac{s_C^{\,2}}{n_C} + \frac{s_F^{\,2}}{n_F}} = \sqrt{\frac{8.1^2}{97} + \frac{6.3^2}{78}} = \sqrt{1.185} \approx 1.09.$$

$$z = \frac{-1.3}{1.09} = -1.19.$$

Since $-1.19 > -1.645$, accept H_o and conclude that there is no difference between the mean mileages of cars from Company C and Company F.

9

Binomial Proportion

M*any of the practical uses of statistics today involve polling a random sample of a large population and deciding how accurately the sample's responses reflect the responses of the entire population. For example, political polls before an election might say that the percentage of people who will vote for Candidate R is 45% with a margin of error of 3%. This result is based on "binomial population proportions."*

Recall from Chapter 6 that a binomial experiment consists of a large number of trials in which there are only two outcomes, success or failure. The polling problem is an example of a binomial experiment, in which success is defined as answering yes to the question, Will you vote for Candidate R next Tuesday? Suppose 453 out of 1000 people asked responded yes. In binomial trials, we would say that there were 453 successful outcomes. In this chapter, we discuss the proportion who answered yes or the number of successes, x, divided by the total number sampled, n. Therefore, the proportion of success in this sample of 1000 people is $\hat{P} = 453/1000 = .453$.

If $\hat{P} = .453$ is the proportion of success in the sample polled, what is the proportion of success in the entire population? That is, if everyone in the voting population were asked if they will vote for Candidate R next Tuesday, what proportion of the population would answer yes; what is the population proportion, p?

Recall that the symbol p was used to represent the probability of success in binomial experiments. Since the proportion of success and the probability of success are two ways of stating the same concept, the symbol p can also be used to represent the population proportion p.

The relationship of p to $\hat{P}$ (sample proportion) is the same as the relationship of μ to $\bar{x}$ or the relationship of σ to s. The first symbol in these pairs represents the "population parameter" and the second represents the "sample statistic."

BINOMIAL PROPORTION DISTRIBUTION

The binomial distribution, which was discussed in Chapter 6, can be approximated by a normal distribution for large numbers of trials. Its mean μ or expectation, $E(x) = np$; its variance $\sigma^2 = npq$, where p is the probability of success in any one trial, $q = 1 - p$, and n is the number of trials.

This binomial distribution can be shrunk by dividing each possible value of the binomial random number (possible number of successes) by the total number of trials. Instead of the whole number of successes x, we get the proportion of successes x/n. The normal approximation is still maintained, since the normal distribution is just smaller, with decimal or fractional values of the variable rather than whole numbers.

In this new binomial proportion distribution, the mean μ_p is not equal to np; it, too, is divided by n: $np/n = p$. Thus, the mean of the binomial proportion distribution $\mu_p = p$.

The variance of the binomial proportion distribution is equal to the variance of the binomial proportion npq divided by n: $npq/n = pq$. Thus, $\sigma_p^2 = pq$. The standard deviation of the binomial proportion distribution is the square root of the variance: $\sigma_p = \sqrt{pq}$.

Sampling Distribution of P

Toss a coin 100 times. Find $\hat{P}1$, the proportion of heads in those 100 tosses. Suppose $\hat{P}1 = .52$. Toss the coin another 100 times. Find $\hat{P}2$, the proportion of heads in that second 100 tosses. Suppose $\hat{P}2 = 49$. Repeat this experiment. It turns out that the sampling distribution of $\hat{P}$, the proportion of heads in 100 tosses of a coin, is approximately normal in shape, similar to the sampling distribution of the mean discussed in Chapters 7 and 8.

The mean of the sampling distribution of $\hat{P}$ is the same as the mean of the binomial proportion from which $\hat{P}$ comes. This mean $\mu_{\hat{p}} = p$ and $\hat{P}$ is an unbiased estimator of p. In the sampling distribution of the coin toss problem, $\mu_{\hat{p}} = p = .5$, the probability of one head in one trial.

The standard deviation of the sampling distribution of $\hat{P}$ is the same as the standard deviation of the binomial proportion divided by the square root of n. Therefore, $\sigma_{\hat{p}} = \dfrac{\sqrt{pq}}{\sqrt{n}} = \sqrt{\dfrac{pq}{n}}$. In the sampling distribution of the coin toss problem, the standard deviation is $\sigma_{\hat{p}} = \sqrt{\dfrac{.5(.5)}{100}} = \sqrt{.0025} = .05$.

We have developed a new sampling distribution: a sampling distribution of proportions, $\hat{P}$. Now we want to apply the Central Limit Theorem to this new kind of sampling distribution.

Central Limit Theorem for Proportions

$\hat{P}$, the proportion of success in a sample, has its own sampling distribution, illustrated in Figure 9.1.

The Central Limit Theorem can be applied to the sampling distribution of $\hat{P}$:

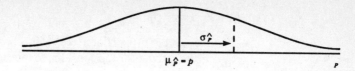

Figure 9.1:

Sampling Distributon of $\hat{P}$ (Proportion) $\mu_{\hat{p}} = p$, $\sigma_{\hat{p}} = \sqrt{\dfrac{pq}{n}}$

1. The mean of the sampling distribution of P is p; therefore, $\hat{P}$ is an unbiased estimator of the mean of the population proportion p.

2. The standard deviation of the sampling distribution of $\hat{P}$ is
$$\sigma_{\hat{p}} = \frac{\sigma_{\hat{p}}}{\sqrt{n}} = \sqrt{pq/n}.$$

3. For large samples, the sampling distribution of $\hat{P}$ is approximately normal. A sample is large enough if the interval $\hat{P} \pm 3\sigma_{\hat{p}}$ does not include 0 or 1.

This last condition is similar to the check for using the normal distribution to approximate the binomial distribution. Recall that in order to use this approximation, we must be certain that the three standard deviation interval around the mean does not go outside the range of possible numbers of successes, $(0, n)$.

For proportions, the range of $\hat{P}$, the sample proportion, and p, the population proportion, must be between 0 and 1, just as in probabilities. Therefore, $(0, 1)$ is the entire range of proportions.

In the sampling distribution of the proportions of heads in 100 coin tosses, recall that we have previously calculated $\mu_{\hat{p}} = \hat{P} = p = .5$ and $\sigma_{\hat{p}} = .05$. $\hat{P} \pm 3\sigma_{\hat{p}} = .5 \% 3(.5) = .5 \% (.15) = (.35, .65) \subset (0, 1)$. Therefore, the sample of 100 tosses of a coin is large enough to use the normal distribution to approximate the sampling distribution of $\hat{P}$.

Confidence Intervals

$\hat{P}$ is a proportion of a single sample, like .453 is the proportion of people who say they will vote for Candidate R. What is the real proportion of all the voters who would say they would vote for Candidate R? Since .453 represents only a sample of 1000, the best we can do to answer that question is to find a confidence interval around the .453 in which we are reasonably confident (95% or so) that the true population proportion will exist.

Calculating the confidence interval for the population proportion p is almost identical to calculating the confidence interval for the population mean. First, a proper confidence level, e.g. 95%, must be set. Subtract the confidence level, .95, from 1 to arrive at α.

The confidence interval is given by the formula

$$(a, b) = \hat{P} \pm z_{\alpha/2} \cdot \sigma_{\hat{P}} \quad \text{where:}$$

$\hat{P}$ is the sample proportion (like .453)

$z_{\alpha/2}$ is the z-score for the confidence interval (like $z_{.05/2} = z_{.025} = 1.96$),

and $\sigma_{\hat{P}}$ is the standard deviation of the sampling distribution of $\hat{P}$.

Recall from the Central Limit Theorem for Proportions that $\sigma_{\hat{P}} = \sqrt{pq/n}$. However, since $\hat{P}$ is an unbiased estimator of p and since $q = 1 - p$, we can replace p in the formula for standard deviation by $\hat{P}$ and q by $\hat{Q} = 1 - \hat{P}$. Then the working formula for the confidence interval for p is

$$(a, b) = \hat{P} \pm z_{\alpha 2} \cdot \sqrt{\hat{P}\hat{Q}/n}.$$

In the case previously cited, out of 1000 people sampled, 453 said they would vote for Candidate R. We can say with 95% confidence that the proportion p in the population who, if asked, would say they would vote for Candidate R is in the interval:

$$(a, b) = .453 \pm 1.96 \cdot \sqrt{(.453)(.547)/1000}$$

($\hat{P} = .453$ so $\hat{Q} = 1 - \hat{P} = 1 - .453 = .547$; $n = 1000$ since .453 was based on a sample of 1000 people.)

$$(a, b) = .453 \pm 1.96 (.0157) = .453 \pm .031 = (.422, .484)$$

Therefore, p is in the interval (.422, .484). The pollsters would report that the proportion of people who say that they will vote for Candidate R is .453 with a margin of error of .031. The *margin of error* is the bound of the interval.

The results of these polls are usually reported in percentages: the percentage of people who say that they will vote for Candidate R is 45.3% with a margin of error of 3.1%.

Exercise 9.1: A random sample of the records of 300 students at XYZ College determines that 213 of them have G.P.A.s greater than 2.5. Find a 90% confidence interval for the proportion of students at XYZ College who have G.P.A.s greater than 2.5.

Answer: The proportion of students in the sample who have G.P.A.s greater than 2.5 is $213/300 = .71$.

$$\hat{P} = .71, \hat{Q} = 1 - \hat{P} = .29$$
$$z_{\alpha/2} = z_{.10/2} = z_{.05} = 1.645 \text{ for a 90\% confidence interval.}$$

The confidence interval for the population proportion is given by the formula

$$(a, b) = \hat{P} \pm z_{\alpha/2} \cdot \sqrt{\hat{P}\hat{Q}/n}$$

$$= .71 \pm (1.645) \sqrt{(.71)(.29)/300}$$

$$= .71 \pm (1.645)(.026) = .71 \pm .043 = (.667, .753)$$

With 90% confidence, we can say that the proportion of students at XYZ College who have G.P.A.s greater than 2.5 is in the interval (.667, .753).

Hypothesis Testing of Proportions

Just as means of samples can be tested to see if they come from the population hypothesized in the null hypothesis, so proportions can also be tested. Suppose that Candidate R's party claims that he will receive 50% of the vote. Is this likely, in view of the value of $\hat{P} = .453$ that was obtained from the sample of 1000? To answer this question requires a hypothesis test.

The null hypothesis is the hypothesized value of p. In this case, since the party claims that 50% of the population will vote for R, $p = .50$. To distinguish this particular p (which the party claims is the population proportion) from the true p, the actual population proportion, we call it p_o, p-null. Therefore, the null hypothesis, H_o, is $p_o = .50$.

The alternative hypothesis is similar to the alternative hypothesis for hypothesis testing of the means. It can be directional or nondirectional, indicating an alternative to the null, either $p_o \neq .50$, $p_o > .50$, or $p_o < .50$. In this case, the party cares only about whether Candidate R has 50% or more of the voting population as supporters. The alternative they do not want to have to accept is that fewer than 50% support their candidate. Therefore, the alternative hypothesis is $p_o < .50$.

TEST STATISTIC FOR HYPOTHESIS TESTING OF PROPORTIONS

The test statistic for hypothesis testing of proportions is z; this time

$$z = \frac{\hat{P} - p_o}{\sigma_{p_o}}$$

The hypothesis test is always done under the assumption that the null hypothesis is true. Therefore, instead of finding the standard deviation of the sampling distribution of $\hat{P}$ (as we did in computing confidence intervals), in hypothesis testing we find the standard deviation of the sampling distribution of p_o, the null hypothesis proportion. Notice that the denominator of the test statistic, the standard deviation, is σ_{p_o}, not $\sigma_{\hat{P}}$.

Therefore, the denominator $\sigma_{p_o} = \sqrt{\dfrac{p_o q_o}{n}}$.

The rejection region is chosen before the experiment is conducted. In this case, let's use $\alpha = .05$. Notice that this is a one-tailed, directional (lower tail) test, so the rejection region comprises all $z < -1.645$.

H_o: $p_o = .50$

H_a: $p_o < .50$

Test Statistic: $z = \dfrac{\hat{P} - p_o}{\sqrt{p_o q_o / n}}$

Region of Rejection (Figure 9.2):

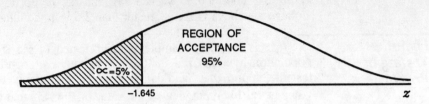

Figure 9.2:
Region of Rejection (Shaded)
$\alpha = .05$
One-tailed (Lower) Directional Hypothesis Test

$$dz = \frac{\hat{P} - p_0}{\sqrt{p_0 q_0 / n}} = \frac{.453 - .5}{\sqrt{(.5)(.5)/1000}} = \frac{-.047}{.0158}$$

so $z = -2.97$.

Since $-2.97 < -1.645$, reject H_0 and conclude that fewer than 50% of the population would say that they would vote for Candidate R.

Notice the wording: just because a person polled *says* he or she will or won't vote for a candidate doesn't mean that he or she will or won't do so. What kind of things must a pollster ask to make this survey more meaningful?

Exercise 9.2: The president of XYZ College claims that 75% of the students have G.P.A.s greater than 2.5. In a random sample of 300 students, it was determined that 71% have G.P.A.s greater than 2.5. Using $\alpha = .05$, test the president's hypothesis against the alternative hypothesis that 75% of the students at XYZ College do not have G.P.A.s greater than 2.5.

Answer: The null (president's) hypothesis is that the proportion of students with high G.P.A.s is .75. The alternative hypothesis is a nondirectional one, so it will be represented as not equal to .75 and the region of rejection will have two tails. Recall that hypothesis tests are set up before the statistic is gathered, so it may be that the statistician had no idea whether the proportion of students with G.P.A.s higher than 2.5 is more or less than .75 when he or she set up the experiment.

$H_0: p_0 = .75$
$H_a: p_0 \neq .75$

Test Statistic: $z = \dfrac{\hat{P} - p_0}{\sqrt{p_0 q_0 / n}}$

Region of Rejection (Figure 9.3):

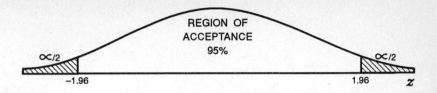

Figure 9.3:
Region of Rejection (Shaded)
$\alpha = .05, \alpha/2 = .025$
Two-tailed, Nondirectional Hypothesis Test

$$z = \frac{\hat{P} - p_0}{\sqrt{p_0 q_0 / n}} = \frac{.71 - .75}{\sqrt{(.75)(.25)/300}} = \frac{-.04}{.025} = -1.6$$

Therefore, $z = -1.6$. Since -1.6 is *not* in the rejection region (it is neither less than -1.96 nor greater than 1.96), do not reject the null hypothesis and conclude that the president's hypothesis is correct.

Determining Sample Size

Earlier we found it was useful to determine how large a sample should be drawn from a population so that the mean of the population would be included and the bound of the interval would be a manageable number. It is even more useful to do this with proportions; that is, it is important to determine how large a sample should be drawn from a population whose proportion is to be found within a certain bound. Recall that the confidence interval of a population is given by

$$(a, b) = \hat{P} \pm z_{\alpha/2} \cdot \sqrt{\frac{pq}{n}} = \hat{P} \pm B,$$

where B is the bound or the margin of error.

FORMULA FOR SAMPLE SIZE OF A PROPORTION

Given the formula for a confidence interval in terms of its bound,

$\hat{P} \pm z_{\alpha/2} \cdot \sqrt{\frac{pq}{n}} = \hat{P} \pm B$, subtract $\hat{P}$ from each side. This means that the formula for finding n is

$$\pm z_{\alpha/2} \cdot \sqrt{\frac{pq}{n}} = \pm B$$

As we did to derive the formula for sample size from the confidence interval of the mean, we can cross-multiply in the above formula:

$$\pm B \cdot \sqrt{n} = \pm z_{\alpha/2} \cdot \sqrt{pq}$$

Dividing by B on each side, and squaring both sides, the formula for determining the sample size needed to locate the mean in an interval whose bound and confidence level are predetermined is

$$n = \frac{(z_{\alpha/2})^2(pq)}{B^2}$$

It is possible that a value of $\hat{P}$ has been found in a previous sample. If so, this number can be used in place of p, since $\hat{P}$ is an unbiased estimator of p. If no previous sample has been drawn, a conservative estimate of $p = .5$ will ensure that a large enough number of random samples will be chosen.

Choosing $p = .5$ guarantees pq the highest possible value. If $p = .5$, $q = .5$ and $pq = .25$. (Suppose $p = .8$. Then $q = 1 - p = .2$ and $pq = .16$.) If pq is a maximum, then n will be the largest possible number, since $z_{\alpha/2}$ and B are the same for all possible choices of p.

Suppose the problem of predicting Candidate R's success is addressed by polling a number of people to ask if they will vote for him. A 95% confidence level with no more than two percentage points on either side of the sample success proportion is desired, whatever the success proportion turns out to be.

This means that the bound of the interval is .02, the width is .04, so the margin of error by taking the midpoint of the interval is 2%. If a previous poll had been conducted, the value of $\hat{P}$ could be used for this. To be conservative, making n the largest possible number for a given $z_{\alpha/2}$ and B, suppose we use p = .5 first.

Substituting in the formula for sample size of a proportion:

$n = (z_{\alpha/2})^2(pq)/B^2 = (1.96)^2(.5)(.5)/.02^2 = 3.8416(.25)/.0004$, so $n = 2401$.

Therefore, 2401 people must be polled to ensure (95%) that the confidence interval has a width of .04, a bound and a margin of error of .02. If the result had been over 2401, say 2401.1, it would have had to be rounded up to the next highest whole number.

Actually, this poll was conducted before, and $\hat{P} = .453$. Using this value as an unbiased estimator of p, $\hat{Q} = .547$ is an unbiased estimator of q. Again, substituting in the formula:

$n = (z_{\alpha/2})^2(pq)/B^2 = (1.96)^2(.453)(.547)/.02^2$

$= 3.8416 (.247791)/.0004 = 2379.8$, so $n \approx 2380$.

Notice that by using the conservative estimate of $p = .5$, twenty-one more people have to be polled to meet the demands of the sample.

Exercise 9.3: In Exercises 9.1 and 9.2, 300 students' G.P.A.s were sampled to determine the proportion of G.P.A.s at XYZ College that were above 2.5. In the sample of 300, there were 231 or a proportion of .71 who had these high G.P.A.s. How many students' G.P.A.s must be sampled to be sure that the width of the 90% confidence interval is .08 or less if:

a. $\hat{P} = .71$ is assumed;
b. $\hat{P} = .71$ is not assumed.

Answers: In both cases, $z_{\alpha/2} = 1.645$ and $B = .04$ (since the bound is half the width).

a. $\hat{P} = .71$, so $\hat{Q} = 1 - \hat{P} = .29$. Therefore, using $p = \hat{P}$ and $q = \hat{Q}$,

$$n = (z_{\alpha/2})^2(\hat{P}\,\hat{Q})/B^2$$

$$= (1.645)^2(.71)(.29)/.04^2$$

$$= .557/.0016 = 348.125 \approx 349.$$

Notice that since the width is narrower than the one found in Exercise 9.1 (.04 in this exercise vs. .043 in 9.1), the number sampled must be higher than the 300 originally sampled.

b. Since $\hat{P} = .71$ is not assumed, use $p = .5$

. $1 - p = q = .5$ also.

Then $n = (z_{\alpha/2})^2(pq)/B^2$

$$= (1.645)^2(.5)(.5)/.04^2$$

$$= .6765/.0016 = 422.8 \approx 423.$$

Notice that not assuming anything about $\hat{P}$ results in a larger sample number being required for the same bound and confidence level.

DIFFERENCES BETWEEN POPULATION PROPORTIONS

In addition to checking whether the sample proportion reflects the presumed population proportion, or whether statements can be made about the population proportion that will be upheld or negated by testing the sample proportion, statisticians are also interested in testing the difference between two population proportions to see whether that difference is zero. That is, are certain sample proportions drawn from different populations really the same proportion, thus showing that the two populations do not differ in the particular measure tested?

For example, suppose men and women are polled to see whether they intend to vote for candidate R in the same proportion. The results are summarized in Table 9.1.

Table 9.1

	Men	Women
Number	450	550
# Voting for R	225	228

The question is whether the proportion of men who say they intend to vote for R and the proportion of women who say they intend to vote for R are different.

Central Limit Theorem for Proportion Differences

As in finding the difference between population means, look at the sampling distribution of $(\hat{P}_M - \hat{P}_W)$. Recall that $\hat{P}$ is the sample proportion, so $\hat{P}_M$ represents the proportion of the sample of men who say they intend to vote for Candidate R, and $\hat{P}_W$ is the proportion of women who intend to do the same. These proportions are obtained by dividing the number voting for R by the total number polled: $\hat{P}_M = x_M/n_M$ and $\hat{P}_W = x_W/n_W$. For the above question concerning men and women's intentions to vote for R, $\hat{P}_M = 225/450 = .5$ and $\hat{P}_W = 228/550 = .415$.

The Central Limit Theorem can be applied to the sampling distribution of $(\hat{P}_M - \hat{P}_W)$ as shown in Figure 9.4.

1. For large sample sizes (recall the guideline for checking that $\hat{P} \pm 3 \cdot \sigma_{\hat{p}}$ does not include 0 or 1), the sampling distribution of $(\hat{P}_M - \hat{P}_W)$ is approximately normal.

2. The mean of the sampling distribution of $(\hat{P}_M - \hat{P}_W)$ is $(p_M - p_W)$. That is, $(\hat{P}_M - \hat{P}_W)$ is an unbiased estimator of $(p_M - p_W)$.

3. The standard deviation of the sampling distribution of $(\hat{P}_M - \hat{P}_W)$ is:

$$\sigma_{(\hat{P}_M - \hat{P}_W)} = \sqrt{\frac{p_M q_M}{n_M} + \frac{p_W q_W}{n_W}}$$

The populations from which the samples are drawn are independent binomial populations. In general, the subscripts 1 and 2 are used in place of M and W, which are specific to this problem.

Hypothesis Testing of Difference Between Proportions

The Central Limit Theorem as applied to the difference between population proportions will help test hypotheses concerning mean population proportions in two groups. For example, using the information about the numbers of men and women who say they intend to vote for R. (See Table 9.1.)

We ask whether the proportion of men and women is different. Use .05 as the level of significance. The null hypothesis is that these proportions are the same, and the alternative hypothesis is that they are different.

$H_o: p_M - p_W = 0$ or $p_M = p_W$

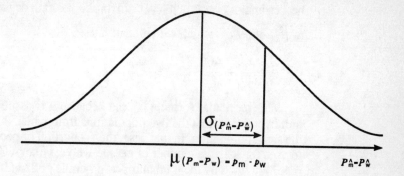

Figure 9.4:

Sampling Distribution of ($\hat{P}_M - \hat{P}_W$)

(Difference of Two Proportions)

$\mu(P\,\hat{}_M - P_W) = p_M - p_W$

$$\sigma_{(P_M - P_W)} = \sqrt{\frac{p_M\,q_M}{n_M} + \frac{p_W\,q_W}{n_W}}$$

Table 9.1

	Men	Women
Number	450	550
# Voting for R	225	228

$H_a: p_M - p_W \neq 0 \quad$ or $\quad p_M \neq p_W$

Test Statistic: $z = \dfrac{\hat{P}_M - \hat{P}_W}{\sigma_{(\hat{P}_M - \hat{P}_W)}}$

Region of Rejection: This is a two-tailed test (see Figure 9.3).

In order to find the test statistic, a good formula for the standard deviation, the denominator of the test statistic, $\sigma_{(\hat{P}_M - \hat{P}_W)}$, is needed. It turns out that the best estimator of $\sigma_{(\hat{P}_M - \hat{P}_W)}$ needed for the standard deviation involves an average of $\hat{P}_M$ and $\hat{P}_W$, which we will call just $\hat{P}$.

$$\hat{P} = \frac{x_M + x_W}{n_M + n_W}$$

This particular formula is used because it is assumed, in keeping with the null hypothesis, that the two populations from which the samples are drawn are the same population. In that case, the proportion of people who say they intend to vote for R is the number of people who say they will vote for R (225 + 228 = 453) divided by the total number of people polled (1000). This proportion is called $\hat{P}$. In the problem cited above, $\hat{P} = 453/1000 = .453$.

$\hat{Q}$, which is also part of the standard deviation formula for hypothesis testing, is calculated by $\hat{Q} = 1 - \hat{P}$. In the problem above, $\hat{Q} = 1 - .453 = .547$.

The standard deviation for hypothesis testing of a single proportion vs. an assumed population proportion is $\sigma \hat{P}_0 = \sqrt{\dfrac{p_0^{\wedge} q_0^{\wedge}}{n}}$. In the difference between two proportions problem, $\hat{P}\,\hat{Q}$ is divided by each of the sample proportion's numbers and added before the square root is taken. Thus, the standard deviation that will be used for the denominator of the test statistic for hypothesis testing is

$$\sigma_{(\hat{P}_M - \hat{P}_W)} = \sqrt{\hat{P}\hat{Q}\left(\frac{1}{n_M} + \frac{1}{n_W}\right)}$$

For the data in Table 9.1 above, the standard deviation is

$$\sigma_{(\hat{P}_M - \hat{P}_W)} = \sqrt{\hat{P}\hat{Q}\left(\frac{1}{n_M} + \frac{1}{n_W}\right)} = \sqrt{(.453)(.547)\left(\frac{1}{450} + \frac{1}{550}\right)}$$

$$= \sqrt{.2478(.0022 + .0018)} \approx .0315.$$

The numerator of the test statistic is $\hat{P}_M - \hat{P}_W$. We previously calculated $\hat{P}_M = .5$ and $\hat{P}_W = .415$. Thus, the numerator of this z-score is $.5 - .415 = .085$.

Therefore, $z = .085/.0315 = 2.70$. Since $2.70 > 1.96$, it is in the rejection region. Reject the null hypothesis and conclude that the proportion of men and women who say they will vote for Candidate R is different.

DIRECTIONAL (ONE-TAILED) HYPOTHESIS TEST

Notice that the previous hypothesis test was a nondirectional one. This test might be followed by a directional one with new data asking, for example, if the proportion of men who say they intend to vote for Candidate R is greater than the proportion of women who say they intend to vote for Candidate R.

This information might be valuable for Candidate R's platform and speaking engagements; i.e., he could target women's issues and groups during the rest of his campaign.

Exercise 9.4: At College XYZ, as first discussed in Exercise 9.1, 231 out of 300 students sampled had G.P.A.s higher than 2.5. At College JKL, 272 out of 400 students sampled had G.P.A.s higher than 2.5. Is the proportion of students with G.P.A.s higher than 2.5 greater at College XYZ than at College JKL? Test using $\alpha = .05$.

Answers: This is a one-tailed hypothesis test of the difference between proportions. The setup is as follows (notice the use of subscripts X and J to indicate College XYZ and College JKL):

$$H_o: p_X - p_J = 0 \quad \text{or} \quad p_X = p_J$$

$$H_a: p_X - p_J > 0 \quad \text{or} \quad p_X > p_J$$

$$\text{Test Statistic: } z = \frac{\hat{P}_X - \hat{P}_J}{\sigma_{(P_x - P_J)}}$$

Region of Rejection: This is a one-tailed test (Figure 9.5).

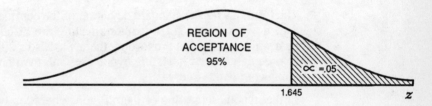

Figure 9.5:
Region of Rejection (Shaded)
$\alpha = .05$
One-tailed (Upper) Directional Hypothesis Test

For the data above, $\hat{P}_X = 231/300 = .77$; $\hat{P}_J = 272/400 = .68$; the numerator of the z-score is $\hat{P}_X - \hat{P}_J = .77 - .68 = .09$. The denominator, the standard deviation, is given by the formula

$$\sigma_{(\hat{P}_X - \hat{P}_J)} = \sqrt{\hat{P}\hat{Q}\left(\frac{1}{n_X} + \frac{1}{n_J}\right)}, \text{ where } \hat{P}\frac{231+272}{300+400} = .719$$

$$\hat{Q} = 1 - \hat{P} = 1 - .719 = .281.$$

Substituting above,

$$\sigma_{(\hat{P}_X - \hat{P}_J)} = \sqrt{(.719)(.281)\left(\frac{1}{300} + \frac{1}{400}\right)}$$

$$= \sqrt{(.202)(.0033 + .0025)} = .034.$$

$$z = .09/.034 = 2.65.$$

Since $2.65 > 1.645$, reject H_o and conclude that the proportion of students at XYZ College with G.P.A.s higher than 2.5 is greater than the proportion of students at JKL College with G.P.A.s higher than 2.5.

Confidence Interval for the Difference Between Proportions

In the previous chapter, we found the confidence interval for the difference between means. Recall that in this interval we would find the true difference between the means of the two different populations. Recall also that the presence or absence of 0 confirmed a hypothesis testing outcome. If the confidence interval contained 0, then a hypothesis test would result in accepting the null hypothesis that there is no difference between the population means for the two sets.

In order to say these same things about the difference between two population proportions, we will also find the confidence interval for the difference between population proportions.

The formulas for the standard deviation of the confidence interval and the standard deviation used for hypothesis testing are different. Recall that in testing a single population proportion, there was also a difference between the standard deviation used in testing hypotheses and the standard deviation used in finding confidence intervals.

In the hypothesis testing of the difference between two populations, it is assumed that the two populations are really the same. Therefore, a success proportion for the entire sample $\hat{P}$ is found by dividing the total number of successes by the total number sampled, disregarding the fact that they were originally in two separate samples.

When a confidence interval is computed, the populations that the samples are drawn from are presumed to be different. Therefore, the standard deviation of the difference between two populations for purposes of finding a confidence interval uses the individual proportions of the samples in its formula.

Again, use the information in Table 9.1 concerning the proportion of men and women who say they will be voting for Candidate R:

The confidence interval is given by a formula similar to the confidence interval for the difference between means. For proportions it is:

$$(a, b) = (\hat{P}_M - \hat{P}_W) \pm z_{\alpha/2} \cdot \sigma_{(\hat{P}_M - \hat{P}_W)}$$

For computing the standard deviation, however,

$$\sigma_{(\hat{P}_M - \hat{P}_W)} = \sqrt{\frac{\hat{P}_M \hat{Q}_M}{n_M} + \frac{\hat{P}_W \hat{Q}_W}{n_W}},$$

Table 9.1

	Men	Women
Number	450	550
# Voting for R	225	228

where $\hat{P}_M$ and $\hat{P}_W$ are the proportions of men and women in each sample; $\hat{Q}_M = 1 - \hat{P}_M$ and $\hat{Q}_W = 1 - \hat{P}_W$. $\hat{P}_M = 225/450 = .5$ so $\hat{Q}_M = 1 - .5 = .5$.

$\hat{P}_W = 228/550 = .415$, so $\hat{Q}_W = 1 - .415 = .585$.

$$\sigma_{(\hat{P}_M - \hat{P}_W)} = \sqrt{\frac{\hat{P}_M \hat{Q}_M}{n_M} + \frac{\hat{P}_W \hat{Q}_W}{n_W}} = \sqrt{\frac{(.5)(.5)}{450} + \frac{(.415)(.585)}{550}}$$

$$= \sqrt{.000997} = .0316.$$

Recall that this is the real standard deviation for the sampling distribution of the difference between binomial proportions, as shown in the Central Limit Theorem for Proportion Differences. The proportions in the Central Limit Theorem are considered from different populations; in hypothesis testing, the proportions are considered to be from the same population (H_o: $p_1 = p_2$), until proven otherwise. $\hat{P}_M$ is an unbiased estimator of p_M and $\hat{P}_W$ is an unbiased estimator of p_W.

Notice that the standard deviation in the hypothesis testing problem, which used a different standard deviation formula, was .0315.

CALCULATING THE CONFIDENCE INTERVAL FOR PROPORTION DIFFERENCES

Continuing the calculation for the confidence interval for the differences between the proportion of men and women favoring Candidate R, assume a 99% confidence interval is required. Then $\alpha = 1 - .99 = .01$;

$$z_{\alpha/2} = z_{.01/2} = z_{.005} = 2.58.$$

Substitute in the formula for confidence interval:

$$(a, b) = (\hat{P}_M - \hat{P}_W) \pm z_{\alpha/2} \cdot \sigma_{(\hat{P}_M - \hat{P}_W)}$$

$$(a, b) = (.5 - .415) \pm 2.58(\sigma_{(\hat{P}_M - \hat{P}_W)}), \text{ where}$$

$$\sigma_{(\hat{P}_M - \hat{P}_W)} = \sqrt{\frac{\hat{P}_M \hat{Q}_M}{n_M} + \frac{\hat{P}_W \hat{Q}_W}{n_W}} = .0316$$

The 99% confidence interval for this problem is $(a, b) = (.5 - .415) \pm 2.58$ $(.0316) = .085 \pm .082$, which yields the interval $(.003, .167)$.

It can be said with 99% confidence that the difference between the population proportions of men and women who say they intend to vote for Candidate R is in the interval (.003, .167). This means that the actual difference between the proportion of men and women who intend to vote for Candidate R is between .003 and .167. Notice that 0 is not in the interval, so a hypothesis test would (and did) lead to rejection of the null hypothesis.

Exercise 9.5:   At College XYZ, 231 out of 300 students sampled had G.P.A.s higher than 2.5. At College JKL, 272 out of 400 students sampled had G.P.A.s higher than 2.5.   Find a 95% confidence interval for the difference between the proportion of higher G.P.A.s at the two colleges.

Answer: The 95% confidence interval for the difference between the proportions is given by

$$(a, b) = (\hat{P}_X - \hat{P}_J) \pm z_{\alpha/2} \cdot \sigma_{(\hat{P}_X - \hat{P}_J)},$$

where $\sigma_{(\hat{P}_X - \hat{P}_J)} = \sqrt{\dfrac{\hat{P}_X \hat{Q}_X}{n_X} + \dfrac{\hat{P}_J \hat{Q}_J}{n_J}}$

$\hat{P}_X = 231/300 = .77$, so $\hat{Q}_X = 1 - .77 = .23$.

$\hat{P}_J = 272/400 = .68$, so $\hat{Q}_J = 1 - .68 = .32$.

$\hat{P}_X - \hat{P}_J = .77 - .68 = .09$. For a 95% confidence interval, $z_{\alpha/2} = 1.96$.

$$\sigma_{(\hat{P}_X - \hat{P}_J)} = \sqrt{\frac{\hat{P}_X \hat{Q}_X}{n_X} + \frac{\hat{P}_J \hat{Q}_J}{n_J}} = \sqrt{\frac{(.77)(.23)}{300} + \frac{(.68)(.32)}{400}}$$

$$= \sqrt{.001134} = .034.$$

The 95% confidence interval for the difference between the proportions is $(a, b) = .09 \pm 1.96 \,(.034) = .09 \pm .067 = (.023, .157)$.

We are 95% sure that the difference between population proportions between the students' high G.P.A.s (over 2.5) at the two colleges is in the interval (.023, .157).

Notice that 0 is not in the interval, which means that in a hypothesis test, the null hypothesis that the two proportions are equal would be rejected.

Also notice that the standard deviation as calculated from the individual $\hat{P}$ s and $\hat{Q}$ s (for the confidence interval) turns out to be identical to three decimal places to the standard deviation using the value of $\hat{P}$ under the assumption that the two populations sampled are the same (which was done for the hypothesis test).

*T*his chapter discussed proportions: hypothesis testing, confidence intervals, and sample sizes. These proportions are based on binomial data: yes or no, pro *or con, good or bad. A proportion distribution is like a binomial distribution divided by the number in the sample.*

Confidence intervals for the population proportion based on the sample proportion can now be found. Hypotheses asking whether a proportion is equal to a certain number can now be tested. Formulas were derived to find how large a sample is needed to be almost certain the population proportion is within a certain interval bound or width.

Another topic in this chapter was sampling from two populations to find if the proportions from these had a nonzero difference (a hypothesis test). Confidence intervals for these differences were also calculated.

The study of proportions is a very important application of large sampling statistics because these proportions or percentages are used in the polls we read about in newspapers and magazines.

Exercise 9.6: The President orders a poll conducted on the following question: Do you favor the current foreign policy? Two groups are polled, Republicans and Democrats. The results are summarized in Table 9.2.

Table 9.2

	Republicans	Democrats
Number Polled	400	500
Number Who Favor Policy	275	225

a. The President claims that 75% of Republicans favor his foreign policy. Does the data confirm this claim? Test using $\alpha = .05$.
b. The President claims that at least 50% of Democrats favor his foreign policy. Does the data confirm this claim? Test using $\alpha = .05$.
c. Is there a difference between the proportion of Republicans and the proportion of Democrats who favor the President's foreign policy? Test using $\alpha = .05$.

Answers:
a. 275 out of 400 Republicans polled favor the President's foreign policy.

$\hat{P} = 275/400 = .6875$; $\hat{Q} = 1 - \hat{P} = .3125$. The standard deviation,

$\sqrt{\hat{P}\hat{Q}/n} = \sqrt{(.6875)(.3125)/400} = .023$.

H_o: $p_o = .75$

H_a: $p_o \neq .75$

(There is nothing in the statement of the problem to indicate a one-tailed test.)

Test Statistic: $z = \dfrac{\hat{P} - p_0}{\sqrt{\hat{P}\hat{Q}/n}}$

Region of Rejection (see Figure 9.3).

$(z_{\alpha/2} = z_{.05/2} = z_{.025} = 1.96)$

Substitute in $z = \dfrac{\hat{P} - p_0}{\sqrt{\hat{P}\hat{Q}/n}} = \dfrac{.6875 - .75}{.023}$

$z = -.0625/.023 = -2.72.$

Since $-2.72 < -1.96$, reject H_0 and conclude that the proportion of Republicans who support the President's foreign policy is not .75.

b. 225 out of 500 Democrats polled favor the President's foreign policy.

$\hat{P} = 225/500 = .45; \hat{Q} = 1 - \hat{P} = .55.$ The standard deviation is

$\sqrt{\hat{P}\hat{Q}/n} = \sqrt{(.45)(.55)/500} = .035.$

H_0: $p_0 = .50$

H_a: $p_0 < .50$

(Since the null hypothesis is really $H_0: p_0 \geq .50$, the alternative hypothesis is that $p_0 < .50$.

Test Statistic: $z = \dfrac{\hat{P} - p_0}{\sqrt{\hat{P}\hat{Q}/n}}$

Region of Rejection (see Figure 9.2).

Substitute in $z = \dfrac{\hat{P} - p_0}{\hat{P}\hat{Q}/n} = \dfrac{.45 - .5}{.035}$

$z = .05/.035 = -1.43.$

Since $-1.43 > -1.645$, do not reject H_0 and conclude that the proportion of Democrats who support the President's foreign policy is .50 or more.

c. $\hat{P}_R = .6875$ and $\hat{P}_D = .45$. Therefore, $\hat{P}_R - \hat{P}_D = .6875 - .45 = .2375$. For the standard deviation, assuming the two samples come from the same population:

$$\hat{P} = \frac{275 + 225}{400 + 500} = \frac{500}{900} = .556.$$

The pooled $\hat{Q} = 1 - \hat{P} = 1 - .556 = .444$. Standard deviation is given by the formula:

$$\sigma_{(\hat{P}_R - \hat{P}_D)} = \sqrt{\hat{P}\hat{Q}\left(\frac{1}{n_R} + \frac{1}{n_D}\right)} = \sqrt{(.556)(.444)\left(\frac{1}{400} + \frac{1}{500}\right)}$$

$$= \sqrt{.001111} = .033$$

H_o: $p_R = p_D$

H_a: $p_R \neq p_D$

Test Statistic: $z = \dfrac{\hat{P}_R - \hat{P}_D}{\sigma_{\hat{P}_R - \hat{P}_D}}$

Region of Rejection (see Figure 9.3).

Substituting: $z = \dfrac{\hat{P}_R - \hat{P}_D}{\sigma_{\hat{P}_R - \hat{P}_D}} = \dfrac{.2375}{.033}$,

so $z = 7.20$. Since $7.20 > 1.96$, reject H_o and conclude that there is a difference between the proportion of Republicans and the proportion of Democrats who support the President's foreign policy.

10

Small Sample Inferential Statistics

*C*hapters 8 and 9 discussed hypothesis testing and confidence intervals for large sample distributions and for proportions, which are defined only for large samples. However, often the sampling procedure allows only small samples to be drawn. Can the same theory and statistics be applied if n = 5 instead of n = 40?

T-DISTRIBUTIONS

The Central Limit Theorem, which describes the mean, standard deviation, and shape of the sampling distribution, depends on large samples (samples where n ≥ 30). What can be said about the mean, standard deviation, and shape of the sampling distribution when small samples are used?

It turns out that if the samples are drawn from approximately normal populations, the mean of the sampling distribution is the same for the sampling distribution of the means of large samples; that is, the mean of the sampling distribution of means from small samples is the same as the mean of the population.

The shape of the sampling distribution of means is symmetric or bell-shaped. The standard deviation of the small sample distribution is not the same as the standard deviation of the large sample distribution.

The *t-statistic* has a sampling distribution quite similar to that of the *z*-statistic. The mean is 0 for both sampling distributions. The shape of both is symmetric, but the *t* is not shaped like the *z*—it is not approximately normal, but its shape differs according to the numbers in the samples. And finally, its standard deviation is also different from $s = 1$, the standard deviation of the z.

Refer to Figure 10.1. The dotted line represents the standard normal distribution (z) and the solid line represents a particular t-distribution.

Figure 10.1:
Dotted Curve —Standard Unit Normal (z) Solid Curve —Particular t-distribution

Multiple t-Distributions

Actually, there are many different t-distributions. As stated above, the mean of each t-distribution is 0. In addition, every t-curve resembles the normal distribution in that it is symmetric and bell-shaped, but each has "fatter" tails than the standard unit normal (the z). This is because the small samples vary more: they are further from the mean of the sampling distribution than are samples in large sample sampling distributions.

The smaller the number in the samples, the more variability occurs and the fatter the tails of the t-distribution. This variability is based directly on the number in the sample. As the number in each sample of the sampling distribution is increased, the tails get slimmer. For large samples, the t-distribution becomes normal.

Figure 10.2 shows three distributions: the dotted line is the normal, the solid line is a t-distribution with samples of size three, and the shaded is a t-distribution with samples of size ten. Notice how the tails differ.

Suppose one wishes to isolate 5% in the upper tail of these three distributions. From the previous chapters on large sample distributions, it is known that the z-score that leaves 5% of the curve in the tail of the standard unit normal is 1.645. This is noted on the diagram by the shaded tail of the normal.

However, the score of 1.645 on the other curves yields an area of more than 5% in their tails. It turns out that a score of 2.92 will leave 5% in the tail of a distribution of means, each of whose sample size is three. To yield a one-tail area of 5% in a sampling distribution of means, each of whose sample size is ten, a score of 1.833 is needed.

These numbers come from tables like the standard normal distribution table (z-scores) that we have been using for several chapters. The new tables, however, are called t-tables or t-score tables; there is a different t-table for each sample size distribution.

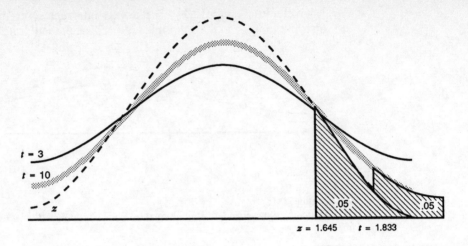

Figure 10.2:
z—Dotted Line, t (Samples of Size 10)—Shaded Line, t (Samples of Size 3)—Solid Line

DEGREES OF FREEDOM

The *t*-tables are not based directly on the sample size but on the number of *degrees of freedom* of the *t*-statistic. The number of degrees of freedom of a sampling distribution of sample means from samples of size *n* is simply $n - 1$. Thus, the number of degrees of freedom (abbreviated df) of a sampling distribution of size three is two, and of size ten is nine. These can be referred to as *t*-distributions with 2 df and 9 df, respectively. The number of degrees of freedom is sometimes symbolized using the Greek letter nu (η).

It is very rare that tables representing individual degrees of freedom (a table for 2 df, one for 3 df, etc.) appear in print. The table is usually a table of *critical values* of *t*; it appears in Appendix B and is partially reproduced below, along with a sketch of a general *t*-distribution (Figure 10.3).

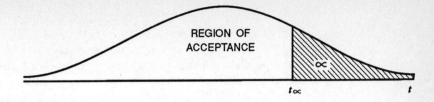

Figure 10.3:
Figure to Accompany Critical Values of t Table
Region of Rejection—Shaded

Notice that the body of this table gives the scores, called *t*-scores or *t*-values, which leave in the tail of the distribution the part of the *t*-distribution indicated in the top row.

Table 10.1 Critical Values of *t*

Degrees of Freedom	$t_{.100}$	$t_{.050}$	$t_{.025}$	$t_{.010}$	$t_{.005}$	df
.	.	.	.	.	.	
2	1.886	2.920	4.303	6.965	9.925	2
3	1.638	2.353	3.182	4.541	5.841	3
4	1.533	2.132	2.776	3.747	4.604	4
.	.	.	.	.	.	.
.	.	.	.	.	.	.
9	1.383	1.833	2.262	2.821	3.250	9
10	1.372	1.812	2.228	2.764	3.169	10
.	.	.	.	.	.	.
.	.	.	.	.	.	.
∞	1.282	1.645	1.960	2.326	2.576	∞

The first column indicates degrees of freedom, or one less than the size of the samples used in the distribution of the means. In a sense, then, this table is used in the opposite way from the standard unit normal (*z*-table). As a matter of fact, it is much easier to use. Once the α-level (part of the *t*-curve that is in the tail) has been established and the degrees of freedom determined, the *t*-score can just be read from the table.

Notice the last line in this table. If *n* is a very large number, here referred to as ∞ (infinity), the *t*-distribution becomes a normal distribution and the *t*-scores become *z*-scores. Do you recognize the numbers 1.645 and 1.96 as two common *z*-scores?

ALPHA VALUES IN THE *t*-TABLE

This table, Critical Values of *t*, was devised to avoid having to make a separate table (like the standard unit normal) for each different degree of freedom possible. As mentioned before, α-levels of 15% or 12% are rarely requested in statistical experiments, but those of 1%, 5%, 10% (and half of those for two-tailed tests of hypotheses and confidence intervals) are usually preset. The critical values in the tables are the alpha-levels that are usually required. If other levels are requested, the problem cannot be done as it could if another level of α in the standard unit normal table was desired.

Suppose you were asked to find the *t*-value that would leave 5% in the tail of a sampling distribution of size three. To use the above table, or the entire table in Appendix B, look up $t_{.05,2}$: find the *t*-value that leaves 5% in the tail of a distribution with 2 df.

In the table above, the first row consists of *t*-values with df = 2. The particular *t*-value requested is $t_{.05,2} = 2.920$. Similarly, $t_{.05,9} = 1.833$, which is the *t*-value for a sampling distribution of means with sample size 10 that leaves 5% in the tail.

Exercise 10.1: Using Table 10.1, or Appendix B, find the following:

  a. $t_{.01,4}$ b. $t_{.001,9}$ c. $z_{.005}$

Answers:

a. $t_{.01,4} = 3.747$ b. $t_{.001,9} = 4.297$ c. $z_{.005} = 2.576$

(The answer to c is found by using the last row, ∞, which gives the *t*-distribution for very large degrees of freedom—the *z*-score or standard unit normal. Notice that the value of $z_{.005}$ previously used was 2.58. This ∞ line gives a better estimate of $z_{.005}$.)

Setting Up the Hypothesis Test—Small Sample

Hypothesis testing using small samples is very similar to hypothesis testing using large samples. In both cases, the mean of the sample is being tested against the presumed population mean.

The setup is the same for the first two parts, H_o and H_a. The test statistic is different: it is *t* instead of *z*. The actual test statistic used is

$t = \dfrac{\bar{x} - \mu}{s/\sqrt{n}}$,   where $\bar{x}$ is the mean of the sample,

μ is the population (hypothesized) mean,

s is the standard deviation of the actual sample, and

n is the sample size

The region of rejection is now based on the *t*-score rather than the *z*-score. However, it is indicated in a similar way—one- or two-tailed.

Small Sample Hypothesis Testing

A previous exercise in Chapter 8 involved the G.P.A.s of students at XYZ College. It was claimed that the mean G.P.A. of students at the college is greater than 2.5. This hypothesis was tested against the null hypothesis that the mean G.P.A. is 2.5 (or less). Forty-two students' G.P.A.s were chosen at random for this problem. Now, suppose only ten students' G.P.A.s were chosen randomly for this test. The G.P.A.s are: 2.23, 2.03, 2.58, 3.02, 1.01, 3.57, 3.65, 3.33, 2.92, 1.98.

Test at .05 level of significance the hypothesis that the mean G.P.A. at XYZ College is higher than 2.5. Assume the G.P.A.s of all students are approximately normally distributed.

$H_o: \mu = 2.5$

$H_a: \mu > 2.5$

Test Statistic: $t = \dfrac{\bar{x} - \mu}{s/\sqrt{n}}$

Region of Rejection (Figure 10.4):

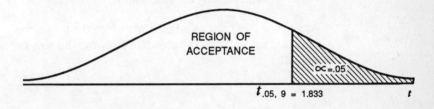

Figure 10.4:
Region of Rejection (Shaded)
$\alpha = .05$; df $= 9$

(Notice that with a sample of ten there are nine df.)

The first step is to calculate $\bar{x}$ and s from the raw data. To calculate $\bar{x}$, find $\Sigma x/n = 26.32/10 = 2.632$, so $\bar{x} = 2.632$. To calculate s using the short formula, find

$$\Sigma x^2 \text{ and } (\Sigma x)^2.$$

$\Sigma x^2 = 75.4938$, $(\Sigma x)^2/10 = 26.32^2/10 = 692.7424/10 \approx 69.2742.$

Then substitute in the formula for standard deviation

$$s = \sqrt{\dfrac{\Sigma x^2 - (\Sigma x)^2/n}{n-1}} = \sqrt{\dfrac{75.4938 - 69.2742}{9}}$$

$$s = \sqrt{6.2196/9} = \sqrt{.6911} = .8313$$

$$t = \frac{\bar{x} - \mu}{s/\sqrt{n}} = \frac{2.632 - 2.5}{.8313/\sqrt{10}} = \frac{.132}{.263} = .502.$$

Since $.502 < 1.833$, accept the null hypothesis and conclude that the mean G.P.A. at XYZ College is not more than 2.5.

Notice how large the denominator of the t-statistic is compared to the denominators of the z-statistics in Chapter 8. This large denominator results in a smaller t, which in turn results in fewer rejections of null hypotheses. Larger deviations from the hypothesized mean are expected using small samples.

Exercise 10.2: I.Q.s of students at JKL College are normally distributed with a mean of 112 and a standard deviation of 12. Professor P believes the I.Q.s of students in her statistics class do not have a mean I.Q. of 112. To prove this point, a random sample of five students from the statistics class is chosen and their I.Q.s are tested.

Their scores are 115, 124, 131, 129, 120. Test the hypothesis that the mean of these scores is the same as that of the population of students at JKL College vs. the alternative that they are not. Use $\alpha = .05$.

Answer: This is a two-tailed test since the professor has not stated in which direction she believes the scores differ from the mean of the population of JKL students.

$H_o: \mu = 112$

$H_a: \mu \neq 112$

Test Statistic: $t = \dfrac{\bar{x} - \mu}{s/\sqrt{n}}$

Region of Rejection (Figure 10.5):

Figure 10.5:
Region of Rejection (Shaded)
$df = 4$, $\alpha = .05$, $\alpha/2 = .025$

(Notice that the 5% alpha-level is divided into two tails with .025 of the area under the curve in each. Since $n = 5$, df $= 4$. $t_{.025,4} = 2.776$.)

VARIANCE AND STANDARD DEVIATION OF THE DISTRIBUTION

The standard deviation of the sampling distribution for the difference of the sample means comes from the individual standard deviations of the samples. The criteria for using the t-statistic for the difference of means of two populations include one we have discussed before: the populations must have approximately normal distributions. Also assumed is that the populations have equal variances and the samples from each population are drawn independently.

It is assumed that the population variances are equal. Therefore, the variance or standard deviation for the sampling distribution for the difference of the sample means should be an average of the individual variances or standard deviations. The formula for the variance of this distribution of differences is called a *pooled variance* and is given by the formula

$$s_p^2 = \frac{(n_B - 1)\, s_B^2 + (n_E - 1)\, s_E^2}{n_B + n_E - 2}$$

where n_B and n_E are the numbers in each sample and s_B^2 and s_E^2 are the variances of each sample.

The variances must be divided individually by the number in their samples, so the actual formula for the standard deviation of the distribution of the difference of two small sample means is

$$\sigma_{(\bar{x}_B - \bar{x}_E)} = \sqrt{s_p^2 \cdot \left(\frac{1}{n_B} + \frac{1}{n_E} \right)}$$

All of the above formulas have 1 and 2 in place of B and E for the subscripts, when presented in their general form.

Hypothesis Testing— Difference of Small Samples

Suppose the null hypothesis is that the I.Q. scores of business and English majors are the same, while the alternative hypothesis is that they differ. Six business majors and seven English majors are chosen at random, and their I.Q.s are tested. The results are:

Business majors: 112, 108, 131, 111, 115, 107
English majors: 114, 102, 119, 113, 110, 123, 103

Is there a difference in the I.Q.s of business and English majors at XYZ College? Test at $\alpha = .05$.

The null and alternative hypotheses are identical to the null and alternative hypotheses for large sample difference of means tests.

$H_o: \mu_B - \mu_E = 0$ or $\mu_B = \mu_E$

$H_a: \mu_B - \mu_E \neq 0$ or $\mu_B \neq \mu_E$

The test statistic is t: its numerator is the difference between the sample means and its denominator is the standard deviation of the sampling distribution of the difference between two sample means.

Test Statistic: $t = \dfrac{\bar{x}_B - \bar{x}_E}{\sigma_{(\bar{x}_B - \bar{x}_E)}}$

The region of rejection must take into account three factors: the α-level, whether it is a one- or two-tailed test, and the degrees of freedom. There are $6 + 7 - 2 = 11$ df. It is a two-tailed test, so $\alpha/2 = .05/2 = .025$. Thus, $t_{.025,11} = 2.201$, or -2.201 for the lower tail.

Region of Rejection (Figure 10.7):

REGION OF
ACCEPTANCE

.025

.025

$t_{.025,11} = -2.201$

$t_{.025,11} = 2.201$

Figure 10.7:
Region of Rejection (Shaded)
df = 11, $\alpha = .05$, $\alpha/2 = .025$

What we need to find now are the means $(\bar{x}_B, \bar{x}_E)$ and the variances (s_B^2, s_E^2) for the two samples. Recall the I.Q. scores:
Business majors: 112, 108, 131, 111, 115, 107
English majors: 114, 102, 119, 113, 110, 123, 103

For B, $\Sigma x = 684$, so $\bar{x} = 684/6 = 114$.

Calculating s^2, $\Sigma x = 684$, so $(\Sigma x)^2/n = 684^2/6 = 77976$.
Also, $\Sigma x^2 = 78364$.

$$s^2 = \frac{\Sigma x^2 - (\Sigma x)^2/n}{n-1} = \frac{78364 - 77976}{(6-1)} = \frac{388}{5} = 77.6$$

Therefore, $\bar{x}_B = 114$ and $s_B^2 = 77.6$.

For E, $\Sigma x = 784$, so $\bar{x} = 784 / 7 = 112$

Calculating s^2, $\Sigma x = 784$, so $(\Sigma x)^2/n = 784^2/7 = 87808$. Also, $\Sigma x^2 = 88168$

$$s^2 = \frac{\Sigma x^2 - (\Sigma x)^2/n}{n-1} = \frac{88168 - 87808}{(7-1)} = \frac{360}{6} = 60$$

Therefore, $\bar{x}_E = 112$ and $s_E^2 = 60$.

To find the pooled variance s_p^2, use the formula

$$s_p^2 = \frac{(n_B - 1) s_B^2 + (n_E - 1) s_E^2}{n_B + n_E - 2} = \frac{(6-1)\,77.6 + (7-1)\,60}{6+7-2}$$

$$= \frac{388 + 360}{11} = \frac{748}{11} = 68$$

so $s_p^2 = 68$.

To find the standard deviation $\sigma(\overline{x}_B - \overline{x}_E)$, use the formula

$$\sigma(\overline{x}_B - \overline{x}_E) = \sqrt{s_p^2 \cdot \left(\frac{1}{n_B} + \frac{1}{n_E} \right)} = \sqrt{68 \left[\frac{1}{6} + \frac{1}{7} \right]}$$

$$= \sqrt{68\,(.3095)} = \sqrt{21.046} = 4.59$$

$$t = \frac{\overline{x}_B - \overline{x}_E}{\sigma(\overline{x}_B - \overline{x}_E)} = \frac{114 - 112}{4.59} = .436$$

Since $t = .436$ is between the t-values for the regions of rejection -2.201 and 2.201, accept the null hypothesis and conclude that the I.Q. scores of business and English majors at XYZ College do not differ.

Exercise 10.5: Random samples of students' G.P.A.s are gathered from XYZ College and JKL College. Table 10.2 summarizes the statistics:

Table 10.2

	XYZ	JKL
Sample Size (*n*)	12	15
Sample Mean ($\overline{x}$)	2.83	2.21
Sample S. D. (*s*)	.728	.819

Test at the .05 level the hypothesis that the mean G.P.A. of students at XYZ College is higher than the mean G.P.A. of students at JKL College.

Answer:

$H_o\colon \mu_X - \mu_J = 0 \qquad$ or $\mu_X = \mu_J$

$H_a\colon \mu_X - \mu_J > 0 \qquad$ or $\mu_X > \mu_J$

Test Statistic: $t = \dfrac{\bar{x}_X - \bar{x}_J}{\sigma_{(\bar{x}_X - \bar{x}_J)}}$

Region of Rejection (this is a one-tailed test with $12 + 15 - 2 = 25$ df. $t_{.05,25} = 1.708$; see Figure 10.8).

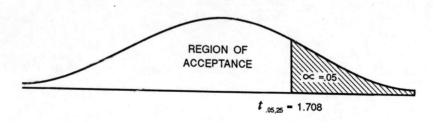

$t_{.05,25} = 1.708$

Figure 10.8:
Region of Rejection (Shaded)
df = 25, $\alpha = .05$

The numerator of the test statistic, the difference of the sample means, is $2.83 - 2.21 = .62$. The pooled variance, s_p^2, is

$$s_p^2 = \frac{(n_X - 1)s_X^2 + (n_J - 1)s_J^2}{n_X + n_J - 2} = \frac{11(.728)^2 + 14(.819)^2}{12 + 15 - 2}$$

$$= \frac{5.8298 + 9.3907}{25} \qquad s_p^2 = 15.2205/25 = .609$$

Therefore, $\sigma_{(\bar{x}_x - \bar{x}_J)} = \sqrt{s_p^2 \left(\dfrac{1}{n_x} + \dfrac{1}{n_J} \right)} = \sqrt{.609 \left(\dfrac{1}{12} + \dfrac{1}{15} \right)}$

$\sqrt{.609\,(.15)} = \sqrt{.09135} = .302$

$t = \dfrac{\bar{x}_X - \bar{x}_J}{\sigma_{(\bar{x}_X - \bar{x}_J)}} = \dfrac{.62}{.302} = 2.05$

Since $2.05 > 1.708$, reject H_o and conclude the mean G.P.A.s at XYZ are higher than those at JKL.

Small Sample Confidence Interval for the Difference of Means

A confidence interval for the difference between two population means given only small samples is found in exactly the same way as a confidence interval for the difference of population means given large samples. We find this confidence interval to place the difference between two population means in an interval with a high degree of certainty. This confidence interval also checks whether these population means might be the same: if the confidence interval contains 0, then a hypothesis test would show the population means are equal.

The formula used is

$$(a, b) = (\bar{x}_1 - \bar{x}_2) \pm t_{\alpha/2} \cdot \sqrt{s_p^2 \left(\frac{1}{n_1} + \frac{1}{n_2} \right)}$$

For example, take the data in the previous section comparing the I.Q.s of business majors and English majors. From the calculations performed in previous sections, the following is a summary table of statistics for this comparison:

Table 10.3

	Business Majors	English Majors
Sample Size (n)	6	7
Sample Variance ($\bar{x}$)	114	112
Sample Variance (s^2)	77.6	60

Find a 90% confidence interval for the difference between the population means.

The formula for finding the confidence interval is

$$(a, b) = (\bar{x}_B - \bar{x}_E) \pm t_{\alpha/2} \cdot \sqrt{s_p^2 \left(\frac{1}{n_B} + \frac{1}{n_E} \right)}$$

(Change the subscripts 1 and 2 to more meaningful ones, B and E.) A 90% confidence interval means an $\alpha = .10$, so $t_{\alpha/2} = t_{.05}$. The df $= n_1 + n_2 - 2 = 11$. $t_{.05,11} = 1.796$.

Recall that s_p^2, which we calculated before, is 68. As a matter of fact, we calculated the entire standard deviation earlier, but let's repeat this calculation by substituting into the formula above.

$$(a, b) = (114 - 112) \pm 1.796 \sqrt{68 \left(\frac{1}{6} + \frac{1}{7} \right)}$$

$$= 2 \pm 1.796 \left(\sqrt{68 \cdot .3095} \right) = 2 \pm 1.796 \left(\sqrt{21.046} \right)$$

$$= 2 \pm 1.796 \, (4.59) = 2 \pm 8.2 = (-6.2, 10.2).$$

Therefore, we are 90% certain that the difference of the mean I.Q.s in the two populations, business and English majors, is between –6.2 and 10.2. Notice that 0 is in the interval, so under a hypothesis testing situation, the null hypothesis would *not* be rejected.

Exercise 10.6: In Exercise 10.5, Table 10.2 compared the G.P.A.s of samples of students from XYZ College and JKL College. Find a 90% confidence interval for the difference of the mean G.P.A.s at the two colleges.

Table 10.2

	XYZ	JKL
Sample Size (n)	12	15
Sample Mean $(\bar{x})$	2.83	2.21
Sample S. D. (s)	.728	.819

Answer: The confidence interval for the difference of two population means, given the small samples above, is

$$(a, b) = (\bar{x}_X - \bar{x}_J) \pm t_{\alpha/2} \cdot \sqrt{s_p^2 \left(\frac{1}{n_X} + \frac{1}{n_J} \right)}$$

$$df = n_X + n_J - 2 = 12 + 15 - 2 = 25.$$

$$t_{\alpha/2} = t_{.10/2} = t_{.05,25} = 1.708.$$

s_p^2, the pooled variance, has already been calculated at .609 and the standard deviation at .302, both in Exercise 10.5. Substituting in the confidence interval formula,

$$(a, b) = (2.83 - 2.21) \pm 1.708(.302)$$
$$= .62 \pm .52 = (.10, 1.14).$$

With 90% confidence we can say that the difference between the mean G.P.A.s at the two colleges is between .10 and 1.14. Notice that 0 is not in the interval; therefore, a hypothesis test with the same data will result in rejection of the null hypothesis.

PAIRED DIFFERENCE T-TEST

Experimental Designs

There are two types of experiments that are the basis for most of the statistics gathering discussed here. *Observational experiments* are the type we have dealt with in this and the two previous chapters. In an observational experiment, a certain phenomenom is observed and noted; then a hypothesis test is performed to prove or disprove this phenomenon within a certain probability.

For example, two populations are examined, and a certain hypothesis is made about the relationship of their means. Samples, large or small, are chosen randomly and we conduct a hypothesis test to see if the sample means (or in the case of binomial populations, the sample proportions) prove or disprove the relationship of the population means (or proportions).

The second type of experiment is called a *designed experiment* . Subjects are chosen at random and in some way matched to each other. In the designed experiments we will discuss here, the subjects will be paired. The pairs can be matched on the basis of some shared characteristic (same I.Q., same weight, same G.P.A) or the paired subjects can be matched intrinsically (identical twins are used frequently in designed experiments). For the closest match of all, subjects can be paired by measures such as a before and after on the same subject (a subject is matched with himself).

After the subjects have been chosen and matched, one subject in each pair gets one treatment and the other one gets another treatment. A measure representing the result of the treatments is taken.

The measures taken after the treatment are then compared in a simple t-test, which is performed on the difference of the two measures, one for each matched pair member. This hypothesis test is called a *paired difference test* .

Hypothesis Testing for Paired Differences

Suppose a new but unconventional "all-you-can-eat" diet is invented. Each dieter can eat normally but takes a pill right before meals to negate some of the calories eaten. This diet is tested, under laboratory conditions, on six matched pairs. Test using $\alpha = .05$ the hypothesis that the pill takers lost more weight.

Assume that in each matched pair are two people of the same sex, age, height, and weight who eat the same food and the same quantity of food for one week. One person from each pair is taking the pill; the other one is not. These assignments were made at random. The results of this test appear below, where each number represents the weight loss for each member of the matched pair, N (for no pill) and P (for pill).

Table 10.4

Subject Pair	Weight Loss N	Weight Loss P
A	2	4
B	1	1
C	0	2
D	2	3
E	4	2
F	3	5

The hypothesis test we want to perform answers the following question: Is there a positive difference in the weight loss between those who are taking the pill and those who are not? That is, when the differences in all matched pairs in the population are taken and the mean of those differences computed, will that mean be positive or zero? Does the weight loss pill work (positive difference) or not (zero difference)?

The numbers to be used in the paired difference t-test are not the means of each of these columns, as in a test of the sampling distribution of the difference of means, but the single mean that represents the difference between each pair of measures.

To Table 10.4, add a column that represents the difference in the weights. Since it is expected that the difference $P-N$ will be positive, take this difference for the last column of the new table.

Table 10.5

Subject Pair	Weight Loss N	Weight Loss P	P – N
A	2	4	2
B	1	1	0
C	0	2	2
D	2	3	1
E	4	2	–2

Notice that for pair E, $2 - 4 = -2$.

The test statistic will be $\quad t_D = \dfrac{\bar{x}_D}{s_D / \sqrt{n_D}}$,

where $\bar{x}_D$ is the mean of the sample differences,

s_D is the standard deviation of the sample differences, and

n_D is the number of sample differences (pairs).

Now set up the hypothesis test, which resembles very closely an ordinary t-test:

$H_o: \mu_D = 0$ $\qquad\qquad$ (The population mean of the differences is 0.)

$t_{.05,5} = 2.015$

Figure 10.9:
Region of Rejection (Shaded)
df = 5, $\alpha = .05$

$H_a: \mu_D > 0$ 　　　　　　　　(The population mean of the differences is greater than 0: the mean is positive so the Ps are, in general, greater than the Ns.)

Test Statistic: $t_D = \dfrac{\bar{x}_D}{s_D / \sqrt{n_D}}$

Region of Rejection (Figure 10.9):

Notice that there are six numbers in the sample, which consists of the differences in weight loss. This is a one-tailed, directional t-test with $n_D - 1 = 6 - 1 = 5$ degrees of freedom; $\alpha = .05$ is in the upper tail. $t_{.05,5} = 2.015$.

The data needed are the mean and standard deviation of the set of six numbers representing weight loss differences: 2, 0, 2, 1, –2, 3. $\Sigma x = 6$ and $\Sigma x^2 = 22$.

$$\bar{x} = \Sigma x / n = 6/6 = 1; \ (\Sigma x)^2 / n = 6^2/6 = 6.$$

$$s_D = \sqrt{\frac{\Sigma x_2 - (\Sigma x)^2 / n}{n-1}} = \sqrt{\frac{22-6}{6-1}} = \sqrt{\frac{16}{5}} = \sqrt{3.2} = 1.79$$

$$t_D = \frac{\bar{x}_D}{s / \sqrt{n}} = \frac{1}{1.79 / \sqrt{5}} = 1.25$$

Since $1.25 < 2.015$, do not reject the null hypothesis and conclude that the mean of the weight loss differences is 0. (The weight loss pill does not work!)

Exercise 10.7:　　Eight pairs of five-year-old identical twins are assigned at random, each twin of a pair going into one of two groups learning to read using two different methods. The twins in Group S are taught by a standard method and those in Group N by a new method.

Table 10.6

Twin Pair	Score of Twin in Standard Method Reading Program (S)	Score of Twin in New Method Reading Program (N)
I	57	59
II	72	75
III	68	67
IV	64	70
V	49	51
VI	62	67
VII	54	62
VIII	71	71

After six months, the same test is given to all the twins. The results are compared with a paired difference hypothesis test. The results are tabulated below. Is there evidence to believe that there is a difference in the test results of the twins in the standard method group from those in the new method group? Test at .05.

Answer:

H_o: $\mu_D = 0$

H_a: $\mu_D \neq 0$

Test Statistic: $t_D = \dfrac{\bar{x}_D}{s/\sqrt{n}}$

Region of Rejection (see Figure 10.10).

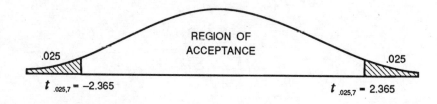

Figure 10.10:
Region of Rejection (Shaded)
df = 7, $\alpha = .05$, $\alpha/2 = .025$

This is a two-tailed test. Given eight pairs, df = 7; $\alpha = .05$. Therefore, $t_{.05/2,7} = t_{.025,7} = 2.365$.

The first task is to calculate the differences. We can do this either by S – N (standard minus new) or by N – S, since this is a nondirectional test. Normally, we would select N – S, since we might assume that the new system will have higher results. However, let's choose S – N to provide practice using negative numbers in the mean and standard deviation formulas. These S – N differences are –2, –3, 1, –6, –2, –5, –8, 0.

To find $\bar{x}$ and s, first find $\sum x = -25$ and $\sum x^2 = 143$.

$\bar{x} = \sum x/n = -25/8 = -3.125$.

$(\sum x)^2/n = (-25)^2/8 = 625/8 = 78.125$.

$$s = \sqrt{\frac{\Sigma x^2 - (\Sigma x)^2/n}{n-1}} = \sqrt{\frac{143 - 78.125}{8 - 1}} = \sqrt{\frac{64.875}{7}}$$
$$= \sqrt{9.27} = 3.04.$$

Substituting in the test statistic: $t = \dfrac{\overline{x}_D}{s/\sqrt{n}} = \dfrac{-3.125}{3.04/\sqrt{8}} = \dfrac{-3.125}{1.07} = -2.92$

Since $-2.92 < -2.365$ (the lower $t_{.025,7}$ value), reject H_o and conclude there is a difference in the two reading methods.

In this chapter we discussed sampling distributions of the means of small samples from approximately normally distributed populations. Hypothesis tests were performed and confidence intervals for the population means were found.

In connection with small sample hypothesis testing, a table of critical values of t, the test statistic for small samples, was introduced. Unlike the standard unit normal (z) table, the t-table is a compendium of thirty or more tables of t-values from sampling distributions whose sizes range from two on up to large samples. Only critical values, those values of α most often needed, appear in the usual t table.

Whereas the z-table has one parameter, α, the t-table has two parameters, α and df. Degrees of freedom (df) is a number one less than the number in each sample, i.e., df = n – 1. The t-table is easy to use; given df and α, the t-score can be read directly from the table.

In addition to hypothesis testing for single small samples, we can compare two small sample means to see if they belong to the same population: the difference between the means is tested against a zero difference to see if they are the same.

This chapter also provided an introduction to designed experiments, illustrated by the paired difference hypothesis test. Designed experiments will be discussed again in the next chapter, "Analysis of Variance."

Exercise 10.8: A large number of high school students take the Scholastic Aptitude Test more than once to raise their mathematics and/or English scores. Many of the students who are retaking the exam prepare by reviewing mathematics. Many prepare by taking a prep course; others form study groups to work practice problems.

A sample of seven students was chosen from those who took the prep course (C) and seven from those who formed study groups (S). After they retook the SAT, the increase of their scores in math (after minus before) was recorded as below:

C: 25, 14, –5, 37, 15, 4, 17

S: 18, –16, 31, 9, 12, 6, 23

[These numbers are determined in the following manner: suppose Student I in Sample C got 560 on the first try and 585 on the retake. The increase in the score, 585 (after) – 560 (before) = 25. Two of the students, one from each sample, did better in their first test: this accounts for the negative numbers, which represent decreases.]

Assume these increases (and decreases) are normally distributed and that the samples were randomly chosen.

a.   The people who teach the prep course claim an average increase in math scores of at least twenty-five points. Test this claim using the above sample C and $\alpha = .05$.

b.   The study group was hoping to increase their scores by at least twenty points. Test whether this hope was realized using the above sample S and $\alpha = .05$.

c.   Is there a difference between the mean increase in group C and group S? Test using $\alpha = .05$.

Answers:

a. H_o: $\mu = 25$ (this is really $\mu \geq 25$)
     H_a: $\mu < 25$

Test Statistic: $t = \dfrac{\bar{x} - \mu}{s/\sqrt{n}}$

Region of Rejection (Figure 10.11):

Figure 10.11:
Region of Rejection (Shaded)
df = 6, $\alpha = .05$

This is a one-tailed, lower (or left) tail test.
Since $n = 7$, $n - 1 = 6$, so $t_{.05,6} = 1.943$.

$\Sigma x = 107$; $(\Sigma x)^2/n = 107^2/7 \approx 1635.57$.

$\bar{x} = \Sigma x/n = 107/7 \approx 15.29$. $\Sigma x^2 = 2745$.

$$s = \sqrt{\dfrac{\Sigma x^2 - \Sigma(x)^2/n}{n-1}} = \sqrt{\dfrac{2745 - 1635.57}{6}} \approx \sqrt{184.9} \approx 13.60.$$

Substituting in the test statistic:

$$t = \frac{15.29 - 25}{13.6/\sqrt{7}} = \frac{-9.71}{5.14} = -1.89$$

Since $-1.89 > -1.943$, accept H_o and conclude that the claim of the prep course teachers is valid.

b. H_o: $\mu = 20$
    H_a: $\mu < 20$

Test Statistic: $t = \dfrac{\bar{x} - \mu}{s/\sqrt{n}}$

Region of Rejection (see Figure 10.11)

$\Sigma x = 83$; $(\Sigma x)^2/n = 83^2/7 \approx 984.14$.

$\bar{x} = \Sigma x/n = 83/7 \approx 11.86$. $\Sigma x^2 = 2331$.

$$s = \sqrt{\frac{\Sigma x^2 - (\Sigma x)^2/n}{n-1}} = \sqrt{\frac{2331 - 984.14}{6}} \approx \sqrt{224.48} = 14.98.$$

Substituting in the test statistic,

$$t = \frac{11.86 - 20}{14.98/\sqrt{7}} = \frac{-8.14}{5.66} = -1.44$$

Since $-1.44 > -1.943$, accept H_o and conclude that the hope of the study group participants is founded.

c. H_o: $\mu_C = \mu_S$
    H_a: $\mu_C \neq \mu_S$

Test Statistic: $\dfrac{\bar{x}_C - \bar{x}_S}{\sqrt{s_p^2\left(\dfrac{1}{n_C} + \dfrac{1}{n_S}\right)}}$

Region of Rejection (Figure 10.12):

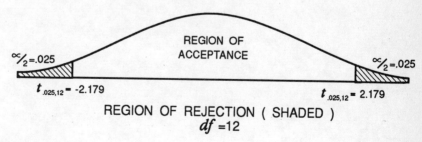

Figure 10.12:
Region of Rejection (Shaded)
df = 12

This is a two-tailed, nondirectional test.

The $df = n_C + n_S - 2 = 7 + 7 - 2 = 12$.

$t_{\alpha/2} = t_{.05/2} = t_{.025,12} = 2.179$.

The numerator of t is $15.29 - 11.86 = 3.43$.

For the denominator, first calculate $s_p{}^2$:

$$s_p{}^2 = \frac{(n_C - 1)s_C{}^2 + (n_S - 1)s_S{}^2}{n_C + n_S - 2} = \frac{6(184.9) + 6(224.48)}{12} = 204.69$$

The denominator then is $\sqrt{204.69\left(\dfrac{1}{6} + \dfrac{1}{6}\right)}$
$= \sqrt{68.23} = 8.26$.

Therefore, $t = 3.43 / 8.26 = .42$. Since .42 is between -2.179 and 2.179, accept the null hypothesis and conclude that the means of point increases in the math SAT are the same for students taking the prep course and those in study groups.

11

Analysis of Variance

In the previous three chapters, we discussed hypothesis testing of means and proportions. In all three chapters, we did the hypothesis tests by testing a sample mean against a presumed population mean or testing two sample means against each other to see if they came from the same population.

When more than two samples are drawn—when the discussion centers around whether three or more samples came from the same population—these techniques for hypothesis testing can no longer be used.

For example, suppose an experiment calls for randomly selecting a number of mice and teaching them to run through a maze. One sample or group of mice receives encouragement in the form of a piece of cheese after correct turns in the maze. Another group of mice receives a slight shock if they turn the wrong way in the maze, a discouragement. A third group does not receive any encouragement or discouragement at all: this is called the "control group." The question we ask is whether the mean time (to run the maze after the training period) of each "population group," treated in the same way that the sample was treated, is different.

One way to do this would be to take each mean and compare it with the other means in pairs. That is, suppose the groups are called C, D, and E for Control, Discouraged, and Encouraged. It would be possible to compare the mean of C with D, C with E, and D with E. But suppose there were five different samples with five different treatments. Then how many comparisons would be necessary? In how many ways can two groups from five be paired for comparison? The answer to this question comes from Chapter 5 (Probability), which turns out to be the combination $_5C_2 = 5!/3!2! = 10$. Therefore, ten comparisons (two at a time) or t-tests would be needed to see if any differences exist among the five treatments.

ANALYZING VARIANCE

Instead of comparing all the different pairs, at least at the outset of a designed experiment, statisticians analyze the variance of each of the different samples: the variance of the individual scores from the sample mean, and the variance of the sample means from the mean of all scores in the experiment.

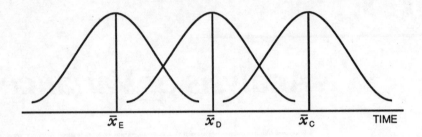

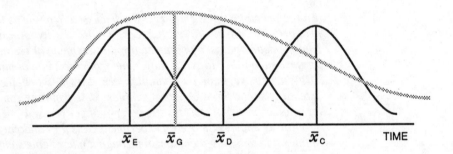

Figure 11.1a (top):
Probability Distributions –Time to Run Maze
(Large Sample Variances)
Figure 11.b:(bottom):
Probability Distributions With Overall (Grand) Mean $\bar{x}_G$

Refer to Figure 11.1a, which represents the probability distribution of time taken by each of the samples of mice that ran the maze. C is the control group, D the discouraged group, and E the encouraged group. The horizontal line represents the time it would take individual mice to run the maze. The means of each of the samples, x_C, x_D, and x_E, are indicated.

Even though these sample means are different, they could conceivably have come from a single population because the variance of each sample is very large. As a matter of fact, these three separate samples could have come from a single sample whose mean, called a grand mean and marked $\bar{x}_G$, is indicated in Figure 11.1b.

Figure 11.1b invites exploration of two types of variances: the sum of the variances of the sample means from the grand mean and the sum of the variances within the individual samples. If we take the ratio of the sum of the variances of each sample mean from the grand mean to the sum of the variances of individual scores from the mean of the sample the scores come from, we would find this ratio to be rather low since both variances are high.

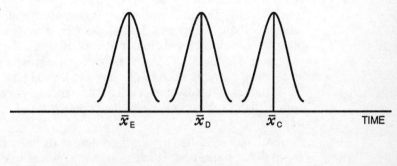

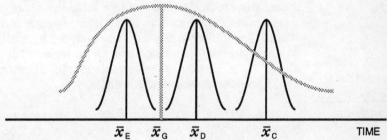

Figure 11.2a (top):
Probability Distribution –Time To Run Maze
(Small Sample Variances
Figure 11.2b (bottom):
Probability Distribution With Overall (Grand) Mean

Now refer to Figure 11.2a. In this scenario, the three sample means are the same as those in the previous figures. What is different? Because the individual sample variances are so small, it seems unlikely that these means came from the same population.

Furthermore, if we divide the sum of the sample variances from the grand mean by the sum of the individual variances, the ratio we get is high (Figure 11.2b). The variances of the observations from their sample means are small, while the variances of the sample means from the grand mean are large, as in Figure 11.2b.

These figures illustrate that we can compare means by examining the variances of the individual samples. This process is called *analysis of variance*, abbreviated ANOVA.

Experimental Design

Designed experiments were first mentioned in the last chapter when we introduced paired *t*-tests. Most analysis of variance experiments follow a design. In such experiments, a random sample of a population is chosen and placed into various treatment groups.

For example, thirty-two mice are randomly selected and divided into three groups, C, D, and E. The groups into which the subjects are divided must also be randomly assigned. One way to do this, for example, is to toss a die for each mouse. If the die lands with a 1 or 2 face up, the mouse goes into treatment group C; if the die shows 3 or 4, the mouse goes into treatment group D; otherwise, the mouse goes into treatment group E. Continuing in this manner, each mouse is placed in a treatment group; the groups should be fairly equal in size: perhaps twelve mice in C, eleven in D, and nine in E. Random number tables (tables of numbers whose digits are randomly generated) can also be used both to choose the sample from the population and to divide the sample into treatment groups.

Each mouse is then trained according to its treatment regime. The control group is not trained but is left to its own devices to explore and conquer the maze. After each group has had the same amount of practice, or training, each mouse runs the maze one last time, and the number of minutes each mouse takes is recorded. These times are then analyzed by treatment group, using techniques of analysis of variance, to see if the means of the times of the three groups are the same. If they are not statistically the same, further techniques can be used to determine which means differ.

Kinds of Variance

The total variance found in this experiment is divided into two kinds: between and within. *Between* variance is the variance between the grand mean (the mean of all three samples treated as a single sample) and each of the treatment means. *Within* variance is the variance within each separate treatment group: i.e., it is the variance between the actual results for each subject (time for each mouse) and the mean of the treatment group the mouse is in.

Between and within variances are averaged by dividing each by the degrees of freedom (one less than the number) in each group. This results in new numbers called *mean variances*. The test statistic used for analyzing the variance is the ratio of the mean between variance to the mean within variance. This ratio is called the *F* statistic (*F*-tables will be discussed later).

ANOVA Tables

Analysis of variance requires a lot of computation, which is best summarized in an analysis of variance table. The contents of the analysis of variance tables depend in part upon the type of problem. The mice running the maze example is called a *completely randomized design* because the mice were divided at random into their three treatment groups.

An analysis of variance randomized design experiment can be summarized in an ANOVA table similar to Table 11.1 for the mice problem. The numbers in the table were invented for purposes of illustration.

Table 11.1

Source	df	Sums of Squares	Mean Squares	F
Treatment (Between)	2 ($k-1$)	5428 (SST)	2714 MST = SST/df	6.21 F = MST/MSE
Error (Within)	29 ($n-k$)	12673 (SSE)	437 MSE = SSE/df	
Total (B +W)	31 ($n-1$)	18101 (SS)		

The degrees of freedom are found as follows. The degrees of freedom of the treatment component (between) is the number of treatments k less 1, or $k-1$ df for treatment. In this case, there were three different treatments (C, D, and E), so $3-1 = 2$ df for treatment.

The degrees of freedom for the total is one less than the number of subjects. Since there are thirty-two mice, df (total) = $n-1 = 32-1 = 31$. To find df (error) (within variance), subtract df (treatment) from df (total). Therefore, $(n-1) - (k-1) = n-k$, which in the case of the mice is given by $32-3 = 29$ or $31-2 = 29$.

The sum of squares for the three kinds of variances, treatment (SST), error (SSE), and total (SS), can be computed in a number of ways that we will discuss later. Usually, SST and SS are calculated, then SSE is found by subtracting SST from SS. Therefore, SSE = SS − SST. This is the only use of the last line in the table, total variance, as a vehicle for finding SSE and df error.

The means squares are calculated by dividing the sum of squares by the degrees of freedom for both treatment and error. Therefore, MST (mean square treatment) = SST/df(T) and MSE (mean square error) = SSE/df(E). Notice it is not necessary to find the mean square for the total sum of squares.

Finally, F, the ratio of MST to MSE (MST/MSE), is calculated and placed in the last column. This is the only number that goes in the last column of an analysis of variance table for a completely randomized design. If this F is large enough (as will be explained below), it will be possible to say that at least two of the means μ_C, μ_D, or μ_E differ. If F is not large enough, it will not be possible to conclude this difference: instead the null hypothesis (that the means of C, D, and E do not differ) will be accepted.

F-Distribution

In order to decide whether F is large enough to reject H_o, we must use the F-distribution and must set up a region of rejection like those in the z- and t-tables. The F-statistic is like the t-statistic in many ways: there are different Fs for different degrees of freedom and for different levels. But there are even more F-distributions than there are t-distributions.

Figure 11.3 is a sketch of an F-distribution. Table 11.2 is a reproduction of a part of the F-distribution table for $\alpha = .05$ (the complete table is found in Appendix C).

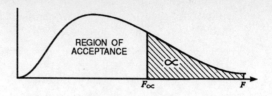

Figure 11.3:
An F -Distribution Curve Region of Rejection (Shaded)

The F-distributions in Table 11.2 represent a ratio of variances, $F = s_1^2/s_2^2$. Each variance in the fraction has a certain number of degrees of freedom associated with it. These different degrees of freedom represent the outward bound of acceptability for the variances being equal: 90% ($\alpha = .10$), 95% ($\alpha = .05$), 99% ($\alpha = .01$). There are many F-distributions for each level, and each F-table has many entries because the degrees of freedom for both the numerator and denominator must be considered.

Table 11.2 F–Distribution for $\alpha = .05$

df for denominator	df for numerator 1	2	3	4	5...
.	.	.	.	.	.
.	.	.	.	.	.
.	.	.	.	.	.
4	7.71	6.94	6.59	6.39	6.26
5	6.61	5.79	5.41	5.19	5.05
6	5.99	5.14	4.76	4.53	5.39
.	.	.	.	.	.
.	.	.	.	.	.
.	.	.	.	.	.
29	4.18	3.33	2.93	2.70	2.55
30	4.17	3.32	2.92	2.69	2.53
40	4.08	3.23	2.84	2.61	2.45
.	.	.	.	.	.
.					

For this book, only one F-table will be presented: the F-table for 95% confidence that the ratio of variances equals one: $s_1^2/s_2^2 = 1$ or, cross multiplying, $s_1^2 = s_2^2$. This is called the F-distribution where $\alpha = .05$.

Notice the shape of the F-distribution. Its actual shape depends on the degrees of freedom of the numerator and denominator, but it is skewed to the right, and since variances are always positive, this curve will exist only for positive values. Only the single right-hand tail, which represents ratios greater than or equal to 1 (≥ 1), is considered for hypothesis testing.

Each F-distribution has three parameters associated with it: α, the number of degrees of freedom in the numerator (v_1), and the number of degrees of freedom in the denominator (v_2). For example, in Table 11.2, $F_{.05,(2,5)}$ is the F-value for $\alpha = .05$, with 2 df for the numerator and 5 df for the denominator. $F_{.05,(2,5)} = 5.79$.

HYPOTHESIS TESTING—ANOVA

Going back to the mouse problem: thirty-two mice are randomly selected and placed into one of three groups, C, D, or E, to receive training (or no training) to run a maze. After a certain number of trials, each mouse runs the maze, and the time for each mouse to complete the maze is recorded. Is there a difference between the mean times of mice from each treatment group? Test using $\alpha = .05$.

The first step in any analysis of variance problem is to fill out an ANOVA table. In the next section, the computational formulas will be introduced, but often the table is presented, either filled out or partially filled out. Computer software can be used to fill in the ANOVA table and, in some cases, actually answer the question as to whether and which means differ. In this case, the ANOVA table has been completed and is again reproduced as Table 11.1.

Table 11.1

Source	df	Sums of Squares	Mean Squares	F
Treatment	2	5428	2714	6.21
(Between)	$(k-1)$	(SST)	MST = SST/df	F = MST/MSE
Error	29	12673	437	
(Within)	$(n-k)$	(SSE)	MSE = SSE/df	
Total	31	18101		
(B + W)	$(n-1)$	(SS)		

The next step is to set up the hypothesis test. It follows the same form as our previous hypothesis tests. The descriptions in brackets are not part of the hypothesis test.

H_0: $\mu_C = \mu_D = \mu_E$ [The population means of the three treatment groups are the same.]

H_a: At least two μ_is are different [This is easier than trying to set up all possible pairs of differences, particularly if there are more than three means to compare.]

Test Statistic: F = MST/MSE [This statistic is the ratio of the mean square treatment to the mean square error in the ANOVA table.]

Region of Rejection (Figure 11.4):

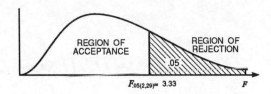

Figure 11.4:
df (Numerator — Treatment) = 2
df (Denominator — Error) = 29

[From the F-table above or Appendix C we find the value of F that separates the acceptance and rejection areas. This value is $F_{.05,(2,29)} = 3.33$, as noted on Figure 11.4. The degrees of freedom of the numerator are equal to the df of MST (2) and the degrees of freedom of the denominator are equal to the df of MSE (29).]

Since the calculated F for this particular problem, according to the ANOVA table, is 6.21 and the region of rejection, according to the F-table, starts at 3.33, reject the null hypothesis. One would write: Since $6.21 > 3.33$, reject H_0 and conclude that there is a difference between the means of C, D, and E — there is evidence to suggest that the times the mice took to run the maze may vary according to the type of training they received.

One big question that remains to be answered is: which times are significantly different? Does the time of the control group differ from both of the other (trained) groups, and do they differ from each other? Answers to questions like these will be discussed later in this chapter.

Exercise 11.1: Twenty-five college freshmen are chosen from all the entering freshmen and randomly assigned to four freshman English classes, those of Professors Q, R, S, and T. At the end of the semester, the same objective exam is given to all students who have taken freshman English. The grades of these twenty-five students are separated, and the variances are calculated and put into the ANOVA table below. Complete it and test the hypothesis that the means of the grades differ by professor. Use $\alpha = .05$.

Table 11.3

Source	df	Sums of Squares	Mean Squares	F
Treatment		1558		
Error				
Total		4851		

Answers: First, the ANOVA table must be completed. There are four treatment groups (each professor's class, Q, R, S, T), so df (treatment) is $k - 1 = 4 - 1 = 3$. There are twenty-five subjects, so df (total) = $n - 1 = 25 - 1 = 24$. Now subtract to get df (error) = $24 - 3 = 21$.

Similarly, SSE (sum of squares error) can be found by subtracting SS $-$ SST = $4851 - 1558 = 3293$.

To find the mean squares, divide the sum of squares by the degrees of freedom: MST = SST/dfT = $1558/3 = 519$. MSE = $3293/21 = 157$.

Finally, F = MST/MSE = $519/157 = 3.31$.

The completed ANOVA table is as follows:

Table 11.3a

Source	df	Sums of Squares	Mean Squares	F
Treatment	3	1558	519	3.31
Error	21	3293	157	
Total	24	4851		

Now the hypothesis test:

H_o: $\mu_Q = \mu_R = \mu_S = \mu_T$

H_a: At least two means (μ_is) differ.

Test Statistic: $F = $ MST/MSE

Region of Rejection (see Figure 11.5).

$F_{.05,(3,21)} = 3.07$, using the F-table in Appendix C.

Since the calculated F, 3.31, is greater than the tabulated F, 3.07, reject H_o and conclude that at least two means differ.

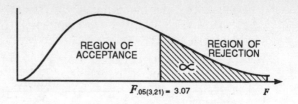

Figure 11.5:
df (Treatment) = 3
df (Error) = 21

Calculating Sums of Squares

The next point we consider is how to calculate the sums of squares necessary to fill out an ANOVA table.

Given the problem, it is fairly simple to fill out the first column (degrees of freedom), which is based only upon the number of treatments and the number of subjects. Given the second column (sums of squares) it is easy to find the two important entries in the third column (mean square treatment and mean square error) by dividing the sums of squares by their degrees of freedom. The only number in the last column, the F-ratio, is calculated by dividing mean square treatment by mean square error. Thus, if the sum of squares column can be filled in from the data, the ANOVA table can be completed.

Referring back to Exercise 11.1, the data from which the partially completed ANOVA table came is found in Table 11.4. Recall that these are the grades of the twenty-five randomly chosen and assigned freshmen on a uniform final. Each treatment group is named for the English professor in whose class the subject was assigned. The raw data, with column totals added, appears in Table 11.4.

Table 11.4

	Professor			
	Q	R	S	T
	74	95	58	72
	69	89	63	83
Grades on Uniform Final	83	76	85	69
	91	85	72	87
	77	79	48	76
	59	92	56	
	38		75	
Totals	491	516	457	387

Recall that the sum of squares treatment is also called the *sum of squares between*. To arrive at this number by the direct method, the grand mean should be calculated along with each sample mean. Then the differences between the grand mean and each sample mean are found, squared, and totaled.

Further, the sum of squares error is defined as the *sum of squares within*. Thus, each score must be subtracted from the mean of its sample, squared, and then totaled. The totals for each sample must also be added.

There are shortcuts for finding SST and SSE. They too require a lot of computation, but not as much as the scenarios outlined above. Start by calculating the *correction to the mean*, CM. This number will be subtracted from the shortcuts to arrive at the necessary sums of squares. CM is given by

$$CM = \frac{(\sum x)^2}{n}$$

Often, the treatment groups' scores have already been totaled; these totals can be called T_Q, T_R, T_S, and T_T. Then these can be added and squared, making the formula for the correction to the mean:

$$CM = \frac{(T_Q + T_R + T_S + T_T)^2}{n}$$

The CM for the problem with the freshman English finals above is CM = $(491 + 516 + 457 + 387)^2 \div 25 = 1851^2/25 = 3426201/25 = 137048$.

The correction to the mean is thus 137,048.

To fill in the last row (total) in the sums of squares column, find SS; its formula is:

$$SS = (\sum x^2) - CM$$

[Each individual score is squared, the squares are all added, and CM is subtracted from that total.]

For the above problem:

$SS = (74^2 + 69^2 + 83^2 + 91^2 + 77^2 + 59^2 + 38^2 + 95^2 + 89^2 + 76^2 + 85^2 +$
$79^2 + 92^2 + 58^2 + 63^2 + 85^2 + 72^2 + 48^2 + 56^2 + 75^2 + 72^2 + 83^2 + 69^2$
$+ 87^2 + 76^2) - 137,048 = 141,899 - 137,048 = 4,851$, so SS = 4,851.

Notice that this number matches exactly the SS entry in ANOVA Table 11.3.

To fill in the first row (treatment) in the sums of squares column, find SST; its formula is

$$SST = \frac{T_Q{}^2}{n_Q} + \frac{T_R{}^2}{n_R} + \frac{T_S{}^2}{n_S} + \frac{T_T{}^2}{n_T} - CM$$

[The total score for each sample T_i is squared and then divided by the number in the sample. These are added and CM is subtracted from their total.]

For the above problem:

$$SST = \frac{491^2}{7} + \frac{516^2}{6} + \frac{457^2}{7} + \frac{387^2}{5} - 137,048$$

$$SST = 34,440 + 44,376 + 29,836 + 29,954 - 137,048$$
$$= 138,606 - 137,048 = 1,558.$$

Notice that this number matches the SST entry in Table 11.3.

To find SSE, use the formula SSE = SS – SST. For the above problem, SSE = 4851 – 1558 = 3293, the entry we found the same way in Table 11.3 for SSE.

Since all the entries in the sum of squares column are sums of squares, they must be positive. If you arrive at negative answers for any of these entries, or any entries in the ANOVA table, you have made an error: go back and check your computations.

Exercise 11.2: Thirty men who were 25 lbs overweight were chosen randomly from a large group of overweight men and then were assigned at random to four groups:

Men in Group C, the control group, ate as they had before and did not increase their amount of exercise.

Men in Group D were put on a low-calorie diet, but did not increase their exercise level.

Men in Group E ate as they had before but were put on an increased exercise regime.

Men in Group F were given a modified fasting diet. They did not increase their exercise level.

After two months in treatment, the men were weighed and their weight loss (–) or gain (+) recorded as indicated in Table 11.5.
Test at .05 significance level to see if there is a difference among the weight loss means in the four groups.

Answers:
This is a hypothesis test. We must do two things: complete an ANOVA table and run the hypothesis test. First, fill out the ANOVA table (although we could set up the hypothesis test first instead).
The first column (degrees of freedom) can be filled in now. The number of degrees of freedom for treatment is $k - 1 = 4 - 1 = 3$ since there are four treatment groups.
df (total) = $n - 1 = 30 - 1 = 29$ since there are thirty total subjects.
df (error) = df (total) – df (treatment) = 29 – 3 = 26.

Table 11.5

	C	D	E	F
	0	−10	−4	−18
	−3	−15	+2	−20
	+2	−6	−7	−12
	−5	−9	+1	−22
	+1	−3	−3	−15
	0	−12	−5	−9
	+2	−5	0	
	−4		+3	
			−8	

Calculating CM:

Once the sums of squares (second column) have been found, the rest of the ANOVA table can be completed. Recall that the first number to calculate is CM, the correction to the mean. Calculate the total number of pounds lost (or gained and lost) in each treatment group. The calculated treatment sums are:

$T_C = -7$; $T_D = -60$;
$T_E = -21$; $T_F = -96$
Therefore, $CM = (T_C + T_D + T_E + T_F)^2/n$
$$= (-7 + -60 + -21 + -96)^2/30$$
$$= (-184)^2/30 = 33,856/30 = 1,128.5$$

Calculating SS:

The sums of squares for each column (i.e., column C sums of squares would be $0^2 + (-3)^2 + 2^2 + (-5)^2 + 1^2 + 0^2 + 2^2 + (-4)^2 = 59$) are:
The sum of the squares of numbers in C is 59;
the sum of the squares of numbers in D is 620;
the sum of the squares of numbers in E is 177;
the sum of the squares of numbers in F is 1,658.

Σx^2, the total of the above numbers, is 2,514.

$SS = \Sigma x^2 - CM = 2,514 - 1,128.5 = 1,385.5$.

Calculating SST:

For SST, go back to the individual column sums above, square each, divide each by the number in its group, add the quotients, and subtract CM.

$$SST = \frac{(-7)^2}{8} + \frac{(-60)^2}{7} + \frac{(-21)^2}{9} + \frac{(-96)^2}{6} - 1,128.5$$

SST $= 6.1 + 514.3 + 49 + 1536 - 1,128.5 = 976.9$
Since SS $= 1385.5$ and SST $= 976.9$,
SSE $=$ SS $-$ SST $= 1,385.5 - 976.9 = 408.6$.

MST $=$ SST/dfT $= 976.9/3 = 325.6$.
MSE $=$ SSE/dfE $= 408.6/26 = 15.7$.
F $=$ MST/MSE $= 325.6/15.7 = 20.74$.

Now the ANOVA table can be completed. (See Table 11.6.)

Table 11.6

Source	df	Sums of Squares	Mean Squares	F
Treatment	3	976.9	325.6	20.74
Error	26	408.6	15.7	
Total	29	1,385.5		

Now the hypothesis test: H_o: $\mu_C = \mu_D = \mu_E = \mu_F$
H_a: At least two means (μ_is) differ.
Test Statistic: $F =$ MST/MSE
Region of Rejection (see Figure 11.6).

$F_{.05,(3,26)} = 2.98$. Since the calculated F from the ANOVA table, 20.74, is greater than $F_{.05,(3,26)} = 2.98$, reject the null hypothesis and conclude that at least two weight loss means differ.

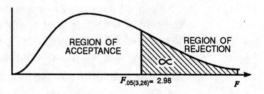

Figure 11.6:
df (Treatment) = 3
df (Error) = 26

BONFERRONI COMPARISONS

The last part of analysis of variance is discussed in answer to the natural question that arises after a hypothesis test: if it is determined that at least two means differ, which means are they? The pairs that differ are found by use of the *Bonferroni comparisons.*

In our first example (the mice running the maze after certain kinds of training), we determined via the hypothesis test that at least two mean times differ. Recall that there were three different training modes: C (control), D (discouragement—mild shocks administered at wrong turns), and E (encouragement—a piece of cheese given at correct turns). An analysis of variance was performed and, since the calculated F-value exceeded the F-value from the table, the null hypothesis (that the means are equal) was rejected. The conclusion was that at least two of the population means μ_C, μ_D, and μ_E differ.

This implies that if these means were compared in pairs, the means in at least one pair would differ. Our first task is to determine how many pairs to compare.

Setting Up a Bonferroni Comparison

NUMBER OF COMPARISONS

The number of comparisons is equal to the number of ways two means can be chosen from the total number, in this case three, for pairing. Recall from Chapter 5 that this is a combination of three items taken two at a time. Ordering is not necessary since comparing μ_C with μ_D is the same as comparing μ_D with μ_C. The formula for choosing r items from n to compare is $_nC_r$. Since for these comparisons the focus is always on pairs, the modified formula is $_nC_2 = n!/(n-2)!2!$.

In the case of the mice, in which there are only three treatment groups, the number of comparisons is $_3C_2 = 3!/1!2! = 3$. Therefore, there are three pairs of means to compare. They are: μ_C with μ_D; μ_C with μ_E; μ_D with μ_E.

Recall the example comparing grades on a final freshman English exam according to the professors who taught the course. In that case, there were four professors. The number of comparisons of pairs of means is $_4C_2 = 4!/2!2! = 6$. In the case of four treatment means, there are six comparisons possible.

CALCULATING t FOR BONFERRONI COMPARISONS

For the Bonferroni comparisons, an interval is formed around the difference of means in one pair. If 0 is in the interval, the means do not differ significantly. The formula used for this interval is very similar to that used to calculate the confidence interval for the difference of two means from small samples. Recall from Chapter 10 that the formula for calculating a small sample confidence interval is

$$(a, b) = (\overline{x}_1 - \overline{x}_2) \pm t_{\alpha/2} \cdot \sqrt{s_p^{\,2}(\frac{1}{n_1} + \frac{1}{n_2})}$$

The t-value in this formula is based on the α-level and on the total number of degrees of freedom for both samples whose means are being compared.

The *t*-value in the Bonferroni comparison is calculated in a different way. The dfs are always the degrees of freedom for error in the ANOVA table for the original problem. The Bonferroni is a follow-up test since the ANOVA hypothesis test must always be done first to determine whether there is a difference in the means.

In the case of the means for the English final exam (Table 11.3), df for error is 21. However, the α-level must be split into a smaller α- level for each of the comparisons. If, as in the case of the means for the English final exam, six comparisons are called for, each alpha is to be 1/6 of the original level set. When all the areas of uncertainty (alphas) are added, the total is not greater than the overall level of significance.

Since each of the comparisons sets a confidence interval, the intervals are always two-tailed. Thus, the alpha-level must be divided by 2. The *t* set for these Bonferroni comparisons will be $t_{\alpha/2c}$, where *c* is the number of comparisons and α is the overall level of significance.

Because the *t*-table is a table of critical values of *t*, when alpha is divided by $2c$ it is likely that the resulting number will not be a critical value. Therefore, the alpha for the Bonferroni comparison will be rounded down so the sum of the alphas for each comparison will not exceed the total level of significance.

For example, suppose the Bonferroni comparison level of significance for the mice in the maze problem ($c = 3$) is .05. Then, each of the comparisons will have a significance level of $\frac{.05}{2 \cdot 3} \approx .0083$. Since there is no .0083 column in the table of critical values of *t* (Appendix B), we round down to .005, the next lowest column in the table. In the case of the mouse problem, the *t*-value used in the Bonferroni comparison would be $t_{.005,29} = 2.756$. Notice that 29 represents the number of degrees of freedom of the error, as found in the ANOVA Table 11.1.

STANDARD DEVIATION FOR BONFERRONI COMPARISONS

The standard deviation for Bonferroni comparisons is much simpler to find than the $s_p^{\,2}$ we had to calculate for the difference of means confidence interval. The *s* that is used is just the error standard deviation, the square root of MSE. For example, in the mouse problem (ANOVA Table 11.1), MSE = 437. Therefore, $s = \sqrt{437} \approx 20.9$.

In the English final exam problem (ANOVA Table 11.3), the variance for the error is MSE = 157. Therefore, *s*, the standard deviation for the error, is $\sqrt{157} \approx 12.53$

FORMULA FOR BONFERRONI COMPARISONS

The actual formula for the Bonferroni comparisons is:

$$(a, b) = (\overline{x}_i - \overline{x}_j) \pm (t_{\alpha/2c})s \cdot \sqrt{\frac{1}{n_i} + \frac{1}{n_j}} \ ,$$

where x_i, x_j are the two sample means of the populations to compare;

n_i, n_j are the numbers in each sample *i*, *j*;

$t_{\alpha/2c}$ is the *t*-value with df from error, overall level of significance α, and number of comparisons *c*; and *s* is $\sqrt{MSE}$.

Using Bonferroni Comparisons

Bonferroni comparisons are performed after the analysis of variance has shown that the null hypothesis should be rejected. For example, in the problem with the freshman English class final exams, the ANOVA table appeared as shown in Table 11.3, reproduced here.

Table 11.3

Source	df	Sums of Squares	Mean Squares	F
Treatment	3	1558	519	3.31
Error	21	3293	157	
Total	24	4851		

Even though the F was quite close to the F from the F-distribution table, the null hypothesis was rejected. This implies that the means in at least one pair differ. The Bonferroni comparison will determine which pair or pairs do differ.

Since each Bonferroni comparison is a confidence interval, finding 0 in the interval would imply that the null hypothesis (that the two population means are equal) is not rejected. Thus, finding 0 in the interval in the Bonferroni comparisons says that if a hypothesis test (a t-test) were run on these two means only, the null hypothesis would be accepted. Conversely, if we do not find a 0 in the interval, then a t-test on these two means would lead to rejection of the null hypothesis: that is, the two means are different.

The Bonferroni comparisons are really a series of t-tests conducted by finding confidence intervals for pairs of means from original data in the analysis of variance. It is a natural follow-up to an analysis of variance that led to rejecting the null hypothesis.

Table 11.4

	Professor			
Grades on Uniform Final	Q	R	S	T
	74	95	58	72
	69	89	63	83
	83	76	85	69
	91	85	72	87
	77	79	48	76
	59	92	56	76
	38		75	
	491	516	457	387

The first step is to calculate the means for each sample. Even though the ANOVA procedure has shown that there is a difference in the means, at no point were they directly calculated. Refer to the table of scores reproduced in Table 11.4.

The means and numbers for each are calculated in the usual way; the results are summarized in Table 11.7. For example, $\bar{x}_Q$ is found by summing the grades from Q and dividing by 7, the number of grades in Q.

Table 11.7

	Q	R	S	T
Means ($\bar{x}_i$)	70.14	86	65.29	77.4
Numbers (n_i)	7	6	7	5

There are $_4C_2$ or 6 comparisons to make. Suppose the overall level of significance requested is .10 (this level is usually larger than the level of significance for the F-test since this number must be divided by the number of comparisons and by 2 for the confidence interval). Then $\alpha/2c = .10/2(6) = .10/12 = .0083$. Therefore, the t-value used will be $t_{.005,21} = 2.831$.

The formula for the Bonferroni comparisons is:

$$(a, b) = (\bar{x}_i - \bar{x}_j) \pm (t_{\alpha/2})\, s\, \sqrt{(\frac{1}{n_i} + \frac{1}{n_j})}$$

We have to use this formula *six* times. The constants for all six are $t = 2.831$ and $s = \sqrt{157} \approx 12.53$. The differences will be in the first part, $\bar{x}_i - \bar{x}_j$, and the last, $\sqrt{\frac{1}{n_i} + \frac{1}{n_j}}$.

I. Starting the six comparisons, first compare μ_Q with μ_R:

$$(a, b) = (\bar{x}_i - \bar{x}_j) \pm (t_{\alpha/2c})s\sqrt{(\frac{1}{n_i} + \frac{1}{n_j})}$$

$$(a, b) = (70.14 - 86) \pm 2.831(12.53)s\sqrt{\frac{1}{7} + \frac{1}{6}}$$

$$= -15.86 \pm 2.831(12.53)(\sqrt{.3095}) = -15.86 \pm 19.73 = (-35.59, 3.87).$$

Since 0 is in this interval, μ_Q and μ_R are *not* significantly different.
II. Next, compare μ_Q with μ_S.

$$(a, b) = (\bar{x}_i - \bar{x}_j) \pm (t_{\alpha/2c})s\sqrt{(\frac{1}{n_i} + \frac{1}{n_j})}$$

$$(a, b) = (70.14 - 65.29) \pm 2.831(12.53)\sqrt{\frac{1}{7} + \frac{1}{7}}$$

$$= 4.85 \pm 2.831(12.53)(\sqrt{.2857}) = 4.85 \pm 18.96 = (-14.11, 23.81)$$

Since 0 is in this interval, μ_Q and μ_S are *not* significantly different.

III. Next, compare μ_Q with μ_T.

$$(a, b) = (70.14 - 77.4) \pm 2.831(12.53)\sqrt{\frac{1}{7} + \frac{1}{5}}$$

$$= -7.26 \pm 2.831(12.53)(\sqrt{.3429}) = -7.26 \pm 20.77 = (-28.03, 13.51)$$

Since 0 is in this interval, μ_Q and μ_T are *not* significantly different.

IV. Next, compare μ_R with μ_S.

$$(a, b) = (86 - 65.29) \pm 2.831(12.53)\sqrt{\frac{1}{6} + \frac{1}{7}}$$

$$= 20.71 \pm 2.831(12.53)(\sqrt{.3095}) = 20.71 \pm 19.73 = (.98, 40.44).$$

Since 0 is *not* in this interval, μ_R and μ_S *are* significantly different.

V.   Next, compare μ_R with μ_T.

$$(a, b) = (86 - 77.4) \pm 2.831(12.53)\sqrt{\frac{1}{6} + \frac{1}{5}}$$

$$= 8.6 \pm 2.831(12.53)(\sqrt{.3667}) = 8.6 \pm 21.48 = (-12.88, 30.08)$$

Since 0 is in this interval, μ_R and μ_T are *not* significantly different.

VI. Last, compare μ_S with μ_T.

$$(a, b) = (65.29 - 77.4) \pm 2.831(12.53)\sqrt{\frac{1}{7} + \frac{1}{5}}$$

$$= -12.11 \pm 2.831(12.53)(\sqrt{.3429}) = -12.11 \pm 20.77 = (-32.88, 8.66).$$

Since 0 is in this interval, μ_Q and μ_T are *not* significantly different.
Thus, only μ_R and μ_S differ, so only these two English class mean final scores are significantly different.

Sometimes, the presentation of such results can be simplified in the following way: the means are placed in ascending order and lines are drawn above those means that are not significantly different. Those *without* a connecting line *are* significantly different. The above results look like this:

65.29	70.14	77.4	86
$\overline{x}_s$	$\overline{x}_Q$	$\overline{x}_T$	$\overline{x}_R$

Since only $\bar{x}_S$ and $\bar{x}_R$ are not joined, only the population means from which these sample means are drawn differ.

Exercise 11.3: In Exercise 11.2, an analysis of variance was performed on groups of overweight men who were given different diet regimes. Recall their

Table 11.5

C	D	E	F
0	−10	−4	−18
−3	−15	+2	−20
+2	−6	−7	−12
−5	−9	+1	−22
+1	−3	−3	−15
0	−12	−5	−9
+2	−5	0	
−4		+3	
		−8	

weight loss statistics:

The ANOVA found that at least two means differ. Using the Bonferroni comparisons, find which pairs of means differ. Use an overall significance level of .10.

Answers: The first step is to find the means of each of the above samples. They are:

$\bar{x}_C = -.875$; $\bar{x}_D = -8.57$; $\bar{x}_E = -2.33$; $\bar{x}_F = -16$.

The formula for the Bonferroni comparisons is

$$(a, b) = (\bar{x}_i - \bar{x}_j) \pm (t_{\alpha/2c}) \, s \cdot \sqrt{\frac{1}{n_i} + \frac{1}{n_j}}$$

The number of comparisons (c) is found by the formula $_4C_2 = 4!/2!2! = 6$. Therefore, the α for the t-value is .10/2(6) = .10/12 = .008, which rounds down to .005. For degrees of freedom, recall the ANOVA table from Exercise 11.2:

Table 11.6

Source	df	Sums of Squares	Mean	F
Treatment	3	976.9	325.6	20.74
Error	26	408.6	15.7	
Total	29	1385.5		

The number of degrees of freedom associated with MSE = 26. Therefore, the t-value for the Bonferroni comparisons is $t_{.005,26}$ = 2.779. The s in the formula is $\sqrt{MSE} = \sqrt{15.7} \approx 3.96$. There are six Bonferroni comparisons we must make:

(I) First, compare μ_C with μ_D:

$$(a, b) = (\bar{x}_i - \bar{x}_j) \pm (t_{\alpha/2c}) \, s \cdot \sqrt{\frac{1}{n_i} + \frac{1}{n_j}}$$

$$(a, b) = (-.875 - (-8.57)) \pm 2.779 \, (3.96) \sqrt{\frac{1}{8} + \frac{1}{7}}$$

$$= (-.875 + 8.57) \pm 2.779(3.96)\sqrt{.268} = 7.70 \pm 5.70 = (2.00, 13.40)$$

Since 0 is *not* in (2.00, 13.40), μ_C and μ_D *are* significantly different.

(II) Next, compare μ_C with μ_E:

$$(a, b) = (\bar{x}_i - \bar{x}_j) \pm (t_{\alpha/2c}) s \cdot \sqrt{\frac{1}{n_i} + \frac{1}{n_j}}$$

$$(a, b) = (-.875 - (-2.33)) \pm 2.779 \, (3.96) \sqrt{\frac{1}{8} + \frac{1}{9}}$$

$$= (-.875 + 2.33) \pm 2.779(3.96)\sqrt{.236} = 1.455 \pm 5.35 = (-3.895, 6.805)$$

Since 0 *is* in (-3.895, 6.805), μ_C and μ_E are *not* significantly different.

(III) Next, compare μ_C with μ_F:

$$(a, b) = (-.875 - (-16)) \pm 2.779(3.96)\sqrt{\frac{1}{8} + \frac{1}{6}}$$

$$= (-.875 + 16) \pm 2.779(3.96)\sqrt{.292} = 15.125 \pm 5.95 = (9.175, \ 21.075)$$

Since 0 is *not* in (9.175, 21.075), μ_C and μ_F *are* significantly different.

(IV) Next, compare μ_D with μ_E:

$$(a, b) = (-.857 - (-2.33)) \pm 2.779 \, (3.96)\sqrt{\frac{1}{7} + \frac{1}{9}}$$

$$= (-8.57 + 2.33) \pm 2.779 \, (3.96) \sqrt{.254} = -6.24 \pm 5.55 = (-11.79, -.69)$$

Since 0 is *not* in (-11.79, -.69), μ_D and μ_E *are* significantly different.

(V) Next, compare μ_D with μ_F:

$$(a,b) = (-.857 - (16)) \pm 2.779 \, (3.96)\sqrt{\frac{1}{7} + \frac{1}{9}}$$

$$= (-8.57 + 16) \pm 2.779(3.96)\sqrt{.310} = 7.43 \pm 6.13 = (1.30, 13.56)$$

Since 0 is *not* in (1.30, 13.56), μ_D and μ_F *are* significantly different.

(VI) Last, compare μ_D with μ_F:

$$(a, b) = (-2.33 - (-16)) \pm 2.779 \, (3.96) \sqrt{\frac{1}{9} + \frac{1}{6}}$$

$$= (-2.33 + 16) \pm 2.779(3.96) \sqrt{.278} = 13.67 \pm 5.80 = (7.87, 19.47)$$

Since 0 is *not* in (7.87, 19.47), μ_E and μ_F *are* significantly different. To summarize these results, put the means in ascending order and connect those that are *not* significantly different with a horizontal line. The only pairs that are joined are $\bar{x}_E$ and $\bar{x}_C$. Therefore, the populations whose means do not differ significantly are the exercisers and the control group. All other pairs show significant differences.

-16	-8.57	-2.33	$-.875$
$\bar{x}_F$	$\bar{x}_D$	$\bar{x}_E$	$\bar{x}_C$

ANALYSIS OF VARIANCE—BLOCK DESIGN

In our previous work on analysis of variance, there were two sources of variance that, when summed, equal the total variance. One of these sources was treatment or between variance, the variation of the treatment means from the grand mean. The other source of variance was error or within variance, the variation of the individual data points from the treatment means. The type of ANOVA whose variance comes from just these two sources is called the completely randomized design.

There is another kind of analysis of variance often found in designed experiments: *block design*. In this design, there are two relationships among the data points: a vertical one, in which all numbers in a column are the results of a single treatment (as was the case in the completely randomized design), and a horizontal one in which all numbers in the same row also have a relationship to each other—they are in the same block.

For example, suppose it is hypothesized that the time when a student takes a certain college class influences his or her grade; perhaps students who take classes earlier in the day do better, or perhaps students do better in late classes,

Table 11.8 — Median Grades in Each Class

Instructor	8:00	10:00	1:00	3:00	Total
Doe	19	20	14	12	65
Jones	18	16	15	10	59
Smith	15	14	11	9	49
Total	52	50	40	31	173

Hour of Class

or perhaps students do best in classes nearer the middle of the day.

To prove or disprove this hypothesis, give the same quiz to a random sample of students in each class (same subject, different hour), take the average (mean or median for the entire class) grades, and see if the means of these averages differ from one class time to another class time. But there may be other factors that could influence the grades: for example, perhaps the teachers of some classes are better or worse than others. Therefore, the experiment can be set up by blocking by instructor as shown in Table 11.8.

In these block variance problems, it is a good idea to total the columns and rows since these totals will be needed in the calculations to follow.

New ANOVA Table

The above numbers are class median grades. Why are these medians different? There are really three sources for these differences (variances). One is that the classes are at different hours; another is that the classes have different instructors; a third source is just the error variance—the extent to which the median grades differ from the treatment mean for each treatment (hour) group. These variances will all be sorted out in an ANOVA table with an additional line (Table 11.9a).

Table 11.9a

Source	df	Sums of Squares	Mean Squares	F
Treatment (Hour)	$k-1$	SST	MST	MST/MSE
Block (Teacher)	$b-1$	SSB	MSB	MSB/MSE
Error	$(k-1)(b-1)$	SSE	MSE	
Total	$n-1$	SS		

Let's fill in the ANOVA table for the class grades by hour problem. First, the degrees of freedom:

df (treatment) is one less than the number of treatments: $k-1 = 4-1 = 3$ since there are four treatments, which correspond to the four hours the class is offered.

df (block) is one less than the number of blocks: $b-1 = 3-1 = 2$ since there are three blocks that correspond to the three instructors.

df (total) is one less than the total number of scores: $n-1 = 12-1 = 11$ since there are twelve numbers in the four treatments and three blocks.

Finally, df (error) is df (total) minus df (treatment) minus df (block): $e = (n-1) - [(k-1) + (b-1)] = 11 - [3+2] = 6$. By the way, df (error) in the block design is also always the product of the dfs for treatment and block: $(k-1)(b-1) = 3 \cdot 2 = 6$.

SUMS OF SQUARES CALCULATION

To calculate sums of squares, first find the correction to the mean. (Notice that the column totals come in handy here.)

$$CM = (T_8 + T_{10} + T_1 + T_3)^2/n = (52 + 50 + 40 + 31)^2/12 = 173^2/12 = 2494.$$

SS is the sum of the squares of each of the numbers (i.e., $19^2 + 18^2 + \ldots + 9^2$), which equals 2629, minus CM:

$$SS = \Sigma x^2 - CM = 2629 - 2494 = 135.$$
$$SST = (T_8{}^2 + T_{10}{}^2 + T_1{}^2 + T_3{}^2)/b - CM$$

(Since this is a block design, each treatment group has the same number of data points in it, namely b, the number of blocks. Therefore, instead of dividing each $T_i{}^2$ by b, we can divide the sum of all the squared treatment sums by b.)

$$SST = (52^2 + 50^2 + 40^2 + 31^2)/3 - 2494$$
$$= 765/3 - 2494 = 2588 - 2494 = 94.$$

The sum of squares for the blocks utilizes the block sums, which are: $B_D = 65$; $B_J = 59$; $B_S = 49$. Notice that the sum of the treatment sums, 173, equals the sum of the block sums.

$$SSB = (B_D2 + B_J2 + B_S2)/k - CM$$
(Again, each block has the same number of data points in it, namely k, the number of treatments.)

$$SSB = (65^2 + 59^2 + 49^2)/4 - 2494 = 10107/4 - 2494 = 2527 - 2494 = 33.$$
$$SSE = SS - SST - SSB = 135 - 94 - 33 = 8.$$

Dividing the sums of squares by the df gives the mean squares. The ANOVA table is completed in Table 11.9b.

Table 11.9b

Source	df	Sums of Squares	Mean Squares	F
Treatment (Hour)	3	94	31.3	24.08
Block(Teacher)	2	33	16.5	12.69
Error	6	8	1.3	
Total	11	135		

Two F-statistics are calculated. The F-statistic for the treatment is equal to MST/MSE, and the F-statistic for the block is equal to MSB/MSE. This second statistic will be important for a follow-up.

Hypothesis Test

Now for the hypothesis test. Using $\alpha = .05$:

H_0: $\mu_8 = \mu_{10} = \mu_1 = \mu_3$
H_a: At least two of the means (by hour) differ.

Test Statistic: $F = MST/MSE$

Region of Rejection (Figure 11.7):

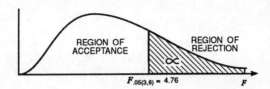

Figure 11.7:
df (Treatment) = 3
df (Error) = 6

Using the F-table, $F_{.05,(3,6)} = 4.76$, where df(T) = 3 and df(E) = 6.

Since the calculated $F = 24.08$ is greater than the F of the region of rejection $F = 4.76$, reject the null hypothesis and conclude that at least two means differ.

TEST FOR SIGNIFICANCE OF BLOCKING

The problem above could have been done without blocking. In that case, the error variance would have been much larger. How do we know that blocking is justified for this problem? To answer this question, a hypothesis test is performed on the blocking. A rejection of the null hypothesis indicates that the blocking is justified in this problem. The new hypothesis test is the reason the F for blocking ($F = MSB/MSE$) was calculated in the ANOVA table.

This hypothesis test will also be done using $\alpha = .05$.

H_o: $\mu_D = \mu_J = \mu_S$
H_a: At least two of the means (by instructor) differ.
Test Statistic: $F = MSB/MSE$
Region of Rejection (see Figure 11.8).

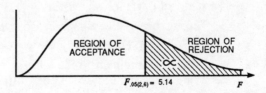

Figure 11.8:
df (Block) = 2
df (Error) = 6

Using the F-table, $F_{.05,(2,6)} = 5.14$, where $df(B) = 2$ and $df(E) = 6$.

The calculated block F (12.69) is greater than the F that delineates the region of rejection, $F = 5.14$. This means, by the hypothesis test above, that the null hypothesis is rejected and there is a difference between at least two of the instructor means.

However, this was not the reason we did this second hypothesis test. We did it to see if the blocking by instructor was justified. Since the instructor means are not the same, the blocking was justified, so the use of a block rather than a completely randomized design was a good choice for the statistician.

BONFERRONI FOLLOW-UP

Our original hypothesis test showed that there is a difference between means of class scores by hour. Now the question is, which hours differ? Again, the Bonferroni comparisons are used, but the formula this time is easier:

$$(a, b) = (\bar{x}_i - \bar{x}_j) \pm (t_{\alpha/2c})\, s \cdot \sqrt{\frac{2}{b}}$$

Since in a block design, all the treatments have the same number of data points, all the comparisons will involve the same numbers. Each n from the previous formula is now a b, which represents the number of blocks. Since the last part of the formula originally contained

$\sqrt{\frac{1}{n_i} + \frac{1}{n_j}}$, this formula is now $\sqrt{\frac{1}{b} + \frac{1}{b}}$ or $\sqrt{\frac{2}{b}}$.

Thus, the latter part of the formula $(\pm t_{/2\,c} \cdot s \sqrt{2/b})$ is the same for all pairs of means. Therefore, it may be easier to calculate this part of the Bonferroni comparisons first.

Since there are four means to compare, the four hours of classes, there are again $_4C_2 = 6$ comparisons.

Using $\alpha = .10$, $\alpha/2c = .10/12 = .0083$, which rounds down to .005. $t_{.005,6} = 3.707$ [Recall that df (error) is used for the number of degrees of freedom.] The standard deviation s is $\sqrt{MSE} = \sqrt{1.3} \approx 1.14$.

The number of blocks is three, so $\sqrt{2/b} = \sqrt{2/3} \approx .82$. $\pm t_{\alpha/2c} \cdot s\sqrt{2/b} = \pm (3.707)(1.14)(.82) = \pm 3.47$.

Now all that remains to be done is to calculate and arrange the means in ascending order and see which ones differ by more than 3.47. The means are $\bar{x}_8 = 17.3; \bar{x}_{10} = 16.7; \bar{x}_1 = 13.3; \bar{x}_3 = 10.3$.

Arranging in ascending order:

10.3	13.3	16.7	17.3
$\bar{x}_3$	$\bar{x}_1$	$\bar{x}_{10}$	$\bar{x}_8$

Now, inspect these to see which ones differ by less than 3.47. Those should be joined by a horizontal line as before. Then the joins should look like this:

10.3	13.3	16.7	17.3
$\bar{x}_3$	$\bar{x}_1$	$\bar{x}_{10}$	$\bar{x}_8$

The following pairs of means *do* differ:

μ_3 differs from μ_{10}.
μ_3 differs from μ_8.
μ_1 differs from μ_8.

The other three pairs do not differ by 3.47 or more. Of course, this problem can be done using the original formula, in which the means are subtracted and the inclusion or exclusion of 0 from the interval is the clue to whether the means do not or do differ. For example, comparing μ_3 and μ_{10}:

$$(a, b) = (\bar{x}_3 - \bar{x}_{10}) \pm (t_{\alpha/2c}) \, s \cdot \sqrt{2/b}$$

$$= (10.3 - 16.7) \pm 3.47 = -6.4 \pm 3.47 = (-9.87, -2.93)$$

Since 0 is not in the interval, these two means differ. Comparing μ_3 and μ_1:

$$(a, b) = (10.3 - 13.3) \pm 3.47 = -3 \pm 3.47 = (-6.47, .47).$$

Since 0 is in the interval, these two means do not differ.

Exercise 11.4: A research physician wishes to test two drugs, A and B, to determine how effective they are against a common cold germ. Eighteen volunteers are chosen, three from each age group: 18 to 25, 26 to 33, 34 to 41, 42 to 49, 50 to 57, and 58 to 65. Then each is infected with the cold virus, and one from each age group is assigned to be given Drug A, one is given Drug B,

Table 11.10a

Age Range	Drug		
	A	B	C
18 – 25	3	4	6
26 – 33	4	4	5
34 – 41	5	6	6
42 – 49	4	5	7
50 – 57	5	5	7
58 – 65	6	6	8

and one a placebo, C (the control group).

The measured response in this experiment is the number of days each volunteer remains symptomatic. The treatments, blocks, and responses are shown in Table 11.10a.

    a.   Is there evidence to indicate that the three treatments differ? Use $\alpha =$ .05 and construct a block ANOVA table to answer this.

    b.   Was the use of blocking justified for this experiment? Test using $\alpha =$ .05.

    c.   Using the Bonferroni comparisons with $\alpha = .10$, determine which pair of means differ.

Answers:

    a.   In order to fill out the ANOVA table, it might be a good idea to total the columns and rows. Thus, Table 11.10b now has an additional column and an additional row for totals.

Table 11.10b

		Drug		
Age Range	A	B	C	Totals
18 – 25	3	4	6	13
26 – 33	4	4	5	13
34 – 41	5	6	6	17
42 – 49	4	5	7	16
50 – 57	5	5	7	17
58 – 65	6	6	8	20
Totals	27	30	39	96

df (treatment) = $k - 1 = 2$
df (block) = $b - 1 = 6 - 1 = 5$
df (error) = $(k - 1)(b - 1) = 2 \cdot 5 = 10$
df (total) = $n - 1 = 18 - 1 = 17$
CM = $(T_A + T_B + T_C)^2/n = 96^2/18$
CM = 512

SS = $\Sigma x^2 - $ CM $= 540 - 512 = 28.$
SST = $(T_A^2 + T_B^2 + T_C^2)/b -$ CM $= (27^2 + 30^2 + 39^2)/6 - 512 = 3150/6$
$- 512 = 525 - 512 = 13.$
(For the subscripts on SSB, we will use the first number in the row. For example, in the first row, the first age is 18, so the total of row 1 is $T_{18} = 13$.)
SSB = $(T_{18}^2 + T_{26}^2 + T_{34}^2 + T_{42}^2 + T_{50}^2 + T_{58}^2) \div k -$ CM
$= (132 + 132 + 172 + 162 + 172 + 202) \div 3 - 512$

$$SSB = 1572/3 - 512 = 524 - 512 = 12.$$
$$SSE = SS - SST - SSB = 28 - 13 - 12 = 3.$$
$$MST = 13/2 = 6.5$$
$$MSB = 12/5 = 2.4$$
$$MSE = 3/10 = .3$$

F for treatment $= MST/MSE = 6.5/.3 = 21.67$
F for block $= MSB/MSE = 2.4/.3 = 8.00$

All these calculations can now be summarized in an ANOVA table (Table 11.11):

Table 11.11

Source	df	Sums of Squares	Mean Squares	F
Treatment (Drug)	2	13	6.5	21.67
Block (Age)	5	12	2.4	8.00
Error	10	3	.3	
Total	17	28		

Now for the hypothesis test.
H_o: $\mu_A = \mu_B = \mu_C$
H_a: At least two (drug) means differ.
Test Statistic: $F = MST/MSE$
Region of Rejection (see Figure 11.9).

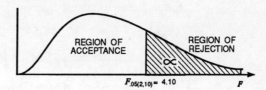

Figure 11.9:
df (Treatment) = 2
df (Error) = 10

$F_{.05,(2,10)} = 4.10$. Since $21.67 > 4.10$, reject H_o and conclude that at least two means differ.

b. To find out if the use of blocking was justified, conduct another hypothesis test.

H_o: $\mu_{18} = \mu_{26} = \mu_{34} = \mu_{42} = \mu_{50} = \mu_{58}$
H_a: At least two (age) means differ.

Test Statistic: $F = MSB/MSE$
Region of Rejection (see Figure 11.10).

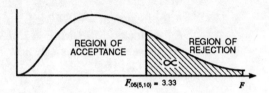

Figure 11.10:
df (Block) = 5
df (Error) = 10

$F_{.05,(5,10)} = 3.33$. Since $8.00 > 3.33$, the use of blocking was indicated in this problem; i.e., the means of the blocks differ.

c. To see which means differ, first calculate the means for each of the treatments. They are: $\bar{x}_A = 4.5$; $\bar{x}_B = 5$; $\bar{x}_C = 6.5$.
Recall the Bonferroni comparison formula:
$$(a, b) = (\bar{x}_i - \bar{x}_j) \pm (t_{\alpha/2c})s \cdot \sqrt{2/b}$$

The number of comparisons is $_3C_2 = 3$. The overall α-level is .10, so .10/2(3) = .10/6 = .0167, which rounds off to .01.
$t_{.01,10} = 2.764$; $s = \sqrt{MSE} = \sqrt{.3} \approx .548$
Since there are six blocks, $\sqrt{2/b} = \sqrt{2/6} \approx .577$

$$\pm t_{\alpha/2c})s \cdot \sqrt{\frac{2}{b}} = \pm (2.764)(.548)(.577) = \pm .87 .$$

Therefore, those means that are less than .87 apart are not significantly different.
Arrange the means in ascending order:

4.5	5	6.5
$\bar{x}_A$	$\bar{x}_B$	$\bar{x}_C$

Join those that are less than .87 apart:

4.5	5	6.5
$\bar{x}_A$	$\bar{x}_B$	$\bar{x}_C$

Therefore, μ_A is different from μ_C and μ_B is different from μ_C. Thus, the drugs significantly lessen the time to cure compared to the control group, but they do not differ from each other.

Exercise 11.5: Three different types of batteries are to be tested to see which, if any, has the longest life. Four of each brand (X, Y, and Z) are chosen at random and placed in four different items. The length of time, in weeks, that the batteries operate each item before failing is measured (Table11.12a). The items used are a toy rabbit (R), a toy airplane (A), a flashlight (F), and a remote control device (D).

Table 11.12a

Item	Battery Brand		
	X	Y	Z
R	4	5	3
A	5	5	4
F	4	5	4
D	5	6	5

a. Use analysis of variance, completely randomized design, to determine if the mean lives of these batteries are different. Use $\alpha = .05$. (Consider only the battery life, not the items.)
b. Now use the randomized block design of analysis of variance to determine if the mean lives of these batteries are different. Use $\alpha = .05$.
c. Use the Bonferroni comparisons, if indicated, to see which battery means are different. Use $\alpha = .10$.

Answers: To do all parts of this problem, we will need the row and column totals (Table 11.12b).

Table 11.12b

Item	Battery Brand			
	X	Y	Z	RT
R	4	5	3	12
A	5	5	4	14
F	4	5	4	13
D	5	6	5	16
CT	18	21	16	55

a. To fill out the ANOVA table, we need the degrees of freedom, the sums of squares, the mean squares, and the F-statistic for the completely randomized design. They are:

df (treatment) = $k - 1 = 3 - 1 = 2$.

df (total) = $n - 1 = 12 - 1 = 11$.

df (error) = $11 - 2 = 9$.

$CM = (T_X + T_Y + T_Z)^2/n = 55^2/12 = 252$

$SS = \Sigma x^2 - CM = 259 - 252 = 7$.

$SST = (T_X^2 + T_Y^2 + T_Z^2)/b - CM$

(Actually, there is no block, but since there are exactly the same number of data points in each treatment, the formula can be written with one division instead of three.)

$SST = (18^2 + 21^2 + 16^2)/4 - 252 = 1021/4 - 252 = 255 - 252 = 3$.

$SSE = SS - SST = 7 - 3 = 4$.

$MST = 3/2 = 1.5$

$MSE = 4/9 = .444$

$F = MST/MSE = 1.5/.444 = 3.38$.

Putting these numbers in the ANOVA table:

Table 11.13

Source	df	Sums of Squares	Mean Squares	F
Treatment	2	3	1.5	3.38
Error	9	4	.444	
Total	11	7		

Now for the hypothesis test.

$H_0: \mu_X = \mu_Y = \mu_Z$

H_a: At least two (battery) means differ.

Test Statistic: F = MST/MSE

Region of Rejection (Figure 11.11):

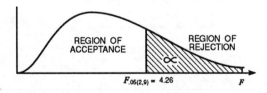

$F_{.05(2,9)} = 4.26$

Figure 11.11:
df (Treatment) = 2
df (Error) = 9
(Completely Randomized Design)

$F_{.05,(2,9)} = 4.26$. Since the calculated F (MST/MSE) of 3.38 is less than the table F of 4.26, accept the null hypothesis and conclude that the battery means are the same.

b. For this part, we do the calculations for a block design. Now, consider degrees of freedom for this design:

df (treatment) = $k - 1 = 3 - 1 = 2$.
df (block) = $b - 1 = 4 - 1 = 3$.
df (total) = $n - 1 = 12 - 1 = 11$.
df (error) = df (total) − df (treatment) − df (block) = $11 - 2 - 3 = 6$.
CM = $(T_X + T_Y + T_Z)^2/n = 55^2/12 = 252$ (This is the same as in the randomized design.)
SS = $\Sigma x^2 - CM = 259 - 252 = 7$.
(This, too, is the same as in the randomized design.)
SST = $(T_X^2 + T_Y^2 + T_Z^2)/b - CM = (18^2 + 21^2 + 16^2)/4 - 252 = 1021/4$
$- 252 = 255 - 252 = 3$.
(This is also the same as in the randomized design.)
SSB = $(T_R^2 + T_A^2 + T_F^2 + T_D^2)/k - CM = (12^2 + 14^2 + 13^2 + 16^2)/3$
$- 252 = 765/3 - 252 = 255 - 252 = 3$.
SSE = SS − SST − SSB = $7 - 3 - 3 = 1$.
MST = $3/2 = 1.5$
MSE = $1/6 = .167$
F =MST/MSE = $1.5/.167 = 8.98$.
MSB = $3/3 = 1$, so F, (for the block) = MSB/MSE =$1/.167 = 5.99$.
These numbers are now put into the ANOVA table (Table 11.14).

Table 11.14

Source	df	Sums of Squares	Mean Squares	F
Treatment	2	3	1.5	8.98
Block	3	3	1	5.99
Error	6	1	.167	
Total	11	7		

Now for the hypothesis test.

H_o: $\mu_X = \mu_Y = \mu_Z$
H_a: At least two (battery) means differ.

Test Statistic: F = MST/MSE
Region of Rejection (Figure 11.12):
$F_{.05,(2,6)} = 5.14$. (Notice that since df [error] is different than in the previous region of rejection, the table F is also different.)

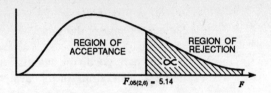

Figure 11.12:
df (Treatment) = 2
df (Error) = 6
Block Design

Since the calculated F (MST/MSE) of 8.98 is greater than the table F of 5.14, reject the null hypothesis and conclude that at least two battery means differ.

c. By part (b) of this exercise, utilizing the randomized block design, the battery means are different. Therefore, Bonferroni comparisons are indicated to determine which battery means differ. Recall the formula for the Bonferroni comparisons:

$$(a, b) = (\bar{x}_i - \bar{x}_j) \pm (t_{\alpha/2c})s \cdot \sqrt{2/b}$$

The number of comparisons is $_3C_2 = 3$. The overall α-level is .10, so .10/2 · 3 = .10/6 = .0167, which rounds down to .01.
$t_{.01,6} = 3.143$; $s = \sqrt{MSE} = \sqrt{.167} \approx .41$
Since there are four blocks, $\sqrt{2/b} = \sqrt{2/4} \approx .71$;
$\pm(t_{\alpha/2c})s \cdot \sqrt{2/b} = \pm(3.143)(.41)(.71) = \pm.91$. Means that are more than .91 apart are significantly different.
The means are: $\bar{x}_X = 4.5$; $\bar{x}_Y = 5.25$; $\bar{x}_Z = 4$. Arranging the means in ascending order:

4	4.5	5.25
$\bar{x}_Z$	$\bar{x}_X$	$\bar{x}_Y$

Joining those that are less than .91 apart:

4	4.5	5.25
$\bar{x}_Z$	$\bar{x}_X$	$\bar{x}_Y$

Therefore, μ_Z is different from μ_Y. This is the only pair of batteries that has different means. However, these differences would not have been revealed in a completely randomized design: it took a block design to show them.

If the Bonferroni comparisons had been tried based on the completely randomized design in (a), there would have been no significant differences among the means. Try it!

*A*nalysis of variance is used extensively in designed experiments when a group of subjects is randomly assigned to three or more treatments. Variance is analyzed by comparing how much of the total variance comes from the differences between the treatment mean and the grand mean and how much comes from the differences between the individual data points and the mean of their treatment group.

These two numbers, MST (mean square treatment) and MSE (mean square error), are compared in a ratio, F. If the numerator (MST) is sufficiently large compared to the denominator (MSE), the null hypothesis that the means of the treatment groups are the same is rejected.

If the null hypothesis is rejected, then the alternative hypothesis, that at least two of the treatment means differ, is investigated further. By using Bonferroni comparisons, which pair or pairs of means differ can be determined. Then the experimenter knows not only that the treatments affect the subjects differently but also which treatments differ.

In some designed experiments, a match across treatments can be made. This design, called experimental block design, reduces the error variance by assigning it to two different classes: the variance that comes from the blocks or divisions and the variance that comes from the error. Since the error variance and thus the denominator of the F-statistic is reduced, an experiment that does not reject the null hypothesis with a completely randomized design, when repeated using a block design, might then produce an F-statistic large enough to be in the region of rejection of the null hypothesis.

12

Chi-Square Tests of Enumerative Data

---

*O*ne type of data we have not yet discussed at length is "enumerative" or "count data." In previous chapters, we used "quantitative data," data measured on a numeric scale. Most of the experiments conducted in the previous chapters involved comparing the means of certain sets of numbers.

In the experiments we will discuss in this chapter, numbers of subjects who fall into certain categories are counted, and these counts are compared with the expected counts in these categories. For the most part, the categories are nominal, not ordered; they may include men and women; Republicans, Democrats, and Independents; blue-eyed, green-eyed, and brown-eyed people.

An example of this type of experiment is as follows. Suppose that three candidates are running for office and a poll is taken to see whether registered voters show a preference for one candidate over another. If 300 registered voters are randomly sampled, one would expect, if no preference exists, that approximately 1/3 of 300 or 100 of the voters would say they prefer Candidate A, 100 would say they prefer Candidate B, and 100 Candidate C.

The poll is taken and the enumerative data shows that 125 of the 300 prefer A, 110 prefer B, and 65 prefer C. Does this mean that the voters show a preference for one candidate over another? In other words, are these numbers (125, 110, and 65) so far away from the expected numbers (100, 100, and 100) under a no preference (null) situation that a preference is indicated? This is the type of question this chapter will answer.

ONE-DIMENSIONAL ENUMERATIVE DATA

The problem above is an example of *one-dimensional* enumerative data. It is a *multinomial experiment*, which is similar to a binomial experiment but has more than two outcomes. As in binomial experiments (Chapter 6), multinomial experiments consist of a large number of identical trials (n). In multinomial experiments, there are more than two possible outcomes, say k possible outcomes, each of which has a probability associated with it. The sum of the probabilities associated with all the outcomes is 1.

The two sets of numbers that are of interest are the actual counts in each cell (like 125, 110, and 65), and the expected numbers in each, each of which is calculated by multiplying the total number of trials (n) by the probability of a certain trial (p_i). The product $n \cdot p_i$ equals $E(n_i)$, the expected value of the ith n. The present problem is set up to indicate both the actual and expected counts (Table 12.1a).

Table 12.1a

	Candidate		
	A	B	C
Preference in Poll	125	110	65
Expected Preferences	100	100	100

We want to determine whether these differences are so great as to imply that the preferences for the three candidates are not in the same proportion; in other words, that the probabilities, p_A, p_B, and p_C are not all equal to 1/3.

To do this, we introduce a new statistic called the *chi-square statistic*.

Chi-Square Distribution

Chi-square (χ^2) is a sampling distribution involving variances of the population and sample when the population is normally distributed. It is the sampling distribution of the ratio of $(n-1)\, s^2$ to σ^2.

The chi-square distribution is similar to the t-distribution in that there are many different χ^2 distributions, each dependent on the number of degrees of freedom. In the case of the χ^2 distribution, the degrees of freedom $= k - 1$, where k is the number of choices, categories, or groups. This aspect is similar to the analysis of variance, in which the degrees of freedom for the numerator of the F-statistic was also equal to $k - 1$, where k is the number of treatment groups.

Because each experiment has the potential of any number of categories, there are many different χ^2 distributions. A few are sketched in Figure 12.1.

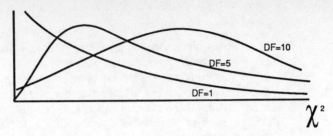

Figure 12.1
χ^2 distributions with df = 1, 5, 10

Note that as the number of degrees of freedom increases, the χ^2 distribution resembles more and more the normal distribution. However, the smallest value for χ^2 is 0. Since this distribution represents the ratio indicated above, in this case either the sample size $n = 1$ (and thus $n - 1 = 0$) or the variance of the sample $s^2 = 0$.

Just as with the t-distribution, the table for the χ^2 distribution represents only a table of critical values of α, those that experimenters use most often. Part of the χ^2 table, which is in Appendix D, is reproduced in Table 12.2.

Table 12.2

Critical Values of χ^2

df		$\chi^2_{.05}$	$\chi^2_{.025}$	$\chi^2_{.01}$	
1	. . .	3.841	5.024	6.635	. . .
2	. . .	5.991	7.378	9.210	. . .
3	. . .	7.815	9.348	11.345	. . .
4	. . .	9.488	11.143	13.277	. . .
5	. . .	11.070	12.832	15.086	. . .
6	. . .	12.592	14.449	16.812	. . .
.	.	.	.	.	.

Table 12.2 gives the numbers that separate the region of acceptance (less than) from the region of rejection (greater than) for all problems involving this distribution (Figure 12.2). Actually, the χ^2 table is often presented with both the left and the right tail values, the left ones being values for $\chi^2_{.99}$, $\chi^2_{.95}$, etc. However, we will work only with that part of the χ^2 table needed for the problems in this book.

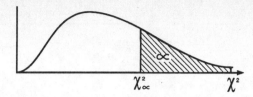

Figure 12.2
χ^2 Distribution — Region of Rejection (Shaded)

CHI-SQUARE STATISTIC IN MULTINOMIAL EXPERIMENTS

The statistic used for hypothesis testing in multinomial experiments like the problem above concerning voter preference for candidates is

$$\chi^2 = \sum \frac{[n_i - E(n_i)]^2}{E(n_i)},$$

where n_i is the actual count in cell i and $E(n_i)$ is the expected number in cell i.

Notice that this number is always positive since the numerator is squared and the denominator is an expected number (positive). Recall that the $\sum$ sign means that all squared differences divided by expectation must be summed. This means that each term adds more to χ^2, and if the statistic gets beyond the table value of χ^2, then the null hypothesis (that the count is as expected) is rejected.

HYPOTHESIS TESTING IN ONE-DIMENSIONAL EXPERIMENTS

Putting all of the above together, now we can solve the problem about the candidates. Recall that a pollster interviews 300 randomly sampled voters to determine if one candidate is preferred over the other two. The results of the poll are repeated in Table 12.1b.

Is there evidence to indicate that the preference probabilities are not as expected? Test using $\alpha = .05$. The null hypothesis is that each $p_i = 1/3$ and the alternative hypothesis is that at least one $p_i \neq 1/3$.

Table 12.1b

	Candidate		
Preference in Poll	A	B	C
	125	110	65

H_{o}: $p_1 = p_2 = p_3 = 1/3$
H_{a}: At least one $p_i \neq 1/3$

Test Statistic: $\chi^2 = \Sigma \dfrac{[n_i - E(n_i)]^2}{E(n_i)}$

Region of Rejection (Figure 12.3):

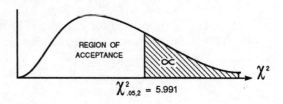

$$\chi^2_{.05,2} = 5.991$$

Figure 12.3
χ^2 Distribution (Region of Rejection Shaded)
— 2 df $\alpha = .05$

There are two degrees of freedom because df $= k - 1$, where k is the number of cells or categories in a one-dimensional multinomial test. According to the chi-square table,

$$\chi^2_{.05,2} = 5.991.$$

FINDING THE TEST STATISTIC

To calculate the expected value in each cell, multiply the total number of subjects in the sample (300) by the probability (1/3) under the null hypothesis that a particular candidate will be chosen. Since $(300)(1/3) = 100$, $E(n_i) = 100$ for each n_i (the null hypothesis is that each $p_i = 1/3$). Then,

$$\chi^2 = \Sigma \frac{[n_i - E(n_i)]^2}{E(n_i)} = \frac{(125-100)^2}{100} + \frac{(110-100)^2}{100} + \frac{(65-100)^2}{100}$$

$$= \frac{25^2}{100} + \frac{10^2}{100} + \frac{(-35)^2}{100} = 6.25 + 1 + 12.25 = 19.5$$

Since $19.5 > 5.991$, reject H_o and conclude that there is a difference in preference for one or more candidates, since at least one $p_i \neq 1/3$.

Exercise 12.1: A die (one of a pair of dice) is tossed sixty times. Table 12.3 shows the number of times each face appeared in the sixty tosses.

Table 12.3

Face #	1	2	3	4	5	6
Frequency	14	5	16	7	15	3

Is there evidence to believe that the die is weighted (unfair)? Test at $\alpha = .05$.

Answer: First, set up the hypothesis test. If a die is fair, then the probability of any number being rolled is equal to 1/6.

H_o: $p_1 = p_2 = \ldots = p_6 = 1/6$

H_a: At least one $p_i \neq 1/6$

Test Statistic: $\chi^2 = \Sigma \dfrac{[n_i - E(n_i)]^2}{E(n_i)}$

Region of Rejection (Figure 12.4)

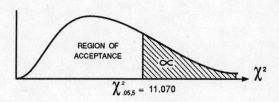

$\chi^2_{.05,5} = 11.070$

Figure 12.4

χ^2 Distribution (Region of Rejection Shaded)
— 5 df $\alpha = .05$

The number of degrees of freedom is $6 - 1 = 5$. The table value of $\chi^2_{.05,5} = 11.070$. Each $E(n_i) = 60(1/6) = 10$. Therefore,

$$\chi^2 = \frac{(14-10)^2}{10} + \frac{(5-10)^2}{10} + \frac{(16-10)^2}{10} + \frac{(7-10)^2}{10}$$

$$+ \frac{(15-10)^2}{10} + \frac{(3-10)^2}{10}$$

$$= \frac{4^2 + (-5)^2 + 6^2 + (-3)^2 + 5^2 + (-7)^2}{10}$$
$$= (16 + 25 + 36 + 9 + 25 + 49)/10 = 160/10 = 16.$$

Since $16 > 11.070$, reject H_o and conclude that the die is not fair, at least one $p_i \neq 1/6$.

Multinomial Experiments with Unequal Probabilities

In a multinomial experiment, the probabilities do not all have to be the same. For example, suppose that in past elections Candidate A's party has gotten 45% of the vote, Candidate B's party 35% of the vote, and Candidate C's party 20% of the vote. Three hundred voters are polled, and the results are repeated in Table 12.1c.

Table 12.1c

	Candidate		
	A	B	C
Preference in Poll	125	110	65

Do these numbers indicate that the past voting percentages (45%, 35%, and 20%, respectively) will be maintained in this election? Test using $\alpha = .05$.

In this problem, the expected numbers differ; therefore, it is a good idea to fill them in the bottom line of the table. $E(n_A) = 300(.45) = 135$; $E(n_B) = 300(.35) = 105$; $E(n_C) = 300(.20) = 60$. This new data appears in Table 12.1d.

Table 12.1d

	Candidate		
	A	B	C
Preference in Poll	125	110	65
Expected Vote	135	105	60

Setting up the hypothesis test:
H_0: $p_A = .45$; $p_B = .35$; $p_C = .20$
H_a: At least one p_i is not as above.

Test Statistic: $\chi^2 = \sum \frac{[n_i - E(n_i)]^2}{E(n_i)}$

Region of Rejection: (See Figure 12.3)

Notice that the region of rejection does not change with the probabilities.

$$\chi^2 = \frac{(125-135)^2}{135} + \frac{(110-105)^2}{105} + \frac{(65-60)^2}{60}$$

$\chi^2 = (-10)^2/135 + 5^2/105 + 5^2/60 = 100/135 + 25/105 + 25/60 = 1.39550.$

Since $1.39550 < 5.991$, do not reject H_o and conclude that the preference poll reflects the expected vote.

Exercise 12.2: Suppose it is known that a die is weighted so that the odd numbers are twice as likely to occur as the even numbers. The die is tossed ninety times; the frequency distribution for the numbers is shown in Table 12.4.

Table 12.4

Face #	1	2	3	4	5	6
Frequency	24	15	14	14	16	7

Is there evidence to believe that the die tosses recorded in Table 12.4 are results of the die weighted as suggested? Test at $\alpha = .05$.

Answer: First determine the probabilities for each toss of the weighted die. If the probability for each even number is $1/x$, then the probability for each odd number is twice that, or $2/x$.

$p_1 + p_2 + p_3 + p_4 + p_5 + p_6 = 1$, so

$2/x + 1/x + 2/x + 1/x + 2/x + 1/x = 1$ and $9/x = 1$.
Cross multiplying, $x = 9$. Therefore, $1/x = 1/9$ and $2/x = 2/9$. The probability of tossing each odd number is 2/9 and of tossing each even number is 1/9. The null hypothesis is:

H_o: $p_1 = p_3 = p_5 = 2/9$ and $p_2 = p_4 = p_6 = 1/9$
H_a: At least one p_i is not as above.

Test Statistic: $\chi^2 = \sum \dfrac{[n_i - E(n_i)]^2}{E(n_i)}$

Region of Rejection: (See Figure 12.4)

Before calculating χ^2 by the formula, find $E(n_i)$ for the odd and even numbers. Recall, $E(n_i) = n(p_i)$. In the case of the odd numbers $E(n_i) = 90(2/9) = 20$. For the even numbers, $E(n_i) = 90(1/9) = 10$. Now these expectations and the frequencies from Table 12.4 can be substituted into the formula for χ^2 above.

$$\chi^2 = \frac{(24-20)^2}{20} + \frac{(15-10)^2}{10} + \frac{(14-20)^2}{20}$$

$$= \frac{(14-10)^2}{10} + \frac{(16-20)^2}{20} + \frac{(7-10)^2}{10}$$

$$= \frac{4^2}{20} + \frac{5^2}{10} + \frac{(-6)^2}{20} + \frac{4^2}{10} + \frac{(-4)^2}{20} + \frac{(-3)^2}{10}$$

$$= .8 + 2.5 + 1.8 + 1.6 + .8 + .9 = 8.4$$

Since $8.4 < 11.070$, do not reject H_o, and conclude that the probabilities are as originally presented: tossing the odd numbers is twice as probable as tossing the even numbers.

CONTINGENCY TABLES

Count data may also be presented in two dimensions. In the one-dimensional problems, the classes were formed according to one criterion, such as candidate preference. For the two dimensional problems, classes are formed with respect to two factors.

For example, suppose again that three candidates (A, B, and C) are running for office. Again, a number of registered voters (150) are asked their preference, but this time those voters are also classified according to political affiliation: Democrats, Republicans, and Independents. The new question is: is there a relationship between a voter's political affiliation and the candidate that he or she prefers? Test using $\alpha = .05$.

The contingency table for this problem is Table 12.5a.

Table 12.5a

	Candidate		
Political Affiliation	A	B	C
Republican	10	35	5
Democrat	50	20	10
Independent	5	5	10

The hypothesis test is conducted similarly to the one-dimensional test, but there are differences in every part of the test. For example, the null hypothesis states that there is no relationship between the two factors, and the alternative hypothesis says that there is a relationship.

The test statistic, while in the same format, must be modified to address not only a row, n_i and $E(n_i)$, but also columns. This contingency table is thus actually a matrix. Recall from Chapter 1 that matrix entries are addressed by their row and column number in a double subscript. For example, the entry in row 1 and column 2 in Table 12.5a is $n_{ij} = n_{12} = 35$; n_{ij} is the general term of the matrix, just as n_i is the general term of the one-dimensional array. We can address every entry by its row and column number. The test statistic for the contingency table problem is

$$\chi^2 = \sum \frac{[n_{ij} - E(n_{ij})]^2}{E(n_{ij})}$$

where n_{ij} is the entry in the ith row and jth column of the contingency table, and $E(n_{ij})$ is the expected value of that entry.

The number of degrees of freedom for the region of rejection is obtained by multiplying the number of rows less one by the number of columns less one; that is, $df = (r-1)(c-1)$ where r is the number of rows and c the number of columns. In the above problem, there are three rows and three columns, so df $= (3-1)(3-1) = 4$. Setting up the hypothesis test for $\alpha = .05$:

H_o: Voter preference and political affiliation are not related.

H_a: There is a relationship between voter preference and political affiliation.

Test Statistic: $\chi^2 = \sum \dfrac{[n_{ij} - E(n_{ij})]^2}{E(_{ij})}$

Region of Rejection (See Figure 12.5)

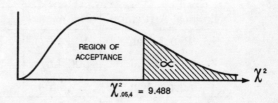

$$\chi^2_{.05,4} = 9.488$$

Figure 12.5

χ^2 Distribution (Region of Rejection Shaded)
—4 df $\alpha = .05$

CALCULATING EXPECTATIONS

To calculate the χ^2 for the test statistic, the expectations for each cell must be calculated. The first step in doing this is to find the row and column totals. Rewriting Table 12.5a with these totals yields in Table 12.5b.

We base the expectations of each entry on the row and column totals. For example, p_{1c} (the probability of a number being in the first row) is 50/150, since 50 of the 150 entries are in the first row. Further, p_{r1} (the probability of a number being in the first column) is 65/150, since 65 of the 150 entries are in the first column. Therefore, $p_{11} = (50/150)(65/150)$ is the probability of an entry being in the first row and first column, under the null hypothesis that these are independent probabilities.

Table 12.5b

	Candidate			
Political Affiliation	A	B	C	Totals
Republican	10	35	5	50
Democrat	50	20	10	80
Independent	5	5	10	20
Totals	65	60	25	150

Recall that the expectation is the product of the total number of subjects and the probability of a certain entry. $E(n_{11}) = n(p_{11}) = 150(50/150)(65/150)$. Canceling the common 150, $E(n11) = 50(65)/150$, which is the total of row one times the total of column one, divided by the total number of entries.

In general, the formula for the expected value of an entry in the ith row and jth column in a contingency table is: $E(n_{ij}) = (T_{ri})(T_{cj})/n$. In Table 12.5c, $E(n_{11}) = (50)(65)/150 = 21.67$.

Table 12.5c

	Candidate			
Political Affiliation	A	B	C	Totals
Republican	10(21.67)	35(20)	5(8.33)	50
Democrat	50(34.67)	20(32)	10(13.33)	80
Independent	5(8.67)	5(8)	10(3.33)	20
Totals	65	60	25	150

Continue to calculate each expectation and put these numbers in parentheses next to the actual numbers in the table. Round all expectations to two decimal places (Table 12.5c).

FINDING THE TWO-DIMENSIONAL TEST STATISTIC

Notice that the totals of the expectations across the rows and down the columns are the same as the totals of the observations, except for rounding errors.

The next step is to calculate χ^2. Recall the formula:

$$\chi^2 = \Sigma \frac{[n_{ij} - E(n_{ij})]^2}{E(n_{ij})}$$

This summation will have nine terms. Listed by their matrix addresses, they are:

11: $(10 - 21.67)^2/21.67$ 12: $(35 - 20)^2/20$

13: $(5 - 8.33)^2/8.33$ 21: $(50 - 34.67)^2/34.67$

22: $(20 - 32)^2/32$ 23: $(10 - 13.33)^2/13.33$

31: $(5 - 8.67)^2/8.67$ 32: $(5 - 8)^2/8$

33: $(10 - 3.33)^2/3.33$

Calculating each of these to two decimal places, they are:

11: 6.28	12: 11.25	13: 1.33
21: 6.78	22: 4.5	23: .83
31: 1.55	32: 1.13	33: 13.36

It is obvious that the sum of these numbers is in the rejection region, but we should sum them anyway. The result is 47.01. Since $47.01 > 9.488$, reject H_o and conclude that political affiliation and candidate preference are related.

Exercise 12.3: One thousand people are asked the following question: Which is your favorite type of television program, comedy (C), drama (D), sports (S), or news (N)? The 1000 people are also asked their age range: under 25, 25–50, or over 50.

The results are summarized in a contingency table (Table 12.6a).

Table 12.6a

Age Range	Viewing Preference			
	C	D	S	N
Under 25	114	61	173	52
26–50	63	88	122	77
Over 50	58	75	49	68

Is there a relationship between the age of the viewer and his or her viewing preference? Test using $\alpha = .01$.

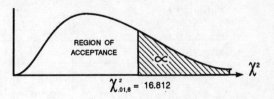

$\chi^2_{.01,6} = 16.812$

Figure 12.6

χ^2 Distribution (Rejection Region Shaded)
— 6 df $\alpha = .01$

Answer: The hypothesis test can be set up first.

H_o: Viewer preference and age are not related.

H_a: There is a relationship between viewer preference and age.

Test Statistic: $\chi^2 = \sum \dfrac{[n_{ij} - E(n_{ij})]^2}{E(n_{ij})}$

Region of Rejection (See Figure 12.6)

df $= (r - 1)(c - 1) = (3 - 1)(4 - 1) = 6$.

The first step in calculating the expected values in each cell is to total the rows and columns of the contingency table (Table 12.6b).

Table 12.6b

Viewing Preference

Age Range	C	D	S	N	Totals
Under 25	114	61	173	52	400
26–50	63	88	122	77	350
Over 50	58	75	49	68	250
Totals	235	224	344	197	1000

The next step is to calculate each $E(n_{ij})$. We compute them using the product of their row and column total divided by the subject total (1000). For example, $E(n_{11}) = 400(235)/1000 = 94$. In a similar manner:

$E(n_{12}) = 89.6$; $E(n_{13}) = 137.6$;

$E(n_{14}) = 78.8$; $E(n_{21}) = 82.25$;

$E(n_{22}) = 78.4$; $E(n_{23}) = 120.4$;

$E(n_{24}) = 68.95$; $E(n_{31}) = 58.75$;

$E(n_{32}) = 56$; $E(n_{33}) = 86$; $E(n_{34}) = 49.25$;

Put these expectations into a modified table (Table 12.6c).

Table 12.6c

Viewing Preference

Age Range	C	D	S	N	Ts
Under 25	114 (94)	61(89.6)	173(137.6)	52(78.8)	400
26–50	63(82.25)	88(78.4)	122(120.4)	77(68.95)	350
Over 50	58(58.75)	75(56)	49(86)	68(49.25)	250
Totals	235	224	344	197	1000

The calculation of χ^2 will have twelve terms:

11: $(114 - 94)^2/94 = 4.26$ 12: $(61 - 89.6)^2/89.6 = 9.13$

13: $(173 - 137.6)^2/137.6 = 9.11$ 14: $(52 - 78.8)^2/78.8 = 9.11$

21: $(63 - 82.25)^2/82.25 = 4.51$ 22: $(88 - 78.4)^2/78.4 = 1.18$

23: $(122 - 120.4)^2/120.4 = .02$ 24: $(77 - 68.95)^2/68.95 = .94$

31: $(58 - 58.75)^2/58.75 = .01$ 32: $(75 - 56)^2/56 = 6.45$

33: $(49 - 86)^2/86 = 15.92$ 34: $(68 - 49.25)^2/49.25 = 7.14$

Therefore, $\chi^2 = 67.78$

Since $67.78 > 16.812$, reject H_o and conclude that viewer preference and age of viewer are related.

Contingency Tables with Fixed Margins

The χ^2 experiments discussed in the previous sections were not designed experiments. A sample of subjects was obtained and certain information taken. In the case of the one-dimensional analysis, one question was asked: who will you vote for among the three candidates? In the two-dimensional case, two questions were asked: who will you vote for, and what is your party affiliation? In that way, the alternative hypothesis states that the answers to the two questions are not independent.

A χ^2 experiment can be designed to try to reach a stronger conclusion. The results of Exercise 12.3 state that viewer age and preference in television programs are not independent. Sometimes, we may prefer a stronger statement. For example, it would be stronger to suggest in what way these two facts are related. What we would like to conclude is that the choice of television programs is specifically related to the age of the viewer. To make the alternative hypothesis this strong, some slight adjustments to the experiment are necessary.

This time, we will fix the size of the samples according to age. That is, instead of asking 1000 people about their viewing preference and their age range, we ask viewing preference while interviewing the same number of subjects in each age range.

Table 12.7a

Age Range	Viewing Preference				
	C	D	S	N	Totals
Under 25	97	51	116	36	300
26-50	53	78	94	75	300
Over 50	58	91	46	105	300
Totals	208	220	256	216	900

In keeping one of the two levels of the contingency table constant, we can make stronger hypotheses about the outcome of the experiment, namely viewer preference is (alternative) or is not (null) related to age.

This *fixing of the margins* will involve the same type of calculation, but it will be much easier because the expectations up and down the nonfixed row or column will be the same; also, when calculating χ^2, all those differences squared will be divided by the same number (the expectation of all entries in that row or column).

For example, suppose the survey in Exercise 12.3 were conducted using 300 people from each age group, with the results as shown in Table 12.7a. Test at $\alpha = .01$ again.

H_o: Viewer preference does not depend on age.

H_a: Viewer preference depends on age of viewer.

Test Statistic: $\chi^2 = \Sigma \dfrac{[n_{ij} - E(n_{ij})]^2}{E(n_{ij})}$

Region of Rejection: (See Figure 12.6)

$E(n_{11}) = (208)(300)/900 = 69.3$. Notice that this is the expectation for all entries in column C. Therefore, $E(n_{r1}) = 69.3$.

Similarly,

$E(n_{r2}) = (220)(300)/900 = 73.3;$
$E(n_{r3}) = (256)(300)/900 = 85.3;$
$E(n_{r4}) = (216)(300)/900 = 72.$

In calculating χ^2, it is easier to work with one column at a time: subtract the expectation from each term in the column, square, and divide by that expectation. For the first column, for example, the calculation is:

$$\frac{(97 - 69.3)^2 + (53 - 69.3)^2 + (58 - 69.3)^2}{69.3}$$

$= (767.29 + 265.69 + 127.69)/69.3 = 16.75$

The second column calculation is:

$$\frac{(51 - 73.3)^2 + (78 - 73.3)^2 + (91 - 73.3)^2}{73.3}$$

$= (497.29 + 22.09 + 313.29)/73.3 = 11.36$

The third column calculation is:

$$\frac{(116 - 85.3)^2 + (94 - 85.3)^2 + (46 - 85.3)^2}{85.3}$$

$= (942.49 + 75.69 + 1544.49)/85.3 = 30.04$

Lastly, the fourth column:

$$\frac{(36 - 72)^2 + (75 - 72)^2 + (105 - 72)^2}{72}$$

$= (1296 + 9 + 1089)/72 = 33.25$

The sum of the column totals is $\chi^2 = 16.75 + 11.36 + 30.04 + 33.25 = 91.4$. Since $91.4 > 16.812$, reject the null hypothesis and conclude that viewer preference depends upon the age of the viewer.

Exercise 12.4: Three candidates (A, B, and C) are running for office. One hundred men and one hundred women are chosen at random from registered voters and asked whom they intend to vote for. The contingency table is Table 12.8a.

Table 12.8a

Gender of Respondents	Candidate			
	A	B	C	Totals
Men	30	45	25	100
Women	50	40	10	100
Totals	80	85	35	200

Test at the .05 level of significance to see if voting preference among the three candidates is dependent upon the gender of the voter.

Answer: First, set up the hypothesis test.

H_o: Candidate preference and gender are not related.

H_a: Candidate preference depends on gender.

Test Statistic: $\chi^2 = \Sigma \dfrac{[n_{ij} - E(n_{ij})]^2}{E(n_{ij})}$

Region of Rejection: (See Figure 12.3)

Notice that the number of degrees of freedom is $(r-1)(c-1) = (2-1)(3-1) = 2$. Now to find the expectations for each entry in the table:

$E(n_{11}) = (80)(100)/200 = 40$.

$E(n_{22}) = (85)(100)/200 = 42.5$.

With just these two entries, the rest of the table can be completed, because we also know the row and column totals.

Table 12.8b

Gender of Respondents	Candidate			
	A	B	C	Totals
Men	30 (40)	45 (45.5)	25 (17.5)	100
Women	50 (40)	40 (42.5)	10 (17.5)	100
Totals	80	85	35	200

For example, since the sum of the first column is 80, and $E(n_{11}) = 40$, then $E(n_{21}) = 40$ also. Similarly, $E(n_{22}) = 42.5$ means that the other second column entry, $E(n_{12}) = 42.5$ also. Since both row totals are 100, the final entry in each position in column 3, $E(n_{13}) = E(n_{23}) = 100 - 40 - 42.5 = 17.5$. Notice that twice 17.5 is 35, the third column total. Table 12.8b includes with the expectations.

Calculating χ^2, both terms in the same column are equal, since there are only two divisions, men and women. Therefore, instead of having to calculate the first column as:

$$\frac{(30 - 40)^2 + (50 - 40)^2}{40}$$

both these numerator differences will be 10^2, so

$$\chi^2 = \frac{2(10)^2}{40} + \frac{2(2.5)^2}{42.5} + \frac{2(7.5)^2}{17.5} = 200/40 + 12.5/42.5 + 112.5/17.5$$

$= 5 + .294 + 6.429 = 11.723$. Since $11.723 > 5.991$, reject H_o and conclude that candidate preference does depend on the voters' gender.

In this chapter, we discussed multinomial experiments and contingency table examples, both of which employ the χ^2 distribution as the test statistic. In both of these examples, the difference between the observed number of occurrences and the expected number of occurrences is calculated for each entry, either in a one-dimensional or two-dimensional table.

These differences are squared, normalized by dividing by their expected value, and summed. If this sum is greater than the corresponding χ^2 value from the table for the appropriate α and df, the null hypothesis is rejected.

In the case of contingency tables, this rejection leads to a statement like "A (row category) and B (column category) are related." To arrive at a stronger statement, keep one of the margin sums constant (either row or column sum). Then, upon rejecting the null hypothesis, one can say that "A depends on B" or "B depends on A."

Table 12.9a

Final Grade	Type of Instruction			
	I	II	III	Totals
A	15	13	12	40
B	34	28	35	97
C	40	36	38	114
D	8	13	7	28
F	3	10	8	21
Totals	100	100	100	300

Count data is used in many different areas of research, particularly in the social sciences. In these types of experiments, counts of subjects in the different categories, rather than measurable and ordered numbers (like the means of scores on finals), are compared.

Exercise 12.5: Three hundred students are randomly divided into three different types of English classes to learn freshman English. In the first type (I) the primary mode of instruction is lecture; in the second type (II) the primary mode of instruction is discussion; in the third type (III) the students primarily use computer assisted instruction. Final grades for each of the 300 students are assigned and the results shown in Table 12.9a.

Test at the .05 level of significance to determine whether final freshman English grades depend on the teaching method employed in the classes.

Answer: First, set up the hypothesis test:

Ho: Final grade does not depend on teaching method.
Ha: Final grade depends on teaching method.

Test Statistic: $\chi^2 = \sum \dfrac{[n_{ij} - E(n_{ij})]^2}{E(n_{ij})}$

Region of Rejection (Figure 12.7):

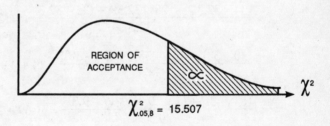

Figure 12.7
χ^2 Distribution (Rejection Region Shaded) — 8 df
$\alpha = .05$

df $= (r-1)(c-1) = (5-1)(3-1) = 8$.

To find the expectations, notice that all the column totals are the same. Therefore, the expectations across each row are equal. They are:

$E(n_{1j}) = (40)(100)/300 = 13.3$
$E(n_{2j}) = (97)(100)/300 = 32.3$
$E(n_{3j}) = (114)(100)/300 = 38$
$E(n_{4j}) = (28)(100)/300 = 9.33$

$E(n_{5j}) = (21)(100)/300 = 7$

Put the expectations into Table 12.9b.

Table 12.9b

Final Grade	Type of Instruction			Totals
	I	II	III	
A	15 (13.3)	13 (13.3)	12 (13.3)	40
B	34 (32.3)	28 (32.3)	35 (32.3)	97
C	40 (38)	36 (38)	38 (38)	114
D	8 (9.3)	13 (9.3)	7 (9.3)	28
F	3 (7)	10 (7)	8 (7)	21
Totals	100	100	100	300

To calculate χ^2, go across the rows:

$$\frac{(15-13.3)^2 + (13-13.3)^2 + (12-13.3)^2}{13.3} = (2.89 + .09 + 1.69)/13.3 = .35$$

$$\frac{(34-32.3)^2 + (28-32.3)^2 + (35-32.3)^2}{32.3}(= (2.89 + 18.49 + 7.29)/32.3 = .89$$

$$\frac{(40-38)^2 + (36-38)^2 + (38-38)^2}{38} = (4 + 4 + 0)/38 = .21$$

$$\frac{(8-9.3)^2 + (13-9.3)^2 + (7-9.3)^2}{9.3} = (1.69 + 13.69 + 5.29)/9.3 = 2.22$$

$$\frac{(3-7)^2 + (10-7)^2 + (8-7)^2}{7} = (16 + 9 + 1)/7 = 26/7 = 3.71$$

Therefore, $\chi^2 = .35 + .89 + .21 + 2.22 + 3.71 = 7.38$.

Since $7.38 < 15.507$, do not reject H_o and conclude that final grades do not depend on teaching method used in the class.

13

Linear Regression

Linear regression analysis presents new types of data: two numbers associated with each subject rather than one. Then new kinds of hypotheses regarding the relationship between these numbers are developed and proved or disproved with a high degree of confidence.

For example, suppose we believe that the higher the price of a new car, the lower its gas mileage. In linear regression analysis, we can hypothesize this relationship. Then we can prove or disprove it by using statistical methods like hypothesis testing and confidence intervals on samples of new cars.

If it turns out that the price/mileage relationship we hypothesized does exist, we will even be able to predict the gas mileage of a new car (within a certain interval) by knowing its price. These are some if the ideas we will discuss in this chapter.

Ordered Pairs of Numbers

Data points for regression analysis are presented in ordered pairs (x, y), where x is the independent variable and y the dependent variable; i.e., the value of y depends on the value of x. In such a case, there is a function or an equation that links x and y; given a value of x, one can find the value of y for that ordered pair. Sometimes, the equation that links the value of x and y is the equation of a line.

Suppose we are given a set of ordered pairs of the form (x, y) to find an equation of a line that links x and y. For example, suppose the set of ordered pairs is (65, 140), (69, 150), (62, 110), (71, 170), (66, 120), (68, 150), (70, 150), (67, 130), (63, 120), (65, 100).

These ten ordered pairs represent the heights (x in inches) and weights (y in pounds) of ten women chosen at random from a large group of women. Is there a linear relationship between x and y? That is, if these points are graphed, will they all lie on the same line?

Equation of a Line

Recall from Chapter 1 that the equation of a line has the form $y = mx + b$, where m is the slope of the line (change in y over change in x) and b is the y-intercept of the line (the point at which the line intersects the y-axis). Recall also that given two points, one can find and graph the equation of the line that joins them and that there is only one such line that joins them (two points determine a line). If more than two points are on the same line, the points are said to be collinear. Are the ten points above collinear? The first step is to graph them.

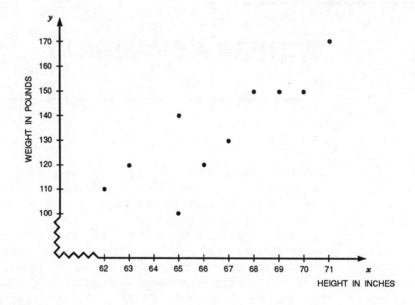

Figure 13.1
Scattergram: x: Height
             y: Weight

Graphing Data Points

Notice that the graph in Figure 13.1 is drawn in only one quadrant since both the x-values of the points (height in inches) and the y-values of the points (weight in pounds) are positive numbers. Further, neither the x-axis nor the y-axis needs to include all values starting at 0. As a matter of fact, the first number needed for the x-axis is 62 (inches), so the part of the x-axis between 0 and 62 is compressed. In a similar way, the part of the y-axis between 0 and 100 (the first weight given) can also be compressed. In that way, the entire graph can appear in a smaller area.

Why did we put these points on a graph? To see if they all lie on the same line, i.e., are collinear. It is obvious that they are not. However, three of the points are on the same horizontal line [(69, 150), (68, 150), and (70, 150)] and two of them are on the same vertical line [(65, 100) and (65, 140)].

On the same (horizontal) line are the coordinates (height and weight) of three points representing women of different heights who have the same weight (150); and on the same (vertical) line are the coordinates of two points representing women of the same height (65) whose weights are different. However, there is no one line on which all ten points lie.

Often such data points seem to be scattered all over the grid. The ones we see here may look as if they are heading in the same direction. No matter how scattered the points are, or how close to a line they seem to lie, such a graph of data points is always called a *scattergram*.

LEAST SQUARES LINE

Note, however, that the above points do tend to change together; as a whole, the taller a woman is, the heavier she is. What remains is to find out whether these heights and weights are linearly related. That is, first we find a line that best fits these data points; then we ask, is the line close enough to the points to say that there is a linear relationship among them?

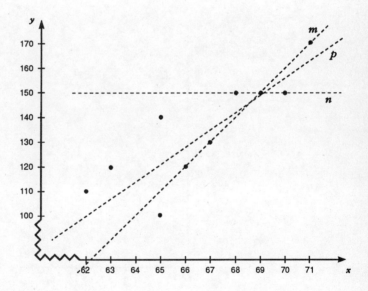

Figure 13.2
Scattergram: *x*: Height *y*: Weight
Candidates for Least Squares Line: *m, n, p*

Therefore, there are two questions we need to answer:

1. What is the equation of the line that is closest to these data points?

2.   Is the line close enough to claim a linear relationship?
These questions will be answered in this chapter.

The line that is closest to the points is called the *least squares line*, the *regression line*, or the *line of best fit* . Examine Figure 13.2 for some possible candidates for this line.

Line *m* is a possibility because it goes through (fits perfectly) several of the data points. Therefore, the fit of the line to those points is perfect. However, many of the data points are very far from the line. The distance from a point to a line in linear regression analysis is measured vertically.

Line *n* goes through the three points that lie on a horizontal line. Many of the other points, though, are quite far away from line *m*.

Line *p* seems to be a good choice for the least squares line since most points are quite close to *n*, although no points are on it.

Exercise 13.1: Graph the following set of data points, and try to find the line that best fits the points (the regression line):   (1, 2), (2, 4), (3, 5), (4, 7), (5, 8).

Answer: Figure 13.3 shows the points and a reasonable choice for a regression line. Other choices for the regression line might also be reasonable, as long as none of the points is too far away from the line. We will define "too far away" and learn how to find the closest line in the next few sections.

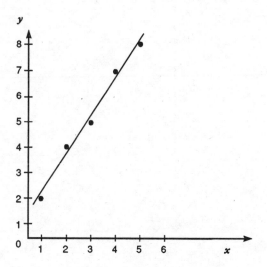

Figure 13.3
Scattergram and Least Squares Line Possibility

FINDING THE LEAST SQUARES LINE

Given the equation of a line (e.g., $y = 2x - 1$), a point on the line can be found by substituting a number for x, the independent value, and finding the corresponding y (dependent value). For example, if $x = 3$, and $y = 2x - 1$, then $y = 5$.

Given two points, a line can be found that contains both of them. But in Exercise 13.1 we have five points that are *not* collinear. We wish to find the least squares line for these points; i.e., the line that comes closest to all of them.

The general equation of a line is $y = mx + b$. For the line $y = 2x - 1$, the slope (m) is 2 and the y-intercept (b) is -1. Graphing this line, it is obvious that it intersects the y-axis at -1 and goes up two units (changes in the y or vertical direction) for every one unit it goes to the right (changes in the x or horizontal direction) (Figure 13.4).

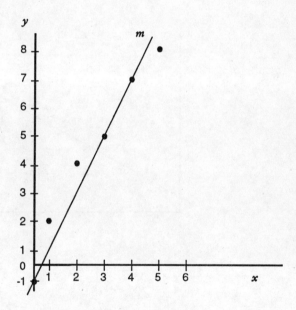

Figure 13.4
Data Points (1, 2) (2, 4) (3, 5) (4, 7) (5, 8)
Line *m*: $y = 2x - 1$

To find the equation of the regression line (i.e., find its slope and y-intercept), we need to find a line that minimizes the distances from the data points to it. Since some of the points are above and some below the line, we will square these distances and establish that the sum of these square distances, otherwise known as SSE, sum of squares error, is smaller than the sum of squares of distances from these same points to any other line. This line is called the least squares line.

Equation of the Linear Model

Two components distinguish one line from another: its slope and its y-intercept. So far we have used the letters m for slope and b for y-intercept. In the case of the least squares line, the population parameters, also called β (beta) parameters, are named β_0 (y-intercept) and β_1 (slope).

In terms of the model (the regression line including an error term epsilon (ε), the equation of the line is $y = \beta_0 + \beta_1 x + \varepsilon$. This means that given the line $y = \beta_0 + \beta_{01} x$, we can arrive at any y-value of a data point by substituting x into the equation and then adding ε, the error term, to y. In a sense, one gets close to the point by using the equation of the line, and then "jumps" to the exact point by adding the error term, the vertical distance between the y-value for x on the line and the actual y-value of the data point (Figure 13.5).

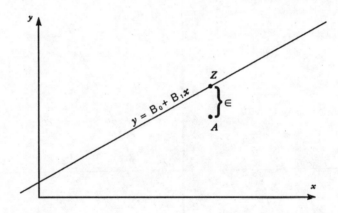

Figure 13.5
A is the data point. Z is the point on the regression line.
$Y = \beta_0 + \beta_1 x$ with the same x-value as A.
ε is vertical distance from A to Z.

Equation of the Least Squares Line

To find the least squares line, we want to calculate b_0 and b_1, estimators for β_0 and β_1 respectively. These estimators are found so that SSE, the sum of all the epsilons squared, will be a minimum for all data points. Thus, the equation of the regression line is $y' = b_0 + b_1 x$, where b_0 is an estimator of the y-intercept that makes SSE minimal; b_1 is an estimator of the slope that makes SSE minimal; and y' is the predictor of y from the model (y' is the value of y on the line, not the value of y at the data point). What remains is to find the values of b_0 and b_1 that will make $y' = b_0 + b_1 x$ the least squares line.

Exercise 13.2: Given the data points from Exercise 13.1, $(1, 2)$, $(2, 4)$, $(3, 5)$, $(4, 7)$, $(5, 8)$, graph them and the line $y' = 2x - 1$ on the same axes. Then find SSE, the sum of squares of the errors (vertical distances) from each of the five points to the corresponding point with the same x-value on the line.

Answers: First graph the points and line on the same axes (Figure 13.6).

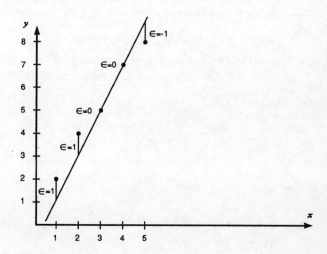

Figure 13.6
Line $y' = 2x - 1$ and data points $(1, 2)$, $(2, 4)$, $(3, 5)$, $(4, 7)$, $(5, 8)$ with εs (epsilon distances) between data points and points on line indicated.

To find the errors, find the y-value of the point on the line and subtract that from the y-value of the data point: this difference is the epsilon (ε). Then square the epsilons and sum them to get SSE.

For $x = 1$, the y-value of the point on the line is obtained by substituting 1 for x in the equation $y' = 2x - 1$. Therefore, $y' = 2(1) - 1 = 1$. The y-value of the first data point $(1, 2)$ is $y = 2$. Therefore, the difference between the actual y of the data point and the predictor y' on the line is $2 - 1 = 1$ and $1^2 = 1$, so the error squared for that point is 1.

For $x = 2$, $y' = 2(2) - 1 = 3$. The difference between the ys is 1 and the error squared is also 1.

For $x = 3$, $y' = 2(3) - 1 = 5$. Since the y-value of the data point is also 5, their difference and difference squared are 0.

For $x = 4$, $y' = 2(4) - 1 = 7$. The y-value of the data point is also 7, so their squared difference is 0.

Finally, for $x = 5$, $y' = 2(5) - 1 = 9$. The actual y-value from the data point is 8, so their squared difference is 1.

The sum of the squared errors, SSE $= 1 + 1 + 0 + 0 + 1 = 3$. The line $y' = 2x - 1$ seems to be a good candidate for the least squares line, the line of best fit, for the points $(1, 2)$, $(2, 4)$, $(3, 5)$, $(4, 7)$, $(5, 8)$. Perhaps we can find a better candidate. If so, it will have a smaller SSE than 3, the SSE of $y' = 2x - 1$.

Finding the Slope and Y-Intercept of the Least Squares Line

The general equation of any least squares line is $y' = b_0 + b_1 x$. Once b_1 and b_0 are found using the given points, the equation of the line will be known.

SLOPE OF THE LEAST SQUARES LINE

The slope of the regression line, b_1, is given by the formula $b_1 = SS_{xy}/SS_{xx}$. SS_{xx} is the numerator of the variance of x. Recall that the formula for the variance of x is

$$x^2 = \frac{\sum x^2 - \dfrac{\left(\sum x\right)^2}{n}}{n-1}$$

The numerator is just $SS_{xx} = \sum x^2 - \dfrac{\left(\sum x\right)^2}{n}$. In turn, SS_{xx} is the denominator of the slope.

SS_{xy} is the numerator of the slope. The formula for SS_{xy} resembles the formula above, except that the main part is $\sum xy$, the sum of the products of the x-value of each data point times its y-value. The formula is

$$SS_{xy} = \sum xy - \left(\sum x\right)\left(\sum y\right)/n.$$

The slope of the regression line is really the ratio of the variance of x and y together to the variance of x. Since both denominators are the same $(n-1)$, they are not included in the formula; they would just cancel each other in the computation. Therefore, the slope of the regression or least squares line is $b_1 = SS_{xy}/SS_{xx}$.

Given the points $(1, 2)$, $(2, 4)$, $(3, 5)$, $(4, 7)$, $(5, 8)$, find the slope of the line of best fit, the regression line. It is easier to display these points in a table for easier computation (Table 13.1).

Table 13.1

x	1	2	3	4
y	2	4	5	7

We should do some preliminary calculations of $\sum x$, $\sum x^2$, $\sum y$, $\sum y^2$, and $\sum xy$. For the above data, we get: $\sum x = 15$; $\sum x^2 = 55$; $\sum y = 26$, $\sum y^2 = 158$; $\sum xy = 1 \cdot 2 + 2 \cdot 4 + 3 \cdot 5 + 4 \cdot 7 + 5 \cdot 8 = 93$. Actually, these formulas do not call for $\sum y^2$, but we will need this computation for later work, so it is best to calculate it now.

$SS_{xx} = \sum x^2 - (\sum x)^2/n = 55 - 15^2/5 = 55 - 45 = 10$. Notice that the number of data points, n, is 5, even though it takes two numbers to describe each point.

$SS_{xy} = \sum xy - (\sum x)(\sum y)/n = 93 - (15)(26)/5 = 93 - 78 = 15$. Since $b_1 = SS_{xy}/SS_{xx}$, $b_1 = 15/10 = 1.5$; the slope of the regression line is 1.5.

Y-INTERCEPT OF THE LEAST SQUARES LINE

Recall from Chapter 1 that to find the y-intercept of a line, substitute m and any ordered pair value of x and y into the equation of the line $y = mx + b$ and solve for b. Since a given pair of points is not necessarily on the least squares line, we substitute the means of x and y, $\bar{x}$ and $\bar{y}$, into the equation of the line and solve for b_0.

To find the y-intercept, substitute into the equation $y' = b_0 + b_1 x$ as follows: let $y' = \bar{y}$, $x = \bar{x}$, and substitute the slope calculated above for b_1. Thus, the formula used to find the y-intercept of the regression line is: $b_0 = \bar{y} - b_1 \bar{x}$.

$\bar{x} = \sum x/n = 15/5 = 3$, $\bar{y} = \sum y/n = 26/5 = 5.2$, and $b_1 = 1.5$; therefore $b_0 = \bar{y} - b_1 \bar{x} = 5.2 - 1.5(3) = 5.2 - 4.5 = .7$. The y-intercept of the least squares line is $b_0 = .7$.

The equation of the least squares line for the above five points is thus $y' = .7 + 1.5x$.

Graph the new line, $y' = .7 + 1.5x$ and the points on the same axis. To graph the line, take two values of x in the data set and find the corresponding values of y. Then join the two points. For the line in Figure 13.7, $x = 1$ and $x = 5$ were used.

This equation is quite different from the first guess of $y' = 2x - 1$, which had an SSE of 3. The SSE of the least squares line, $y' = .7 + 1.5x$ should be smaller. Nevertheless, the line in Figure 13.4 looks to be as good a fit to the scattergram as the least squares line in Figure 13.7 is to the same points. We now want to check out the error, SSE, point for point, starting with $x = 1$ and $x = 5$, the points that were used to graph the line.

For $x = 1$, $y' = .7 + 1.5(1) = 2.2$. Notice that the difference between the actual y from the data point (1, 2) and the y' on the line (2.2) is .2.

For $x = 5$, $y' = .7 + 1.5(5) = 8.2$. Notice that the difference here, between 8.2 and 8, is also .2.

To find the other differences:

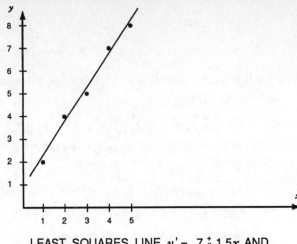

LEAST SQUARES LINE $y' = .7 + 1.5x$ AND
DATA POINTS $(1,| 2)$ $(2,| 4)$ $(3,| 5)$ $(4,| 7)$ $(5,| 8)$

Figure 13.7
Least Squares Line $y' = .7 + 1.5x$ and
Data Points $(1, 2), (2, 4), (3, 5), (4, 7), (5, 8)$

For $x = 2$, $y' = 3.7$, which yields a difference of $- .3$ from 4.
For $x = 3$, $y' = 5.2$, giving a difference of .2 from 5.
For $x = 4$, $y' = 6.7$, giving a difference of $- .3$ from 7.

If all these differences are summed before squaring, the sums should equal 0 since the line is supposed to be a closest fit between the data points.

The sum of the errors is $.2 + (- .3) + .2 + (- .3) + .2 = 0$. The sum of the squares of the errors is:

$$SSE = (.2)^2 + (-.3)^2 + (.2)^2 + (-.3)^2 + (.2)^2$$
$$= .04 + .09 + .04 + .09 + .04 = .3.$$

Notice how much smaller this SSE is than the SSE using the other line $y' = 2x - 1$, whose SSE from these five points was 3. As a matter of fact, this SSE is smaller than any other SSE obtained by using a different line, because $y' = .7 + 1.5x$ is the least squares line.

Exercise 13.3: Recall earlier data points (x, y) in which x was the height in inches and y the weight in pounds of ten randomly chosen women. Those points are repeated here:

$(65, 140), (69, 150), (62, 110), (71, 170), (66, 120), (68, 150), (70, 150),$
$(67, 130), (63, 120), (65, 100)$

Find the equation of the least squares line, plot it and the points on the same graph.

Answers: First put the points in a table for easier computation (Table 13.2).

Table 13.2

x	65	69	62	71	66	68	70	67	63	65
y	140	150	110	170	120	150	150	130	120	100

To find the equation of the regression line, we must make some preliminary calculations:

$$\sum x = 666; \bar{x} = 66.6; \sum x^2 = 44,434$$

$$\sum y = 1340; \bar{y} = 134; \sum y^2 = 183,800*$$

$$\sum xy = 89,730.$$

*We do not need this number, $\sum y^2$, for this exercise, but we will need it in future exercises.

The general equation of the least squares line is $y' = b_0 + b_1 x$. To find the slope, b_1, use the formula $b_1 = SS_{xy}/SS_{xx}$.

$$SS_{xx} = \sum x^2 - \left(\sum x\right)^2/n$$
$$= 44,434 - (666)^2/10 = 44434 - 44355.6 = 78.4.$$

$$SS_{xy} = \sum xy - \left(\sum x\right)\left(\sum y\right)/n$$
$$= 89,730 - (666)(1340)/10 = 89,730 - 89244 = 486.$$

$b_1 = SS_{xy}/SS_{xx} = 486/78.4 = 6.20$. The slope of the least squares line is 6.20.

To find the y-intercept, use the equation $b_0 = \bar{y} - b_1\bar{x} = 134 - 6.20(66.6) = -278.92$. Therefore, the equation of the regression line is $y' = -278.92 + 6.20x$.

To graph this line, take two values of x that are in the set of values, one small and one large. For example, take $x = 62$ and $x = 70$. For $x = 62$, $y' = -278.92 + 6.20(62) = 105.48$, so one point on the regression line is (62, 105.48). For $x = 70$, $y' = -278.92 + 6.20(70) = 155.08$, so a second point on the regression line is (70, 155.08).

Figure 13.8 shows the regression line and the data points.

Notice that this line does not fit the data points as well as the previous line fit its data points. The error terms, the epsilons, are larger, since the points are further from the line.

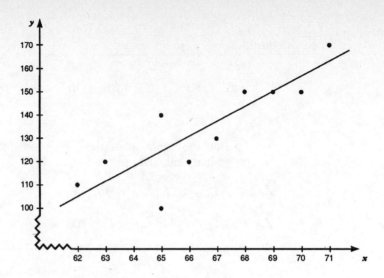

Figure 13.8
Regression line $y' = -278.92 + 6.20x$ for ten data points (x, y) x: Hts y: Wts

VARIANCE OF THE ERROR DISTRIBUTION

We can think of the regression line in terms of a number of probability distributions, one at each point of the line. These distributions represent the probability distributions of epsilon (ε), the error. One of the assumptions we make when using the techniques of linear regression is that the probability distribution of each ε is normal.

Refer to Figure 13.9. This is the true population regression line, whose equation is $y = \beta_0 + \beta_1 x$. y is the expected value of y over a large number of observations, given that the mean value of the random error is 0. Each of these normal probability distributions, therefore, has a mean of 0, a variance σ^2, and a standard deviation σ. Each of the little normal probability distributions contains the ε-term for each point.

Recall that the model has the equation $y = \beta_0 + \beta_1 + \varepsilon$. It is these epsilons ($\varepsilon$) that are included in the probability distributions. The distance from the actual y-values of the data points to the y-values on the least squares line are in keeping with the normal probabilities of the curve. For example, 95% of the data points will be within two standard deviations (2σ on either side) of the point on the line with the same x-value.

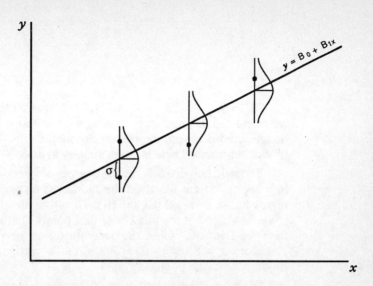

Figure 13.9
Regression Line $y = \beta_0 + \beta_1 x$, Showing Probability Distributions of ε

In order to find s^2 and s, first find SSE, which is the sum of squares of all the errors. Recall that we have calculated SSE before by finding the actual y-values of the data points, subtracting them from the y' values on the least squares line, then squaring and summing. We now present an easier way to compute.

Calculating SSE, s^2, and s

SSE is defined as $\sum (y - y')^2$ for all y-values of the data points. That is the way we calculated SSE for the two lines $y = 2x - 1$ and $y' = .7 + 1.5x$ that were fitted to the five data points.

However, there is another formula that also yields the sum of squares of the epsilons. This formula for SSE is $\text{SSE} = \text{SS}_{yy} - b_1 \cdot \text{SS}_{xy}$. SS_{yy} is calculated in the same way as is SS_{xx}; its formula is $\text{SS}_{yy} = \sum y^2 - \left(\sum y \right)^2 / n$.

Recall the example with the five data points from Table 13.1, repeated on the next page.

Recall also that $\text{SS}_{xy} = 15$ and the equation of the least squares line is $y' = .7 + 1.5x$. To find SSE (if we hadn't already found it the hard way), first calculate SS_{yy}. $\sum y^2 = 158$ and $\sum y = 26$. Therefore,

$$\text{SS}_{yy} = \sum y^2 - \left(\sum y \right)^2 / n = 158 - 26^2/5 = 22.8.$$

Table 13.1

x	1	2	3	4	5
y	2	4	5	7	8

$SSE = SS_{yy} - b_1 SS_{xy} = 22.8 - (1.5)(15) = .3$. Note that .3 is the same number we calculated the long way: finding each difference between the actual y and its predicted point (on the regression line), then squaring and summing. The formula introduced here is much simpler to use.

To find s^2, divide SSE by the degrees of freedom. The degrees of freedom in a regression are based on the number β of parameters, which in a linear regression is always 2 (β_0 and β_1). Therefore, the df for all linear regressions is $n - 2$, where n is the number of data points. In the example above in which there are five data points, the denominator of the s^2 calculation is $5 - 2 = 3$. Therefore, $s^2 = SSE/(n - 2) = .3/3 = .1$. The variance of the regression model for the above data points is $s^2 = .1$.

To find s, the standard error of the regression model, take the square root of s^2: $\sqrt{.1} \approx .316$, so $s = .316$. This means that one would be 95% certain that the actual y-values for each x of the data points is within two standard deviations, $2(.316) = .632$, of the y' on the line for the same x. Notice that the line is very close to the points (Figure 13.7), so a small s is expected.

Exercise 13.4: Find the sum of squares errors (SSE), the variance of the model (s^2) and the standard error of the model (s) for the data in Exercise 13.3. Table 13.2 is repeated here:

Table 13.2

x	65	69	62	71	66	68	70	67	63	65
y	140	150	110	170	120	150	150	130	120	100

Answers:

Recall from the Exercise 13.3 calculation that $\Sigma y = 1340$ and $\Sigma y^2 = 183{,}800$. Also recall that $SS_{xy} = 486$ and $b_1 = 6.20$. $SSE = SS_{yy} - b_1 SS_{xy}$, so we need to calculate SS_{yy}.

$$SS_{yy} = \Sigma y^2 - (\Sigma y)^2/n = 183{,}800 - (1340)^2/10 = 4240.$$

Substituting: $SSE = SS_{yy} - b_1 SS_{xy} = 4240 - 6.2(486) = 1226.8$.
Therefore, $SSE = 1226.8$.
$s^2 = SSE/(n - 2) = 1226.8/8 = 153.35$. Thus, $s = \sqrt{s^2} = \sqrt{153.35} = 12.38$.

(Refer to Figure 13.8.) Comparing the actual values of y from the data points with the values of y for the same values of x on the least squares line, most of the distances should be no more than two standard deviations or $2(12.38) \approx 25$. Almost all of the data points should be no more than 25 units vertically from the least squares line. Are they?

HYPOTHESIS TESTING USING THE REGRESSION LINE

A least squares line can be fitted to any set of data, even if the points are not linearly related. Then the question becomes whether the line is a true picture of the relationship between the points. Are they linearly related or not? When *x* increases, does *y* either increase or decrease predictably? Or does *y* increase or decrease capriciously, without pattern, or not change much at all? One key to the answer to this question is the slope of the regression line, b_1.

Suppose the data points are more or less randomly scattered, as in Figure 13.10. A least squares line can be fitted, but the line is almost horizontal. (Recall that the slope of a horizontal line is 0.) In Figure 13.10, it seems that

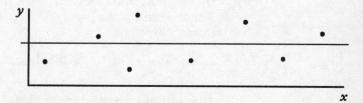

Figure 13.10
Horizontal Regression Line ($\beta_1 = 0$)
x and *y* are not linearly related.

the values of *y* have no linear relation to the values of *x* since they are neither generally increasing nor decreasing as *x* gets larger. So even if a regression line can be fitted, its slope is close enough to 0 to negate any hypothesis about the linear relationship between *x* and *y*. In this section, slopes of least square lines will be tested to see if they are close enough to 0 to say that no linear relationship between *x* and *y* exists.

Hypothesis Testing of the Slope of the Least Squares Line

The hypothesis test will be a test of the slope of the regression line against a zero slope (the null hypothesis). The test statistic used is the t since the sample of points is almost always small. The region of regression will be based on the alpha-level and the number of degrees of freedom. The df will always be two less than the number of data points.

The dean of a college hypothesizes that the more credits a student takes during a semester, the lower his or her grade point average is for that semester. In order to test that theory, eight students are chosen at random and the number of credits and G.P.A.s for each for the previous semester are reported (Table 13.3). Test the dean's hypothesis at .05 level of significance.

Table 13.3

Student	A	B	C	D	E	F	G	H
# of Credits (x)	10	18	12	15	16	16	22	9
G.P.A. (y)	3.5	2.8	3.3	3.7	2.9	3.0	2.4	3.1

This is a hypothesis test of the slope of the line. The test statistic used is t since the number of data points is small (8). The set-up is as follows:

H_o: $\beta_1 = 0$

H_a: $\beta_1 < 0$ [The expectation here is for a negative slope since the higher x (number of credits) is, the lower y (G.P.A.) is expected to be according to the dean's hypothesis.]

Test Statistic: $t = \dfrac{b_1}{s_{b_1}}$ where b_1 is the slope of the least-squares line and

s_{b_1} is the standard deviation of the slope. $s_{b_1} = \dfrac{s}{\sqrt{SS_{xx}}}$ where s is the

standard deviation of the regression model and SS_{xx} is the sum of squares x.

Region of Rejection (See Figure 13.11)

REGION OF REJECTION

REGION OF ACCEPTANCE

$t_{.05,6} = -1.943$

Figure 13.11
t = Distribution: 6 df

This is a one-tailed, lower or negative tail t-test with $\alpha = .05$. The number of degrees of freedom is $n - 2$, based on the fact that there are two parameters, β_0 and β_1, for the linear regression. There are eight data points, so $8 - 2 = 6$: $t_{.05,6} = -1.943$.

To calculate the t-value for the test statistic requires most of the steps needed to find the equation of the line and SSE. Preliminarily, calculate the same sums of squares as in the previous examples for linear regression.

$$\Sigma x = 118;\ \bar{x} = 14.75;\ \Sigma x^2 = 1870$$

$$\Sigma y = 24.7;\ \bar{y} = 3.0875;\ \Sigma y^2 = 77.45$$

$$\Sigma xy = 355.6$$

$$SS_{xx} = \Sigma x^2 - \left(\Sigma x\right)^2/n = 1870 - (118)^2/8 = 129.5$$

$$SS_{yy} = \Sigma y2 - \left(\Sigma y\right)^2/n = 77.45 - (24.7)^2/8 = 1.19$$

$$SS_{xy} = \Sigma xy - \left(\Sigma x\right)\left(\Sigma y\right)/n = 355.6 - (118)(24.7)/8 = -8.725$$

Notice that SS_{xy} is negative. This occurs when x and y are inversely related. Since $SSxy$ is the numerator of the slope and SS_{xx} is always positive, the slope of this least squares line will be negative. To calculate the slope:

$$b_1 = SS_{xy}/SS_{xx} = -8.725/129.5 = -.067$$

For the hypothesis test, we want to find out if this number is close enough to 0 to say that the hypothesized relationship between x and y is not true.

The first step in finding s_{b_1} is to find SSE.

$$SSE = SS_{yy} - b_1 \cdot SS_{xy} = 1.19 - (-.067)(-8.725) = 1.19 - .584575 = .605$$

$$s^2 = SSE/(n - 2) = .605/6 = .101;\ \text{therefore,}\ s = .318.$$

$$s_{b_1} = \frac{s}{\sqrt{SS_{xx}}} = .318/\sqrt{129.5} = .028.$$

The test statistic $t = b_1/s_{b_1}$ calculates the t-value for the slope. The t-value places the slope in the sampling distribution of slopes of least squares lines. The test is to see if this slope is within the acceptance region, in view of the given α and df.

$$t = b_1/s_{b_1} = -.067/.028 = -2.39.\ \text{Since}\ -2.39 < -1.943,\ \text{reject}\ H_o\ \text{and}$$

conclude that the more credits a student carries, the lower is his/her G.P.A. This conclusion comes from the fact that the regression line has a significant negative slope.

Exercise 13.5: In the previous two exercises, ten women's heights and weights were given. Suppose the hypothesis is that there is a linear relationship between the heights and weights of women. Test this hypothesis at the .05 level of significance, using the data in Table 13.2.

Table 13.2

x	65	69	62	71	66	68	70	67	63	65
y	140	150	110	170	120	150	150	130	120	100

Answer: Recall that the equation of the regression line for this data is $y' = -278.92 + 6.20x$. We will test the slope (6.20) to see if it is significantly different from 0.

$H_o: \beta_1 = 0$

$H_a: \beta_1 \neq 0$ (Note the nondirectional test. This is because the hypothesis is that there is a linear relationship between the heights and weights, not, as might have been stated for a stronger hypothesis, that taller women are heavier, which would be a directional hypothesis.)

Test Statistic: $t = \dfrac{b_1}{s_{b_1}}$

Region of Rejection (Figure 13.12):

$t_{.025,8} = -2.306$ $t_{.025,8} = 2.306$

Figure 13.12
t-Distribution — 6 df

Note the nondirectional, two-tailed test: $\alpha = .05$, $\alpha/2 = .025$. $t_{.025,8} = 2.306$ or -2.306. From the previous exercises, we have already calculated $b_1 = 6.20$, $s = 12.38$, and $SS_{xx} = 78.4$.

Since $s_{b_1} = \dfrac{s}{\sqrt{SS_{xx}}}$, $s_{b_1} = 12.38/\sqrt{78.4} = 1.4$.

$t = 6.2/1.4 = 4.43$. Since $4.43 > 2.306$, reject H_o and conclude that there is a linear relationship between the heights and weights of women.

Coefficient of Correlation

When two variables are very closely related, such as height and weight, they are said to be *correlated*. A numerical value of the amount of correlation, r, is called the *Pearson product moment coefficient of correlation*. Its formula is

$$r = \frac{SS_{xy}}{\sqrt{SS_{xx} \cdot SS_{yy}}}$$

The value of r can range between -1 and $+1$. The only way that r can equal 0 is if $SS_{xy} = 0$, in which case $b_1 = 0$, since SS_{xy} is the numerator of the slope b_1. The closer r is to -1 or $+1$, the stronger the linear relationship between x and y. If r is close to 1, a strong positive linear relationship exists, and if r is close to -1, a strong negative linear relationship exists.

The problem in the previous section involved a hypothesis (which was proven) that the more credits a student takes in a semester, the lower is his or her G.P.A. Recall the data set from that problem (Table 13.3).

Table 13.3

Student	A	B	C	D	E	F	G	H
# of Credits(x)	10	18	12	15	16	16	22	9
G.P.A. (y)	3.5	2.8	3.3	3.7	2.9	3.0	2.4	3.1

The sums of squares calculated for the work in the previous section were $SS_{xx} = 129.5$; $SS_{yy} = 1.19$; $SS_{xy} = -8.725$.

Calculating the coefficient of correlation:

$$r = \frac{SS_{xy}}{\sqrt{SS_{xx} \cdot SS_{yy}}} = \frac{-8.725}{\sqrt{(129.5)(1.19)}} = -.703$$

This says that for these subjects, the negative linear correlation is fairly high: as the number of credit hours students take increases, their G.P.A.s tend to decrease.

Instead of testing β_1 to see if it equals 0, as we did in the previous section, ρ (rho) can also be tested to see if it is close to 0. Rho (ρ) is the population correlation coefficient, while r is the sample correlation coefficient, just as β_1 is the slope of the least squares line fitted to the entire population while b_1 is the slope of the line fitted to the sample. Since the test of β_1 and the test of ρ both will confirm or deny the null hypothesis (i.e., there is no linear relationship between x and y) for the same data, it is not necessary to test both: the test to see if $\beta_1 = 0$ is sufficient.

Coefficient of Determination

Another number that indicates to what extent x and y are linearly related is called the *coefficient of determination*. It measures the proportion of variability in y that is explained by x. Recall that the model in terms of the population parameters β_0 and β_1 is given by the equation $y = \beta_0 + \beta_1 x + \varepsilon$. To go from a given x to y, substitute x into the model.

When the epsilons (ε) are all squared and summed for a given data set, the result is SSE, which represents the error or unexplained sample variability. SS_{yy} is the total sample variability for y. Therefore, SS_{yy} – SSE refers to the total variability minus the unexplained sample variability, or the explained variability. The proportion of variability that is explained is, therefore, (SS_{yy} – SSE)/SS_{yy}. This number is called the coefficient of determination and is represented by r^2.

Notice that this coefficient of determination is the same as the square of the coefficient of correlation. It can be shown algebraically that

$$r^2 = \left(\frac{SS_{xy}}{\sqrt{SS_{xx} \cdot SS_{yy}}} \right)^2 = \frac{SS_{yy} - SSe}{SS_{yy}}$$

Therefore, to find the coefficient of determination r^2, all that must be done is to square the coefficient of correlation r. In the previous section, we showed that semester grade point averages were negatively correlated with the number of credits taken that semester ($r = -.703$). Therefore, $r^2 = (-.703)^2 = .4942$. The proportion of total variability of the sample (the fact that the ys differ from their mean, $\bar{y}$) is .4942.

Thus 49.42% of the variability in the G.P.A.s (y) is explained by the number of semester hours taken (x). Of course, this means that 50.58% of the variability in y is not explained by x. Therefore, there are other factors that are also responsible for the G.P.A. differences. Can you think of any other factors that influence grade point averages?

Notice that since $-1 \le r \le 1$, then $r^2 \le 1$. If $r^2 = 1$, there would be no points off the least squares line and 100% of the variability in y would be explained by x.

Exercise 13.6: Recall from previous exercises the heights and weights of ten randomly chosen women. Find and interpret the coefficients of correlation and determination for this data set.

Answers: Recall from the previous solutions that $SS_{xx} = 78.4$; $SS_{xy} = 486$ and $SS_{yy} = 4240$. Therefore, $r = \dfrac{SS_{xy}}{\sqrt{SS_{xx} \cdot SS_{yy}}} = \dfrac{486}{\sqrt{(78.4)(4240)}} = .8429$. This means that there is a strong positive linear relationship between the heights and weights of these women.

$r^2 = (.8419)^2 = .7105.$

This means that the proportion of variability in weights that is explained by the heights is .7105: 71.05% of thevariability in the weights of these women is explained by their heights. Notice that 28.95% of this variability is not explained by their heights. What other factors might explain this variability? A few candidates might be diet, exercise, and metabolism.

USING THE MODEL TO PREDICT AND ESTIMATE

Finding a Prediction Interval

The most important use of the equation of the least squares line is to predict y from x. For example, recall the data set from a previous example in which number of credits carried during a semester was the independent variable, x, and G.P.A. was the dependent variable y (Table 13.3).

Table 13.3

Student	A	B	C	D	E	F	G	H
# of Credits (x)	10	18	12	15	16	16	22	9
G.P.A.(y)	3.5	2.8	3.3	3.7	2.9	3.0	2.4	3.1

To get the equation of the regression line, recall that $b_1 = -.067$ has already been calculated for the hypothesis test. Also,

$$\sum x = 118 \text{ and } \bar{x} = 118/8 = 14.75$$

$$\sum y = 24.7 \text{ and } \bar{y} = 24.7/8 = 3.0875.$$

$b_0 = \bar{y} - b_1(\bar{x}) = 3.0875 - (-.067)(14.75) = 3.0875 + .98825 = 4.076$. The equation of the least squares line is $y' = 4.076 - .067x$.

Suppose John is taking ten credits this semester. Predict his semester's grade point average. Using the regression equation, $y' = 4.076 - .067(10) = 3.406$ by substituting 10 for x in the equation of the line.

But (10, 3.406) is just a point on the regression line. It is likely that the point that represents John's G.P.A. is not on the line but within a certain interval of the line. How far away from the line that point might be depends on two things: the standard error s and how far the x-value of the point (x_p) is from the mean of the xs ($\bar{x}$).

Using these facts, a prediction interval around 3.406 is calculated such that we are quite confident that John's actual G.P.A. is in that interval.

The formula for this interval, called the *prediction interval*, is

$$(a, b) = y' \pm t_{\alpha/2} \cdot \sqrt{1 + \frac{1}{n} + \frac{(x_p - \bar{x})^2}{SS_{xx}}}$$

where $t_{\alpha/2}$ has $n - 2$ degrees of freedom,

x_p is the x value of the point whose y is to be predicted, and

x is the mean of the x-values.

Suppose we want a 95% prediction interval for the value of y when $x = 10$, i.e., a 95% prediction interval for John's semester G.P.A. when he is taking ten credits. Then, the interval (a, b) is

$$3.406 \pm t_{.025,6} \cdot .318\sqrt{1 + .125 + \frac{(10 - 14.75)^2}{129.5}}$$

$$= 3.406 \pm 2.447(.318)(\sqrt{1.125 + .174})$$

$$= 3.406 \pm 2.447(.318)(1.14) = 3.406 \pm .887 = (2.519, 4.293)$$

With 95% certainty, John's G.P.A. will be between 2.519 and 4.293. Notice how large this interval is, which is due to several factors: the standard deviation was very large, the number of credits (ten) was very far from the mean (14.75), the certainty for the interval was high (95%), and, most important, this prediction was for a single person.

Estimating the Mean

Suppose we changed the problem above to find another kind of interval: not an interval for John's G.P.A. during the semester in which he carries ten credits, but an interval for the mean grade point average of every student who carries ten credits. Such an interval is not called a prediction interval, but a confidence interval for the mean. The formula is slightly altered. It now reads:

$$(a, b) = y' + t_{\alpha/2} \cdot s \sqrt{\frac{1}{n} + \frac{(x_p - \bar{x})^2}{SS_{xx}}}$$

Notice that the 1 is no longer under the square root sign. Since all other terms are the same, the confidence interval of the mean is narrower than the prediction interval.

Finding the confidence interval (a, b) for the mean of all students taking ten credits, using the same data as above:

$$3.406 \pm t_{.025,6}(.318)\sqrt{.125 + \frac{(10 - 14.75)^2}{129.5}}$$

$$= 3.406 \pm 2.447(.318)(\sqrt{.125 + .174})$$

$$= 3.406 \pm 2.447(.318)(.547) = 3.406 \pm .426 = (2.98, 3.832)$$

With 95% certainty, we can say that the average semester G.P.A. for everyone who is taking ten credits will be between 2.98 and 3.832. Notice how much narrower the confidence interval is for the mean G.P.A. than is the prediction interval for a single person's G.P.A. This is because points on the line of means are usually within a much shorter distance of the least squares line than is a single data point.

The major use of linear regression is to predict a y for a given x or to estimate the mean of all ys for all those points with a given x. Be sure that the x for which the prediction or estimation is given is not outside the domain (values) of the xs of those points in the sample that were used to find the least squares line. For example, this prediction or estimation would be very faulty if used for $x =$

6 or $x = 25$ (where x is the number of credits carried in a semester) since the range of xs in the sample used to find the least squares line is only from 9 to 22.

Exercise 13.7: Recall one more time the height and weight table used in previous exercises:

Table 13.2

x	65	69	62	71	66	68	70	67	63	65
y	140	150	110	170	120	150	150	130	120	100

a. Predict Ann's weight if her height is 68 inches. Use a 95% prediction interval.
b. Find a 95% confidence interval for the mean of the weights of all women who are 68 inches tall.

Answers: For both (a) and (b), we will require the following numbers, all of which have been calculated in previous exercises.

$s = 12.38$; $SS_{xx} = 78.4$; $\overline{x} = 66.6$;
$y' = -278.92 + 6.20x$

To find y' for $x = 68$, $y' = -278.92 + 6.2(68) = 142.68$. It is this number around which the prediction and estimation intervals will be determined. Also, since $\alpha = .05$, $\alpha/2 = .025$; df $= n - 2 = 10 - 2 = 8$. $t_{\alpha/2} = t_{.025,8} = 2.306$ for both parts of the problem.

a. The 95% prediction interval is given by

$$(a, b) = y' \pm t_{\alpha/2} \cdot s \sqrt{1 + \frac{1}{n} + \frac{(x_p - \overline{x})^2}{SS_{xx}}}$$

$$(a, b) = 142.68 \pm 2.306 \, (12.38) \sqrt{1 + .1 + \frac{(68 - 66.6)^2}{78.4}}$$

$= 142.68 \pm 2.306 \, (12.38)\sqrt{1.125} = 142.68 \pm 30.28 = (112.40, 172.96)$.
We are 95% certain that Ann's weight (she is 68 inches tall) is between 112.40 and 172.96 pounds.

b. The formula for the 95% confidence interval for the mean weight for all women 68 inches tall is

$$(a, b) = y' + t_{\alpha/2} \cdot s \sqrt{\frac{1}{n} + \frac{(x_p - \overline{x})^2}{SS_{xx}}}$$

$$(a, b) = 142.68 \pm 2.306 \, (12.38) \sqrt{.1 + \frac{(68 - 66.6)^2}{78.4}}$$

$$= 142.68 \pm 2.306\,(12.38)\sqrt{(.125)} = 142.68 \pm 10.09 = (132.59, 152.77).$$

We are 95% certain that the mean weight of all women 68 inches tall is between 132.59 and 152.77 pounds. Notice how much narrower (20 pounds vs. 60) is the width of the confidence interval for the mean than the width of the prediction interval.

Multiple Regression Analysis

In a multiple regression, there is more than one independent variable: x_1, x_2, x_3. Each of these variables contributes something to finding y. For example, several factors contribute to grade point average, one of which, as discussed, is number of credits taken. Other factors (x_is) might be a student's year in school (first, second, etc.), number of hours worked on an outside job, S.A.T. scores, or high school grade point average. Each of these factors is a contributor to the prediction of college grade point averages.

Thus, a multiple regression best fit equation might look like

$$y' = 17 - 3.8x_1 + .45x_2 + .007x_3 - .93x_4 + .22x_5$$

Generating all those beta parameters (b_is) is beyond the ability of a hand calculator but can be accomplished by a computer using data points. These data points are not ordered pairs but ordered triples or quadruples or quintuples of the form $(x_1, x_2, \ldots, x_i, \ldots, y)$. We can find results in multiple regression analysis that are similar to those in linear regression analysis, except that the analysis is done with the aid of a computer.

Exercise 13.8: It is widely believed that the more years of education a person has, the higher is his or her starting salary for the first job out of school. Seven people starting their first job are randomly selected and their number of years of schooling (x) to the nearest full year and their starting salary (y) in thousands of dollars per year to the nearest thousand are recorded in Table 13.4.

Table 13.4

# of Years of School	9	11	12	12	14	16	16
Starting Salary	12	15	14	17	19	16	21

Using the data in Table 13.4, perform a complete linear regression analysis. Test the slope of the line at .05 level of significance. Find and interpret the coefficients of correlation and regression.

Then find a 95% prediction interval for the starting salary of a person with fifteen years of schooling, and a 95% confidence interval for the mean of the starting salaries for all people who have had fifteen years of school.

Answers: In order to do a complete linear regression analysis, review the steps indicated in the summary above. First, draw a scattergram of the data points and find and graph the least squares line for the data points.

To find the equation of the least squares line, first calculate SS_{xx} and SS_{xy}.

$$\sum x = 90; \bar{x} = 12.86; \sum x^2 = 1198;$$

$$\sum y = 114; \bar{y} = 16.29; \sum y^2 = 1912;$$

$$\sum xy = 1503.$$

$$SS_{xx} = \sum x^2 - \left(\sum x\right)^2/n = 1198 - 90^2/7 = 40.86.$$

$$SS_{xy} = \sum xy - \left(\sum x\right)\left(\sum y\right)/n = 1503 - 90(114)/7 = 37.29.$$

$b_1 = SS_{xy}/SS_{xx} = 37.29/40.86 = .913$

$b_0 = \bar{y} - b_1\bar{x} = 16.29 - .913(12.86) = 4.55$

Therefore, the equation of the least squares line is $y' = 4.55 + .913x$.

The next step is to graph the data points and the least squares line together. To graph the least squares line, substitute two values of x, say $x = 10$ and $x = 15$, in the equation $y' = 4.55 + .913x$.

For $x = 10$, $y' = 4.55 + .913(10) = 13.68$, so (10, 13.68) is one point of the least squares line.

For $x = 15$, $y' = 4.55 + .913(15) = 18.25$, so (15, 18.25) is a second point on the least squares line (Figure 13.13).

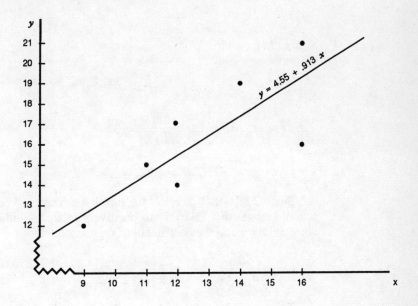

Figure 13.13
Least Squares Equation $y' = 4.55 + .913x$
with Data Points (x, y) Where x Is Years in School and y Is Starting Salary in Thousands

In order to test the slope β_1 to see if it is 0, first find s. The first step in calculating s is to find SSE.

Calculating $SS_{yy} = \Sigma y^2 - (\Sigma y)^2/n = 1912 - 114^2/7 = 55.43$.

$SSE = SS_{yy} - b_1 \cdot SS_{xy} = 55.43 - .913(37.29) = 21.4$.

$s^2 = SSE/(n-2) = 21.4/5 = 4.28$.

$s = \sqrt{4.28} = 2.07$.

Next, an appropriate hypothesis test of the slope.

H_o: $\beta_1 = 0$

H_a: $\beta_1 > 0$ (The more schooling, the larger the starting salary: a positive linear relationship is being tested here.)

Test Statistic: $t = b_1/s_{b_1}$

Region of Rejection (Figure 13.14):

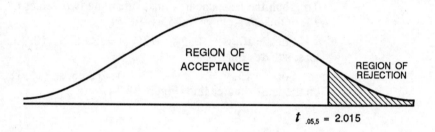

REGION OF ACCEPTANCE

REGION OF REJECTION

$t_{.05,5} = 2.015$

Figure 13.14
t - Distribution—5 df

Recall $s_{b_1} = \dfrac{s}{\sqrt{SS_{xx}}} = \dfrac{2.07}{\sqrt{40.86}} = .324$

$t = b_1/s_{b_1} = .913/.324 = 2.82$.

Since $2.82 > 2.015$, reject the null hypothesis and conclude that years of school and starting salaries are positively related. Finding the coefficient of correlation (r) and the coefficient of regression (r^2):

$r = \dfrac{SS_{xy}}{\sqrt{SS_{xx} \cdot SS_{yy}}} = \dfrac{37.29}{\sqrt{40.86\,(55.43)}} = .784$

The coefficient of correlation, .784, indicates a fairly high positive correlation between x and y.

$r^2 = (.784)^2 = .615$. Therefore, 61.5% of the variation in the starting salaries (y) can be explained by the number of years in school (x). Recall that this leaves 38.5% of the starting salary variations to be explained by other factors.

To find a prediction interval for a person with fifteen years of schooling and a confidence interval for the mean of all persons who have had fifteen years of school, first find y' for $x = 15$. Recall that $x = 15$ was used to graph the least squares line, so $y' = 18.25$.

$t_{.025,5} = 2.571$ for both parts of the problem.

Now put a 95% prediction interval around 18.25.

$$(a, b) = y' \pm t_{\alpha/2} \cdot s \sqrt{1 + \frac{1}{n} + \frac{(x_p - \bar{x})^2}{SS_{xx}}}$$

$$= 18.25 \pm 2.571(2.07) \sqrt{1 + \frac{1}{7} + \frac{(15 - 12.86)^2}{40.86}}$$

$$= 18.25 \pm 2.571 \, (2.07) \sqrt{1.255} = 18.25 \pm 5.96$$

$$(a, b) = (12.29, 24.21)$$

The 95% prediction interval for the starting salary for a person with fifteen years of schooling is between 12.29 and 24.21 thousand dollars a year, (i.e., between \$12,290 and \$24,210).

Now, the 95% confidence interval for the mean of the starting salaries of all people with fifteen years of schooling:

$$(a, b) = y' \pm t_{\alpha/2} \cdot \sqrt{\frac{1}{n} + \frac{(x_p - \bar{x})^2}{SS_{xx}}}$$

$$= 18.25 \pm 2.571 \, (2.07) \sqrt{.255} = 18.25 \pm 2.69.$$

$$(a, b) = (15.56, 20.94).$$

The 95% confidence interval for the mean starting salary for people with fifteen years of schooling is between 15.56 and 20.94 thousand dollars a year (i.e., between \$15,560 and \$20,940).

*T*his *chapter discussed linear regression analysis. To perform a complete linear regression analysis given a number of data points, the following steps are required:*

1. *Graph the data points (this is called a scattergram).*
2. *Find the least squares line for these data points: $y' = b_0 + b_1 x$.*
3. *Test the slope of the line (b_1) to see if the variables are linearly related. This will require finding the estimated standard error of the regression model, s.*
4. *Find the coefficient of correlation, r, and the coefficient of determination, r^2. Interpret them as applied to the linear relationship between x and y.*
5. *Use the least squares line to predict a value for y, given an x in the domain of the data set. Find a prediction interval and a confidence interval for the mean.*

Almost all these steps are incorporated into computer programs that find the regression line and supply data in order to complete the regression analysis. All the user need do is enter the data, tell the computer which prediction interval or confidence interval for the mean is desired, and read the printout. The computer does all the computation in fitting the line to the data, testing the slope for significance, finding the coefficient of determination, and supplying the prediction or confidence interval for the mean, given an x-value and a percent age for confidence.

14

Nonparametric Statistics

*A*ll *the statistical tests we have discussed in previous chapters, except the chi–square test and the linear regression analysis, have compared the means of two or more samples with each other, the mean of a single sample with the presumed population mean, or the mean of the difference of two matched sets with 0. The assumption we have made throughout these statistical experiments is that the populations from which small samples are drawn are normally distributed.*

DATA IN NONPARAMETRIC STATISTICS

There are many instances in which we cannot assume normality of the population distribution. Often it is known that the population is skewed; for example, the salaries of people working for a large corporation are not normally distributed. Sometimes we do not know whether or not the population distribution is normal.

In addition, instead of actual numbers for data, often data takes the form of rankings or preferences (e.g., rate items in order of your preference). There is a way to determine whether a certain hypothesis is true or not despite not having data that meet all the criteria in previous chapters. This data can be analyzed by nonparametric (nonmeasured) methods.

When to Use Nonparametric Statistics

When a data set is skewed, like the salaries of people working for a large corporation, the median rather than the mean provides a better estimation of the "middle" of the data set since a few people in the corporation might be earning seven-figure incomes, but the majority are not. If the incomes of all the employees are added together and divided by the number of employees, the $1,000,000+ incomes become a part of the mean income for all employees and may skew the mean to reflect a much higher salary than most employees earn.

On the other hand, if the incomes are ranked and the middle rank number, the median, is used to represent this estimation of the middle, it makes no difference how high the highest few salaries are: they are just the highest ranked numbers, but their size does not influence the value of the median.

Nonparametric statistical methods compare medians in sets of ranked data. The data is ranked, and the ranks are compared. The hypotheses for nonparametric statistics tests are not as strong as those for the parametric tests. The hypotheses in nonparametric statistics state only that the entire population distributions are the same or that they differ.

In a parametric hypothesis, most conclusions are that the means are the same or that they differ. When population distributions differ, they can be different in many ways: their means, their variances, their shapes. The conclusion we reach after a nonparametric hypothesis test is not as strong as the comparable conclusion from parametric statistical analysis methods, like a t-test, an analysis of variance, or a linear regression test of the slope.

Ranking

All nonparametric statistical methods depend upon the ranks of the data. Recall from Chapter 2 that to find the median of a set of numbers, rank the numbers from 1 to n and choose the number with the middle rank as the median.

In Chapter 10, we worked a problem in which I.Q.s of business and English majors were compared to see if there was a difference. These I.Q.s were:

Business majors: 112, 108, 131, 111, 115, 107
English majors: 114, 102, 119, 110, 113, 123, 103

A t-test was performed to see if the means of the populations from which these I.Q.s were drawn differed. The underlying assumption in using the t-test in this problem was that the I.Q.s in the populations of business and English majors were normally distributed. This may not be a correct assumption since there may be some very high I.Q.s among business and English majors, but probably not an equal number of very low ones. In order to compensate for that, a nonparametric test can be performed. The first step is to rank these thirteen data points (I.Q.s,) from 1 to 13. The results are in Table 14.1 (the original scores are in parentheses).

It is important that the sum of the ranks be a constant for a certain number of scores. The formula for this is $S = \sum_{i=1}^{n} i = \dfrac{n(n+1)}{2}$. In this problem,

$$S = \sum_{i=1}^{13} i = 1 + 2 + 3 + \ldots + 13 = \frac{13\,(14)}{2} = 91.$$

Table 14.1

Business Majors		English Majors	
(112)	7	(114)	9
(108)	4	(102)	1
(131)	13	(119)	11
(111)	6	(113)	8
(115)	10	(110)	5
(107)	3	(123)	12
		(103)	2

In order not to violate these rules for ranking, if two of the raw scores are the same, the ranks are assigned by adding the two ranks dividing by two. For example, if the first two I.Q.s are both 101, the rank assigned to each would be obtained by adding 1 and 2, the ranks of the first two, and dividing by 2. Therefore, each number would be given the rank of 1.5. Since ranks 1 and 2 have now been used, the next lowest number would be ranked 3. Note that the sum of $1.5 + 1.5$ is the same as the sum of $1 + 2$.

Suppose the 11th-, 12th-, and 13th-lowest numbers (the highest three) are all the same, say 120. All three would be assigned the same rank, which would be obtained by adding the three available ranks, $11 + 12 + 13$, and dividing by 3, yielding 12. Notice that the sum of the three ranks, $11 + 12 + 13$, is the same as $12 + 12 + 12$.

This procedure for ranking data is followed for all nonparametric tests, five of which will be presented in this chapter.

WILCOXON RANK SUM TEST

The next step is to see if the sum of the ranks for each of the two groups (in this case, business and English majors) differs from the sum of the ranks one might find in two randomly ranked groups, both drawn from the same population.

The *Wilcoxon Rank Sum Test* is the nonparametric equivalent of the *t*-test, in which the means of two small samples are tested to see if they differ. The Wilcoxon Rank Sum Test tests entire population distributions, or their representations, by their ranks, to see if they differ.

The basis of the Wilcoxon Rank Sum Test is that if a certain ordered set of numbers is ranked 1 to n, their sum will always be the same number. This sum is given by the formula $S = n(n + 1)/2$. The formula for S is derived from the formula for the sum of an arithmetic series of n numbers in which the first term is 1, the last term is n, and the difference between terms is equal to 1.

For example, if $n = 10$, the sum of the numbers 1 to 10 is $S = 10(11)/2 = 55$. Adding the numbers 1, 2, 3, 4, 5, 6, 7, 8, 9, and 10 together results in 55.

Suppose that these ten numbers, which are actually ten ranks, are divided into two sets, A and B. Suppose also that five numbers are assigned to each set. If the ranks are randomly assigned to set A and set B, we would expect each set to have equal rank sums; T_A (the total of the ranks in set A) would equal 27.5 and T_B (the total of the ranks in set B) would equal 27.5, half of the 55 total for the sum of the ranks of ten numbers.

How much different do the actual rank sums have to be from 27.5 to conclude that the ranks are not just random, but that one set (say, business majors) has more low or high ranks? The answer to this question can be found in the Wilcoxon Rank Sum Test Tables found in Appendix E.

Wilcoxon Rank Sum Test Tables

The tables in Appendix E are critical value tables. The top one can be used for one-tailed ($\alpha = .025$) or two-tailed ($\alpha = .05$) tests, and the bottom one for one-tailed ($\alpha = .05$) or two-tailed ($\alpha = .10$) tests.

Part of the first table is reproduced as Table 14.2.

In Table 14.2, n_1 is the number of data points in the first sample and n_2 is the number of data points in the second sample. T_L represents the lower limit and T_U the upper limit of the rank sum in the sample with the smaller number of elements. Either sample can be used if the numbers of elements are equal.

In particular, if the test with the ten numbers divided into two sets of five

Table 14.2   Critical Values of T_L and T_U for Wilcoxon Rank Sum Test
($\alpha = .025$ one-tailed; $\alpha = .05$ two-tailed)

$n_1 \ldots$	4		5		6		7 $\ldots$	
n_2	T_L	T_U	T_L	T_U	T_L	T_U	T_L	T_U
3	6	18	6	21	7	23	7	26
4	11	25	12	28	12	32	13	35
5	12	28	18	37	19	41	20	45
6	12	32	19	41	26	52	28	56
7	13	35	20	45	28	56	37	68
8	14	38	21	49	29	61	39	73
.	.	.	.	.	.	.	.	.

were being conducted as a two-tailed test with $\alpha = .05$, according to Table 14.2 ($n_1 = n_2 = 5$), T_L (the lower limit value of the sum) is 18 and T_U (the upper limit value of the sum) is 37.

This means that if the total of one of the sets, T_A or T_B, is between 18 and 37 exclusive (the total is neither 18 nor 37), then the null hypothesis about the probability distributions of A and B (that they are the same) will be accepted. If $T_A \leq 18$ or $T_A \geq 37$, then the null hypothesis will be rejected. In that case, the alternative hypothesis, that the probability distributions of A and B are different, will be accepted. The upper bound of the lower rejection region for the null hypothesis is 18, and the lower bound of the upper rejection region for the null hypothesis is 37.

Notice that the table provides for cases when the two sets do not have equal numbers. When the sets are of unequal size, the calculation uses the rank sum T from the set that has the fewer numbers. Also notice that it makes no difference whether, for example, $n_1 = 4$ and $n_2 = 7$ or $n_1 = 7$ and $n_2 = 4$. In both these cases, $T_L = 13$ and $T_U = 35$.

The table in Appendix E, and thus the Wilcoxon Rank Sum Test, can be used only when the number of samples from each population is between 3 and 10.

Wilcoxon Rank Sum Hypothesis Test

We can now set up a hypothesis test for the above problem about the I.Q.s of business and English majors. The test will help determine if the probability distributions of the two sets of I.Q.s are the same, using $\alpha = .05$.

H_o: The probability distributions of the I.Q.s of population B and population E are the same.

H_a: The probability distributions of the I.Q.s of population B and population E are different. (This is a two-tailed test, since one probability distribution was not presumed to be to the right or left of the other.)

Test Statistic: T_B (there are fewer business majors in the survey).

Region of Rejection (Figure 14.1):

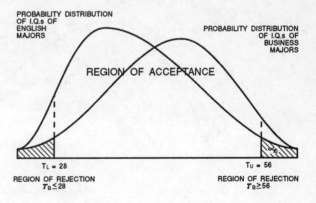

Figure 14.1
Rejection and Acceptance Regions
Wilcoxon Rank Sum Test ($n_B = 6$; $n_E = 7$)
Two-tailed with $\alpha = .05$

$T_L = 28$ and $T_U = 56$, the starting points of the two-tailed rejection regions, come from Table 14.2 for $n_1 = 6$ and $n_2 = 7$ or vice versa. The region of rejection diagram represents the two population distributions (B the population of the business majors' I.Q.s and the other the population of the English majors' I.Q.s). Both populations may come from the same (I.Q.) population, and thus their distributions would be identical.

If the area of overlap of the two curves is very large, then the two populations are considered to have come from the same population. If the area of overlap is small, then the populations are not considered to have come from the same population. The rejection region when $\alpha = .05$ is that part of Figure 14.1 where the areas under the curves overlap.

T_B, the rank sum of the business majors from Table 14.1, is $7 + 4 + 13 + 6 + 10 + 3 = 43$. Since 43 is between 28 and 56, in the acceptance area, accept the null hypothesis and conclude that the population distributions of B and E are the same, i.e., the I.Q.s of business and English majors come from the same population distribution.

DIRECTIONAL HYPOTHESIS IN WILCOXON RANK SUM TEST

A directional hypothesis can also be tested using the Wilcoxon Rank Sum Test. For example, the alternative hypothesis in the problem above could be that the probability distribution of the I.Q.s of business majors is to the right of the probability distribution of the I.Q.s of English majors. This really means that the median (and thus the ranks) of the population of business majors' I.Q.s is higher than the median (and the ranks) of the population of English majors' I.Q.s.

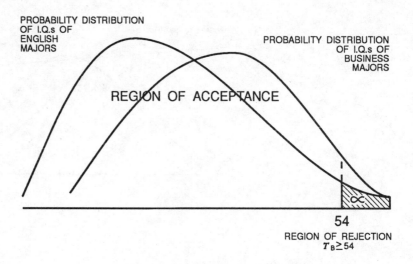

Figure 14.2
Rejection and Acceptance Regions
Wilcoxon Rank Sum Test ($n_B = 6$; $n_E = 7$)
One-tailed with $\alpha = .05$

The hypothesis test looks like this:

H_o: The probability distributions of the I.Q.s of population B and population E are the same.

H_a: The probability distribution of the I.Q.s of population B is to the right of the probability distribution of the I.Q.s of population E.

Test Statistic: T_B (there are fewer business majors in the survey).

Region of Rejection (See Figure 14.2)

(In this hypothesis test, assuming the same $\alpha = .05$, we use the lower table in Appendix E since it covers the one-tailed $\alpha = .05$ test. Again looking up $n_1 = 6$ and $n_2 = 7$, we find $T_U = 54$. This is the upper limit for the total of the set with the fewest numbers (B) for accepting the null hypothesis. If T_B, the total of the ranks of the business majors' I.Q.s, is any number up to (but not including) 54, then the null hypothesis will be accepted. If $T_B \geq 54$, the null hypothesis will be rejected.)

Since $T_B = 43$ and $43 < 54$, accept the null hypothesis and conclude that the probability distribution of the I.Q.s of business majors is the same as the probability distribution of the I.Q.s of English majors: the I.Q.s of business majors are the same as those of English majors.

Note the limitations on the number of ranked numbers. The maximum that the Wilcoxon Rank Sum Test can handle is ten in each set. If one or both sets have more than ten numbers in them, other tests will have to be performed. Later in this chapter, we will discuss a test that could be used for sets with more than ten numbers in each (the Kruskal-Wallis H Test).

Exercise 14.1: A mathematics class has taken a final exam. The scores of the nine boys in the class are 58, 44, 68, 89, 75, 98, 62, 73, 75. The ten girls in the math class scored: 75, 62, 97, 86, 88, 93, 82, 94, 77, 83. Is there evidence to suggest that the probability distribution of the population of the girls' scores is to the right of that of the boys' scores (i.e., the median of the girls' scores is greater than the median of the boys' scores in the population of final exam scores)? Test at $\alpha = .05$.

Answer: The first step is to rank the nineteen numbers, keeping the ranks separated into the two sets B and G (Table 14.3).

Table 14.3

B (Scores)	58	44	68	89	75	98	62	73	75	
B (Ranks)	2	1	5	15	8	19	3.5	6	8	
G (Scores)	75	62	97	86	88	93	82	94	77	83
G (Ranks)	8	3.5	18	13	14	16	11	17	10	12

Since 62 is the 3d– and 4th–smallest test score, each 62 gets a rank of 3.5 and the next lower number (68) is ranked 5th.

Also notice that the three 75s are in the 7th, 8th, and 9th rank, so they all get rank 8, and the next lower number (77) is ranked 10th.

The last rank (unless there is a tie in the last two scores) should reflect the total number of numbers to be ranked, 19 in this case.

H_o: The probability distributions of the population of girls' and boys' scores is the same.

H_a: The probability distribution of the population of the girls' scores is to the right of that of the boys' scores.

Test Statistic: T_B (there are fewer boys' scores)

Region of Rejection (See Figure 14.3):

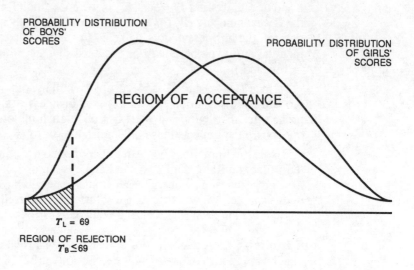

Figure 14.3
Rejection and Acceptance Regions
Wilcoxon Rank Sum Test ($n_B = 9$; $n_G = 10$)
One (Left) Tail with $\alpha = .05$

The second table is used, where $\alpha = .05$ in a one- tailed test. Since it is expected that the boys' ranks are to the left of the girls', and the boys' total is the one we are using, that total must be less than or equal to 69 to reject the null hypothesis.

$T_B = 2 + 1 + 5 + 15 + 8 + 19 + 3.5 + 6 + 8 = 67.5$. To check on the accuracy of your rankings, G also, add the totals for B and G, check with the formula for the sum of ranks 1 to 19: $S = 19(20)/2 = 190$. Since $T_G = 122.5$ and $122.5 + 67.5 = 190$, the rankings are accurate.

Since $67.5 < 69$, reject H_o and conclude that the probability distribution of the girls' scores is to the right of the probability distribution of the boys' scores; thus the median of the population distribution of girls' final exam scores is higher than the median of the population distribution of boys' final exam scores —the girls did better than the boys!

WILCOXON SIGNED RANK TEST

In Chapter 10 we discussed the paired difference t-test, a parametric test. In the paired difference t-test, measures of paired samples were subtracted and the mean of their difference, x_D, was found and tested against 0. It was assumed that the populations from which these measures were sampled were normal.

Recall Exercise 10.7 in which eight pairs of identical twins were sampled, and one of each pair randomly assigned to each of two different reading groups. A reading test was subsequently given to each of the sixteen children, and the difference in scores for each pair of twins was calculated. The mean and standard deviation of these differences were found, and a t-difference test was performed to see if μ_D differed significantly from 0. Table 14.4 repeats the data.

Table 14.4

Twin Pair	Score of Twin in Standard Method Reading Program (S)	Score of Twin in New Method Reading Program (N)
I	57	59
II	72	75
III	68	67
IV	64	70
V	49	51
VI	62	67
VII	54	62
VIII	71	71

The *Wilcoxon Signed Rank Test* is the nonparametric equivalent of the t-test for paired differences. This test begins as does the parametric one, but once the differences are found, their *absolute values* are ranked. For example, the differences found in Exercise 10.7 between the matched twins, scores by subtracting the new reading method (N) twin's score n from the standard reading method (S) twin's score were $-2, -3, 1, -6, -2, -5, -6, 0$.

The Wilcoxon Signed Rank Test checks to see if the probability distributions of the two methods (S and N) differ. To perform this test, the absolute value of each of these differences is found; these absolute values are ranked; and the ranks are summed.

These sums are indicated by T_+, the sum of the ranks of the absolute values that came from positive differences, and T_-, the sum of the ranks of the absolute values that came from negative differences.

Recall from Chapter 1 how to find the absolute value of a number. If the number is already positive, then its absolute value is just the number: $|7| = 7$. If the number is negative, then its absolute value is the negative of the number: $|-5| = 5$. In the Wilcoxon Signed Rank Test, if the difference between two numbers is 0, those numbers and that difference are thrown out of the random sample. Therefore, the difference in twin pair VIII's scores is thrown out of the sample set.

The absolute values of the remaining seven sample differences are 2, 3, 1*, 6, 2, 5, and 6. The (*) next to the 1 is to remind us that this number was already positive before its absolute value was found.

Next, rank the seven absolute values:

Number	-2	-3	1	-6	-2	-5	-8
Absolute Value	2	3	1*	6	2	5	8
Rank	2.5	4	1*	6.5	2.5	5	6.5

$T_+ = 1$ since only the number 1, which has rank 1, is the absolute value of a positive difference. $T_- = 27$, which represents the total of the ranks of the absolute values of the negative differences. $T_+ + T_- = 28$, and the sum of the ranks of seven numbers is $S = 7(8)/2 = 28$ also.

Wilcoxon Signed Rank Table

We are going to compare these totals using the Wilcoxon Signed Rank Table in Appendix F, which is partially reproduced in Table 14.5.

The table in Appendix F covers up to fifty paired differences, though the part reproduced above covers only nine pairs. Use the table as follows: first, note the number of differences remaining, n. In this case, n = 7 since one of the eight differences was 0.

Table 14.5   Critical Values of T_0 in the Wilcoxon Paired Difference Signed Rank Test

One-tailed	Two-tailed	$n = 5$	$n = 6$	$n = 7$	$n = 8$	$n = 9$
$\alpha = .05$	$\alpha = .10$	1	2	4	6	8
$\alpha = .025$	$\alpha = .05$		1	2	4	6
$\alpha = .01$	$\alpha = .02$			0	2	3
$\alpha = .005$	$\alpha = .01$				0	2

Then, decide the α level. Let us suppose that $\alpha = .05$ and that the hypothesis test is two-tailed. For a two-tailed test, the minimum of T_+ and T_- (the smaller of the two numbers T_+ and T_-) is used to calculate T to compare with the critical value (denoted T_0) in the table. In the above example, the minimum of T_+ and T_- is the smaller of the sums 1 and 27, which is 1. Therefore, the test statistic $T = 1$.

For the problem above involving seven paired differences with a two-tailed $\alpha = .05$, the value of T_0 from Table 14.5 (or from Appendix F) is 2 ($T_0 = 2$). If $T \leq 2$ (or in general, if $T \leq T_0$) the null hypothesis of identical probability distributions is rejected.

Hypothesis Tests Involving Paired Differences

Now we will set up a hypothesis test using the data above to test to see if these reading score differences imply that the scores of the standard and new method readers come from different populations.

H_0: The probability distributions of S (standard) and N (new) reading method test results are the same.

H_a: The probability distributions of S and N test results are different. (This will be repeated as a directional alternative hypothesis test later.)

Test Statistic: $T = \text{Min}(T_+, T_-)$ (This represents the smaller of the sum of the ranks of absolute values from positive differences $[T_+]$ and the sum of the ranks of absolute values from negative differences $[T_-]$.)

Region of Rejection (See Figure 14.4)

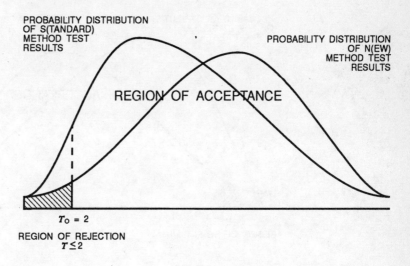

PROBABILITY DISTRIBUTION OF S(TANDARD) METHOD TEST RESULTS

PROBABILITY DISTRIBUTION OF N(EW) METHOD TEST RESULTS

REGION OF ACCEPTANCE

$T_0 = 2$

REGION OF REJECTION
$T \leq 2$

Figure 14.4
Rejection and Acceptance Regions
Wilcoxon Signed Rank Test ($n = 7$)
Two-tailed, $\alpha = .05$; $T = \text{Min}(T_-, T_+)$

The region of rejection ends at 2, according to the Wilcoxon Signed Rank Table 14.5. A rank sum T, where $T = \text{Min}(T_+, T_-)$, that is less than or equal to 2 will allow us to reject the null hypothesis.

Since $\text{Min}(T_+, T_-) = \text{Min}(1, 27) = 1$, and since $1 \leq 2$, reject the null hypothesis and conclude that the probability distributions of S and N are different.

Directional Hypothesis Testing Using Signed Ranks

In the original signed difference problem (Exercise 10.7), the new reading method scores were subtracted from the standard reading method scores. Almost all these differences were negative. This suggests that the new (N) scores are higher than (probability distribution to the right of) the standard (S) scores. Thus, the hypothesis test might well have been a directional hypothesis test with $\alpha = .05$ and the test set up as follows:

H_o: The probability distributions of S (standard) and N (new) reading method test results are the same.

H_a: The probability distribution of the test results of students who learned by the new reading method (N) is to the right of the probability distribution of test results of students who learned by the standard reading method (S).

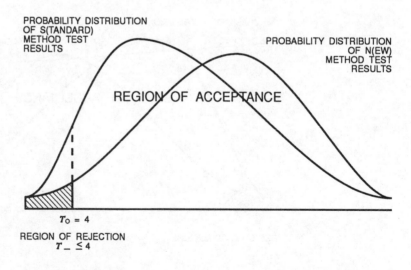

PROBABILITY DISTRIBUTION OF S(TANDARD) METHOD TEST RESULTS

PROBABILITY DISTRIBUTION OF N(EW) METHOD TEST RESULTS

REGION OF ACCEPTANCE

$T_O = 4$

REGION OF REJECTION
$T_- \leq 4$

Figure 14.5
Rejection and Acceptance Regions
Wilcoxon Signed Rank Test ($n = 7$)
One (Left) Tailed, $\alpha = .05$

Test Statistic: T_-. (This assumes that the measures in S are subtracted from those in N. If the alternative hypothesis is true, most of these differences will be positive. The negative ones are flagged and compared with the number in the Wilcoxon Signed Rank Table for a one-tailed test.)

Region of Rejection (See Figure 14.5)

Here, $n = 7$ (one of the differences = 0) and this will be a one-tailed hypothesis test, $\alpha = .05$. According to Table 14.4, the region of rejection ends at 4.

Therefore, if $T_- \leq 4$, the null hypothesis will be rejected. That is, when the differences are taken such that most of them are positive, the sum of the ranks of the absolute values of negative numbers (T_-) will be compared with 4.

To do this problem, we will have to redo the subtractions because the original set, $-2, -3, 1, -6, -2, -5, -6, 0$, were the results of subtracting the S twin's score from the N twin's score. If the subtraction is done in the opposite order, in keeping with the alternative hypothesis and the test statistic, the differences are $2, 3, -1, 6, 5, 2, 6, 0$.

Again, 0 is eliminated from the sample; then, absolute values are taken and ranked. This time the (*) is on the rank of the negative difference. The ranks are:

Number	2	3	−1	6	2	5	6
Absolute Value	2	3	1*	6	2	5	6
Rank	2.5	4	1*	6.5	2.5	5	6.5

$T_- = 1$, since the only negative number has a rank of 1. Since $1 \leq 4$, reject H_o and conclude that the probability distribution of N is to the right of that of S, i.e., the median score of all children who learned to read by the new method is higher than the median score of children who learned to read by the standard method.

Exercise 14.2: Six matched pairs of people of the same sex, age, height, and weight are monitored while they eat the same foods for one week. One group (P) takes an experimental pill right before each meal, which is supposed to negate some of the calories eaten. Table 14.6a shows the weight losses in the control (C) group, which did not take the pill, and the P group, which did.

Test at the .05 level the hypothesis that the weight loss of those taking the pill is greater than that of those in the control group. Use a nonparametric test since there is no reason to believe these samples were drawn from weight loss populations with normal probability distributions.

Answer: First, set up the hypothesis test. This will indicate which way to take the differences in the table. Also, one of the differences is 0, which must be eliminated from the sample, so $n = 5$ for the region of rejection.

H_o: The probability distributions of weight losses for C (control group) and for P (pill group) are the same.

H_a: The probability distribution of weight losses for P is to the right of the probability distribution of weight losses for C. (A higher weight loss is expected from the P group.)

Table 14.6a

Pair	Weight Loss C	Weight Loss P
A	2	3
B	1	1
C	0	2
D	2	3
E	4	2
F	3	5

Test Statistic: T_-. (This assumes that the measures in C are subtracted from those in P. Since most of these differences should be positive, the test statistic flags the negative differences' ranks. If there are enough of these, the null hypothesis will be accepted.)

Region of Rejection (See Figure 14.6)

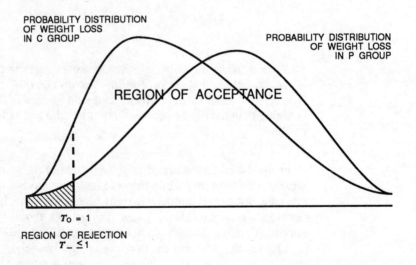

Figure 14.6
Rejection and Acceptance Regions
Wilcoxon Signed Rank Test ($n=5$)
One (Left) Tail, $\alpha = .05$

This is a one-tailed, $\alpha = .05$, $n = 5$ test. The region of rejection starts at 1.

Let's rewrite the table, adding three more columns: a P — C column, an |P — C| column, and a rank column (Table 14.6b).

Table 14.6b

Pair	C	P	P–C	|P–C|	Rank
A	2	3	1	1	1.5
B	1	1	0	0	(eliminated)
C	0	2	2	2	4
D	2	3	1	1	1.5
E	4	2	–2*	2*	4*
F	3	5	2	2	4

The ranks of the 1s are 1.5 each since they share ranks 1 and 2. The ranks of the 2s are each 4 since they share ranks 3, 4, and 5.

$T_- = 4$. Since $4 \geq 1$, the null hypothesis is accepted and the conclusion is that the probability distributions of the weight losses with (P) or without (C) the pill are the same.

NONPARAMETRIC STATISTICS FOR THREE OR MORE DATA SETS

The two previous nonparametric tests compared the population distributions of two sets. The Wilcoxon Rank Sum Test is used when two small samples of data are picked randomly from two populations to see if they are really the same. The Wilcoxon Signed Rank Test is used to test two matched populations that have been administered different treatments to see if the results of the two treatments are the same.

The above two tests have their parametric equivalents in two types of small sample comparison of the means tests discussed in Chapter 10. The two tests we will discuss now are the nonparametric equivalents of the two analysis of variance tests discussed in Chapter 11, the completely randomized design and the block design.

NonParametric Test for Completely Randomized Design Data

Recall (Exercise 11.2) from Chapter 11 in which thirty men who were 25 lbs overweight were chosen randomly from a large group of overweight men and assigned at random to four groups: C was the control group; men in D were dieting but did not increase their exercise levels; those in E ate as before but were put on an increased exercise regime; group F men were given a modified fast, but did not increase their exercise level. After two months, each man's weight loss (−) or gain (+) was recorded (See Table 14.7a).

Table 14.7a

C	D	E	F
0	−10	−4	−18
−3	−15	+2	−20
+2	−6	−7	−12
−5	−9	+1	−22
+1	−3	−3	−15
0	−12	−5	−9
+2	−5	0	
−4		+3	
		−8	

Determine if the probability distributions of the four weight loss groups are different, using $\alpha = .05$.

Notice that this question involves a nonparametric hypothesis. This seems logical since it is doubtful that the weight loss populations are normally distributed for each method, even though we assumed this in solving the problem using analysis of variance in Chapter 11.

KRUSKAL-WALLIS H TEST

The *Kruskal-Wallis H Test* is used to test the nonparametric equivalent of the ANOVA completely randomized design. This H statistic measures the extent to which the ranks of the samples differ; it is similar to the Wilcoxon Rank Sum Test but can be used for more than two samples, e.g., for the four samples in the above example.

The statistic itself is given by the formula

$$H = \frac{12}{n(n+1)} \cdot \sum \frac{R_k^2}{n_k} - 3(n+1)$$

where n = total sample size,

n_k = number of measurements in sample k (e.g., C contains 8 measures so $n_C = 8$),

R_k = sum of the ranks in sample k, where all n samples are ranked together (1 to 30 in above example).

Also, j is the number of treatments (e.g., $j = 4$ in the problem above).

This statistic is actually an equivalent form for one that more closely resembles the χ^2 statistic but is more difficult to use. Its derivation is beyond the scope of an introductory statistics course.

In using the Kruskal-Wallis H test, we compare H with the χ^2 statistic for the appropriate α-level and the appropriate number of degrees of freedom—the number of treatments minus one, $j-1$. Therefore, the region of rejection will be similar to the region of rejection for the χ^2 test in Chapter 12.

Setting up the above problem for hypothesis testing:

H_0: The probability distributions of the weight losses of people on plans C, D, E, and F are the same.

H_a: At least two of C, D, E, and F have different probability distributions.

Test Statistic: $H = \dfrac{12}{n(n+1)} \cdot \sum \dfrac{R_k^{\;2}}{n_k} - 3(n+1)$

Region of Rejection (See Figure 14.7)

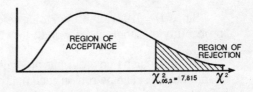

Figure 14.7
$\alpha = .05$; $df = 4 - 1 = 3$
Kruskal-Wallis H-Test

The value of the Kruskal-Wallis H is compared with χ^2, with $j-1$ degrees of freedom. For the above rejection region, $\alpha = .05$, $j = 4$, so $\chi^2_{.05,3} = 7.815$.

The first step is to rank all thirty weight losses or gains from 1 to 30. Be very careful since there are many pairs and triples that are the same, and there are negative and positive numbers to rank. The data, along with the rankings, is shown in Table 14.7b. The actual weight losses or gains are in parentheses.

Recall that the sum of all the numbers from 1 to n is given by the formula $S = n(n+1)/2$. If $n = 30$, then $S = 30(31)/2 = 465$. Notice that the sum of the rank sums, $R_C + R_D + R_E + R_F = 180 + 76.5 + 182 + 26.5 = 465$. This is a check on the accuracy of the rankings.

Now, substituting these rank sums in the test statistic:

$$H = \dfrac{12}{n(n+1)} \cdot \sum \dfrac{R_k^{\;2}}{n_k} - 3(n+1)$$

$$= \dfrac{12}{(30)(31)} \left[\dfrac{180^2}{8} + \dfrac{76.5^2}{7} + \dfrac{182^2}{9} + \dfrac{26.5^2}{6} \right] - 3(30+1)$$

$$= .0129\,(4050 + 836.04 + 3680.44 + 117.04) - 3(31)$$

$$= .0129\,(8683.52) - 93 = 112.02 - 93 = 19.02$$

Table 14.7b

C		D		E		F	
(0)	23	(−10)	8	(−4)	17.5	(−18)	3
(−3)	20	(−15)	4.5	(+2)	28	(−20)	2
(+2)	28	(−6)	13	(−7)	12	(−12)	6.5
(−5)	15	(−9)	9.5	(+1)	25.5	(−22)	1
(+1)	25.5	(−3)	20	(−3)	20	(−15)	4.5
(0)	23	(−12)	6.5	(−5)	15	(−9)	9.5
(+2)	28	(−5)	15	(0)	23		
(−4)	17.5			(+3)	30		
				(−8)	11		
$\sum R_k$	180		76.5		182		26.5

Since $H = 19.02 > \chi^2 = 7.815$, reject H_o and conclude that at least two probability distributions of weight loss by program differ.

Wilcoxon Rank Sum Follow-Up

To find which two programs produce different weight losses, the Wilcoxon Rank Sum Test can be run on each pair of programs. For example, suppose we wish to see if the probability distributions of D and F, diet and fast, differ, again using $\alpha = .05$. These seem the closest because all the samples showed negative numbers (weight losses).

H_o: The probability distributions of the weight losses of people in programs D and F are the same.

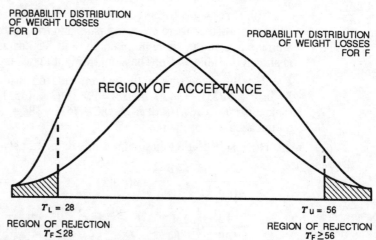

PROBABILITY DISTRIBUTION OF WEIGHT LOSSES FOR D

PROBABILITY DISTRIBUTION OF WEIGHT LOSSES FOR F

REGION OF ACCEPTANCE

$T_L = 28$

REGION OF REJECTION
$T_F \leq 28$

$T_U = 56$

REGION OF REJECTION
$T_F \geq 56$

Figure 14.8   Rejection and Acceptance Regions
Wilcoxon Rank Sum Test ($n_D = 7$; $n_F = 6$
Two-tailed with $\alpha = .05$

H_a: The probability distributions of weight losses of people in programs D and F differ.

Test Statistic: T_F (there are fewer fasters in the survey)

Region of Rejection (See Figure 14.8)

If T_F is between 28 and 56, H_o will not be rejected.

The weight losses in D and F from Table 14.7a have to be ranked, since only the thirteen ranked losses in the D and F columns will be used in this hypothesis test (see Table 14.8).

Table 14.8

	D	(Rank)	F	(Rank)
	(–10)	8	(–18)	3
	(–15)	4.5	(–20)	2
	(–6)	11	(–12)	6.5
	(–9)	9.5	(–22)	1
	(–3)	13	(–15)	4.5
	(–12)	6.5	(–9)	9.5
	(–5)	12	()	
Totals		64.5		26.5

Since $T_F = 26.5 \leq 28$, reject H_o and conclude that the probability distributions of weight loss by dieting (D) and fasting (F) differ.

Exercise 14.3: Recall from Chapter 11 the problems involving the grades on a uniform final of twenty-five freshmen assigned randomly to four different English instructors. The instructors were Q, R, S, and T (the table of grades is reproduced as Table 14.9a).

Table 14.9a   Grades on Uniform Final

		Professor	
Q	R	S	T
74	95	58	72
69	89	63	83
83	76	85	69
91	85	72	87
77	79	48	76
59	92	56	
38		75	

Test, using $\alpha = .05$, the hypothesis that the probability distributions of the four professors' final grades differ.

Answer: This problem requires the ranking of the twenty-five grades from 1 to 25 and the use of the Kruskal-Wallis H test. Set up the hypothesis test first:

H_o: The probability distributions of the grades of students in Q, R, S, and T's classes are the same.

H_a: At least two of Q, R, S, and T have different probability distributions.

Test Statistic: $H = \dfrac{12}{n(n+1)} \cdot \sum \dfrac{R_k^2}{n_k} - 3(n+1)$

Region of Rejection (See Figure 14.7)

Now rank the final grades from Table 14.9a (see Table 14.9b). The original scores are in parentheses.

Table 14.9b   Grades on Uniform Final

				Professor			
Q	(R_k)	R	(R_k)	S	(R_k)	T	(R_k)
(74)	11	(95)	25	(58)	4	(72)	9.5
(69)	7.5	(89)	22	(63)	6	(83)	17.5
(83)	17.5	(76)	13.5	(85)	19.5	(69)	7.5
(91)	23	(85)	19.5	(72)	9.5	(87)	21
(77)	15	(79)	16	(48)	2	(76)	13.5
(59)	5	(92)	24	(56)	3		
(38)	1			(75)	12		
$\sum R_k$	80		120		56		69

Checking the ranking, the sum of the ranks of twenty-five numbers is

$S = n(n+1)/2 = 25(26)/2 = 325$.

$R_Q + R_R + R_S + R_T = 80 + 120 + 56 + 69 = 325$ also.

Substitute these rank sums into the test statistic:

$$H = \dfrac{12}{n(n+1)} \cdot \sum \dfrac{R_k^2}{n_k} - 3(n-1)$$

$$= \dfrac{12}{(25)(26)} \left[\dfrac{80^2}{7} + \dfrac{120^2}{6} + \dfrac{56^2}{7} + \dfrac{69^2}{5} \right] - 3(25+1)$$

$$= 0.185 \, (914.3 + 2400 + 448 + 952.2) - 3(26)$$

$$= .0185 \, (4714.5) - 78 = 87.22 - 78 = 9.22$$

Since $H = 9.22 > \chi^2 = 7.815$, reject H_o and conclude that at least two probability distributions of grades by professor differ.

Tests Using Block Data

Recall that in Chapter 11 we discussed two analysis of variance designs, the completely randomized and the block design. The nonparametric equivalent to the analysis of variance completely randomized design (i.e., the nonparametric test on the same data) is the Kruskal-Wallis *H* Test. The analysis of variance block design is characterized by data linked in two ways, vertically by treatment and horizontally by block or common elements. There is a nonparametric equivalent of this test called the *Friedman-R*.

A problem we analyzed in Chapter 11 by using a block design ANOVA concerned whether the time at which a student took a particular class influenced his or her test grades (perhaps students taking earlier or later classes don't do as well as those taking classes in the middle hours of the day). Thus, the hour the class was held was the treatment. However, it was thought that the instructor of the class might have an influence on the students' grades as well, so the data

Table 14.10a

Instructor	Hour of Class			
	8:00	10:00	1:00	3:00
Doe	19	20	14	12
Jones	18	16	15	10
Smith	15	14	11	9

was blocked by instructor. The table of median test grades by class is reproduced in Table 14.10a.

Friedman-R Test

When a blocked table is presented for a nonparametric statistical analysis, the Friedman-R statistical test is used. In this test, as in the blocked analysis of variance, three or more treatments (hours of class in the above case) are presented and there is blocking by some common element across the columns (instructor). These are the same constraints as in the ANOVA, but this time we do not assume a normal population distribution and do not test the means. Instead, we test to see if the population distributions for the treatments are the same. Use $\alpha = .05$.

For the Friedman-R test, the ranking is done a little differently: the numbers are ranked across the blocks. In this example, there are four treatments, so across each of the three blocks the grades are ranked 1, 2, 3, 4, from lowest to highest grades in the block. In case of ties, the usual method of ranking prevails. Table 14.10a is rewritten to include only the ranks in each block, i.e., for each instructor (see Table 14.10b).

Notice that the sum of each row is $1 + 2 + 3 + 4 = 10$, so the sum of all the ranks is $3(10) = 30$. These block problems are easier to rank than the completely randomized design since in the latter case, all the numbers must be ranked in order.

Table 14.10b

Instructor	Ranks by Hour of Class			
	8:00	10:00	1:00	3:00
Doe	3	4	2	1
Jones	4	3	2	1
Smith	4	3	2	1
ΣR_k	11	10	6	3

The test statistic used to perform the hypothesis test on the probability distribution resembles the Kruskal-Wallis H: it is called the Friedman-R and is designated F_r.

$$F_r = \frac{12}{bj(j+1)} \cdot \Sigma R_k{}^2 - 3b(j+1) \quad \text{where}$$

b is the number of blocks (three here),

j is the number of treatments (four here), and

R_k is the sum of the ranks of the kth treatment.

Setting up the hypothesis test for the problem above:

H_o: The probability distributions of median grades in the 8:00, 10:00, 1:00, and 3:00 classes are the same.

H_a: The probability distributions of grades in at least two of the classes are different.

Test Statistic: $F_r = \dfrac{12}{bj(j+1)} \cdot \Sigma R_k{}^2 - 3b(j+1)$

Region of Rejection (See Figure 14.9)

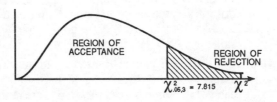

Figure 14.9
$\alpha = .05$; df $= 4 - 1 = 3$
Friedman-R Test

Notice that if $F_r > \chi^2$ with $j - 1$ degrees of freedom and $\alpha = .05$, the null hypothesis is rejected.

$$F_r = \frac{12}{bj(j+1)} \cdot \sum R_k{}^2 - 3b(j+1)$$

$$= \frac{12}{3 \cdot 4 \cdot 5}\left[11^2 + 10^2 + 6^2 + 3^2\right] - 3 \cdot 3 \,(5)$$

$$= .20\,(121 + 100 + 36 + 9) - 45$$

$$= .20\,(266) - 45 = 53.2 - 45 = 8.2.$$

Since 8.2 > 7.815, reject H_o and conclude that at least two probability distributions of median grades by time of class differ.

The Wilcoxon Signed Rank Test can often be used to compare two of the treatments to see if their probability distributions are among the probability distributions that differ, according to the outcome of the above hypothesis test.

Recall that the smallest number of pairs for which the Wilcoxon Signed Rank Test can be run is $n = 5$. Since there are only three pairs (blocks or instructors), this follow-up cannot be done here.

Exercise 14.4: Recall that in Exercise 11.4 a research physician was testing two drugs for effectiveness against a common cold germ. Volunteers were chosen, three from each of six age groups, infected with the cold virus, and given drugs A or B, or a placebo, C. The number of days until they were cured is given in Table 14.11a.

Table 14.11a

Age Range	Drug		
	A	B	C
18 – 25	3	4	6
26 – 33	4	4	5
34 – 41	5	6	6
42 – 49	4	5	7
50 – 57	5	5	7
58 – 65	6	6	8

Test at $\alpha = .05$ the hypothesis that the probability distributions (for the number of days it takes to recover from a cold) differ for some treatment groups.

Answer: First, rank across the blocks (ages) from 1 to 3 (Table 14.11b).

Notice that the sum of the ranks should be $6(1 + 2 + 3) =$ or 36, and $7.5 + 11 + 17.5 = 36$.

H_o: The probability distributions of recovery time in the three treatment groups is the same.

H_a: The probability distributions of recovery time in at least two of the groups are different.

Table 14.11b

Age Range	Drug		
	A	B	C
18 – 25	1	2	3
26 – 33	1.5	1.5	3
34 – 41	1	2.5	2.5
42 – 49	1	2	3
50 – 57	1.5	1.5	3
58 – 65	1.5	1.5	3
$\sum R_k$	7.5	11	17.5

Test Statistic: $F_r = \dfrac{12}{bj(j+1)} \cdot \sum R_k{}^2 - 3b(j+1)$

Region of Rejection (See Figure 14.10)

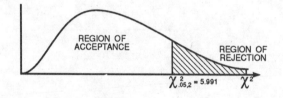

Figure 14.10
$\alpha = .05$; df $= 3 - 1 = 2$
Friedman-R Test

$$F_r = \frac{12}{bj(j+1)} \cdot \sum R_k{}^2 - 3b(j+1)$$

$$= \frac{12}{6 \cdot 3 \cdot 4} \cdot \left[7.5^2 + 11^2 + 17.5^2\right] - 3 \cdot 6(4)$$

$$= .167\,(56.25 + 121 + 306.25) - 72$$

$$= .167\,(483.5) - 72 = 80.74 - 72 = 8.74$$

Since $8.74 > 5.991$, reject H_o and conclude that the probability distributions of recovery time in at least two of the groups are different.

Note that this analysis can be followed up by comparing either A or B with C by using the Wilcoxon Signed Rank Test on their differences.

A and B cannot be compared, because the number of ties (0 differences) would put the count of the number of pairs (*n*) below 5.

Suppose we compare A with C. Subtracting the numbers in A from those in C results in all positive ranks; therefore, $T_- = 0$. For a one-tailed test in which $\alpha = .05$, if $n = 6$, then $T_0 = 2$. Since $0 \le 2$, we reject the null hypothesis and conclude that the probability distribution of C is to the right of the probability distribution of A.

Therefore, the Wilcoxon Signed Rank Test shows not only that A and C produce different probability distributions, but that it takes fewer days to recover from a cold if Drug A is taken than if no drug is taken. A similar result can be found comparing B with C.

NONPARAMETRIC TEST FOR LINEAR CORRELATION

The last of the nonparametric tests we will discuss is a test for correlation, similar to the Pearson Product Moment Coefficient of Correlation (*r*) found as part of the complete linear regression analysis in Chapter 13.

This test for linear correlation is used in much the same way that the coefficient of correlation was used in the linear regression analysis; it is a way to find out whether *x* and *y* are linearly related, and, if so, to what degree. The test performed here, finding the Spearman Rank Coefficient of Correlation, is used when the error distribution is not necessarily normal.

Spearman Rank Coefficient of Correlation

The number to be computed, r_s, is called the *Spearman Rank Coefficient of Correlation*. It is tested to see if the ranks of two sets of data are closely related. This coefficient is found by using the formula

$$r_s = 1 - \frac{6 \cdot \sum d^2}{n(n^2 - 1)} \quad \text{where}$$

d is the difference between the ranks of *x* and *y*, and *n* is the number of pairs.

This formula is actually an approximation for a more complicated formula that resembles the one used for calculating *r* in the parametric test. Recall from Chapter 13 that $r = \dfrac{SS_{xy}}{\sqrt{SS_{xx} \cdot SS_{yy}}}$

Just as $-1 \le r \le 1$, so $-1 \le r_s \le 1$, i.e., r_s is between -1 and 1. If $r_s = -1$, there would be complete negative rank correlation, and if $r_s = 1$, there would be complete positive rank correlation. How close does r_s have to be to -1 or 1 to be able to say that a negative or a positive rank correlation exists? This depends upon two factors, the number of pairs (points: x, y values) in the data set and the $\alpha-$ value set by the problem.

Recall from Chapter 13 a problem in which the hypothesis is that the more credits a student is taking during a semester, the lower will be his or her grade point average. Eight students were chosen at random and the number of credits each took and each student's G.P.A. for the semester are tabulated. This information is repeated in Table 14.12.

Table 14.12

Student	Number of Credits	Grade Point Average
A	10	3.5
B	18	2.8
C	12	3.3
D	15	3.7
E	16	2.9
F	16	3.0
G	22	2.4
H	9	3.1

We want to know, using $\alpha = .05$, whether there is a negative rank correlation between the number of credits students carry and their grade point average.

Spearman's Rank Correlation Coefficient Table

We introduce here a new table (Appendix G), which outlines the critical values of the Spearman Rank Correlation Coefficient. The first few lines are reproduced as Table 14.13.

These are the numbers that begin the region of rejection for a one-tailed test, either $\rho_s > 0$ or $\rho_s < 0$ (with a negative in the case of $\rho_s < 0$). Recall that ρ_s is the population coefficient of rank correlations, as r_s is the sample coefficient of rank correlation. As in the case of the critical values of t-table, if the

Table 14.13   Critical Values of Spearman's Rank Correlation Coefficient

n	$\alpha = .05$	$\alpha = .025$	$\alpha = .01$	$\alpha = .005$
5	.900	—	—	—
6	.829	.886	.943	—
7	.714	.786	.893	—
8	.643	.738	.833	.881
9	.600	.683	.783	.833
10	.564	.648	.745	.794

hypothesis test is two-tailed, the α level should be halved. The Spearman table is read and interpreted similarly to the *t*-table.

Hypothesis Testing Using Spearman Rank

The hypothesis test for the problem whose data appears in Table 14.12 is set up below:

H_0: $\rho_s = 0$ (There is no rank correlation between number of credits and grade point average.)

H_a: $\rho_s < 0$ (There is a negative rank correlation between number of credits and G.P.A.)

Test Statistic: $r_s = 1 - \dfrac{6\sum d^2}{n(n^2 - 1)}$

Region of Rejection (See Figure 14.11)

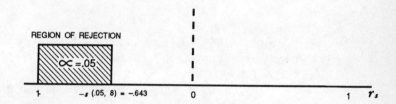

Figure 14.11
Spearman Rank Correlation
One-tailed, $\alpha = .05$; $n = 8$

Assuming the test is at $\alpha = .05$, the region of rejection is $r_{s(.05,\ 8)} < -.643$. According to Table 14.12, .643 begins the rejection region for a one-tailed test at $\alpha = .05$ for $n = 8$ (pairs of numbers). Since the alternative hypothesis checks for a negative correlation, .05 is in the left tail, which begins at $-.643$. Since this function is not a continuous function (not a smooth curve), only the rejection region is pictured.

In order to calculate r_s, both the number of credits and the G.P.A.s must be ranked separately and subtracted. Then the differences are squared (d^2) and summed $\left(\sum d^2\right)$. This is done in Table 14.14.

Note that the sum of the differences $\left(\sum d\right)$ is always equal to 0. This is a check on the correctness of the rankings and the subtraction.

Substituting into the test statistic:

$$r_s = 1 - \frac{6\,(148.5)}{8\,(63)} = 1 - \frac{891}{504} = 1 - 1.768 = -.768$$

Table 14.14

Student	Credit Rank	G.P.A Rank	d	d^2
A	2	7	−5	25
B	7	2	5	25
C	3	6	−3	9
D	4	8	−4	16
E	5.5	3	2.5	6.25
F	5.5	4	1.5	2.25
G	8	1	7	49
H	1	5	−4	16

$$\sum d^2 = 148.5$$

Since −.768 < −.643, reject the null hypothesis and conclude that there is a negative rank correlation between the number of credits carried and the semester G.P.A. ($\rho_s < 0$).

If the ranks of both number of credits and grade point average were identical, then each difference would be 0, so $\sum d^2 = 0$ and $r_s = 1$—perfect rank correlation. However, if the ranks were *exactly* opposite from each other (e.g., the first set ranked 1 to 8 and the second ranked 8 to 1), $r_s = -1$—perfect negative correlation. In this problem, there was a low negative correlation of the sample, −.768, which was close enough to −1 to allow us to reject H_o (at $\alpha = .05$ level) and affirm the negative correlation.

Notice how much less work we must do to calculate and test the rank correlation r_s than to calculate the Pearson Product Moment r by linear regression analysis. In order to calculate r, we must find SS_{xx}, SS_{yy}, and SS_{xy}. However, the Spearman Rank Coefficient Correlation test is not as powerful as

Table 14.15a

Person	# Years School	Salary (1000's)
I	9	12
II	11	15
III	12	14
IV	12	17
V	14	19
VI	16	16
VII	16	21

a linear regression test since its conclusion deals with ranks of x and y rather than actual numbers x and y.

Exercise 14.5: In Exercise 13.8 a complete linear regression analysis was done on the question of whether the more years of education a person has, the higher the starting salary on the first job out of school. Using the data in Table 14.15a, test at $\alpha = .05$ whether the ranks are positively correlated.

Answer: First, set up the hypothesis test:

$H_o: \rho_s = 0$

$H_a: \rho_s > 0$

Test Statistic: $r_s = 1 - \dfrac{6 \cdot \sum d^2}{n(n^2 - 1)}$

Region of Rejection (See Figure 14.12)

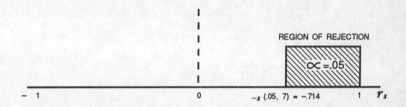

Figure 14.12
Spearman Rank Correlation
One-tailed, $\alpha = .05$; $n = 7$

The region of rejection starts after $r_{s\,(.05,\,7)} = .714$.

Table 14.15b:

Person	Rank Years	Rank Salary	d	d^2
I	1	1	0	0
II	2	3	−1	1
III	3.5	2	1.5	2.25
IV	3.5	5	−1.5	2.25
V	5	6	−1	1
VI	6.5	4	2.5	6.25
VII	6.5	7	−.5	.25

$$\sum d^2 = 13$$

Now, rank number of years of school and starting salary. Take the difference d, square, and sum $\sum d^2$. These are calculated in table 14.15b.

Substituting $\sum d^2 = 13$ into the formula for r_s:

$$r_s = 1 - \frac{6(13)}{7(48)} = 1 - \frac{78}{336} = 1 - .232$$

so $r_s = .768$. Since $.768 > .714$, reject the null hypothesis and conclude that the number of years of school and the starting salary on the first job are positively rank correlated.

Exercise 14.6: A statistics professor gives two one-hour exams during the semester. She wishes to know if the grades on the exams are related. Ten of her students are chosen at random, and their scores on Exam I and Exam II are recorded (Table 14.16a). Test at $\alpha = .05$ the following hypotheses, using the appropriate tests:

Table 14.16a

Student	Exam I	Exam II
Alice	82	87
Billy	91	78
Carl	88	93
David	75	75
Emily	68	74
Frank	79	80
Gwen	57	73
Howard	82	80
Inez	77	87
Jonathan	85	94

a. The grades on the second exam are higher than those on the first exam. (The probability distribution of the grades on the second test is to the right of the probability distribution of the grades on the second test.)
b. The higher the first test grade, the higher the second test grade. (There is a positive correlation between the ranks of the grades on the first and second tests.)

Answers:
a. To test whether the probability distribution of grades in Exam II is to the right of the probability distribution of grades in Exam I, the Wilcoxon Signed Rank Test is used. Recall that the grades are subtracted (II – I), and their absolute values are found and ranked.

It is expected, if the Exam II grades are higher than the Exam I grades, that most of these differences (II – I) will be positive. Therefore, star (*) the negative differences. (See Table 14.16b.)

Table 14.16b

Student	II – I	|II – I|	Rank
Alice	5	5	3.5
Billy	–13*	13*	8*
Carl	5	5	3.5
David	0	0	eliminated
Emily	6	6	5
Frank	1	1	1
Gwen	16	16	9
Howard	–2*	2*	2*
Inez	10	10	7
Jonathan	9	9	6

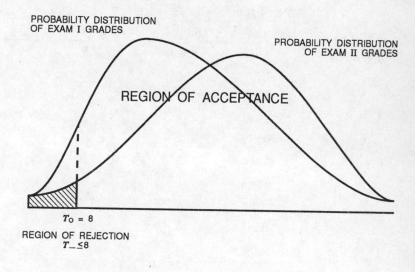

Figure 14.13
Rejection and Acceptance Regions
Wilcoxon Signed Rank Test ($n = 9$)
One-tailed with $\alpha = .05$

Recall that in this type of problem, if there is no difference (0) between two numbers, that sample is eliminated. Our interest is in T_- or T_+ only.

H_o: The probability distributions of the Exam I grades and the Exam II grades are the same.

H_a: The probability distribution of the Exam II grades is to the right of the probability distribution of Exam I grades. (The grades on Exam II are higher.)

Test Statistic: T_-

Region of Rejection (See Figure 14.13)

This is a one-tailed test, $n = 9$, $\alpha = .05$. $T_- = 2 + 8 = 10$. Since $10 > 8$, 10 falls in the acceptance region. Therefore, accept H_o and conclude that the probability distributions of the grades in the two exams are the same.

b. For this part of the problem, we want to know if the grades are positively rank correlated. That is, do higher grades on Exam I mean higher grades on Exam II? The Spearman Rank Correlation Coefficient, r_s, must be found.

Each of the sets of exam grades, I and II, is ranked separately, the ranks are subtracted, their differences squared and summed. Table 14.16c represents this work.

Table 14.16c

Student	Rank I	Rank II	d(II − I)	d^2
Alice	6.5	7.5	1	1
Billy	10	4	−6	36
Carl	9	9	0	0
David	3	3	0	0
Emily	2	2	0	0
Frank	5	5.5	.5	.25
Gwen	1	1	0	0
Howard	6.5	5.5	−1	1
Inez	4	7.5	3.5	12.25
Jonathan	8	10	2	4

$$\sum d^2 = 54.5$$

In the Spearman Rank Correlation, the ranks with 0 difference are retained, so n = 10.

H_o: $\rho_s = 0$ (The ranks of the exams are not correlated.)

$H_a: \rho_s > 0$ (The ranks of the exams are positively correlated.)

Test Statistic: $r_s = 1 - \dfrac{6 \sum d^2}{n(n^2 - 1)}$

Region of Rejection (See Figure 14.14)

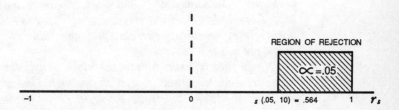

Figure 14.14
Spearman Rank Correlation
One-tailed, $\alpha = .05$; $n = 10$

The region of rejection is one-tailed with $\alpha = .05$. $r_{s(.05, 10)} = .564$, according to the table in Appendix G.

$$r_s = 1 - \frac{6 \sum d^2}{n(n^2 - 1)}$$

$$n_s = \left| -\frac{6(54.5)}{10(99)} \right| = -\frac{327}{990} = 1 - .330 = .670$$

Since $.670 > .564$, reject H_o and conclude that the ranks of the exams are positively correlated: the higher one's grade on the first exam, the higher the grade on the second.

*I*n this final chapter we have discussed five nonparametric hypothesis tests, each of which is equivalent (in data presentation) to a parametric test discussed in earlier chapters. For each of these five tests, ranking the data is the first step in solving the problem.

The Wilcoxon Rank Sum Test is performed when the data resembles a two-sample t-test for the difference between means, but the populations from which the samples are drawn are not necessarily normal. The Wilcoxon Signed Rank Test is the statistical test of choice for matched pairs of data. If the populations from which these pairs were drawn are not necessarily normally distributed, then the nonparametric test rather than the t-difference hypothesis test of means is performed. New tables of critical values were introduced for both these tests.

The nonparametric equivalents to two analysis of variance hypothesis tests were also discussed in this chapter. If the data is the same as that used in a completely randomized design, the Kruskal-Wallis H Test is the nonparametric choice; if the data is randomized block data, the nonparametric hypothesis test is the Friedman-R. In both these tests, the calculated test statistic is compared with a χ^2 statistic.

In Chapter 13, complete linear regression analyses were explained and performed. The same data (x and y values) can be analyzed using the Spearman Rank Correlation Coefficient test to see if the ranks of the pairs of numbers are positively or negatively correlated. A new table of critical values was introduced for this test as well.

Nonparametric statistics tie the whole of hypothesis testing together. Each of the previous hypothesis tests of the mean and linear regression analysis were revisited in discussing these alternatives to parametric tests. Most of the problems in this chapter were solved in previous chapters as parametric tests, assuming normality of the population distributions or, in the case of linear regression, a normal distribution of errors. Even though the hypotheses were weaker in the nonparametric methods, the acceptances or rejections of the null hypotheses were the same as in the original parametric problems.

Appendix A: Normal Curve Areas

Table II: Areas under the standard normal curve

z	0.00	0.01	0.02	0.03	0.04	0.05	0.06	0.07	0.08	0.09
					Second decimal place in z					
0.0	0.0000	0.0040	0.0080	0.0120	0.0160	0.0199	0.0239	0.0279	0.0319	0.0359
0.1	0.0398	0.0438	0.0478	0.0517	0.0557	0.0596	0.0636	0.0675	0.0714	0.0753
0.2	0.0793	0.0832	0.0871	0.0910	0.0948	0.0987	0.1026	0.1064	0.1103	0.1141
0.3	0.1179	0.1217	0.1255	0.1293	0.1331	0.1368	0.1406	0.1443	0.1480	0.1517
0.4	0.1554	0.1591	0.1628	0.1664	0.1700	0.1736	0.1772	0.1808	0.1844	0.1879
0.5	0.1915	0.1950	0.1985	0.2019	0.2054	0.2088	0.2123	0.2157	0.2190	0.2224
0.6	0.2257	0.2291	0.2324	0.2357	0.2389	0.2422	0.2454	0.2486	0.2517	0.2549
0.7	0.2580	0.2611	0.2642	0.2673	0.2704	0.2734	0.2764	0.2794	0.2823	0.2852
0.8	0.2881	0.2910	0.2939	0.2967	0.2995	0.3023	0.3051	0.3078	0.3106	0.3133
0.9	0.3159	0.3186	0.3212	0.3238	0.3264	0.3289	0.3315	0.3340	0.3365	0.3389
1.0	0.3413	0.3438	0.3461	0.3485	0.3508	0.3531	0.3554	0.3577	0.3599	0.3621
1.1	0.3643	0.3665	0.3686	0.3708	0.3729	0.3749	0.3770	0.3790	0.3810	0.3830
1.2	0.3849	0.3869	0.3888	0.3907	0.3925	0.3944	0.3962	0.3980	0.3997	0.4015
1.3	0.4032	0.4049	0.4066	0.4082	0.4099	0.4115	0.4131	0.4147	0.4162	0.4177
1.4	0.4192	0.4207	0.4222	0.4236	0.4251	0.4265	0.4279	0.4292	0.4306	0.4319
1.5	0.4332	0.4345	0.4357	0.4370	0.4382	0.4394	0.4406	0.4418	0.4429	0.4441
1.6	0.4452	0.4463	0.4474	0.4484	0.4495	0.4505	0.4515	0.4525	0.4535	0.4545
1.7	0.4554	0.4564	0.4573	0.4582	0.4591	0.4599	0.4608	0.4616	0.4625	0.4633
1.8	0.4641	0.4649	0.4656	0.4664	0.4671	0.4678	0.4686	0.4693	0.4699	0.4706
1.9	0.4713	0.4719	0.4726	0.4732	0.4738	0.4744	0.4750	0.4756	0.4761	0.4767
2.0	0.4772	0.4778	0.4783	0.4788	0.4793	0.4798	0.4803	0.4808	0.4812	0.4817
2.1	0.4821	0.4826	0.4830	0.4834	0.4838	0.4842	0.4846	0.4850	0.4854	0.4857
2.2	0.4861	0.4864	0.4868	0.4871	0.4875	0.4878	0.4881	0.4884	0.4887	0.4890
2.3	0.4893	0.4896	0.4898	0.4901	0.4904	0.4906	0.4909	0.4911	0.4913	0.4916
2.4	0.4918	0.4920	0.4922	0.4925	0.4927	0.4929	0.4931	0.4932	0.4934	0.4936
2.5	0.4938	0.4940	0.4941	0.4943	0.4945	0.4946	0.4948	0.4949	0.4951	0.4952
2.6	0.4953	0.4955	0.4956	0.4957	0.4959	0.4960	0.4961	0.4962	0.4963	0.4964
2.7	0.4965	0.4966	0.4967	0.4968	0.4969	0.4970	0.4971	0.4972	0.4973	0.4974
2.8	0.4974	0.4975	0.4976	0.4977	0.4977	0.4978	0.4979	0.4979	0.4980	0.4981
2.9	0.4981	0.4982	0.4982	0.4983	0.4984	0.4984	0.4985	0.4985	0.4986	0.4986
3.0	0.4987	0.4987	0.4987	0.4988	0.4988	0.4989	0.4989	0.4989	0.4990	0.4990
3.1	0.4990	0.4991	0.4991	0.4991	0.4992	0.4992	0.4992	0.4992	0.4993	0.4993
3.2	0.4993	0.4993	0.4994	0.4994	0.4994	0.4994	0.4994	0.4995	0.4995	0.4995
3.3	0.4995	0.4995	0.4995	0.4996	0.4996	0.4996	0.4996	0.4996	0.4996	0.4997
3.4	0.4997	0.4997	0.4997	0.4997	0.4997	0.4997	0.4997	0.4997	0.4997	0.4998
3.5	0.4998	0.4998	0.4998	0.4998	0.4998	0.4998	0.4998	0.4998	0.4998	0.4998
3.6	0.4998	0.4998	0.4999	0.4999	0.4999	0.4999	0.4999	0.4999	0.4999	0.4999
3.7	0.4999	0.4999	0.4999	0.4999	0.4999	0.4999	0.4999	0.4999	0.4999	0.4999
3.8	0.4999	0.4999	0.4999	0.4999	0.4999	0.4999	0.4999	0.4999	0.4999	0.4999
3.9	0.5000[†]									

[†]For $z \geq 3.90$, the areas are 0.5000 to four decimal places.

Appendix B: Critical Values of t

Values of t_α

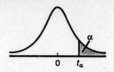

df	$t_{0.10}$	$t_{0.05}$	$t_{0.025}$	$t_{0.01}$	$t_{0.005}$	df
1	3.078	6.314	12.706	31.821	63.657	1
2	1.886	2.920	4.303	6.965	9.925	2
3	1.638	2.353	3.182	4.541	5.841	3
4	1.533	2.132	2.776	3.747	4.604	4
5	1.476	2.015	2.571	3.365	4.032	5
6	1.440	1.943	2.447	3.143	3.707	6
7	1.415	1.895	2.365	2.998	3.499	7
8	1.397	1.860	2.306	2.896	3.355	8
9	1.383	1.833	2.262	2.821	3.250	9
10	1.372	1.812	2.228	2.764	3.169	10
11	1.363	1.796	2.201	2.718	3.106	11
12	1.356	1.782	2.179	2.681	3.055	12
13	1.350	1.771	2.160	2.650	3.012	13
14	1.345	1.761	2.145	2.624	2.977	14
15	1.341	1.753	2.131	2.602	2.947	15
16	1.337	1.746	2.120	2.583	2.921	16
17	1.333	1.740	2.110	2.567	2.898	17
18	1.330	1.734	2.101	2.552	2.878	18
19	1.328	1.729	2.093	2.539	2.861	19
20	1.325	1.725	2.086	2.528	2.845	20
21	1.323	1.721	2.080	2.518	2.831	21
22	1.321	1.717	2.074	2.508	2.819	22
23	1.319	1.714	2.069	2.500	2.807	23
24	1.318	1.711	2.064	2.492	2.797	24
25	1.316	1.708	2.060	2.485	2.787	25
26	1.315	1.706	2.056	2.479	2.779	26
27	1.314	1.703	2.052	2.473	2.771	27
28	1.313	1.701	2.048	2.467	2.763	28
29	1.311	1.699	2.045	2.462	2.756	29
∞	1.282	1.645	1.960	2.326	2.576	∞

Appendix C: F-distribution; $\propto$ = .05

Values of $F_{0.05}$

					df for numerator				
	1	*2*	*3*	*4*	*5*	*6*	*7*	*8*	*9*
1	161.4	199.5	215.7	224.6	230.2	234.0	236.8	238.9	240.5
2	18.51	19.00	19.16	19.25	19.30	19.33	19.35	19.37	19.38
3	10.13	9.55	9.28	9.12	9.01	8.94	8.89	8.85	8.81
4	7.71	6.94	6.59	6.39	6.26	6.16	6.09	6.04	6.00
5	6.61	5.79	5.41	5.19	5.05	4.95	4.88	4.82	4.77
6	5.99	5.14	4.76	4.53	4.39	4.28	4.21	4.15	4.10
7	5.59	4.74	4.35	4.12	3.97	3.87	3.79	3.73	3.68
8	5.32	4.46	4.07	3.84	3.69	3.58	3.50	3.44	3.39
9	5.12	4.26	3.86	3.63	3.48	3.37	3.29	3.23	3.18
10	4.96	4.10	3.71	3.48	3.33	3.22	3.14	3.07	3.02
11	4.84	3.98	3.59	3.36	3.20	3.09	3.01	2.95	2.90
12	4.75	3.89	3.49	3.26	3.11	3.00	2.91	2.85	2.80
13	4.67	3.81	3.41	3.18	3.03	2.92	2.83	2.77	2.71
14	4.60	3.74	3.34	3.11	2.96	2.85	2.76	2.70	2.65
15	4.54	3.68	3.29	3.06	2.90	2.79	2.71	2.64	2.59
16	4.49	3.63	3.24	3.01	2.85	2.74	2.66	2.59	2.54
17	4.45	3.59	3.20	2.96	2.81	2.70	2.61	2.55	2.49
18	4.41	3.55	3.16	2.93	2.77	2.66	2.58	2.51	2.46
19	4.38	3.52	3.13	2.90	2.74	2.63	2.54	2.48	2.42
20	4.35	3.49	3.10	2.87	2.71	2.60	2.51	2.45	2.39
21	4.32	3.47	3.07	2.84	2.68	2.57	2.49	2.42	2.37
22	4.30	3.44	3.05	2.82	2.66	2.55	2.46	2.40	2.34
23	4.28	3.42	3.03	2.80	2.64	2.53	2.44	2.37	2.32
24	4.26	3.40	3.01	2.78	2.62	2.51	2.42	2.36	2.30
25	4.24	3.39	2.99	2.76	2.60	2.49	2.40	2.34	2.28
26	4.23	3.37	2.98	2.74	2.59	2.47	2.39	2.32	2.27
27	4.21	3.35	2.96	2.73	2.57	2.46	2.37	2.31	2.25
28	4.20	3.34	2.95	2.71	2.56	2.45	2.36	2.29	2.24
29	4.18	3.33	2.93	2.70	2.55	2.43	2.35	2.28	2.22
30	4.17	3.32	2.92	2.69	2.53	2.42	2.33	2.27	2.21
40	4.08	3.23	2.84	2.61	2.45	2.34	2.25	2.18	2.12
60	4.00	3.15	2.76	2.53	2.37	2.25	2.17	2.10	2.04
120	3.92	3.07	2.68	2.45	2.29	2.17	2.09	2.02	1.96
∞	3.84	3.00	2.60	2.37	2.21	2.10	2.01	1.94	1.88

df for denominator

Appendix D: Critical Values of χ^2

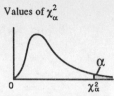

Values of χ^2_α

df	$\chi^2_{0.995}$	$\chi^2_{0.99}$	$\chi^2_{0.975}$	$\chi^2_{0.95}$	$\chi^2_{0.05}$	$\chi^2_{0.025}$	$\chi^2_{0.01}$	$\chi^2_{0.005}$	df
1	0.000	0.000	0.001	0.004	3.841	5.024	6.635	7.879	1
2	0.010	0.020	0.051	0.103	5.991	7.378	9.210	10.597	2
3	0.072	0.115	0.216	0.352	7.815	9.348	11.345	12.838	3
4	0.207	0.297	0.484	0.711	9.488	11.143	13.277	14.860	4
5	0.412	0.554	0.831	1.145	11.070	12.832	15.086	16.750	5
6	0.676	0.872	1.237	1.635	12.592	14.449	16.812	18.548	6
7	0.989	1.239	1.690	2.167	14.067	16.013	18.475	20.278	7
8	1.344	1.646	2.180	2.733	15.507	17.535	20.090	21.955	8
9	1.735	2.088	2.700	3.325	16.919	19.023	21.666	23.589	9
10	2.156	2.558	3.247	3.940	18.307	20.483	23.209	25.188	10
11	2.603	3.053	3.816	4.575	19.675	21.920	24.725	26.757	11
12	3.074	3.571	4.404	5.226	21.026	23.337	26.217	28.300	12
13	3.565	4.107	5.009	5.892	22.362	24.736	27.688	29.819	13
14	4.075	4.660	5.629	6.571	23.685	26.119	29.141	31.319	14
15	4.601	5.229	6.262	7.261	24.996	27.488	30.578	32.801	15
16	5.142	5.812	6.908	7.962	26.296	28.845	32.000	34.267	16
17	5.697	6.408	7.564	8.672	27.587	30.191	33.409	35.718	17
18	6.265	7.015	8.231	9.390	28.869	31.526	34.805	37.156	18
19	6.844	7.633	8.907	10.117	30.144	32.852	36.191	38.582	19
20	7.434	8.260	9.591	10.851	31.410	34.170	37.566	39.997	20
21	8.034	8.897	10.283	11.591	32.671	35.479	38.932	41.401	21
22	8.643	9.542	10.982	12.338	33.924	36.781	40.289	42.796	22
23	9.260	10.196	11.689	13.091	35.172	38.076	41.638	44.181	23
24	9.886	10.856	12.401	13.848	36.415	39.364	42.980	45.558	24
25	10.520	11.524	13.120	14.611	37.652	40.646	44.314	46.928	25
26	11.160	12.198	13.844	15.379	38.885	41.923	45.642	48.290	26
27	11.808	12.879	14.573	16.151	40.113	43.194	46.963	49.645	27
28	12.461	13.565	15.308	16.928	41.337	44.461	48.278	50.993	28
29	13.121	14.256	16.047	17.708	42.557	45.722	49.588	52.336	29
30	13.787	14.953	16.791	18.493	43.773	46.979	50.892	53.672	30

Appendix E: Critical Values of T_L and T_U for Wilcoxon Rank Sum Test

a. $\alpha = .025$ one-tailed; $\alpha = .05$ two-tailed

n_2	n_1 3		4		5		6		7		8		9		10	
	T_L	T_U	T_L	T_U	T_L	T_U	T_L	T_U	T_L	T_U	T_L	T_U	T_L	T_U	T_L	T_U
3	5	16	6	18	6	21	7	23	7	26	8	28	8	31	9	33
4	6	18	11	25	12	28	12	32	13	35	14	38	15	41	16	44
5	6	21	12	28	18	37	19	41	20	45	21	49	22	53	24	56
6	7	23	12	32	19	41	26	52	28	56	29	61	31	65	32	70
7	7	26	13	35	20	45	28	56	37	68	39	73	41	78	43	83
8	8	28	14	38	21	49	29	61	39	73	49	87	51	93	54	98
9	8	31	15	41	22	53	31	65	41	78	51	93	63	108	66	114
10	9	33	16	44	24	56	32	70	43	83	54	98	66	114	79	131

b. $a = .05$ one-tailed; $\alpha =$ two-tailed

n_2	n_1 3		4		5		6		7		8		9		10	
	T_L	T_U	T_L	T_U	T_L	T_U	T_L	T_U	T_L	T_U	T_L	T_U	T_L	T_U	T_L	T_U
3	6	15	7	17	7	20	8	22	9	24	9	27	10	29	11	31
4	7	17	12	24	13	27	14	30	15	33	16	36	17	39	18	42
5	7	20	13	27	19	36	20	40	22	43	24	46	25	50	26	54
6	8	22	14	30	20	40	28	50	30	54	32	58	33	63	35	67
7	9	24	15	33	22	43	30	54	39	66	41	71	43	76	46	80
8	9	27	16	36	24	46	32	58	41	71	52	84	54	90	57	95
9	10	29	17	39	25	50	33	63	43	76	54	90	66	105	69	111
10	11	31	18	42	26	54	35	67	46	80	57	95	69	111	83	127

Appendix F: Critical Values of T_0 for Wilcoxon Signed Rank Test

One-tailed	Two-tailed	$n = 5$	$n = 6$	$n = 7$	$n = 8$	$n = 9$	$n = 10$
$\alpha = .05$	$\alpha = .10$	1	2	4	6	8	11
$\alpha = .025$	$\alpha = .05$		1	2	4	6	8
$\alpha = .01$	$\alpha = .02$			0	2	3	5
$\alpha = .005$	$\alpha = .01$				0	2	3
		$n = 11$	$n = 12$	$n = 13$	$n = 14$	$n = 15$	$n = 16$
$\alpha = .05$	$\alpha = .10$	14	17	21	26	30	36
$\alpha = .025$	$\alpha = .05$	11	14	17	21	25	30
$\alpha = .01$	$\alpha = .02$	7	10	13	16	20	24
$\alpha = .005$	$\alpha = .01$	5	7	10	13	16	19
		$n = 17$	$n = 18$	$n = 19$	$n = 20$	$n = 21$	$n = 22$
$\alpha = .05$	$\alpha = .10$	41	47	54	60	68	75
$\alpha = .025$	$\alpha = .05$	35	40	46	52	59	66
$\alpha = .01$	$\alpha = .02$	28	33	38	43	49	56
$\alpha = .005$	$\alpha = .01$	23	28	32	37	43	49
		$n = 23$	$n = 24$	$n = 25$	$n = 26$	$n = 27$	$n = 28$
$\alpha = .05$	$\alpha = .10$	83	92	101	110	120	130
$\alpha = .025$	$\alpha = .05$	73	81	90	98	107	117
$\alpha = .01$	$\alpha = .02$	62	69	77	85	93	102
$\alpha = .005$	$\alpha = .01$	55	61	68	76	84	92
		$n = 29$	$n = 30$	$n = 31$	$n = 32$	$n = 33$	$n = 34$
$\alpha = .05$	$\alpha = .10$	141	152	163	175	188	201
$\alpha = .025$	$\alpha = .05$	127	137	148	159	171	183
$\alpha = .01$	$\alpha = .02$	111	120	130	141	151	162
$\alpha = .005$	$\alpha = .01$	100	109	118	128	138	149
		$n = 35$	$n = 36$	$n = 37$	$n = 38$	$n = 39$	
$\alpha = .05$	$\alpha = .10$	214	228	242	256	271	
$\alpha = .025$	$\alpha = .05$	195	208	222	235	250	
$\alpha = .01$	$\alpha = .02$	174	186	197	211	224	
$\alpha = .005$	$\alpha = .01$	160	171	183	195	208	
		$n = 40$	$n = 41$	$n = 42$	$n = 43$	$n = 44$	$n = 45$
$\alpha = .05$	$\alpha = .10$	287	303	319	336	353	371
$\alpha = .025$	$\alpha = .05$	264	279	295	311	327	344
$\alpha = .01$	$\alpha = .02$	238	252	267	281	297	313
$\alpha = .005$	$\alpha = .01$	221	234	248	262	277	292
		$n = 46$	$n = 47$	$n = 48$	$n = 49$	$n = 50$	
$\alpha = .05$	$\alpha = .10$	389	408	427	446	466	
$\alpha = .025$	$\alpha = .05$	361	379	397	415	434	
$\alpha = .01$	$\alpha = .02$	329	345	362	380	398	
$\alpha = .005$	$\alpha = .01$	307	323	339	356	373	

Appendix G: Critical Values of Spearman Rank Correlation Coefficient

n	$r_{s,0.05}$	$r_{s,0.025}$	$r_{s,0.01}$	$r_{s,0.005}$	n
5	0.900	—	—	—	5
6	0.829	0.886	0.943	—	6
7	0.714	0.786	0.893	—	7
8	0.643	0.738	0.833	0.881	8
9	0.600	0.683	0.783	0.833	9
10	0.564	0.648	0.745	0.794	10
11	0.523	0.623	0.736	0.818	11
12	0.497	0.591	0.703	0.780	12
13	0.475	0.566	0.673	0.745	13
14	0.457	0.545	0.646	0.716	14
15	0.441	0.525	0.623	0.689	15
16	0.425	0.507	0.601	0.666	16
17	0.412	0.490	0.582	0.645	17
18	0.399	0.476	0.564	0.625	18
19	0.388	0.462	0.549	0.608	19
20	0.377	0.450	0.534	0.591	20

Values of r_s, $\alpha 0.900$

Index

$\bar{x} = \Sigma x/n = 619/5 = 123.8$

To calculate s, find $\Sigma x^2 = 76803$. Since $\Sigma x = 619$, $(\Sigma x)^2 = 619^2 = 383161$

$(\Sigma x)^2/n = 383161/5 = 76632.2$.

$$s = \sqrt{\frac{\Sigma x^2 - (\Sigma x)^2/n}{n-1}} = \sqrt{\frac{76803 - 76632.2}{4}} \qquad s = \sqrt{170.8/4} \approx 42.7 = 6.53.$$

Calculating t:

$$t = \frac{\bar{x} - \mu}{s/\sqrt{n}} = \frac{123.8 - 112}{6.53/\sqrt{5}} = \frac{11.8}{2.92} = 4.04$$

Since $4.04 > 2.776$, reject H_o and conclude that the mean I.Q. for students in Professor P's statistics class is different from the mean I.Q. of the students in JKL College.

OBSERVED SIGNIFICANCE LEVEL FOR *t*-TESTS

After a hypothesis test has been completed, a common follow-up is to find the observed significance level. Recall that the observed significance level places the calculated statistic on the distribution and finds the area in the tail or tails that start at this number. It is helpful to calculate the observed significance level to plan the region of rejection for future tests involving the same population.

For example, in the example concerning G.P.A.s above, the null hypothesis was $\mu = 2.5$ and the alternative hypothesis was $\mu > 2.5$. The calculated *t*-value for this test was .502. If tables were available that list *t*-values for every possible curve area, as the standard unit normal (*z*-table) does, then it would be simple to find the area under the curve between 0 and .502 in the table for 9 df. This would be subtracted from .5 to find the tail beginning at .502.

However, the Critical Values of *t* Table lists only the tail areas for what are considered critical values of *t*, those leaving .05, .01, .025, etc., in the tail. The best that can be done to find the observed significance level after a *t*-test is to place it either between two values in the table (e.g., $x \le p < y$), less than (<) .001, or greater than (>) .10, the smallest and largest alpha-values in Table 10.1 respectively. For example, in the line for nine degrees of freedom,

df	$t_{.100}$	$t_{.050}$	$t_{.025}$	$t_{.010}$	$t_{.005}$
9	1.383	1.833	2.262	2.821	3.250

The *t*-value of .502 is less than the smallest value in the 9 df line (1.383), which is the $t_{.10}$ tail. Consider Figure 10.6, which represents the *t*-distribution for df = 9.

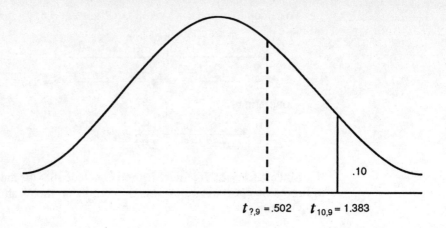

$t_{?,9} = .502$ $t_{10,9} = 1.383$

Figure 10.6:
t-Distribution for df = 9
Observed Significance Level

Notice that .10 of the area under the curve is in the 1.383 tail and more than .10 in the tail starting at .502. We do not know *how much* more since $t_{.10}$ is the first column of our table. So the observed significance level of .502 is greater than (>) .10.

Exercise 10.3:   In Exercise 10.2, $H_o : \mu = 112$, $H_a : \mu \neq 112$, and the test statistic was $t = 4.04$, with a sample size of five. Find the observed significance level of t.

df	$t_{.100}$	$t_{.050}$	$t_{.025}$	$t_{.010}$	$t_{.005}$
4	1.533	2.132	2.776	3.747	4.604

Answer: Consider the line in the Critical Values of t Table for df = 4.
The calculated $t = 4.04$. This value in the appropriate line (since $n = 5$, df $= n - 1 = 4$) in the table is between 3.747 and 4.604, 3.747 < 4.04 < 4.604. Therefore, the tail area is between $t_{.010}$ and $t_{.005}$.

However, since the alternative hypothesis was nondirectional ($\neq$), both upper and lower tails have to be examined. Therefore, the alpha-levels of .01 and .005 must be doubled. The observed significance level of t is between 2(.010) and 2(.005) or between .02 and .01. Recall that for $\alpha = .05$, the level of the hypothesis test, H_o was rejected. That was because the observed significance was much smaller than .05: it was between .02 and .01.

Small Sample Confidence Interval for the Mean

In Chapter 8, we showed that a confidence interval for the population mean can be generated given the sample mean and standard deviation of a large sample. A confidence interval for the population mean can also be found using a small sample of that population, given also that the population is approximately normally distributed.

Recall that the confidence interval is an interval in which, with a preset high degree of confidence, the population mean occurs. The formula for the small sample confidence interval is

$$(a, b) = \bar{x} \pm t_{\alpha/2}(s/\sqrt{n}) \text{ where } t_{\alpha/2} \text{ has } n - 1 \text{ df.}$$

Recall the ten G.P.A.s chosen at random from the G.P.A.s at XYZ College. They were 2.23, 2.03, 2.58, 3.02, 1.01, 3.57, 3.65, 3.33, 2.92, 1.98. Find a 99% confidence interval for the mean of all G.P.A.s at XYZ College. Recall that $\bar{x}$ = 2.632 and s = .8313.

Since there are ten data points, df = 9. A 99% confidence interval would require α = .01, so $\alpha/2$ = .005. Therefore, $t_{\alpha/2}$, df = $t_{.005,9}$ = 3.250.

Substituting in the above formula yields

$$(a, b) = \bar{x} \pm t_{\alpha/2}(s/\sqrt{n}) = 2.632 \pm 3.250 (.8313/\sqrt{10}) =$$

$$2.632 \pm 3.25 (.263) = 2.632 \pm .855 = (1.777, \ 3.487)$$

With 99% confidence we can say that the mean G.P.A. of students at XYZ College is between 1.777 and 3.487. Notice the large width of the confidence interval, since the sample is so small and the t-value for a small $\alpha/2$ and a small df is very large.

Exercise 10.4: In Exercise 10.2, five statistics students' I.Q. tests yielded $\bar{x}$ = 123.8 and s = 6.53. Find a 90% confidence interval for the mean I.Q. of the population of statistics students.

Answer: The formula for a small sample confidence interval is

$$(a, b) = \bar{x} \pm t_{\alpha/2} \cdot \left(\frac{s}{\sqrt{n}}\right). \quad \bar{x} = 123.8, \ s = 6.53,$$

$n = 5$, and $t_{.05,4} = 2.132$. Substituting:

$$(a, b) = 123.8 \pm 2.132 (6.53/\sqrt{5})$$

$$= 123.8 \pm (2.132)(2.92)$$

$$= 123.8 \pm 6.2 = (117.6, 130.0)$$

We are 90% confident that the mean I.Q. of students in statistics is between 117.6 and 130.0.

DIFFERENCES BETWEEN MEANS—SMALL SAMPLES

In Chapters 8 and 9 we developed procedures to compare the means (or proportions) of two large samples in order to make inferences about the populations from which the samples were drawn; that is, to decide: are the population means (or proportions) really from the same population? In a similar way, the means of two small samples can be used to locate an interval in which the difference of the population means exists or to test whether the population means are the same.

For example, suppose a statistician wants to find out whether the I.Q.s of business majors and English majors at XYZ College are the same. This problem may seem familiar, since we already did this with random samples of fifty from each major. But this time, we will solve it with small random samples taken from students in each major. Will the small samples be enough to say within a certain α whether the I.Q.s of business and English majors are the same?

Assume that there are six business majors' I.Q.s and seven English majors' I.Q.s in the sample. Let us first look at the sampling distribution of the means.

Sampling Distribution of the Difference of Small Sample Means

DEGREES OF FREEDOM OF THE SAMPLING DISTRIBUTION

The sampling distribution of the difference of two small sample means resembles a t-distribution as long as the populations from which the samples are drawn are approximately normally distributed.

The number of degrees of freedom in the sampling distribution of the difference of two small sample means is equal to the sum of the degrees of freedom in each sample. Sample B has $n_B - 1 = 6 - 1 = 5$ degrees of freedom, and Sample E has $n_E - 1 = 7 - 1 = 6$ degrees of freedom. The number of degrees of freedom of the sampling distribution of the differences of the means is $(n_B - 1) + (n_E - 1) = (n_B + n_E - 2)$ degrees of freedom.

MEAN OF THE SAMPLING DISTRIBUTION

This sampling distribution of the difference of two small sample means $(\bar{x}_B - \bar{x}_E)$ has a mean equal to the difference of the population means, $\mu_B - \mu_E$, which is estimated by the difference of the two sampled means, $\bar{x}_B - \bar{x}_E$.